A Hobbes Dictionary

THE
BLACKWELL PHILOSOPHER DICTIONARIES

A Hobbes Dictionary

A. P. Martinich

First published 1995

Blackwell Publishers Inc.
238 Main Street
Cambridge, Massachusetts 02142, USA

Blackwell Publishers Ltd
108 Cowley Road
Oxford OX4 1JF
UK

Library of Congress Cataloging-in-Publication Data

Martinich, Aloysius.
    A Hobbes dictionary / A. P. Martinich.
        p.   cm. — (The Blackwell philosopher dictionaries)
    Includes bibliographical references (p.   ) and index.
    ISBN 0–631–19261–1 (hbk. : alk. paper). — ISBN 0–631–19262–X (pbk. : alk. paper)
    1. Hobbes, Thomas, 1588–1679—Dictionaries.   I. Title.
II. Series.
    B1246.M37   1995   94–43256
    192—dc20   CIP

ISBN 0–631–19261–1 (hardback) ISBN 0–631–19262–X (pbk)

British Library Cataloguing in Publication Data

A CIP catalogue record for this book is available from the British Library.

Typeset in 10 on 12pt Baskerville   ·
by Graphicraft Typesetters Ltd., Hong Kong
Printed in Great Britain by T.J. Press, Padstow, Ltd.

This book is printed on acid-free paper

Contents

Preface

Goals and Organization

The primary purpose of this book is to explain the key concepts in Hobbes's thought and those subsidiary concepts that are important but not well known. Occasionally, I shall raise objections to Hobbes's views and sometimes suggest how he might have responded. The reason for doing so is to help the reader to understand what I take Hobbes to mean by considering the implications of his thought. Where there are apparent contradictions in Hobbes's thought, I have noted them and sometimes suggest reasons for them or ways of eliminating them without trying to force an interpretation on the text. Interpretations of Hobbes's thought vary widely. I have tried to steer a course between being partisan and being uncritical. The secondary purpose of this book is to refer the reader to the chief discussions of those concepts in Hobbes's own work.

Two kinds of people are most likely to use this book. First, there are those who, in the process of reading Hobbes, are not quite sure what he means. Second, there are those who come across an allusion to Hobbes's thought in another context and need background information in order to understand it. Either kind of reader may want to follow up my treatment of Hobbes with a study of the text first hand. My references to Hobbes's works should allow the reader to do this with little trouble. In order to maximize the intelligibility of Hobbes's text, I have modernized some of his punctuation and spelling.

My goal has been to make this book as helpful as possible to all students of Hobbes's thought. That goal has guided its organization and content. The book contains five parts.

(1) A biography of Hobbes with a selective history of seventeenth-century England. The history emphasizes the religious and political beliefs of James I, the events leading up to the English Civil Wars, and the events of the first decade of the Restoration. Later events in Stuart history are dealt with in the most cursory way. An account of the political and

intellectual context of the seventeenth century is necessary to get a full understanding of what Hobbes was trying to do.

(2) A chronology of Hobbes's life and works.

(3) A detailed chronology of (mainly) seventeenth-century events in English history with correlations to Hobbes's discussion of them in *Behemoth*. Since Hobbes's discussion is often oblique, this should help non-historians to understand this work.

(4) A dictionary of about 140 entries covering the main concepts in Hobbes's metaphysics, epistemology, science, philosophy of language, politics, and theology. Most words are indexed according to a noun, even in phrases that begin with an adjective. Thus, "fundamental law of nature" is listed as "law of nature, fundamental." Hobbes's Latin term is given in parentheses for some of the more important or interesting words.

(5) An annotated bibliography. The first part lists the most important early editions and manuscripts of his works and important recent editions. The second part lists important seventeenth-century books relevant to his philosophy. The third part contains a select bibliography of twentieth-century works.

Dictionary and Encyclopedia

Although dictionaries are defined as books that give the meanings of words, and encyclopedias as books that give information about things, they are deceptively similar kinds of books. To define a word, say, "apple" or "justice," is to say what an apple or justice is. To say what an apple or justice is is to explain how to use the words "apple" and "justice." The basic reason that dictionaries and encyclopedias are closely related is that most words are used for saying something about reality. When a book comprehensively covers a specific subject in small pieces, the line between a dictionary and an encyclopedia is even more blurred. It would be difficult to judge solely on the basis of its contents which book, say, is titled *A Dictionary of Mythology* and which *An Encyclopedia of Mythology*. While it is possible to emphasize the difference between a dictionary and an encyclopedia by their focus and mode of presenting each entry, it is natural for one to blend into the other. The *Hobbes Dictionary* is a natural blend. Its reader will want to know how Hobbes uses a word to talk about reality.

For most entries, I have tried to answer three questions – How did Hobbes use the word? Where did he use it? and Why did he use it? – roughly in that order. Many entries begin with a succinct description of how the word is used by Hobbes. Readers who need no more information can stop there. Those who need a more elaborate explanation can read on.

Two Trilogies

In considering how Hobbes's doctrines may have developed or otherwise changed, it is important to keep in mind that he wrote in effect two trilogies. The first consists of three separate treatments of his political philosophy:

Elements of Law, Natural and Politic (manuscript, 1640; published in two parts, 1650)
De Cive (1642; expanded in 1647)
Leviathan (1651).

For entries related to his political theory, references have been given to each discussion where it is helpful to do so, but the organization is guided by what I consider the best-developed treatment. For important concepts that have an interesting variation on the theme, I shall often discuss both explicitly. This is especially true for parallel passages in *Leviathan* and *De Cive*. When multiple references are cited for some idea, the order is usually determined by their importance. When a quotation is followed by multiple references, the first one gives the location of the quotation.

Hobbes's other trilogy is his complete system of philosophy in Latin. It is called *Elementa Philosophiae* (*The Elements of Philosophy*) but the three works have never been published together and each is better known as an individual work:

De Corpore (1655)
De Homine (1658)
De Cive (1642; expanded in 1647).
Notice that *De Cive* is part of both trilogies.

References

For more than 100 years, Sir William Molesworth's edition of the collected works of Hobbes has served scholars. In the last thirty years, the discovery of new manuscripts and the advancement of scholarship, especially in the production of more-accurate editions, have made Molesworth's edition much less important although it remains crucial when there is no more contemporary edition of a text. Because there is no longer any one standard edition for such works as *Leviathan, De Cive*, and *The Elements of Law*, among others, I have referred to passages in them either by chapter and paragraph number or by part, chapter and section number, as appropriate. Virtually all editions have the same paragraphing; for *Leviathan*, where there may be some minor variations, I have used Macpherson's edition as the standard.

The numbers in square brackets in the headings for dictionary entries on individual works by Hobbes, and in some bibliographic references in the text, refer to the numbered entries in the list of works by Hobbes given in the first section of the Bibliography.

Generic Pronouns

I typically use the feminine form for pronouns used to refer generically to persons. There are a few notable exceptions. When the interaction of two generic people is being described, masculine pronouns are used for one and feminine pronouns are used for the other. Masculine pronouns are always used when "sovereign" or "God" is the antecedent in order to avoid conflict with Hobbes's usage; but feminine pronouns are used otherwise, for example, with "monarch."

Acknowledgements

Mark Bernstein commented on the entire manuscript. Leslie Martinich, Max Rosenkranz, Avrum Stroll, and John Walchak commented on parts of it. Stephen Ryan has my deepest gratitude and greatest admiration for providing incisive philosophical comments and masterly stylistic suggestions on the entire manuscript. I also want to thank Bob Harverstick. I have enjoyed working with the staff of Blackwell Publishers, especially Steve Smith and Deborah Yuill, who have been extremely helpful and supportive. I am overdue in publicly thanking David Johnston for his help on an earlier project. My research was supported by the University Research Institute, University of Texas at Austin. I dedicate this book to my brothers: Tony, John, Joe, and the memory of Charley.

Abbreviations

AW = Anti-White (aka *Hobbes's Critique of Thomas White's* De Mundo)
B = Behemoth, ed. Tönnies
BCL = An Answer to Bishop Bramhall's Book, Called "The Catching of the Leviathan" EW 4
DC = De Cive
DCL = A Dialogue between a Philosopher and a Student of the Common Laws of England EW 6
DCo = De Corpore EW 1
DH De Homine OL 2
EL = The Elements of Law, Natural and Politic
EW = English Works, ed. Molesworth
HH = An Historical Narration Concerning Heresy, and the Punishment Thereof EW 4
L = Leviathan
LN = Of Liberty and Necessity EW 4
ODM = Objections to Descartes's Meditations
OL = Opera Latina, ed. Molesworth
PW = The History of the Peloponnesian War, ed. Grene
QLNC = The Questions Concerning Liberty, Necessity, and Chance EW 5
RLM = Considerations upon the Reputation, Loyalty, Manners, and Religion of Thomas Hobbes EW 4
SL = Six Lessons to the Savilian Professors of Mathematics EW 7

Thomas Hobbes in Stuart England

For without some general notions of these first times, many places of the history are the less easy to be understood; as depending upon the knowledge of the original of several cities and customs, which could not be at all inserted into the history of the text itself, but must be either supposed to be foreknown by the reader, or else be delivered him in the beginning as a necessary preface.

"Of the Life and History of Thucydides," in *PW*

Thomas Hobbes was born a twin with Fear, as he says of himself, because his mother, frightened about the impending invasion of the Spanish Armada, gave birth to him prematurely, on April 5, 1588. His home village was Westport, near Malmesbury, in the eastern part of the Cotswolds. Hobbes was proud of his native region and published under the name "Thomas Hobbes of Malmesbury." He spoke with a West Country accent, for which he was sometimes ridiculed. Hobbes's father, also named Thomas, was a poorly educated minister of the Church of England and an intemperate man. According to one story, the father, who had spent Saturday night playing cards, was sleeping during Sunday worship when he cried out that Clubs were trumps. He later physically fought with another cleric, fled to the west of London and never returned. Hobbes's education was supported by his uncle Francis, a successful glove-maker. Hobbes began to

---

Most of the historical information in this biography concerns early and middle Stuart England, that is, 1603 to 1660. The period after 1660 is dealt with briefly, but some mention of it is appropriate since many of the practical and theoretical problems that exercised Hobbes continued to be played out at least until 1689.

In the seventeenth century, there were two calendars: the Gregorian, used on the Continent and called New Style, and the Julian, used in England and called Old Style. The Julian calendar was ten days behind the Gregorian. Thus, January 10 in England was January 20 on the Continent. Another complication is that the new year in England was taken to begin on March 25. It is conventional for historians to give dates according to Old Style but to date the new year from January 1; that convention is followed here.

1

read and write at an early age and knew Greek and Latin before he went to Magdalen Hall, Oxford at the age of thirteen. (Magdalen Hall has since been absorbed into Hertford College.)

The beginning of Hobbes's university career roughly coincided with beginning of the Stuart monarchy. James I, the first Stuart king of England, Wales, and Ireland, was already king of Scotland under the title James VI when he succeeded Elizabeth I. He was the son of Mary (Stuart) Queen of Scots, whom Elizabeth had executed in 1587. As soon as he became king of England, James was faced with the complaints of some ministers of religion against the practices and structure of the Church of England. There were two major sorts of complaints. One was the claim that the liturgy needed further reformation in order to eliminate what were considered superstitious practices left over from the Roman Catholic Church. Roughly this meant that the ministers wanted less ritual, less emphasis on the eucharistic part of the Sunday service, and more emphasis on preaching. Let's call these puritan reforms – although the term "puritan" has many uses, it shall be used here only in the restricted sense just described. The other major area of reform urged by some ministers concerned the government of the church. They wanted to get rid of the episcopacy and replace it with a democratic form of church government, according to which congregations would elect elders to represent them at area councils (classes), each of which would elect representatives to county-wide provincial assemblies, which in turn would elect representatives to a national synod. We shall call people favoring such a structure "presbyterians." Most puritans were presbyterians, but not all. For example, in Elizabethan England, John Whitgift and Edmund Grindal, two archbishops of Canterbury, were puritans but not presbyterians. Virtually all puritans in 1603 were members of the Church of England and wanted to reform it, not to separate from it.

James I was willing to consider some puritan reforms, and in 1604 at the Hampton Court Conference, over which he presided, he made a few concessions to the puritans. But James would not tolerate any tampering with the episcopal system and believed that his own kingship was inextricably tied to it. When it was proposed to discuss the possibility of eliminating the episcopacy, he became angry and reminded the participants of how his mother had been persecuted by the Scottish Presbyterians. He said that his own monarchy depended upon the episcopate, and ended with the memorable phrase, "No Bishop, no King."

Like James, Hobbes was relatively liberal about the form that the liturgy could appropriately take. He prescribed only that prayers and thankgivings be "not sudden, nor light, nor plebeian, but beautiful, and well composed" (*L* 31.34). He expressed his preference for the liturgy prescribed by the Book of Common Prayer of the Church of England over any other. He was also like James in detesting the presbyterians, against whom he often rails in *Leviathan*. His objection to them is that they try to undermine the authority of the king by making the king subordinate to church councils.

Concerning episcopacy, he was less ardent than James. He preferred it, probably because he thought there was at least a strong causal connection between episcopacy and monarchy, which he strongly favored over any other form of government. Nonetheless, like many religious Englishmen, he thought that many of the bishops were personally corrupt. He also thought that Christian churches were not necessarily episcopal. When the abolition of the episcopacy was being debated in the early 1640s, just prior to the outbreak of the English Civil War, Hobbes conceded that another form of church government was acceptable if the people wanted it. During the Commonwealth, when monarchy no longer existed in England, Hobbes suggested that Independency (that is, the view that individual congregations should be relatively autonomous) was perhaps the best form of church government for that time (L 47.20).

Presbyterianism, as I have described it, espoused a democratic or bottom-up form of church government. Roman Catholicism espoused a top-down form. The pope was at the top; the bishops were below him, the priests below the bishops, and the laity at the bottom. Hobbes thought that a top-down structure was the best kind, but that the Roman Catholics had the wrong institutional person at the top. The pope did not have the right to rule anyone outside the Papal States, according to Hobbes. The leader of the church ought to be the civil sovereign because otherwise there can be no political stability. If the sovereign had to compete with any other authority, there could be no peace. The Bible, he pointed out, concurred: "No man can serve two masters". It is often said that Hobbes subordinated the religious to the secular; but that is not quite right. Religious and political authority are united in the civil sovereign, as the illustrated title page of *Leviathan* shows: the civil sovereign holds the secular sword in one hand and the episcopal crosier in the other.

In addition to his theoretical objections to Roman Catholicism and Presbyterianism, Hobbes had practical objections. His complaints against Presbyterians will be discussed below. Concerning the Roman Catholics, he had several complaints, beginning with the circumstances of his birth and extending virtually to his death. Hobbes blamed his premature birth and his lifelong timidity on the impending attack of the Armada of Catholic Spain. He pointed to the Gunpowder Plot of November 1605, the second year of James's reign, as evidence of the perfidy of Roman Catholics. Like James, Hobbes detested Jesuits, partly because Jesuit theologians

3

like Robert Bellarmine and Francisco de Suarez defended revolution against tyrants (*B*, p. 20). For all of his anti-Catholic sentiment, he nonetheless had many Catholic friends, such as Marin Mersenne, Pierre Gassendi, Kenelm Digby, and Thomas White; but none was a Jesuit. Finally, although he did not write about it, Hobbes could have cited the Popish Plot of 1678, in which Catholics allegedly had arranged to assassinate Charles II and install his Catholic brother James on the throne, as further evidence of Catholic perfidy.

The most lasting achievement of the Hampton Court Conference was the commissioning of a new biblical translation to replace the Bishops' Bible, which few read, and the popular Geneva Bible, which had marginal notes that James thought subversive (*B*, p. 22). The result was the Authorized Version or King James Bible, which appeared in 1611. Hobbes's own attitude toward vernacular translations of the Bible was ambivalent. If everyone read and interpreted the Bible according to her own lights, then discord would result from the inevitable diversity of interpretations. On the other hand, Hobbes thought that there was so much "true faith and good morality" in it that to forbid the reading of the Bible would do "great damage to them [the people] and the commonwealth" (*B*, p. 53).

In addition to the contrast between puritanism and presbyterianism, a third category needs to be introduced: calvinism. For our purposes a calvinist of the English variety is one who was in sympathy with the theological, though not the political, views of John Calvin, most conspicuously the doctrine of double predestination, that is, the doctrine that from all eternity God had decided who would go to heaven and who would go to hell and that God's decision was unrelated to the apparent merits of human actions. People are saved not by good works but by the grace of God. This was a hard doctrine but James supported it, albeit with some ambivalence. The issue was pressing because Jacobus Arminius in the Netherlands had challenged the doctrine, and there was some fear that the religious controversy would get translated into social and political unrest in England, as it had in the Netherlands. James sent observers to the Council of Dort (Dordrecht), held in 1618–19, which discussed the relevant issues. The orthodox calvinists dominated the proceedings. They reaffirmed predestination and denied the existence of free will.

Hobbes was logically committed to predestination by his adherence to divine determinism: the propositions that everything has a cause and that God causes everything, even the sins that people commit. Yet God is not culpable since to sin is to break a law, and God, not being subject to law, cannot break one. Human beings have no free will because the concept itself is incoherent. Although his views suggest that Hobbes was a calvinist

4

on this point, he thought that the debates about predestination were useless and offensive. There is no record of his views on the matter until the middle 1640s when he debated the issue in Paris with the Arminian bishop John Bramhall. Although predestination was the prevalent view among the educated during the reign of James, the Arminian view became more influential in the early 1620s and dominated the hierarchy of the Church of England by the later 1630s. This issue will be discussed further below.

Two other doctrines characteristic of calvinism are the belief that the work of human redemption was purely an act of the mercy of God, not justice, and the belief that Jesus died only for those selected to go to heaven ("the elect") and not for all human beings.

In seventeenth-century England, there were several competing theories about what makes government legitimate. The divine right of kings was only one of these theories, but it was the one that James espoused on several occasions. Hobbes recites the formula of divine-right theory in *Leviathan*, but he was not a divine-right theorist, because he did not believe one of the central tenets of that theory, namely, that the legitimacy of a leader is due to God's direct selection of a monarch. Hobbes probably gave lip-service to the divine-right formula to show his solidarity with the king and because he agreed with another, equally important feature of James's version of it, namely, the claim that monarchs are obliged or answerable only to God, and not to any human being.

Both James and Hobbes believed in absolute sovereignty. For our purposes, this may be explained as meaning that the sovereign's power is unlimited in depth and breadth. Its depth is unlimited in the sense that power is not shared with any other political entity. In particular, a monarch does not share power with her parliament, according to Hobbes. The power of an absolute sovereign is broad in the sense that it can extend in theory to any area of life. In *Behemoth*, when Hobbes had the opportunity to reflect upon his idea of absolutism, he committed himself to the view that a child has the obligation to kill her father if so ordered by the sovereign. He denies, however, that any sovereign would act so brutally (*B*, p. 51; cf. *DC* 6.13). One may be able to excuse Hobbes's inability to imagine the likes of Hitler, Stalin, or Pol Pot, but he should have remembered Caligula. For Hobbes, the freedom a subject enjoys under a government is restricted to those matters about which the sovereign chooses not to legislate (*L* 21.6). He compared the civil sovereign to God when he described Leviathan as "that *mortal god*, to which we owe under the immortal God, our peace and defence" (*L* 17.13). One of James's most famous statements of his absolutism is contained in his "Speech to the Lords and Commons of the Parliament at White-Hall" of 1610:

5

> The state of monarchy is the supremest thing on earth. For kings are not only God's lieutenants upon earth, and sit upon God's throne, but even by God himself they are called gods. . . . Kings are justly called gods for that they exercise a manner or resemblance of divine power upon earth. For if you will consider the attributes of God, you shall see how they agree in the person of a king. God has the power to create, or destroy, make, or unmake at his pleasure, to give life, or send death, to judge all, and to be judged nor accountable to none; to raise low things, and to make high things low at his pleasure, and to God are both soul and body due. . . . And the like power have kings: they make and unmake their subjects; they have power of raising and casting down, of life and of death; judges over all their subjects, and in all cases, and yet accountable to none but God only. They have power to exalt low things and abase high things, and make of their subjects like men at the chess: a pawn to take a bishop or a knight, and to cry up or down any of their subjects, as they do their money. And to the king is due both the affection of the soul and the service of the body of his subjects . . . (quoted from Wootton (ed.), *Divine Right and Democracy*, p. 107)

There are other circumstances that relate James and Hobbes. The speech from James that was just quoted was part of his response to Bellarmine, who had argued that the pope had the right to depose monarchs, and it was clear that Bellarmine had James in mind as one target. At about the same time, James was having trouble with Chief Justice Edward Coke, who was asserting the supremacy of the common law over the authority of the king. Hobbes received his Bachelor of Arts degree in 1608, the same year in which James I published a book attacking the Catholic position that the pope had the authority to depose a monarch whose policies conflicted with true Christianity. The debate was not academic. Pope Pius V had excommunitated Queen Elizabeth in 1570; in 1606 parliament had passed a bill requiring Catholics to take an oath of allegiance to the monarch. James was defending the English position against such distinguished Catholic theologians as Suarez and Bellarmine. In 1613, Suarez wrote *Defensor Fidei*, which was an attack on James's *Apologia*. The religious and political views of James I seem to have had a profound effect on Hobbes. He rarely discussed the work of others; yet he picked out Bellarmine and Coke for special attack, and often took potshots at Suarez as well. The longest chapter in *Leviathan*, chapter 42, is devoted to refuting Bellarmine's views about the papacy, and *A Dialogue between a Philosopher and a Student of the Common Laws of England* is an attack on Coke (see also *L* 26.10–11).

Although James aspired to be an absolute ruler, in fact English monarchs depended upon parliament to approve taxes, and James's parliaments were reluctant to approve them without concessions that James thought undermined his authority. There was no standing army in England until

6

the disastrous reign of his grandson James II in the 1680s. If a monarch wanted to go to war, she had to go to parliament for the funds to wage it. As it was, near the end of his reign, parliament voted funds for a war against Spain that James did not want to fight.

In general, James preferred peace and unity in all areas. He wanted to unite his two kingships. Neither the Scots nor the English were eager for this, and the unification did not occur until the Act of Union was passed in 1707, under Queen Anne, the last of the Stuart monarchs. Hobbes supported James's view that Scotland and England were or should have been one state and said that the union probably would have prevented civil war (*L* 19.23). There certainly were troubles between England and Scotland relevant to the Civil War, but it is unlikely that union would have solved them.

Shortly after leaving Oxford, probably in the early summer of 1608, upon the recommendation of the master of Magdalen Hall, John Wilkinson, Hobbes was employed by William Cavendish, the wealthy Baron Cavendish of Hardwick, to tutor his son William. The elder Cavendish became first earl of Devonshire in 1618; the son (Hobbes's tutee) became second earl of Devonshire in 1626; and the grandson, a third William, whom Hobbes would also tutor, became third earl of Devonshire in 1628 when his father, a rather dissolute person, died. There was yet a fourth William Cavendish in Hobbes's life; he was the nephew of the first earl. This William, who was also a patron of Hobbes, became earl, marquis, and eventually duke of Newcastle. He was an important military leader for Charles I during the Civil War, but, ashamed of his role in the defeat of the royalist forces at Marston Moor, he left England. On the Continent he was the governor of the Prince of Wales, the future Charles II.

Between 1610 and 1615, Hobbes toured the Continent with his tutee William Cavendish. In Venice, they associated with Fulgenzio Micanzio, who opposed the pope's claims to supremacy. In 1618, the Thirty Years' War, the last of the religious wars of Europe, broke out between Catholic and Protestant countries. Sometime between 1618 and 1626, Hobbes served as a secretary to Francis Bacon. Bacon thought that Hobbes was one of the few people who understood his thoughts.

James died in 1625 and was succeeded by his son Charles I (1600–49), who was much less learned than his father but equally devoted to the divine right of kings and the pretensions of an absolute monarchy, at least until 1642 when he did an about-face and conceded in his "Reply to the Nineteen Propositions" that England had a mixed government, in a vain attempt to avoid civil war. Charles stuttered; he was shy, taciturn, devious, and mendacious. Although he was personally committed to the Church of England, of which he was of course the legal head, he was religious in a way that alienated many of his subjects. Too much about him smacked of the Roman Catholicism detested by his Protestant subjects. His wife, Henrietta Maria, the sister of Louis XIII of France, was Catholic. Also, Charles preferred elaborate liturgical practices that in the opinion of the puritans too closely resembled Roman Catholicism. Perhaps worst of all, he promoted the career and policies of William Laud.

Laud (1573–1645) became a royal chaplain in 1611 and advanced under the patronage of the duke of Buckingham, whom Charles came to depend upon during the first years of his reign. He became a privy councillor in 1627, bishop of London the next year, chancellor of Oxford University the next, and archbishop of Canterbury in 1633. In his role as bishop, he persecuted puritans, often through the jurisdiction of the Courts of Star Chamber and High Commission, and promoted what his opponents took to be Roman Catholic practices. He tried to improve the financial condition of the church, which had suffered during the Reformation in England, and believed that supporting the king was the only way to do that. It was as if he took James's remark, "No Bishop, no King," personally.

Charles met his first parliament in June 1625. He needed money to continue the war against Spain that he and Buckingham had helped to instigate. But parliament distrusted Buckingham. It also wanted Charles to grant it more power and wanted greater leniency extended to puritans. When Charles refused to accede to these demands, it refused to do what traditionally had been *pro forma* for a new monarch, namely, to grant him the right to collect tonnage and poundage (an import tax on wine and grain) for life. Instead, parliament approved the taxes for only one year. Charles dissolved that parliament, but called another for February 1626 because the English position in the war against Spain had continued to deteriorate.

The results of this parliament were worse. Buckingham had blundered into an additional war, this one with France. When parliament took steps to impeach Buckingham for treason, Charles dissolved it in June, before it granted him any additional revenues. Desperate for money, Charles forced his wealthy subjects to lend him money. (Hobbes, in the service of the earl of Devonshire, helped to collect the money.) About seventy who refused were imprisoned. Hobbes later implicitly justified Charles's actions in *Leviathan* (*L* 21.19). In order to justify the loan, Charles commanded the bishops to have the clergy preach in favor of it. One of these was Roger Manwaring, a royal chaplain, who argued that the king could do whatever he wanted to do because he was an absolute monarch. Charles liked the argument and ordered the sermon to be printed. Many parliamentarians were offended by it, and a complaint was filed against

Manwaring in March 1628. Manwaring was arrested, imprisoned, and fined. Charles himself was pressured into condemning the book but later absolved Manwaring and made him bishop of St David's in 1636. Hobbes, who had been at Oxford at the same time as Manwaring, later said that Manwaring "preach'd his doctrine." (See also *L* 21.19; *DC* 8.5.) The context in Aubrey's biography suggests that Hobbes was claiming to have influenced Manwaring.

Charles opened his third parliament, in March 1628, with the same hope that motivated his calling of the first two, namely, that of getting additional revenues approved. Unhappy with Charles's practices, Parliament proposed granting Charles the funds he needed if he would accept the Petition of Right, which declared the following practices illegal: forced loans, arbitrary arrest, housing soldiers in private homes, and martial law. Charles accepted the Petition in the hopes of getting the money he needed. When Parliament maintained that Charles did not yet have approval to collect tonnage and poundage, Charles prorogued (recessed) parliament. Shortly afterwards, his chief adviser, Buckingham, was assassinated (August 23, 1628). Charles was despondent.

Again hoping to be granted money, Charles recalled the third parliament in January 1629. A new complaint was raised against the "popish practices" promoted by Laud, then bishop of London. Laud was accused of Arminianism, but that is a misnomer. It was not so much his beliefs on free will and predestination that his opponents objected to; it was such liturgical practices as having a communion altar in the eastern end of the church, railed off from the people. Charles, the official head of the Church of England, was fed up with such interference in church affairs and dissolved parliament, but not before parliament condemned the changes in liturgical practice and the collection of tonnage and poundage. No other parliament met from 1629 to 1640.

Although the years between 1608 and 1628 were politically difficult for England, Hobbes later remembered them as the happiest of his life. He had ample time to read ancient Greek and Roman poets, playwrights, and historians. Of these, he liked Thucydides the best, and translated his history of the Peloponnesian War in order to warn Englishmen of the dangers of democracy and rhetoric used for subversive purposes. It was published in 1629, the year that Charles's third parliament, a failure like the first two, was dissolved.

After the second earl of Devonshire died in 1628, Hobbes took a position with Sir Gervase Clifton. He toured the Continent for the second time, now with the younger Clifton, in 1629–30. It is plausible that Hobbes's interest in geometry began sometime during this tour. As Aubrey tells the story,

> Being in a gentleman's library in . . . , Euclid's Elements lay open, and 'twas the 47 *El. libri I.* He read the proposition. "By G—," said he, "this is impossible!" So he reads the demonstration of it, which referred him back to such a proposition; which proposition he read. That referred him back to another, which he also read. Et sic deinceps, that at last he was demonstratively convinced of that truth. This made him in love with geometry.

He would later hold the position that geometrical proof should be the paradigm of scientific demonstration.

Back in England, Hobbes resumed employment with the Cavendish family, partly as tutor to the third earl of Devonshire. As a member of the household, he also associated during the 1630s with the earl's cousin, William Cavendish, the earl of Newcastle, and the latter's scientific friends: Robert Payne, Walter Warner, and John Pell. During the same period, Hobbes had discussions with the members of the intellectual circle associated with Lucius Cary's (Viscount Falkland's) estate, Great Tew, such as Edward Hyde (Lord Clarendon), William Chillingworth, John Hales, and Dudley Digges.

In the fall of 1634, Hobbes began his third trip to the Continent, this time with the third earl of Devonshire. He met Galileo, who was then a prisoner of the Inquisition, and Marin Mersenne, who brought together many of the greatest thinkers of the age, such as Descartes and Pierre Gassendi. Hobbes returned to England in October 1636. Another of Hobbes's Catholic friends was the English scientist and statesman Kenelm Digby. Digby admired both Hobbes and Descartes and sent Hobbes a copy of Descartes's *Discourse on the Method.* In an essay that accompanied the *Discourse,* Descartes argued that color is not a quality in objects but is caused by motions in the nerves. Later, Hobbes was at some pains to insist that he had had this idea first, in 1630. In any case, in 1637, Hobbes wrote extensive comments on the *Discourse* and the accompanying essays. On the strength of them, Mersenne invited him to write a reply to Descartes's *Meditations.*

Descartes's dualism and Hobbes's materialism notwithstanding, their theories of the world are very similar in that each tried to give a mechanistic explanation of all physical phenomena. They felt a rivalry and personally did not like each other. In a letter to Mersenne of March 4, 1641, Descartes says,

> I think the best thing would be for me to have nothing more to do with him. . . . For if his temperament is what I think it is, it will be hard for us to exchange views without becoming enemies. . . . I beg you, moreover, not to tell him any more than you have to of what you know of my unpublished

views; for unless I am very much mistaken, this is someone who is looking to acquire a reputation at my expense.

In 1644, Hobbes refused to meet Descartes when the latter visited Paris. Hobbes thought that Descartes was a good geometer and could have been the best in the world if he had focused on it, but that "his head did not lie for philosophy." Hobbes also downplayed the fruitfulness of algebraic geometry. For his part, Descartes thought that Hobbes was a better moral philosopher than metaphysician.

Charles was short of revenues throughout the 1630s. In order to raise the money he needed, he devised several ingenious, though devious, schemes. All were accepted if resented. One of these was Ship Money. In 1634 Charles imposed the tax, which was traditionally applied to coastal towns with the purpose of providing war ships, or money to pay for them, in times of emergency. Charles claimed that piracy was the emergency; in 1635, he extended the levy of Ship Money to inland towns, and renewed the tax the next year (*B*, p. 85). John Hampden, a respected parliamentarian, refused to pay his tax. He was arrested and narrowly convicted by a split vote of the judges in 1637. The vote was 7–5 in favor of the king, but three of the votes against the king were based upon a technicality, and that may explain why Hobbes records the vote as 10–2 in favor of the king (*B*, pp. 36–7; see also *L* 21.19). The conviction was nonetheless perceived as a political defeat for the king, because some judges had ruled against him.

Charles had even worse problems with Scotland. In 1637, in conjunction with the Scottish bishops, he forced a revised version of the English Book of Common Prayer on Scotland. The largely Presbyterian Scots vehemently opposed it (*B*, p. 28). The incident led in 1638 to the formulation of the National Covenant, in which the Scots proclaimed their allegiance both to the king and to presbyterianism. Hobbes was particularly offended that the Scots "impudently" called it "a *Covenant with God*" (*B*, p. 28; *L* 18.3).

In 1639, Charles led an abortive campaign against the Scots (the First Bishops' War). In 1640, he called his first parliament in eleven years in order to raise money to fight the Scots again (the Second Bishops' War). Parliament was not inclined to authorize money to wage a war against fellow Protestants. Thus, in May, the Short Parliament of 1640 was dissolved, and Charles's privately financed army went off to lose another campaign against the Scots (*B*, pp. 32–3).

Slow to learn, Charles called a second parliament, for November 1640, the Long Parliament. The next two years are a story of almost unrelieved wretchedness for the monarchy. Parliament acted to take away many of

11

the king's prerogatives, and Charles gave away others in a vain attempt to preserve himself (*B*, pp. 72, 74). Thomas Wentworth, Lord Strafford, one of Charles's most competent advisers, was impeached on November 10, 1640 and executed the next May (*B*, pp. 64–6, 69, 71; cf. *L* 25.5); Laud was impeached in December 1640, convicted, but not executed until January 10, 1645. In February 1641, Charles signed the Triennial Act, which required that parliament meet at least every three years (*B*, pp. 74, 85); and in May, he signed a bill requiring that parliament be dissolved only with its consent (*B*, pp. 74, 117). Parliament declared Charles's innovative taxing schemes to be illegal, abolished the Courts of Star Chamber and High Commission, and dissolved the Councils of Wales and of the North.

Hobbes was not oblivious to or unconcerned about the events of 1640. In May 1640, he circulated in manuscript *The Elements of Law, Natural and Politic*, the first version of his political philosophy. In it, he defended established governments in general and argued for the superiority of monarchy over other forms of government. Some parliamentarians were unhappy with the work. Having seen what had happened to some others who had questioned the authority of parliament, and no doubt anticipating the kind of fate that awaited Archbishop Laud and Lord Strafford, Hobbes left England about November 15, 1640, "the first of all that fled," as he said of himself (*EW* 4:414). He was later criticized for abandoning his king. In his defense, it is worth remembering that several people who shared his views were prosecuted by parliament, that he was fifty-two years old, and that he had no military training or political position. Hobbes defended the king in the best way he could, with his pen. In 1642, he published *De Cive* anonymously in France. Its political argument is substantially the same as that in the *Elements*, and it also includes an extended discussion of the nature and role of religion in civil society. It was envisioned as the third part of his projected trilogy to be entitled *The Elements of Philosophy*; indeed, its formal title is *Elementorum Philosophiae Sectio Tertia De Cive*. A second, expanded edition was published by Elzevir in Amsterdam in 1647. (The first section of the trilogy, *De Corpore*, was published in 1655; the second section, *De Homine*, in 1658.)

Not all of Hobbes's thoughts were on politics while in France. He claimed that he had already thought out, if not written, the first two sections of his trilogy, which was to be a comprehensive system of philosophy. Also, Hobbes associated with many in Mersenne's intellectual circle. He contributed the Third Set of Objections to Descartes's *Meditations*. In late 1642 and early 1643, Hobbes drafted a critique of Thomas White's *De Mundo*. Many of the ideas in the critique later found their way into *De Corpore*. He also wrote treatises on optics and aesthetics, studied anatomy and participated in

12

dissections with William Petty, and engaged in a famous debate on free will with Bishop Bramhall. The debate eventually led to the publication of Hobbes's *Of Liberty and Necessity* and *Questions Concerning Liberty, Necessity, and Chance.*

In October 1641, a rebellion broke out in Ireland for which Charles needed to raise an army. But, fearing that the army might be used, not against the Irish, but against Charles's English enemies, parliament did not want it to be under Charles's command (*L* 18.8, 18.12). To this point, public opinion tended to favor parliament against the king. But sympathy for Charles increased within parliament and London in reaction to the strong attack on him in the Grand Remonstrance of December 1641 (*B*, p. 87). Twelve bishops had been impeached shortly thereafter, and there was some talk of impeaching Charles's queen, Henrietta Maria (*B*, p. 61). Charles reacted clumsily. He resolved to arrest Lord Mandeville and five MPs, including John Pym. When he took the unprecedented step of entering the House of Commons to arrest the MPs, he discovered to his embarrassment that they had already fled (*B*, pp. 87, 96). Fearing more than ever for himself and his family, he left London in January 1642. Between then and August 22, when he raised his standard, marking the official beginning of the English Civil War (*B*, p. 121), Charles refused to sign the Militia Bill, which would have turned control of the militia over to parliament; but he did sign the Bishops' Exclusion and Clergy Disqualification Bill, which removed bishops and clerics of all governmental positions, including membership of the House of Lords. The episcopacy was suspended in September 1642 (but not abolished until October 1646). Charles was twice refused entry to the city of Hull, where he intended to get munitions (*B*, p. 103). Political relations were in a shambles when parliament on June 1, 1642 sent Charles the Nineteen Propositions, which included the following items:

(1) That all the king's counselors must be approved by, and take an oath formulated by, parliament (*L* 18.13).

(2) That no private persons may counsel the king and all public business must be discussed in parliament (*L* 18.13).

(3) That certain high officials, such as Lord Chancellor and Lord Treasurer, must be approved by parliament (*L* 18.13).

(4) That the education of the king's children must be approved by parliament.

(5) That no marriage of the king's children may be arranged without approval of the parliament.

(8) That the church be reformed in government and liturgy.

(9) That parliament have control of the militia (*L* 18.12).

(12)   That all judges be subject to review by parliament (L 18.11).
(15)   That commanders of forts and castles be approved by parliament (L 18.12).
(16)   That the king remove the military forces protecting him.
(17)   That the king form alliances with the United Provinces (the Netherlands) and other Protestant countries.

In his chapter on the rights of sovereigns by institution, Hobbes explicitly rejects many of the demands of the Nineteen Propositions, as the references above indicate. Hobbes makes the relevance of his views to the English Civil War explicit: "If there had not first been an opinion received of the greatest part of England, that these powers were divided between the king and the Lords and the House of Commons, the people had never been divided and fallen into this Civil War" (L 18.16).

Charles rejected the Nineteen Propositions, but at the same time he gave up the claim of absolute sovereignty. England, the response said, was a limited and mixed monarchy. Hobbes must have thought that the response unwittingly disclaimed an essential power of sovereignty and would have considered the attempted self-limitation void for that reason: "in whatsoever words any of them [essential powers] seem to be granted away, yet if the sovereign power itself be not in direct terms renounced . . . the grant is void" (L 18.17).

Charles's response was delivered in the middle of June and war officially began in August. The causes of the English Civil War have been debated since the Restoration. Hobbes's analysis in *Behemoth* was one of the first. He thought that it was a structural weakness of the monarchy that it did not have a sufficient and independent source of money but had to rely upon parliament for it. Also, the subjects had been corrupted in six ways. Religious groups make up the first three ways: (1) Presbyterians, (2) Roman Catholics, and (3) Independents, Anabaptists, Quakers, Fifth Monarchy Men, and Adamites. Also, (4) educated people had become corrupted by Greek and Roman political theory; (5) Londoners, inspired by rebellion in the Low Countries, thought that economic prosperity would result from overthrowing the monarchy; and (6) few people understood their duty to obey the king (B, pp. 2–6).

During the Civil War, areas of the country were taken and given back by armies; but in general, the parliamentary forces controlled the east and south of England with London as their headquarters, and the king controlled the north and west with Oxford as his headquarters. The royalist forces had the advantage until the spring of 1644. The tide began to turn when the Scots entered the war in September 1643 (B, p. 110) on the side of the parliamentarians, who in exchange for that support promised to institute a presbyterian system into the Church of England. The royalists also hurt their own cause through poor military decisions.

The king suffered serious defeats at Marston Moor in 1644 (*B*, p. 129) and Naseby in 1645 (*B*, p. 132). Nonetheless, the anti-royalists were dissatisfied with the performance of the parliamentary forces. There was consequently a move in the fall and winter of 1644 to reorganize the army under a single field commander (the New Model Army) and not to allow anyone to hold both a military command and a place in parliament (Self-Denying Ordinance) (*B*, pp. 130–1).

In May 1646, Charles surrendered to the Scots. In early 1647, parliament paid off the Scottish army, who then handed Charles over to the English. A serious rift subsequently opened up between parliament and the army. Parliament feared the power of the army, and the army was upset at not having been paid. Also, a majority of the parliament wanted to negotiate with Charles to resolve their disputes; the army, however, wanted to impose a solution on him. In time, the army began to develop broader political demands of a democratic sort. Within the parliament there was also a rift between those generally sympathetic to presbyterianism, who feared the army, and Independents, who opposed a narrowly presbyterian system and sympathized with the army.

In November 1647, Charles escaped to Carisbrook Castle on the Isle of Wight. Although he was almost immediately captured, he was able to negotiate with the Scots, who agreed to support him in exchange for his promising to try presbyterianism in England for three years. The royalist forces never had much chance of success, and the fighting ended in August 1648. Many MPs still wanted to negotiate a settlement with Charles, who remained uncooperative.

In December 1648, Colonel Thomas Pride, acting on behalf of the army council, prevented those MPs who were sympathetic to the idea of negotiating with the king, most of whom were presbyterians, from entering parliament (Pride's Purge). Charles was brought to trial by a High Court appointed by the Rump Parliament – that is, what was left of the Long Parliament, without the royalists, presbyterians, and others who were conciliatory towards the king – and beheaded on January 30, 1649. Hobbes may have been obliquely referring to this event when he wrote, "And though sovereignty in the intention of them that make it be immortal, yet . . . it has in it . . . many seeds of a natural mortality by intestine discord" (*L* 21.21). And he may have had his own situation in mind when he wrote immediately after that a person "in a foreign country" may accept the victor as her sovereign (*L* 21.22). The House of Lords was abolished on February 6 and the monarchy the next day.

In August 1647, Hobbes became very ill. He confessed to the Arminian

15

John Cosin and received the eucharist from Dr John Pierson. He rejected Mersenne's urgings that he become a Catholic. He later appealed to his behavior in the face of death as part of the evidence that he was not an atheist but a sincere member of the Church of England.

Leviathan was published in London during the spring of 1651. Much of *Leviathan* implicitly defends Charles's behavior and attacks the ideas of limited sovereignty and mixed monarchy, the ideas upon which parliament relied to justify its actions. Hobbes held that any legislative action of a sovereign that would have the consequence of weakening his authority is void (*L* 18.17). This would void much of the legislation reluctantly approved by Charles between 1640 and 1642. In particular, an alleged law depriving the sovereign of the power to dissolve parliament when it suited him would be void (*L* 26.10).

Hobbes returned to England in February 1652 and took the Oath of Engagement, which was a pledge of loyalty to the Commonwealth. Hobbes's apparent abandonment of the royalist cause angered many in the exiled court of Charles II. During the Restoration, both John Wallis and Edward Hyde (Lord Clarendon) claimed that *Leviathan* was a betrayal of the royalist cause and that Hobbes had written it in order to ingratiate himself with Oliver Cromwell. Wallis, a professor of geometry at Oxford with whom Hobbes debated about mathematical issues primarily, made this charge in *Hobbius Heauton-timorumenos* in 1662. Yet Clarendon also reports that Hobbes presented Charles II with a copy of *Leviathan* in October 1651. It is implausible that the timorous Hobbes would have had the audacity to risk presenting Charles with a treatise that justified the actions of Cromwell or parliament against Charles's father. In fact, *Leviathan* is suffused with defenses of Charles I. What is indisputable is that Hobbes had a knack for rubbing people the wrong way. Many others who had sided with the king also took the Oath but suffered much less animosity. His impolitic manner and notoriety also contributed to his exclusion from membership of the Royal Society.

Under the Commonwealth, the state was initially run, badly, by a series of Councils of State, representing parliament. In 1653, Cromwell dissolved the Rump Parliament when it failed to enact legislation that the army wanted. He then selected his own members of parliament to form the Nominated or Barebones Parliament, which was ineffective and quickly dissolved. In December 1653, he accepted the title of Lord Protector, which he held until his death in 1658.

Cromwell was succeeded as Lord Protector by his son Richard. But Richard Cromwell was unable to control the army and he resigned in May 1659. The resignation made the Restoration of the monarchy in 1660 a relatively easy matter. Charles returned to England with a promise of forgiveness for the regicides of his father and toleration for dissenting religious groups. Few regicides were executed, but the Cavalier Parliament, which met periodically from 1661 until 1678, dealt harshly with dissenters. During this time, Charles was trying to rule as much as possible without the influence of parliament. Keeping the Cavalier Parliament in existence was a way of preventing new elections from producing a parliament less amenable to Charles's policies.

A Latin version of *Leviathan*, which differs in significant ways from the English version, was published in Amsterdam in 1668. *Behemoth*, his history of England between 1640 and 1660, probably written in the middle to late 1660s, was first published on the Continent in 1679, without his permission.

Hobbes spent most of his time in London in the company of such people as John Selden and William Harvey, although he was still employed by the Cavendishes. Over the years, Hobbes had acquired enough money and property, largely through the beneficence of the Cavendish family, to allow him to live comfortably and to bestow various gifts on friends and relatives. Although Hobbes had become alienated from Charles II in 1651, largely because of the machinations of the Arminian clergy in Charles's court, their friendship was mended after 1660. The king enjoyed his discussions with Hobbes and kept a portrait of him in his private room. The king called him "the bear" and would say, "Here comes the bear to be baited." Charles shared Hobbes's views about absolute sovereignty but refused Hobbes's request to publish any works on politics. My guess is that Charles, who preferred to work surreptitiously, saw no advantage in allowing the promulgation of inflammatory theories of absolute sovereignty. He was more likely to achieve his ends by working for them politically.

In 1674, when Anthony Wood was publishing his *History and Antiquities of the University of Oxford*, John Fell, the dean of Christ Church, who oversaw the press, inserted disparaging remarks into the text of Wood's biography of Hobbes. When Hobbes protested, Fell remarked to Wood that "he [Hobbes] was an old man, had one foot in the grave, that he should mind his latter end, and not trouble the world any more with his papers."

In 1675, Hobbes retired to Chatsworth and Hardwick Hall in Derbyshire with the third earl of Devonshire: "In his old age he used to sing prick-song every night (when all were gone and sure nobody could hear him) for his health, which he did believe would make him live two or three years longer." He also credited his longevity to eating fish, and he gave up drinking wine after the age of sixty. In his youth he was sickly, but became healthier after the age of forty. His hair was black when he was young, and one of his nicknames at school was "Crow." Bald in his old age, he said "the greatest trouble was to keep off the flies from pitching on the baldness." He occasionally played tennis even at the age of seventy-five, and he enjoyed massages.

In October 1679, Hobbes was struck with "the strangury," some affliction making urination painful and difficult. Hobbes was told that it was unlikely that he would recover, which moved him to say, as reported by a member of the household, that he would "be glad to find a hole to creep out of the world at." The remark seems to continue the analogy Hobbes used in his verse autobiography of being a worm. In late November 1679, the Cavendish family was moving from Chatsworth to Hardwick Hall. Hobbes, seemingly too sick to travel, was to be left behind. He refused and insisted on accompanying the family. Warmly wrapped and laid on a feather bed, he was transported by coach to Hardwick. Shortly afterwards, he apparently suffered a stroke and virtually stopped eating. He died at Hardwick Hall on December 4, 1679 and was buried in the parish church of Hault Hucknall, according to the rites of the Church of England.

Hobbes was probably little aware of the significant political developments occurring in London during the late 1670s. Charles's efforts to put into effect an absolute sovereign rule were threated by the Popish Plot of 1678. The miscreant Titus Oates invented the story that some Roman Catholics had hatched a plot to assassinate Charles II and install his Roman Catholic brother James on the throne. The earl of Shaftesbury exploited Oates's groundless story in order to further his attempts to have James excluded from the monarchical succession. After three years of maneuvering, Shaftesbury was finally defeated when the Oxford Parliament was suddenly dissolved by Charles and popular feeling turned against Shaftesbury and the Whigs.

When Charles died in 1685, James became king. In a series of high-handed and politically suicidal decisions that favored Roman Catholics, James destroyed the support he initially received from his subjects, especially the Anglicans. William of Orange, who was invited by some Englishmen to supervise a fair election of parliament, brought a small army with him. James, at the brink of a nervous breakdown, fled for his life to France. Thus occurred the virtually bloodless Glorious Revolution of December 1688. A confused intellectual and political establishment, trying to understand what was happening, variously judged that James was legally dead, had abdicated or had vacated the throne. No one appealed to Hobbes's political theory to solve the theoretical morass. In any event, a Convention was assembled, which in January 1689 made William and his wife Mary (a Protestant daughter of James) co-monarchs but with all the power of the monarchy in William alone. After the deaths of William and Mary, Anne (Mary's sister) became queen; and when she died in 1714, the Stuart monarchy ended.

A Chronology of Hobbes's
Life and Works

1588:   April 5, born
1602:   goes to Magdalen Hall, Oxford
1608:   February, receives his BA; later that year becomes tutor to
           William Cavendish
1610–15:   tours the Continent with William Cavendish (his tutee)
1615:   returns to England
1626:   first earl of Devonshire dies
1628:   June, second earl of Devonshire dies
1629:   translation of Thucydides published
1630:   resumes employment with family of the earl of Devonshire
1634–6:   third trip to the Continent; with the third earl of Devonshire
1635:   begins association with Marin Mersenne, Pierre Gassendi, and
           other French philosophers
1636:   visits Galileo (probably that year); returns to England in October
1640:   May, *The Elements of Law* circulated in manuscript; published
           1650 in two parts without Hobbes's permission, as *Humane
           Nature* and *De Corpore Politico*; mid-November, flees to France
1641:   Third Set of Objections to Descartes's *Meditations* published
1642:   *De Cive* published; English translation published in 1651 as
           Philosophical Rudiments Concerning Government and Society
1642–3:   writes critique of Thomas White's *De Mundo*
1645:   debates with John Bramhall about free will; writes *Of Liberty
           and Necessity* at the request of the marquis of Newcastle
1646:   becomes tutor in mathematics to the future King Charles II
1647:   second edition of *De Cive* published; Hobbes becomes seriously
           ill
1651:   *Leviathan* published
1652:   February, returns to England
1655:   *De Corpore* published; English translation approved by Hobbes
           but probably not done by him
1658:   De *Homine* published

1666:   writes *A Dialogue between a Philosopher and a Student of the Common Laws of England*; published posthumously in 1681

1668:   Latin version of *Leviathan* published in Amsterdam from revised text

1668–70: the writing of *Behemoth* completed; first authorized edition published posthumously in 1682

1673:   translation of the *Odyssey* published

1676:   translation of the *Iliad* published

1679:   December 4, dies at Hardwick Hall; buried at Hault Hucknall

A Chronology of English History for the Study of Hobbes's Thought

1534:	Act of Supremacy: the monarch (Henry VIII) is officially named head of the Church of England
1553:	Mary I becomes queen (*B*, p. 20)
1555:	Marian exile: some Protestants go into exile, many to Geneva to escape persecution (*B*, pp. 20, 22)
1628:	Petition of Right (*B*, p. 27)
1634–8:	Controversy over Ship Money (*B*, pp. 36–7)
1637:	William Prynne, Bastwick, and Burton punished by Court of High Commission for their puritan writings and sermons (*B*, pp. 64, 69) Imposition of a Book of Common Prayer on the Scots (*B*, p. 28)
1638:	National Covenant (*B*, p. 28)
1639:	First Bishops' War (*B*, p. 29)
1640:	Apr.–May, Short Parliament (*B*, pp. 32–3)
	July–Sept., the Scottish army invades northern England in Second Bishops' War (*B*, p. 35)
	Nov. 3, Long Paliament opens (*B*, pp. 71, 120)
	Nov. 10, Strafford impeached (*B*, pp. 64–6)
	Dec. 18, Archbishop Laud impeached (*B*, p. 72)
1641:	Feb. 16, Triennial Act: parliament to meet at least every three years (*B*, pp. 73–4)
	May 10, Act Against Dissolution (of parliament without its consent) (*B*, pp. 74, 117)
	May 12, Strafford executed (*B*, pp. 66, 69, 71)
	July, High Commission and Star Chamber abolished (*B*, p. 74)
	Aug., Charles goes to Scotland and settles dispute with the Scots (*B*, p. 78)
	Fall, Irish rebel against Protestant settlers (*B*, p. 79)
	Nov., Charles is welcomed back to London by its citizens (*B*, p. 80)
	Dec. 1, Grand Remonstrance presented to the king (*B*, pp. 81–7)
	Dec. 30, twelve bishops impeached

1642: Jan. 4, Montagu Lord Mandeville (Lord Kimbolton) and five MPs (Hollis, Haselrig, Hampden, Pym, and Stroud) flee from the king (*B*, pp. 87, 96)

Jan., members of the House of Lords allied with the king leave London with him (*B*, p. 88)

Feb. 13, Bishops' Exclusion and Clergy Disqualification Act (*B*, p. 88)

Mar., Militia Ordinance: the king commanded to hand over to parliament control of the militia (*B*, pp. 97–8)

Apr. 23, Charles denied entrance to Hull (*B*, p. 103)

June 1, the Nineteen Propositions (*B*, pp. 27, 101, 105–7)

June 11, Commission of Array of the king (*B*, p. 115)

July 14, Charles refused admission to Hull for the second time (*B*, p. 120)

Aug, 22, Charles raises his standard at Nottingham (*B*, pp. 108, 121)

Sept. 22, episcopacy suspended

Oct., battle of Edgehill (*B*, p. 121)

1643: Feb., Henrietta Maria lands in Burlington to promote her husband's cause (*B*, p. 123)

Feb., Sidney Godolphin killed

July 1, opening of the Assembly of Divines

Sept., Charles becomes despondent when he fails to take Gloucester (*B*, p. 126)

Sept. 20, Lord Falkland killed at Newbury

Sept. 25, Solemn League and Covenant sworn by English (*B*, p. 124)

Dec. 8, John Pym dies

1644: Jan. 19, the Scots enter England and pursue the earl of Newcastle (*B*, p. 128)

Jan. 22, Oxford Parliament opens (*B*, p. 131)

June, the earl of Newcastle is besieged in York by the Scots and the army of Thomas Fairfax (*B*, p. 129)

July 2, Oliver Cromwell defeats Prince Rupert and the earl of Newcastle at Marston Moor; Newcastle flees to Hamburg (*B*, p. 129)

July 14, Henrietta Maria leaves England

Oct., second battle of Newbury, another victory for the parliamentary army (*B*, p. 130)

Nov., New Model Army (*B*, p. 130)

1645: Jan. 10, Laud executed (*B*, pp. 72, 131)

Jan. 29–Feb. 22, Uxbridge negotiations (*B*, p. 131)

June 14, battle of Naseby, a decisive royalist defeat (*B*, p. 132)

1646: Mar., Charles, Prince of Wales, escapes to Paris (*B*, p. 132)
May, Charles I surrenders to the Scots (*B*, p. 133)
July 11, Newcastle Propositions (*B*, p. 134)
Oct., episcopacy abolished

1647: Jan. 30, the Scots hand Charles over to the English (*B*, p. 134)
June, Charles taken from Holmby House to Newmarket (*B*, pp. 137–8)
June 16, army brings charges against eleven Presbyterian MPs (*B*, p. 13)
Nov. 11, Charles escapes from Hampton Court (*B*, p. 143)
Nov. 13, Charles arrives at Isle of Wight (*B*, p. 143)
Dec. 26, Charles and the Scots enter into Engagement

1648: Jan. 3, Vote of No Addresses (*B*, p. 145)
Aug. 24, Repeal of No Addresses (*B*, p. 151)
Sept. 18, Newport negotiations begin (*B*, p. 151)
Dec. 6, Pride's Purge: Col. Thomas Pride prevents Presbyterians (parliamentarians sympathetic to the king) from entering parliament (*B*, p. 151)

1649: Jan. 20–7, trial of Charles (*B*, pp. 153–4)
Jan. 30, Charles beheaded (*B*, pp. 95, 154)
Feb. 6, Commons resolves to abolish House of Lords (*B*, p. 155)
Feb. 7, Commons resolves to abolish kingship (*B*, p. 157)
Feb. 14–15, first Council of State chosen (*B*, p. 157)
Aug.–Oct., Cromwell puts down the rebellion in Ireland (*B*, pp. 162–3)

1650: Jan. 2, Engagement Act: government officials required to swear allegiance to the Commonwealth(*B*, p. 164)
Apr., defeat of the marquis of Montrose's royalist forces in Scotland (*B*, pp. 165–6)
June, General Fairfax resigns his commission in order to avoid fighting the Scots (*B*, p. 166)
June–Sept., Cromwell's campaign against the Scots (*B*, pp. 166–8)

1651: Jan. 1, Charles II crowned in Scotland
July–Sept., Charles II enters England from Scotland with an army and is defeated at Worcester (*B*, pp. 170–1)

1652–4: First Dutch War (*B*, pp. 175–9, 183–4)

1653: Apr. 20, Cromwell dissolves the Rump Parliament (*B*, pp. 179–80, 181)
Apr. 29, new Council of State formed (*B*, p. 181)
June 8, plans for a Nominated (Barebones) Parliament (*B*, p. 181)

July 4, opening of the Nominated or Barebones Parliament (*B*, p. 181)

Aug. 24, act requiring marriages to take place before a justice of the peace (*B*, p. 182)

Dec. 12, Nominated (Barebones) Parliament dissolved

Dec. 16, Cromwell becomes Lord Protector (*B*, pp. 183, 188–9)

1654: Sept. 3, opening of first parliament of the Protectorate (*B*, p. 184)

1655: Jan. 22, first parliament of the Protectorate dissolved (*B*, p. 185)

Aug., division of country in major-generalships (*B*, p. 186)

Dec., Manasseh ben Israel discusses readmission of the Jews with Cromwell

1656: Sept. 17, opening of the second parliament of the Protectorate (*B*, p. 186)

Oct., the Quaker James Naylor enters Bristol as the Messiah (*B*, p. 187)

1657: Mar. 31, the kingship offered to Cromwell (*B*, p. 188)

Apr. 3, Cromwell refuses the kingship (*B*, p. 189)

May, 25, Cromwell accepts the amended Humble Petition without the kingship (*B*, p. 190)

1658: Jan. 20, second parliament of the Protectorate reassembles (*B*, p. 190)

Feb. 4, second parliament of the Protectorate dissolved (*B*, p. 190)

Sept. 3, Cromwell dies; his son Richard becomes Lord Protector (*B*, p. 191; see also p. 183)

1659: Jan., parliament of Richard Cromwell meets

Mar., vote to transact business with the "Other House" (*B*, p. 193)

May 7, Rump Parliament reassembles (*B*, pp. 194–5)

May 24, Richard resigns as Lord Protector (*B*, p. 194)

Aug., Booth's Rebellion (*B*, pp. 196–7)

1660: Feb. 3, Monk enters London (*B*, p. 201)

Apr. 4, Declaration of Breda: Charles II states his intentions for ruling

Apr. 25, Convention Parliament begins (*B*, p. 203)

May 25, Charles II enters London

1667: Clarendon dismissed as minister

1678: Popish Plot

1678–81: Exclusion Crisis

1685:   Charles II dies; James, duke of York, becomes king
1688:   Glorious Revolution: William of Orange invades; James II flees
1689:   William of Orange and Mary Stuart (daughter of James II) become co-monarchs

A

absurdity In ordinary speech an absurdity is often called an "error." But Hobbes thinks that a distinction should be made between the two. An error that involves a misapplication of a name to an object will result in some sentence being false, but an absurdity involves a contradiction or an incoherence in the way that words are used, such that it yields a sequence of words that does not even deserve to be categorized as false (*L* 5.22).

As part of his contrast between error and absurdity, Hobbes distinguishes two kinds of error: linguistic and nonlinguistic. A nonlinguistic error is some deception such as thinking that some event happened in the past when it did not, or thinking that some event will occur in the future when it will not. Hobbes does not think that there is any philosophical significance to this sort of error. A linguistic error occurs when a name is mistakenly used to refer to something that does not have that name. Hobbes's example is of a person who sees the sun in the sky and its reflection in the water and says that there are two suns (*DCo* 5.1). That is, the person in error is using "sun" as a name for a reflection. Another example would be that of a person who mistakenly says of some object, say, a chair, that it is a table. Since "table" is not a name for chairs, a linguistic error has occurred. Linguistic error, like nonlinguistic error, is not philosophically important to Hobbes (*DCo* 5.1). Anyone can fall into error. What Hobbes is worried about is absurdity. Only human beings can embrace an absurdity, because only human beings have language, and philosophers are more susceptible to it than others (*L* 5.7).

Although Hobbes is reluctant to say that absurd propositions are false, that they are follows from his definition of falsity. A false proposition, according to Hobbes's characterization, is a proposition in which the subject names something that is not named by the predicate (*DCo* 3.7; *L* 4.11). (This characterization obviously does not work for negative sentences. A negative (subject–predicate) proposition is true when the subject and predicate name different things, for example, "A cat is not a dog.") An absurd proposition is one in which it is impossible for the predicate to name what the subject names. The impossibility alluded to here arises from combining

27

the name of something that belongs to one kind or category of thing with the name of something that belongs to a different kind or category of thing (*DCo* 5.2).

Hobbes's mature account of absurdity is in *De Corpore*. There he says that there are four kinds of things: bodies, accidents, phantasms, and names. Absurdity results when a name from one category is combined with a name from another category (*DCo* 5.2; cf. *L* 4.14–18). Gilbert Ryle discussed the type of problem that Hobbes had in mind under the rubric of a "category mistake." There are thus seven types of absurdity:

(1) Combining the name of a body with the name of an accident, for example, "Existence is a being" and "The intellect acts." The order of the names does not matter. In the examples just given, the name of an accident ("existence," "intellect") is the subject and the name of the body is the predicate. (For Hobbes, a verb like "acts" is a name of all the bodies that act.) But absurdity also results if the name of the body is the subject and the name of the accident is the predicate: "A being is existence." Scholastic philosophy is replete with this sort of absurdity, according to Hobbes (*DCo* 5.3).

(2) Combining the name of a body with the name of a phantasm, for example, "A ghost is a body" and "A shadow moves." In both of these examples, the name of the phantasm occurs as the subject, and the name of the body occurs as the predicate (*DCo* 5.4).

(3) Combining the name of a body with the name of a name, for example, "A genus is a thing" or "A universal is a thing." The word "thing" is a name for every body. The words "genus" and "universal" are words for words (*DCo* 5.5). The two sample sentences say in effect that a word is a body. (For a nominalist like Hobbes, it is strictly true that a word is a body, but Hobbes is not thinking of the sentence in that way, nor would platonists. *See* UNIVERSALS.)

(4) Combining the name of an accident with the name of a phantasm, for example, "Color appears to a perceiver." In this example, "color" is the name of an accident, that is, what it is about a body that produces the visual experience of color, and "appears to a perceiver" is the name of a phantasm (*DCo* 5.6).

(5) Combining the name of an accident with the name of a name, for example, "A definition is the essence of a thing." This example is taken from Aristotle, who holds the view expressed by it (*DCo* 5.7).

(6) Combining the name of a phantasm with the name of a name, for example, "The idea of a man is a universal." To attribute absurdity to this kind of example is to reject conceptualism, a view often closely associated with nominalism. According to conceptualism, an individual

28

idea such as the idea of a man is a universal because it stands for any man. Hobbes rejects conceptualism on two grounds. First, an idea cannot be a universal. An idea is one individual thing; but a universal cannot be an individual thing because by its nature it is supposed to explain what makes something to be one thing or an individual. If a universal were one thing, then it would presuppose the very thing it is supposed to explain. Second, every idea is directed towards or is about only one thing, but a universal by its very nature is directed towards or is about many things. The first reason that Hobbes gives against conceptualism is not one that he can legitimately use, for he holds that names are universals, and names are every bit as individual as ideas are. Concerning the second reason, he is in a slightly better position, but still does not have a refutation of conceptualism. Hobbes thinks that ideas are different from words in such a way that while ideas cannot be universals, words can. But this is not at all obvious. Given the way Hobbes describes ideas and words, ideas, like words, can be marks and signs. The difference between an idea and a word is that an idea is natural and a word is conventional. A conceptualist may claim that Hobbes has begged the question as to whether ideas can be universals (*DCo* 5.8).

(7) Combining the name of a thing with the name of a speech act, for example, "Some entities are beings *per se*" and "Some entities are beings *per accidens.*" Hobbes thinks that these sentences are absurd. He holds that beings *per se* are necessary beings and that the only things that are necessary are PROPOSITIONS. In other words, there is only *de dicto* necessity and no *de re* necessity.

Hobbes's diagnosis of how scholastic philosophy fell into absurdity is incredible. He says, "because 'Socrates is a man' is a necessary proposition, and 'Socrates is musical' is a contingent one, for that reason they [scholastics] make some entities necessary or *per se*, others contingent or *per accidens*" (*DCo* 5.9). In fact that is not true. No scholastic ever held that either Socrates or man or being a man is a necessary entity. Scholastics distinguished two kinds of necessity. A proposition such as "Either it is raining or it is not raining" has *de dicto* or linguistic necessity. In contrast, God has necessity *de re* or with respect to the kind of thing He is. God is necessary because He must exist and it is impossible for Him not to exist. And He must exist, because nothing causes Him to exist; so nothing could prevent Him from existing. In contrast, it is possible for a contingent being not to exist, because its existence is always caused by something, and that cause for existence may be withdrawn. That is, a contingent being exists through something other than itself or *per aliud*. Since a necessary

29

being does not exist through anything other than itself, it exists through itself, that is, *per se*. The entire explanation of this view is nonlinguistic, and does not depend upon the alleged necessity of sentences like "Socrates is a man." Some scholastic philosophers talked about the fact that certain sentences contain "*per se* predication." For example, sculpting is predicated *per se* in the sentence, "A sculptor sculpts," in contrast with its use in "Polydorus sculpts." But they did not infer the necessary existence of anything based upon *per se* predication in general.

Be that as it may, Hobbes proposes a method of detecting absurdities. Every name in a proposition is resolvable into its basic components. A complete resolution of each term would reveal whether those components belong to the same or different categories (*DCo* 5.10).

The attack on absurd propositions is part of Hobbes's commitment to the new science of Galileo and Harvey and his rejection of the scholastic philosophy that had dominated Europe for the previous 500 years. The examples that Hobbes gives for all of the types of absurdity except the second are direct rejections of some Aristotelian or scholastic proposition, and one of the examples for the second type ("A ghost is a body") is rooted in what Hobbes would take to be a medieval mentality. Hobbes's strategy seems to be that if he can show people that the medieval doctrines are absurd, an important obstacle to accepting the new science has been removed.

In *Leviathan*, Hobbes has a less tenable treatment of absurdity. He claims that any false general proposition is absurd: "when we make a general assertion, unless it be a true one, the possibility of it is unconceivable" (*L* 5.5). This means that "All dogs bark" (which happens to be false) is absurd. I would suggest that Hobbes holds this view because he thought of all general propositions as at least partial definitions and hence, if true, necessarily true. The opposite of a necessarily true proposition is a contradiction and hence an absurdity.

Hobbes lists seven causes for absurdity in *Leviathan*. Four of them correspond to the absurdities enumerated above, namely, (1), (3), (4), (5). The first cause mentioned in *Leviathan*, but not in *De Corpore*, is the lack of a correct methodology. The sixth is the use of metaphors. The seventh is the use of names that signify nothing, such as "hypostatical" and "transubstantiate" (*L* 5.7–15).

actor   *See* AUTHOR

alienation   *See* AUTHORIZATION

angels   *See* SPIRITS

anger Anger is sudden COURAGE; that is, the sudden or abrupt belief that one will not be hurt by an object that one is resisting (*L* 6.18). One might object to this definition in at least three ways. First, it seems odd to think of anger as a belief, rather than a passion or emotion. Second, it rules out cases in which people slowly get angry. Third, people sometimes get angry even when they know that it may increase their chances of being injured by whatever is causing them to get angry. It is not clear to me what Hobbes would say in reply to these. Sometimes he gives the impression that some of his definitions are stipulative; but at other times he seems to want them to be descriptive. And I would expect a definition of anger to be closer to a descriptive definition than to a stipulative one.

appetite *See* DESIRE

artificial and natural People standardly divide things into what is natural and what is artificial. What is natural is typically taken to be better than what is artificial. Hobbes challenges both of these ideas. He begins *Leviathan* by undermining the distinction with the phrase, "Nature, the art whereby God hath made and governs the world . . ." That is, nature is an artifact because it is made by God. In several key contrasts, the item or condition that is natural is clearly inferior to and less desirable than the artificial item or condition. Human life in the state of nature, which is natural, is "solitary, poor, nasty, brutish, and short" (*L* 13.9). Human life in the civil state, which is artificial, is unquestionably better. The sovereign or Leviathan is artificial, because it is made by human beings; it is "that mortal God, to which we owe, under the immortal God, our peace and defence" (*L* 17.13).

What is good in the state of nature is whatever a person desires. But because these desires conflict with those of others, almost everything that is naturally desired has destructive consequences. An exception is the natural desire for self-preservation. This exceptional natural good, combined with rationality, leads one to substitute an artificial good as the object of one's desire, namely, the desires of the sovereign. These desires of the sovereign, when expressed, are his commands or laws. Thus, Hobbes holds that it is in the interests of people to desire something artificial, the law.

atheism The cognitive meaning of "atheist" is a person who believes that God does not exist or that there is no God. It had this meaning even in the seventeenth century, even though it was considered appropriate to apply the term to people who believed that God exists but is not providential, that is, that He does not govern or care for the universe. It was also applied to people who believed that God exists but who also held some

31

beliefs that unwittingly were inconsistent with belief in God (*DC* 14.19 note, 15.2, 18.11; *L* 31.17; *OL* 3:548–9). The criterion for applying the word "atheism" then did not fit the cognitive meaning of the term. This sort of discrepancy has led to many errors in determining who was an atheist in the early modern period. One further point about usage is important. Since belief in God was considered essential for morality and uprightness, the term "atheist" was usually applied as a term of abuse. As Hobbes says, "*atheism, impiety,* and the like are words of the greatest defamation possible" (*BCL*, p. 282). Very often when religious groups were bitterly opposed, at least one thought of the other as atheistic. Roman Catholics and Protestants called each other atheists. Calvinists called Arminians atheists, and so on. Usually, the group making the charge knew that the other group did not expressly affirm atheism or consciously believe that God did not exist. Rather, the point was that the principles of the offensive group led to atheism. So, Catholics thought that the Protestant denial of the authority of the pope and the efficacy of the sacraments would lead to more and more denials of doctrine until the very existence of God would be denied. Protestants thought that distinctively Roman Catholic beliefs were superstitious and that when people discovered this, they would reject not only those beliefs but all religious beliefs.

Many of Hobbes's definitions are idiosyncratic because he tries to relate the definition of every word to other words which ultimately will be analyzed in terms of the motion of bodies; and this project sometimes requires some intuitively strained analyses. With regard to "atheism," he defines it in relation to "true religion" and "superstition." (*See* RELIGION.) True religion is fear of powers invisible when the beliefs about the powers that are feared are correct. Superstition is "fear without right reason"; that is, to be superstitious is to be mistaken about what ought to be feared. Playing off the definition of "superstition," Hobbes defines "atheism" as "opinion of right reason without fear." What he means is that an atheist thinks she is being rational in not fearing any invisible power (because she believes that there is none) when in fact there is such a power. Hobbes's use of "opinion" to modify "right reason" implies that the opinion of atheists is mistaken. (*DC* 16.1). Replying to Bishop Bramhall's criticisms of his definitions, Hobbes says, "And is not atheism boldness grounded on false reasoning such as this, *the wicked prosper, therefore there is no God*? . . . I deny that there is any reason either in the atheist or in the superstitious" (*BCL*, p. 291; see also pp. 289–90).

The most common kind of atheism according to Hobbes is that which logically follows from some philosophical propositions. For example, atheism logically follows from identifying God with either the world or the soul of the world. The reason is that God is supposed to be the cause of the world. Since a cause must temporally precede its effect, if God were identical with the whole world or any part of it, then He could not be its cause and hence would not exist (*L* 31.15; *OL* 3:549). For a similar reason, if the world were eternal, then God would not exist; for if it were eternal, then it would not be created and hence there would be no creator (*L* 31.16). Hobbes gives no sense of being aware that this is a controversial opinion even among Christian thinkers. Thomas Aquinas, for example, thought that there is no logical impossibility involved in holding that God created the world from eternity; it is only through revelation that humans know that the world is not eternal. It may be that one reason that Hobbes does not accept the view of Aquinas is their difference about the concept of cause. For Aquinas a cause need not temporally precede its effect; indeed, a cause in its proper sense ("causa per se") is simultaneous with its effect. Hobbes, in contrast, holds the modern view that a cause must temporally precede its effect. (*See* CAUSE AND EFFECT.) For this reason, no being cotemporal with the world can be the cause of the world.

Hobbes calls those doctrines that logically lead to atheism "atheism by consequence." But this is not a genuine atheism: "though by ignorance of the consequence they [many philosophers, especially scholastics] said that which was equivalent to atheism, yet in their hearts they thought God a substance and would also, if they had known what *substance* and what *corporeal* meant, have said he was a corporeal substance. So that this *atheism by consequence* is a very easy thing to be fallen into, even by the most godly men of the church" (*BCL*, pp. 383–4). Bramhall in his criticism of the doctrine of *Leviathan* accused Hobbes of espousing principles that led to atheism. In his response, Hobbes denied the accusation. He says that Bramhall "has not yet found the place where I contradict either the existence, or infiniteness, or incomprehensibility, or unity, or ubiquity of God. I am therefore yet absolved of atheism" (*BCL*, p. 286).

In *De Cive*, after talking about the nature of law in general and SIN in particular, Hobbes has a brief comment to make about the sin of atheists. He imagines an atheist arguing as follows: All sin is breaking some law; there is no law unless the lawgiver is acknowledged by the subject; atheists do not acknowledge the existence of God as a lawgiver; so atheists cannot sin. (If the premise that there is no law unless the lawgiver is acknowledged by the subject seems dubious, one should recognize that Hobbes holds it because he is a radical democrat in political theory. *See* COVENANT.) Hobbes unequivocally asserts that God or an earthly sovereign will or should punish atheists for "sins of impudence" or shamelessness. But that response does not comment on the argument itself. Indeed, Hobbes seems to be committed to its soundness. Atheists are not sinners. Instead, they are enemies of God in the same sense in which any person who does not acknowledge the authority of a civil sovereign is not a criminal but an enemy. And many of Hobbes's critics were not satisfied to have him say that atheists were enemies of God. They wanted him to assert that atheism was a sin of "injustice." Hobbes thought that the criticism was unfair because he thought his description of atheists as enemies of God was "somewhat sharper" than a description of them as "unjust" (*DC* 14.19 note; *BCL*, pp. 290–5). However, the sharpness of the language is not really relevant. The objection is whether Hobbes had correctly categorized the failing of the atheists.

If atheists are genuine sinners, then I think that Hobbes does not have an adequate reply. If the laws of nature are not genuine laws, as Hobbes holds in *De Cive*, then even if an atheist were not to follow them, the atheist would not have sinned, since to sin is to break a law (*DC* 17.25). Further, an atheist could not sin by breaking any covenant with God, because one can make a covenant only if one thinks the other party exists.

Even if the laws of nature are genuine laws, as Hobbes seems to regard them in *Leviathan*, he still does not have an explanation for how atheism could be a sin. To recognize that a law exists presupposes that one acknowledges the existence of the lawgiver, in this case, God. But this is exactly what the atheist does not acknowledge. Thus, even if an atheist is not in conformity with the laws of nature, her behavior does not count as breaking a law. Hence an atheist cannot sin.

Hobbes could of course continue to hold that the atheist is the enemy of God, because in the state of nature all persons are enemies. God would then have the right to punish atheists, even if they are not sinners. There is something unsatisfactory about this general position if one insists that atheism is a sin.

A speculative way to adjust Hobbes's theory in order to explain how atheism could be a sin would be to distinguish between formal and material violations of laws. A material violation would be any nonobservance of the content of a law. A formal violation would be any nonacknowledgment of the authority of the lawgiver. Given this distinction, one could hold that atheists are sinners because they formally break the laws of nature (even if they were to observe the content of all of them). It is plausible that an absolute sovereign would consider it a crime not to accept his authority even if the person's behavior were otherwise blameless. God may be the same. Something like this reasoning seems to motivate Hobbes's remark in *De Cive* when he is speaking of "the kingdom of God by nature." There he calls atheism "treason against the Divine Majesty" on the grounds that since everyone should "absolutely obey" God, anyone who does not "might be said to be guilty of treason" (*DC* 15.19). The point here is that even if an atheist is not violating the content of any specific law of nature, she is violating the laws of nature if she does not acknowledge God as the lawgiver.

What penalty should a civil state inflict on atheists? Almost all of his contemporaries thought that a painful execution would be appropriate. Hobbes is much more merciful. He thought that they should be exiled because they are a danger to the state, not being able to swear an oath. It would not be good to kill them, because there is always the hope that they may be converted to belief in God (*OL* 3:549). Hobbes is not however opposed to capital punishment in principle. The sovereign has the right of nature, which includes the right to kill anyone who is perceived to be a threat.

Many of Hobbes's contemporaries called him an atheist. He always denied the charge and defended himself against it explicitly in several works. He says that if he were an atheist he would have to know it; and knowing it, he would not have made it known in his works. One of the main reasons for the charge was his view that no substance is incorporeal. The standard Christian view is that God is necessarily incorporeal or immaterial. This is what makes Him a spirit. If it were true both that, if there is a God, then He is incorporeal, and that nothing is incorporeal, then it would follow that God does not exist. Bramhall says that the view that "there is no incorporeal spirit is that main root of atheism" (*BCL*, p. 301). Hobbes reasons the opposite way. He holds that nothing incorporeal exists; God exists; therefore, God is corporeal.

What kind of evidence could settle the dispute between Hobbes and the overwhelming majority of Christians who believe that God is incorporeal? Most Christians rely upon the views of ancient Greek metaphysicians and Roman Catholic theologians, Hobbes would point out. Why should English Protestants rely upon pagans and Catholics? On Hobbes's side, Tertullian is the only church father who maintained that all substances are bodies (*BCL*, p. 305; *EW* 4:429); but that claim was not condemned at Nicaea. More significantly, Hobbes has the Bible on his side. The word "incorporeal" does not appear in it.

author The term "author" needs to be understood in conjunction with its correlative "actor." An actor is a person whose behavior – Hobbes uses the term "action" – is attributed to someone or something else. The author is the person to whom the action is attributed whether or not she is the one who performed the behavior that resulted in the action. When a human being acts for herself, she is both the actor and the author (*L* 16.4–5; *DH* 14.2). It is unlikely that Hobbes used these two terms primarily because of their use in the dramatic arts. Hobbes rarely mentions drama or the theater at all, and since the theater was considered disreputable by a large portion of the population, it is unlikely that he would have taken an aspect of it as his model. In the seventeenth century, independently of each other, "actor" had the sense of an agent or representative and "author" had the sense of one who causes an action or authorizes another. Nonetheless, the analogy to the theater is apt. A stage actor recites the lines written for her by the play's author, and those lines may be attributed to the author even though they are spoken by the actor.

Hobbes's brief description of an actor does not make it clear whether the physical behavior of an actor can be attributed to a nonhuman. My guess is that it cannot. Hobbes introduces the idea of an actor at the end of his treatment of what natural and artificial PERSONS are. He says, "Of persons artificial, some have their words and actions owned by those whom they represent. And then the person is the actor; and he that owns his words and actions is the author" (*L* 16.4). The word "some" in the first sentence of this quotation has perplexed commentators. Perhaps Hobbes says, "some," in order to divide the class of artificial persons into two. The first group of artificial persons represents inanimate objects, like hospitals, schools, and bridges. They get their authority from the "owners or governors of those things," not from those things themselves; for "things inanimate cannot be authors" (*L* 16.9). The second group of artificial persons represents one or more human beings; the people they represent are the authors of the actions.

Hobbes uses the correlative terms author/actor in order to explain the nature of sovereignty only in *Leviathan* (cf. *BCL,* p. 375). For Hobbes, the sovereign is an actor. He acts on the AUTHORIZATION of his subjects and on their behalf. The subjects are the authors of the sovereign's behavior. For Hobbes's purposes, this way of talking about the sovereign has two major advantages. First, it seems to explain how the sovereign has authority. For Hobbes, a human being becomes an actor by being authorized by the authors; and authorization is the process by which a person acquires authority. Second, it gives to the sovereign a way of forestalling any objections that might be raised against his policies by his subjects. If the subjects are the authors of the sovereign's behavior and the sovereign is nothing but an actor, then the subjects have no right to complain since they authorized the sovereign to act for them (*L* 18.6; *DH* 15.3). One might object to these supposed advantages. First, while an actor may have authority to act for an author, this cannot give her authority over the author, *pace* Hobbes. A person does not lose her power over another when she authorizes him to act for her. Second, Hobbes's description of authorization does not seem to fit the facts. Subjects often complain because the sovereign acts in way that they had not authorized but which they lack the power to undo. (*See also* PERSON.)

In addition to the two supposed major advantages of the concept of authorization, there is a minor one. Hobbes thinks it justifies obedience to a sovereign in matters of the ritual celebration of religion. Hobbes was an Erastian. He thought that religion ought to be a function of the civil state and hence controlled by it. Christians under a Muslim sovereign ought to observe the same ritual obligations of Islam that a Christian sovereign may require of Muslims under his control. Such a position seems to violate the rights of CONSCIENCE. Many early Christians became MARTYRS precisely because they refused to worship according to pagan Roman rituals. Hobbes's solution is that Christians perform the religious rituals commanded by their sovereign as a matter of the obedience owed to him. Moreover, they can do so in good conscience because their physical behavior does not result in an action attributable to them but to the sovereign. According to Hobbes, the ritualistic behavior is the action of the sovereign; the subjects are only actors. Now, Hobbes's position here is inconsistent with what he said earlier. According to his earlier claims, if the subjects authorize the sovereign, then what he does, they do; so if they make-as-if to pray to Allah at the sovereign's command, then they are in fact praying to Allah.

authorization Hobbes has two ways of explaining the authority of the sovereign in *Leviathan*. One involves the idea of authorizing a person or persons to be the sovereign; the other involves the idea of alienating one's rights to some things. Each way has some advantages for establishing what Hobbes wants to make of sovereignty, and he tries to meld them into one account. But his account is arguably inconsistent.

Let's consider authorization first. Hobbes's theory of authorization depends upon his distinction between actors and authors. An actor is a person whose actions are not owned by her but by someone else. The actions of a stage actor, for example, may be said to be owned by the author of the lines that the actor recites. However, by an actor, Hobbes means something more like an agent, as in the terms, "real estate agent" or "talent agent," that is, a person who represents another person in some business dealing or other practical affair. (The theory being discussed here is sometimes called "the agency model" (Hampton, *Hobbes and the Social Contract Tradition*, pp. 264–5).) By an AUTHOR, Hobbes means not so much a published writer as a person who has the responsibility for some action. An author then is the human being who owns the actor's action or to whom an action is attributed. When a human being acts for herself, she is both the actor and the author (*L* 16.4–15).

According to Hobbes, people trying to get out of the state of nature by forming a civil state are the authors of their action. They achieve their

37

desired goal by authorizing some person to represent them. This person is the sovereign, who, insofar as he acts for them, is an actor. According to Hobbes's view, an actor, by being authorized, acquires authority. Thus, the sovereign, by being authorized, acquires his authority. In establishing a civil state, each prospective subject in effect expresses the following formula: "I authorize and give up my right of governing myself to this man or to this assembly of men on this condition that thou give up thy right to him and authorize all his actions in like manner" (*L* 17.13). The import of part of this formula is clear. Whoever says it authorizes someone (the sovereign) to act on her behalf. Although it is not stated here, the sovereign's authorization has as its aim the protection of the life of the subject.

But there is another part of this formula that does not seem to have anything to do with authorization, namely, "I . . . give up my right of governing myself to this man or to this assembly of men . . ." This part is relevant to the issue of alienation. Hobbes usually talks about laying down or giving up a right, when he means "alienation." (*See* RIGHTS, LAYING DOWN.) I use "alienation" here because it is more convenient and has become standard in the secondary literature. According to his theory of alienation, which is his second way of explaining sovereignty, human beings trying to get out of the state of nature alienate or give up their right to all things. The core of alienation is the idea that something that has been alienated cannot be taken back unilaterally by the person who alienated it. When rights are alienated to a sovereign, there are only two ways in which they can be regained, either through the voluntary return of those rights by the sovereign, or by his destruction. In either case, people return to the state of nature.

The phrase "give up their right to all things," which was just used above, is ambiguous. It may have the consequence that (1) the person has no right to anything, or the consequence that (2) the person has the right to some things but not to everything. When Hobbes first introduces the idea of giving up the right to everything, he clearly intends it to have consequence (2). It is sensible to hold that a necessary condition for founding a civil state is that the subjects give up some of their rights. But later in the presentation of his theory, Hobbes shifts the sense of "giving up the right to everything" such that it has consequence (1). He makes this shift because he wants the sovereign to be absolute in the sense of having control, in principle, over every aspect of life, except those things that concern the immediate preservation of a person's life.

Both authorization and alienation have an advantage. The advantage of authorization is that it makes the subjects responsible for the behavior of their sovereign and thereby immunizes him from blame. The advantage of alienation is that it gives a theoretical reason for why governments ought to be stable and removes the right of rebellion from subjects. One may say that authorization removes the motivation to rebel, and alienation removes the right. Given Hobbes's obsession with political stability, it is no wonder that he would want to combine the advantages of each. The problem is that he does not acknowledge their apparent incompatibility.

Any authorization is revocable, but nothing alienated is recoverable at will. Typically, authorizations are revocable at will when they do not terminate after a fixed period of time. A real estate agent, say, may be authorized to represent a party for only six months and the buyer (author) cannot end the authorization at will before the end of that period. Such cases of authorization always require a contract between the author and the actor in order to protect the rights of each. But Hobbes cannot think of authorization in this way since he refuses to have the sovereign be a party to the contract. Thus, if a person authorizes a sovereign to act for her defense, she must retain the natural right to withdraw the authorization, at least under certain conditions. To object that only the sovereign can judge whether the conditions are met or that the right to withdraw authorization jeopardizes the stability of the government is simply to abandon the idea of authorization (*L* 17.5). Hobbes fears that a subject would be inclined to revoke her authorization of the government just when the government wants to impose some tax or other hardship on her. That is why he also uses the idea of alienation, which prevents subjects from exempting themselves from the authority of the government.

One symptom of the incompatibility between authorization and alienation is a grammatical incoherence in the sovereign-making formula quoted above and given here again: "I authorize and give up my right of governing myself to this man or to this assembly of men on this condition, that thou give up thy right to him and authorize all his actions in like manner" (*L* 17.13). There is no direct object for the first occurrence of "authorize." Neither the phrase "this man" nor the phrase "this assembly of men" can serve that purpose since they are indirect objects for the verb phrase "give up my right." Further, "authorize" needs an infinitive phrase, not the gerund phrase "governing myself," to specify what actions are to be done, as in "authorize you to buy a house." What Hobbes means presumably is "I authorize all his [the sovereign's] actions to govern me." This clause however is objectionable for at least two reasons. First, since the sovereign-making formula is supposed to clarify what being governed by someone means, neither "govern" nor its cognates can be legitimately used.

The second objection will be developed at some length. When a person's life is at stake, it is absurd for that person to give someone else *carte blanche*, and Hobbes makes a point of this in other contexts. There are some things that one can never authorize a person to do, such as to kill one. Authorization has its limits. Hobbes says that "if a man by words or other signs seem to despoil himself of the end for which those signs were intended, he is not to be understood as if he meant it or that it was his will; but that he was ignorant of how such words and actions were to be interpreted" (L 14.8). The sovereign-making formula seems to despoil the subject of the end of self-preservation. So, she cannot mean what she seems to say. But what else could she mean? The answers are as various as the interpreters. (Also, some scholars claim that there is no incompatibility between authorization and alienation, and no problem with the sovereign-making formula.)

Hobbes returns to this issue when he talks about the liberty of subjects (after his discussion of sovereignty by institution and sovereignty by acquisition). There he says that a person cannot give up the right to defend her own body. It follows that a subject cannot be commanded to kill, wound, or otherwise injure herself, say, by self-incrimination (L 21.11–13). What is wrong with this seemingly sober view is that, combined with the principle that whoever has a right to an end has a right to the means to that end, retention of the right to self-defense in principle excludes giving up anything. By Hobbes's own reasoning, one can never know when something may be necessary to preserve one's life (L 14.4); so giving up anything may frustrate one's inalienable right to life. This is a genuine problem in Hobbes's theory.

While it is not appropriate here to press a specific interpretation of Hobbes, it may aid understanding to consider his view that two of the disadvantages of the state of nature are that power is distributed equally among people and that everyone has a right to everything. These disadvantages are eliminated when each person gives up enough of her rights to the sovereign to make him strong enough to ensure the safety of all the subjects. In other words, each subject alienates enough rights to allow the sovereign to do the job he is authorized to do, namely, to ensure the safety of the subjects. Giving up these limited rights is supposed to enhance the chances of preserving a person's life in the long run. If the sovereign failed to fulfill his mission, then the people could withdraw their authorization and would have sufficient reserved rights and powers to make that withdrawal effective. This is roughly Locke's theory, not Hobbes's. Hobbes would not like my suggestion because he wants an absolute sovereign, not a limited one.

Some attempts have been made to reconcile authorization with alienation. David Gauthier concedes that Hobbes gives no good argument for the position that authorizations of the sovereign are irrevocable. Yet he thinks that such an argument can be constructed with nothing but principles that Hobbes does espouse. The crucial premise is that, in establishing a sovereign, each subject incurs an obligation to every other subject not to withdraw her own authorization. He thinks this premise is necessary in order to have a sovereign at all: "For if the sovereign must act under the continual threat of deposition by his subjects releasing each other from their covenants to authorize him, then his efforts to fulfil the intention of the authorization, by guaranteeing the internal and external security of the commonwealth, will be jeopardized" (Gauthier, *The Logic of Leviathan*, p. 160). As a matter of fact, Gauthier seems to be wrong. John Locke uses authorization in his political theory. He raises and cogently answers Gauthier's very objection:

> But 'twill be said, this hypothesis lays a ferment for frequent rebellion. To which I answer,
> First, no more than any other hypothesis. For when the people are made miserable, and find themselves exposed to the ill usage of arbitrary power, cry up their governours, as much as you will for the sons of Jupiter, let them be sacred and divine, descended or authorized from heaven; give them out for whom or what you please, the same will happen. The people generally ill treated and contrary to right will be ready upon any occasion to ease themselves of a burden that sits heavy upon them. . . . He must have lived but a little while in the world who has not seen examples of this in his time; and he must have read very little who cannot produce examples of it in all sorts of governments in the world. (Locke, *Two Treatises of Government* 2.224)

Locke is right; political theories neither foment nor forestall rebellion.

Authorization is part of a democratic theory of government, in the sense that the origin of all political power is located in the subjects, and they are free to establish either a monarchy, an aristocracy, or a democracy. The word "democracy" is obviously ambiguous. It can refer either to a theory about the source of political power or to a form of government. Hobbes uses democratic premises in his discussion of the origin of government, in contrast with, say, patriarchal or divine-right premises.

In a late work that Hobbes did not allow to be published, *A Dialogue between a Philosopher and a Student of the Common Laws of England*, he distinguishes between transferring a right and committing one. These are tantamount respectively to alienating a right and authorizing the exercise of one. A transferred right is lost to the original owner; a committed right remains in her possession. Hobbes uses the distinction in order to explain that the king, in appointing judges to various courts, does not lose the right to judge any case himself. The king authorizes people to act for him; he does not alienate any of his rights, contrary to the claim of the great common law theorist Edward Coke (*DCL*, pp. 52, 54). Thus, when

41

it suited his purposes, Hobbes saw that alienation and authorization were incompatible.

aversion *See* DESIRE

B

Behemoth (1679) [37]   *Behemoth* is Hobbes's history of the English Civil Wars and the Interregnum, that is, the history of England from 1640 to 1660. In addition to a narrative of the events, it contains his analysis of the causes of the Civil War. The causes were both political and religious, according to Hobbes. The political ones were that the king did not have his own source of revenues to conduct state business, but had to rely upon parliament for subsidies, and that the people did not know that they had an obligation to obey the sovereign in all matters. The religious problems were due to subversive doctrines taught by three main groups: the Roman Catholics, the Presbyterians, and the Independents. (*See* CATHOLICS AND PRESBYTERIANS.)

Behemoth was completed sometime between 1668 and 1670, but not published until 1679, in a pirated edition. Hobbes's publisher, William Crook, put out the first authorized edition in 1682, three years after Hobbes's death. Hobbes had wanted to publish the book earlier, but Charles II had refused permission (*EW* 4:411). Charles himself pursued a policy of toleration and did not want to keep the animosities of the 1640s alive. The inflammatory perspective of Hobbes's narrative and analysis was inconsistent with that policy.

Behemoth is a series of four dialogues between two characters, namely, "A," someone who lived through the wars, and "B," a younger person. The first dialogue is the most interesting because it discusses the political and religious background of the Civil Wars and its basic causes. Hobbes establishes the legitimacy of the Stuart monarchy by tracing it back in England to William the Conqueror in 1066 and back in Scotland to Henry II, king of Ireland. (There was some controversy at this time over whether William should be referred to as the Conqueror or as William of Normandy. Some parliamentarians and democrats, not wanting conquest to justify any government for fear of legitimizing tyranny, denied that William conquered England and asserted that he was the legitimate claimant to the throne. Hobbes, not having any scruples about conquest preceding a legitimate government, is quite comfortable with the name "William the Conqueror.")

The Roman Catholics receive detailed criticism for their involvement in the Gunpowder Plot and the Jesuits are attacked (*B*, pp. 20, 61); and there is a history of pre-Reformation abuses of the church. The political dimension of priestly celibacy and auricular confession, the absurdity of transubstantiation, and the nature of heresy are all detailed (*B*, pp. 9–15, 46). Later, he mentions that the English feared the re-establishment of Catholicism because of the foreign Catholics connected to the court and especially to the queen, such as the papal envoys Fr George Con and Count Rosetti (*B*, pp. 60–1). Other facts may have been playing in Hobbes's mind subconsciously. Many Protestants thought that England was being run by papists. Catholicism was practiced at court by Henrietta Maria and her entourage. The king was encouraged to wage war against Scotland by such Catholics as the earl of Worcester and the marquis of Winchester. The earl of Arundel, the head of a family that had many Catholics in it, was the commander in chief of the English forces. And the earl of Strafford was in charge of an Irish Catholic army that the English Protestants were afraid might be used against them. Much of the evidence for Roman Catholic meddling in English affairs is detailed in the Grand Remonstrance of 1641.

The evils of the Presbyterians are traced back to the reign of the Catholic Queen Mary I. Her persecutions of Protestants sent many of them to Geneva, where a group of them produced the Geneva Bible, which contained some seditious marginal notes and encouraged people to devise their own interpretations of the Bible. The Marian exiles also picked up democratic ideas in Geneva and imported them when they returned to England (*B*, pp. 135–6). Finally, the Presbyterians became a strong influence in the universities and parliament and corrupted both (*B*, pp. 21–7, 41–3, 55–8). In addition to the English Presbyterians, Scottish Presbyterians contributed to the outbreak of war, because of their refusal to accept the prayer book imposed on them in 1637 (*B*, pp. 28–31). Hobbes presents a narrative of the problems in Scotland from 1638 to 1640 (*B*, pp. 31–9).

The second dialogue is part analysis and part narrative of the events between 1640 and the outbreak of war in 1642. Hobbes defends the behavior of the three people closest to the king who were often blamed for corrupting Charles's judgement: Henrietta Maria, Thomas Wentworth (Lord Strafford), and archbishop William Laud. About Henrietta Maria, he says that she was only following her religious beliefs. About Wentworth, he says that he was conducting the king's policies (*B*, pp. 64–9). About Laud, he rejects the charge that he was a "papist." Laud only wanted to promote "the Church-government by bishops, and . . . desired to have the service of God performed, and the house of God adorned, as suitable as was possible to the honour we ought to do to the Divine Majesty"

(*B*, p. 73; see also pp. 62, 72–4). Considering the grief he suffered at the hands of Laud's colleagues, Hobbes's defense of Laud and his attack on the puritan emphasis on preaching in preference to the celebration of the eucharist are evidence of his commitment to the Church of England (*B*, p. 64). In addition to the defense of these people, there is an extended discussion of the impropriety of the Grand Remonstrance of December 1641 (*B*, pp. 80–5) and the Nineteen Propositions of June 1642 (*B*, pp. 105–7).

Hobbes says that the third and fourth dialogues are based upon "Mr. Heath's chronicle" (*B*, pp. [v], 119–20). This is either or both of James Heath's *A Brief Chronicle of All the Chief Actions So Fatally Falling out in these Three Kingdoms* etc. (1662) and his greatly expanded *Brief Chronicle of the Late Intestine Warr* (1663), which Anthony Wood described as "being mostly compiled from lying pamphlets, and all sorts of news-books" and as containing "innumerable errors . . . especially as to name and time" (quoted from Macgillivray, *Restoration Historians and the English Civil War*, p. 12). This would explain some, though not all, of the factual errors in Hobbes's account. For example, Hobbes seems mistakenly to think that the Oxford Parliament met in 1645 instead of 1644 (*B*, p. 131).

The third dialogue is largely a narrative of the war from the outbreak of fighting to the execution of Charles I. At the beginning of the dialogue, he criticizes unnamed counselors of the king who did not believe that England was an absolute monarchy (*B*, pp. 114–15). Hobbes probably had in mind the authors of Charles's conciliatory answer to the Nineteen Propositions on June 18, 1642. The reply is usually now attributed to John Culpepper. It might have served Hobbes's purpose to suggest that someone other than Charles I had been its author.

Hobbes also thought that Charles should have acted with more force against parliament when it first opposed him. He thought that decisive and crushing force would have been the best argument about who held the sovereignty (*B*, p. 116). (Presumably Hobbes thinks that *argumentum ad baculum* is a valid argument form when used by an absolute sovereign.) In effect, Charles gave away his sovereignty. When the issue is raised about where sovereignty resided when Charles was held captive by the English, a very un-Hobbesian answer is given: "the right was certainly in the King, but the exercise was yet in nobody" (*B*, p. 135). In his theoretical works, irresistible power is a necessary condition for sovereignty. Sovereign right without power for Hobbes is as contradictory as the idea of immaterial substance.

After Charles was defeated and turned over to the army, a power struggle ensued between the army and parliament. Within parliament itself, this was a struggle between the Presbyterians, who were the anti-army contingent, and the Independents, with Cromwell emerging as their leader. In this struggle, Londoners felt threatened by the army. While he does not sympathize with the Presbyterians, Hobbes seems better disposed towards Londoners, and he criticizes the army and the Independents (*B*, pp. 140–2).

To Hobbes, Cromwell's rise to power was the result of his own elaborate and single-minded scheme. Even the appointment of Sir Thomas Fairfax as general of the entire parliamentary army is interpreted by Hobbes as in fact benefiting primarily Cromwell (*B*, p. 142). Hobbes also accepts the royalist view that Cromwell instigated Charles's escape from Hampton Court. But he draws the line there. He does not accept the implausible view, expressed by Andrew Marvell in "An Horatian Ode Upon Cromwell's Return from Ireland," that Cromwell had even schemed to have Charles flee to the Isle of Wight, where he would be captured (*B*, p. 143).

Hobbes does not seem to think that there was a second civil war. He does not mention the Engagement that Charles made with the Scots. The uprising of the apprentices, the revolt in Wales, and the invasion of the Scots, under the duke of Hamilton, are dismissed as the actions of people using the name of the king without genuinely being royalists. The third dialogue closes with the trial and execution of Charles. Hobbes's narration of these events contains no special rhetorical flourishes or highlights, which strikes me as strange, given his royalist leanings and the fact that he probably wrote *Behemoth* to ingratiate himself with the king, Charles's son (*B*, pp. 153–4).

The fourth dialogue covers the years 1649–60, that is, the Commonwealth and Protectorate. It begins with a discussion of the nature of the Rump Parliament. It was, says Hobbes, an oligarchy (*B*, p. 156). Hobbes continues to blame the Presbyterians, more than anyone else, for destroying the monarchy, even though they opposed the execution of Charles I and often urged the restoration of the monarchy (*B*, p. 159). His analysis of their strategy is that they wanted a democratic government, because once it was obtained, they could then institute a democratic church, which he thinks was their primary goal all along. Thus, Hobbes is able to apply his theoretical views about the proper relationship between religion and politics and the subversiveness of false religious beliefs to an actual situation. Roman Catholics are hardly mentioned, probably because, as Hobbes was then writing, they were in favor in the royal court. In the narrative, Hobbes still represents Cromwell implausibly as stage directing every event leading up to his assumption of the Protectorate. At the end of *Behemoth*, Hobbes has a fairly elaborate statement of the mythic understanding of political revolutions as literally circular actions. He sees "in this revolution a circular motion . . . from King Charles I to the Long Parliament; from thence to the Rump; from the Rump to Oliver Cromwell; and then back again from Richard Cromwell to the Rump; thence to the Long Parliament; and thence to King Charles II, where long it may remain" (*B*, p. 204). Fairness perhaps requires that it be mentioned that the parliamentarians interpreted the Civil War as the completion of a revolution from a pre-Stuart age of representative government, to the Stuart tyranny, to the Commonwealth.

benevolence Benevolence is a desire that the desires of another person will be satisfied (*L* 6.22). (*See* DESIRE.)

Bible The Bible is made up of two main parts, according to Christians: the Old Testament and the New. For Hobbes, the similarities between them are more important than the differences, since he, as a Christian, considers each to contain the revelation of God to human beings. The principal difference between them is that, while the Old Testament was written over a very long period of time and usually long after the events it reports, the New Testament was written within the span of a century and shortly after the events it reports. Hobbes points out that most of the Old Testament was not accepted as revelatory until after the Babylonian Captivity ended in 538 BC.

Hobbes first discusses biblical criticism in *De Cive*, but his discussion of the topic there is limited and not essential to the argument of the book (*DC* 16.12). By far his fullest and most important treatment of the accuracy, canonicity, and composition of the Bible occurs in part three of *Leviathan*, as part of his discussion of the nature of a Christian commonwealth. The rest of this entry will be divided into three parts: (1) the accuracy of the Bible; (2) the canonicity of the Bible; (3) the authorship of the Bible.

(1) The first topic can be dealt with rather briefly. Hobbes points out that the text of the Bible was under the exclusive control of clerics during the early part of its existence. If the clerics had changed anything substantive, they certainly would have changed those parts that are critical of them:

> I am persuaded they [the priests] did not therefore falsify the Scriptures, though the copies of the Books of the New Testament were in the hands only of the ecclesiastics; because if they had had an intention to do so, they would surely have made them more favorable to their power over Christian princes and civil sovereignty than they are. I see not therefore any reason to doubt but that the Old and New Testament, as we have them now, are the true Registers of those things which were done and said by the prophets and apostles. (*L* 33.20)

(2) Canonicity, that is, the status of the Bible as law, is the defining feature of the Bible (*L* 33.1). The obvious question to ask is, "What makes certain books law and not others?" Indeed, this is the first question that Hobbes asks about the Bible. His answer is that the sovereign determines it, because the sovereign is the only person who can make laws (*L* 33.1).

One might object that since God is the one who speaks in the Bible and since He is "the Sovereign of all sovereigns," He ought to decide which books are canonical and which are not (*L* 33.1). God ought to be obeyed no matter what an earthly sovereign may command. Consider how blasphemous it would be, the objection might continue, to have some book containing the word of God excluded from the Bible simply because some earthly sovereign did not include it. Hobbes thinks the objection misses the point. He does not doubt that every command of God ought to be obeyed. It goes without saying that God ought to be obeyed if there is any conflict between divine commands and human ones. The relevant issue then is not the metaphysical or theological question of whether God or man ought to be obeyed. Rather, it is the epistemological issue of determining which books are the ones that contain the word of God (*L* 33.1). Hobbes's point here should be compared with his treatment of PROPHETS, MIRACLES, and REVELATION. In each case, Hobbes affirms that the phenomenon exists (that is, there are true prophets, miracles, and revelation) but points out epistemological problems with determining which they are in the midst of false pretenders. And in each case, his solution to the epistemological problem is the same. Instead of trying to find some epistemological foundation to answer the skeptical challenge, "How do we know?", Hobbes opts for a practical solution, intended to sidestep dissension. A subject should rely upon the decision of her sovereign. In other words, an epistemological problem is given a political solution.

One might ask a related question, "What is the mechanism by which one determines that the decision of the sovereign rather than something else is the right procedure to follow?" The answer is of the first importance. One uses one's natural reason (*L* 33.1). There is no other way. Since virtually no one has the privilege of direct supernatural revelation, the only way people have of determining what to do is to employ natural reason. What this means is that ultimately our belief in what books constitute the Bible, what revelation is, when miracles occur, and who is a prophet rests on reason. Revelation cannot suggest the criterion without begging the question, because it is revelation that is at issue. Also, for any criterion that revelation might suggest, one might always legitimately ask, "Why is that the right criterion?" And to ask such a question is to ask for a reason. It is reason alone that evaluates the acceptability of criteria.

People sometimes ask, "How do we know the Bible is the word of God?"

and sometimes "Why do we believe the Bible is the word of God?" Each question incorporates a confusion, though not the same one according to Hobbes. The first question is defective because it presupposes that the Bible is known to be the word of God when in fact knowledge does not figure in the acceptance of it at all. The only person who could have known that God revealed something is the person who received the immediate revelation; and none of us belongs to that category. The second question is defective because it presupposes that there is one explanation for why people believe the Bible when in fact there are many. Some believe it because they were taught it when they were children; some because they trust their pastors or parents; some because they like the stories. The proper question to ask about why the Bible is accepted by a community is "By what authority is it made law?" (*L* 33.21). To this, there are three answers. First, to the extent that the Bible teaches the laws of nature, "they [the Scriptures] are the law of God and carry their authority with them, legible to all men that have the use of natural reason" (*L* 33.22). Second, as laws which God has given to some specific people, such as the Jews, they depend upon being promulgated through His representatives (*L* 33.23). Third, the only other authority that can make anything law is the sovereign. So, if the Bible is a law, it is made a law by one's own sovereign (*L* 33.24).

To return to the issue of canonicity, Hobbes says that in particular he acknowledges as the Old Testament only the books that the Church of England has commanded (*L* 33.1). (When he says "the Church of England" he does not mean the archbishop of Canterbury or all the bishops of England. He means the sovereign of England.) Concerning the New Testament, Hobbes, perhaps echoing the Thirty-Nine Articles, says that all Christians accept the same books (*L* 33.2).

(3) The authors of the Bible are unknown and cannot be determined either by historical evidence or by reason alone. Any evidence about authorship must come consequently from the books themselves (*L* 33.3). This is usually called internal evidence. Such evidence never permits a precise identification of the author; but it does indicate roughly when the book was written.

Hobbes begins with the question of the authorship of the Pentateuch, that is, the first five books of the Old Testament. These are also known as the books of Moses, and traditionally people have thought that Moses wrote them. Hobbes is the first person to argue in a systematic way that Moses could not have written most of this material. To begin with, there is no reason to think that Moses wrote any of the Pentateuch if we rely merely on the title "books of Moses." A phrase of the form "books of Y" can mean "books written about Y" as easily as it can mean "books written by Y." Thus, the book of Joshua is a book written about Joshua, not by him. The books of Judges, the book of Ruth, and the books of Kings are other examples of books that everyone admits are written about the people mentioned and not by them (*L* 33.4).

A reason for doubting that Moses wrote everything in the Pentateuch is the fact that the Pentateuch records events that happened after Moses died. The last chapter of Deuteronomy contains the clause "no man knows of his [Moses'] sepulcher to this day." It seems obvious that Moses did not write these words: "For it were a strange interpretation to say Moses spoke of his own sepulcher (though by prophecy)" (*L* 33.4). One might object that these words occur at the very end of the Pentateuch; so that if Moses wrote everything except the last seven verses of the work, Hobbes would not have succeeded in proving very much. The point is well taken but not damaging to Hobbes's position because he in fact goes on to show that large portions of the Pentateuch cannot be Mosaic. His purpose in first questioning the authorship of the last part of the Pentateuch is to get the thin edge of the wedge into the wood. Once it is shown that part of the Pentateuch has a doubtful authorship, it is easier to show that other parts do also.

Further, Hobbes is not especially concerned with who wrote about the sepulcher; he is more concerned with illustrating a certain kind of literary criticism. He focuses on the precise phrasing of the passage being considered, in particular, the phrase "to this day." This phrase would be used only by someone who was writing long after the death of Moses. Whoever wrote these words would not have said that the location of Moses' burial is unknown "to this day" if he were writing the day after or even the year after Moses died. This literary analysis forestalls another objection that might have been made. One cannot try to defend the Mosaic authorship of the "sepulcher" passage by suggesting that God could have revealed to Moses before he died that his burial place would not be discovered; for, if God had done this, Moses would have written something like, "No man will know of his sepulcher for centuries."

Hobbes deploys his sensitivity to the phrasing of the Bible to uncover other passages with a problematic authorship. In the book of Genesis (12:6), it is reported that, "Abraham passed through the land to the place of Sichem, unto the plain of Moreh, and the Canaanite was then in the land." It may seem that nothing very telling would be revealed if this passage were shown to have been written long after the time of Abraham. Since Moses lived centuries after Abraham, the passage would have to have been written long after the death of Abraham. But all of this is irrelevant to maintaining that Moses wrote the passage. What the passage reveals is not only that it was written long after Abraham lived, but also that it was written long after Moses lived. To explain this, I shall give a list of dates. In order to sidestep issues about chronology, each is part of a pair. The first in each pair will be the date assigned to the biblical events by archbishop James Ussher, a famous seventeenth-century chronologist; the second, placed in parentheses, will be the date widely accepted today. All of the following dates are of course BC. Hobbes's argument goes through whichever set is used. Abraham lived in about 1900 (c.1850); Moses lived in about 1500 (c.1300); Joshua destroyed the Canaanites in about 1450 (c.1250).

The crucial phrase of the biblical text is "the Canaanite was then in the land." No author would have used this phrase when the Canaanites still lived in Canaan. For example, Christopher Columbus would not have written that, "the Indian was still in the land," because American Indians were living there when he wrote. Someone writing in the nineteenth or twentieth century however might write those words after the Indians had been massacred or displaced. The phrase "the Canaanite was then in the land" consequently would only have been used if the Canaanites had not lived in Canaan for a long time. When would this have been? It could not have been any time from 1900 (1850) to 1450 (1250), since the Canaanites were still living there. It would have to have been some time long after 1450 (c.1250), the time when Joshua reportedly exterminated them, and thus long after Moses had died. So Moses could not have written that passage and presumably none of the connected stories that seem to have had the same author.

There are other problems with holding that Moses wrote most of the Pentateuch. A passage in the book of Numbers (21:14) indicates that its author relied upon another book, now lost, called "The Book of the Wars of the Lord," in which some of Moses' exploits were reported. Since Moses would not have relied upon someone else's account of what he had done, he should not be considered the principal author of this part of the Pentateuch. Hobbes's conclusion is, "It is therefore sufficiently evident, that the five Books of Moses were written after his time, though how long after it be not so manifest" (L 33.4).

Given that Moses certainly did not write most of the Pentateuch, did he write any of it, and if so what? Hobbes's answer is that Moses wrote just those parts of the Pentateuch that the Bible says he wrote, for example, Deuteronomy, chapters 11 through 27. This is the same material that the high priest Hilkiah discovered in the Temple in the seventh century. (Contemporary scholars would deny that Moses is responsible for this material. But Hobbes was giving a best guess based upon the information available to him.)

Hobbes uses reasoning similar to that discussed with regard to the

Pentateuch in order to conclude that virtually all of the other books of the Old Testament were written long after the events they report. Concerning the book of Joshua, Hobbes analyzes the phrase "unto this day" in the same way as he had "to this day." Also, Hobbes points out that certain names of places are used that only came into existence long after the events recorded (*L* 33.6). In the book of Judges, which concerns events in about 1200 (*c.*1150), Jonathan and his sons are reported to have been priests "until the day of the captivity of the land." Since the Babylonian Captivity began in 587/6, this passage was written about 700 years after the events of the book of Judges occurred (*L* 33.7). Evidence in the two books of Samuel, the two books of Kings and the two books of Chronicles, the books of Ezra and Nehemiah, and others shows that they were written after or during the Babylonian Captivity, since they refer to or discuss it (*L* 33.8–11).

Hobbes thinks that Job was probably a real person, even though the book about him is not a history since no one suffering as Job does and no one coming to comfort a person in great pain as his friends do would speak in verse. The prose preface and epilogue were "added." Hobbes does not say explicitly that they were added later, rather than added from independent and possibly older sources, but that is implied (*L* 33.12). The book is a philosophical treatise on the ancient problem of evil. Hobbes discusses this problem in several places and solves it by saying that God can do whatever He wants, without injustice, in virtue of His overwhelming power (*DC* 15.6; *L* 31.6; *LN*, p. 249; *QLNC*, pp. 16, 114, 118, 133, 143). From Hobbes's frequent use of and reference to the book of Job, one may conjecture that it was his favorite. The epigraph on the illustrated title page of *Leviathan* is a quotation from it.

The book of Psalms was put into its present form after the Babylonian Captivity. The oldest prophets are Sophoniah, Jonas, Amos, Hosea, Isaiah, and Michaiah, all of whom lived in the eighth century (*L* 33.13, 33.16). The Old Testament was put into its present form by Esdras (Ezra), if the Apocrypha can be used as evidence (*L* 33.19).

In contrast with the Old Testament, Hobbes does not question the dating or authorship of the New Testament at all. He says it was written soon after the events reported occurred and all by people who had "seen our Saviour or been his disciples, except St. Paul and St. Luke" (*L* 33.20). But there's a difference between when a book is written and when it becomes canonical. The first enumeration of all the books of the Old and New Testaments was supposedly done by Clement, the first bishop of Rome after Peter. But this is doubted by some, and the council of Laodicea of about AD 364 is the first time that the Bible is recommended to the Christian churches (*L* 33.20).

Spinoza carried on and greatly expanded the work that Hobbes started in biblical criticism. His analysis of the authorship of the Bible is much more detailed and devastating, but it builds upon foundations that Hobbes laid.

bodies and accidents Hobbes defines a body as that which does not depend for its existence upon human thought and which coincides with some space (*DCo* 8.1). The first clause of the definition coincides with Aristotle's definition of substance. The second clause differentiates Hobbes's doctrine from Aristotle's. For Hobbes all substances are material, that is, bodies. The phrase "immaterial substance" is "contradictio in adiecto," a contradiction in terms. As an alternative to saying that body coincides with space, he sometimes says that it fills it up (*L* 34.2; *AW*, p. 311).

Hobbes does not distinguish between the form and matter of a substance as Aristotelians do. Rather, he distinguishes between body and accidents. Aristotelians distinguish between substances and accidents, but the similarity between Hobbes's distinction and the Aristotelian one is purely verbal. An accident for Aristotelians is an objective, nonrelational part of a substance. A red substance does not merely appear red when it is perceived, it is red in itself. A central part of Hobbes's commitment to modern science is his denial of this Aristotelian doctrine. For Hobbes, accidents are not in bodies in the way Aristotelians represent it: "When an accident is said to be in a body, it is not so to be understood, as if any thing were contained in that body; as if, for example, redness were in blood, in the same manner as blood is in a bloody cloth" (*DCo* 8.3; *AW*, p. 312).

According to Hobbes, it is difficult to say what an accident is. When he explains the concept, he seems to give two different, though related, explanations of it. First he says that accidents are not parts of the body, but are relative to a perceiving subject. An accident is a way of conceiving an object. This makes an accident a psychological reality (*DCo* 8.2). But he then goes on to say that an accident is a power a body has to cause sensations in animals, or alternatively, it is the way a body is conceived (*DCo* 8.2). The word "accident" etymologically refers to how a body is "falling" or moving; so differences in accidents are differences in how the bodies are moving (*L* 34.2; *AW*, pp. 313–14). It would seem that "accident" is equivocal; it can mean either that structure of a body that causes a certain perception or the qualitative perception itself.

As anti-Aristotelian as he is concerning the nature of body, Hobbes nonetheless thinks that the idea of prime matter is useful:

> it signifies a conception of body without the consideration of any form or other accident except only magnitude or extension, and aptness to receive

53

form and other accident. So that whensoever we have use of the name "body in general" if we use that of "*materia prima*", we do well. . . . *Materia prima*, therefore, is body in general, that is, body considered universally, not as having neither form nor any accident, but in which no form nor any other accident but quantity are at all considered, that is, they are not drawn into argumentation. (*DCo* 8.24; *AW*, pp. 80–1)

Two bodies cannot occupy the same place at the same time, because a body cannot be separated from its magnitude and the magnitude fills up the whole of a place, so there is no room for another body in the same place at the same time. Also, the same body cannot be in two places at once, because when a body is divided the place at which it exists also divides. That is, the body and the place go together. Each body has one and only one place (*DCo* 8.8). Hobbes would have held this position independently of his rejection of TRANSUBSTANTIATION. But his views about bodies and places provide a theoretical basis for rejecting it.

Unlike Descartes, Hobbes does not identify matter with extension. In introducing his explanation of what an accident is, he takes it as obvious that, when a body fills a space, it is coextended with the space but "coextension is not the coextended body" (*DCo* 8.2).

C

Catholics and Presbyterians Many religious groups in seventeenth-century England had some subversive tendencies according to Hobbes, such as Fifth Monarchy Men, Quakers, and Baptists. And while it is important to be aware of this religious diversity, two denominations were particularly obnoxious to Hobbes: Roman Catholicism and Presbyterianism, partly because they were more powerful than others, but largely because each involved politico-religious theories that wove an important truth together with a subversive falsehood. Roman Catholicism and Presbyterianism represented the two main ways in which a religious group espousing a form of church government with a structural flaw could jeopardize peace.

Roman Catholicism can be described as espousing a top-down form of church government. Full authority resides in the pope; the bishops have authority below him; priests are below them; and laymen are at the bottom. Top-down authority is the proper form according to Hobbes. He approves of a strong hierarchy in church government and preferred the episcopal system within the Church of England. (When the episcopacy was being considered for abolition in the early 1640s, Hobbes reconciled himself to the acceptability of Independency, that is, the system that gave autonomy to each congregation as long as it was approved by and posed no threat to the sovereign (*L* 47.20).) His objection to Roman Catholicism is that it misidentifies who should be at the top of the chain of command. By the Act of Uniformity, the monarch of England is the head of the Church of England. The pope, who is a foreigner, has no legal standing in England and thus cannot have authority over any English subject. To separate the religious ruler from the secular ruler would be to violate the biblical aphorism, "No man can serve two masters."

Presbyterianism is the opposite of Roman Catholicism in this respect. It has a bottom-up theory of church government. Each congregation was to elect representatives to an area council called a class. Each class was to elect representatives to county-wide provincial councils. These provincial groups in turn were to elect members to a nationwide synod. Presbyterianism then is democratic. Hobbes's own theory of the origin of political authority is bottom-up and democratic. The government is established by having each subject covenant with every other. So its democratic foundation is not the objectionable feature of Presbyterianism. Rather, it is the belief that the monarch is simply a member of some congregation and hence subject to the judgement of the religious rulers. Hobbes considers this view intolerable. Religion is one of the principal causes of dissension in a civil state. If a sovereign could not control what was taught about religion, civil war would inevitably ensue. When Hobbes eventually came to write his history of the English Civil War in the middle to late 1660s, he blamed the Presbyterians more than any other group. (Hobbes would also find it objectionable that Presbyterians typically believed that the authority of a ruler was revocable for malfeasance or misfeasance; but that issue is not directly relevant here. *See* AUTHORIZATION.)

cause and effect   A cause is something that produces a new accident in another body. Hobbes is not squeamish about using terms such as "produce" and "accident" in his account of causality, as David Hume would be; nor is he shy about saying that one body causes another, rather than one event causing another. Yet, his views about causality are more sophisticated than this loose language may suggest.

The primary discussion of causality occurs in Part II of *De Corpore* after the discussion of body and accident. This is the logical place for it, because, according to Hobbes, only bodies cause things, and they are often said by him to cause accidents in virtue of their own accidents (*DCo* 9.3).

For Hobbes, only moving bodies cause effects; and every effect is the motion of some other body. Hobbes considers this his own revolutionary discovery, notwithstanding the work of Galileo, upon which it is probably based. A body is a cause "not because it is a body, but because [it is] . . . so moved" (*DCo* 9.3). All changes, qualitative or quantitative, are explainable in terms of the motions of bodies. (*See* MOTION.)

All causality occurs by contact (*DCo* 9.7). There is no action (causality) at a distance. When one body moves another body with no other body intervening, the first body is the immediate cause of the second. If there is one or more intervening body, then the first cause is the mediate cause of the last in the chain (*DCo* 9.1). In mediate causation, the first body of the chain is an agent and not a patient. ("Agent" here means simply an object that does something, not necessarily a human being, while "patient" means an object that is being caused by something.) The last body caused is a patient and not an agent. Each intermediate body is both a patient, because it has been caused by some preceding body, and an agent, because it is the cause of the following body. Hobbes does not discuss a problem in this area that has an untoward consequence for his belief in God. Since he subscribes both to the principle that every cause moves and to the principle that every object that is in motion is caused to be in motion, he should also believe that there could not be any agent that is not also a patient in some chain or other. That is, there cannot be a first unmoved mover. So, if God were to exist, there would have to be a cause of Him. In one place, Hobbes indicates that this issue cannot be settled by human beings, and that God should neither be said to be moved nor be said to be at rest (*DC* 15.14).

The entire cause of something is all the conditions that are sufficient to produce the effect. If one of those conditions is not satisfied, then the remaining conditions are not sufficient, the effect does not occur, and the remaining conditions are not a cause (*DCo* 9.5). It is contradictory to say that some (entire) cause failed to do something: "where there is no effect, there can be no cause" (*DCo* 9.4; *LN*, pp. 274–5; *QLNC*, pp. 382–3). If someone says something like, "The cause was prevented from acting because of the wetness," what she is saying is literally false or absurd.

In place of "entire cause," Hobbes sometimes uses the term "necessary cause." The term is pleonastic since for Hobbes every cause is necessary: "all the effects that have been, or shall be produced, have their necessity in things antecedent" (*DCo* 9.5; *AW*, p. 424). In other words, everything happens by necessity. This view is relevant to his views about free will and determinism. (*See* LIBERTY AND NECESSITY.) Hobbes is a compatibilist. Since every event is caused, acts of will are caused. Yet human beings are free, because being free concerns how something is caused and not whether it is caused.

The idea of a necessary cause should not be confused with the idea of a "cause necessary by supposition" (*causa sine qua non*) (*DCo* 9.3; *AW*, p. 423). The latter is a condition that is necessary but not sufficient for an effect. In the ordinary speech of people, such necessary conditions are sometimes called causes, but such a use is inexact. Someone may say that the cause of a fire is the striking of a match; but the striking is only a cause necessary by supposition, where what is further supposed but unmentioned are such other conditions as oxygen, sulphur, and dryness, all of which collectively are the cause.

One of the principal tenets of the medieval doctrine of causality is that an effect exists only so long as one of its causes (*per se* essential causes) operates. Hobbes rejects this idea completely. An effect does not cease as soon as its cause ceases (*EL* 1.3.1). If a ball strikes another ball and causes it to move, then the first ball is the cause of the motion of the second even if the first ball stops before the second one does. Another consequence of Hobbes's rejection of the scholastic idea of *per se* essential causes is his belief that a cause always temporally precedes its effect.

57

Hobbes discusses the four Aristotelian causes: final, formal, efficient, and material. So-called "final causes" are not causes at all, because they are not in MOTION: "rest does nothing at all, nor is of any efficacy; nothing but motion gives motion to such things as be at rest, and takes it from things moved" (*DCo* 15.3; cf. *AW*, pp. 401, 436; *EW* 7:3). Formal causes are not causes, because, according to Aristotle, they have their efficacy simultaneously with their effect, and Hobbes holds that a cause must precede its effect. Hobbes reinterprets the idea of efficient and material causes. For him, the efficient cause is the moving or active object while the material cause is the moved or passive object (*AW*, pp. 315–16). In one place, he says that the term "efficient cause" is used when the cause is an agent (that is, God, angels, human beings, or beasts), and "natural cause" when it is not (*AW*, p. 423).

Christ, offices of In one sense, Christ has one office, that of messiah. But this is typically sub-divided into three offices. The first is variously described as redeemer or savior, the second as pastor, counselor, or teacher, the third as eternal king (*L* 41.1). For Hobbes, these three offices correspond to three historical moments or epochs. The first was the event of Christ's death on the cross. That is the event that saved human beings. The second is achieved through the work of his ministers. This period extends from Christ's death until his second coming, which is sometime in the indefinite future. Hobbes equates Christ's ministers with pastors, counselors, and teachers. The equation is not accidental. He is exploiting the etymological sense of "minister" as a subordinate or servant. The point is that ministers do not have any authority of their own; in particular, they have no authority to coerce. They may counsel and teach, but not command. The authority to command is reserved to the sovereign. Sovereignty also relates to the third office. When Christ returns to earth, he will reign as king(*L* 41.6). Until that time, one's own secular sovereign is the only sovereign to whom obedience is owed.

In *De Cive*, Hobbes had given a complementary treatment of the matter. There he listed the offices of Christ in this way: (1) to teach the means and way to salvation; (2) to forgive sins; (3) to "teach the commandments of God whether concerning his worship or those points of faith which cannot be understood by natural reason" (*DC* 17.13). Concerning (1), Christ's teaching is that the way to salvation is to obey the sovereign. Concerning (2), there never would have been any sin if people had obeyed their sovereigns; in the first instance Adam and Eve should have obeyed God. Concerning (3), God reveals His will about the proper mode of worship and belief through the sovereign. Hobbes summarizes the doctrine in this way: "The sum of our Saviour's office was to teach the way and all the means of salvation and eternal life. But justice and civil obedience and observation of all the natural laws is one of the means to salvation" (*DC* 17.13).

Christianity, essence of   The essence of Christianity (sometimes described as the things necessary to salvation) can be considered broadly and narrowly. In the broad sense, its essence is (1) to obey God, and (2) to have faith in Christ or to believe that Jesus is the Messiah. These two points are put in various ways, sometimes as "obedience to laws" and "faith in Christ," respectively (*L* 43.3). They are also presented in an abbreviated form as the requirement that people exhibit two virtues, obedience and faith (*DC* 17.7, 18.2, 18.12). In the narrow sense, the essence of Christianity is item (2) alone.

Hobbes discusses the essence of Christianity in all three of his political works. In *Leviathan*, the topic is discussed prominently in the last chapter of part three, "Of a Christian Commonwealth," just before the last part, "Of the Kingdom of Darkness." The rationale is that it is appropriate to know what the truth about a Christian commonwealth is before going on to diagnose and categorize its corruption in the kingdom of darkness. In *De Cive*, the topic is introduced as part of the explanation of the second prophetic KINGDOM OF GOD. But it is not discussed as an explicit theme until the last chapter of the book in the third part, "Of Religion." In *The Elements of Law*, he had raised the issue in the context of arguing that there should be no conflict for a Christian between obeying God's laws and obeying the laws of a Christian sovereign (*EL* 2.6.6). Between the circulation of this work in manuscript in 1640 and the publication of *De Cive* (in 1642, revised in 1647), religious dissension intensified and the space Hobbes devoted to the issue increased. In chapter 17, the second to last one in the book, Hobbes discusses the role of Jesus within the context of what people are supposed to do until the second prophetic kingdom of God is established at the end of the world. He says that two things are to be done: to obey God and to have faith in Jesus. To hold this second tenet is tantamount to believing that Jesus is the Messiah. In the last chapter, what is essential to Christianity is raised as an explicit theme.

In *Leviathan*, the essence of Christianity is presented, not as a theological issue, but as a political one. Civil wars in Christian commonwealths are usually caused by people who are mistaken about what the essence of Christianity is. They mistakenly disobey their sovereign because they benightedly believe that God is commanding them to do so. There is no question but that a person should obey God if He commands one thing and the sovereign commands another. As Jesus said, "Fear not those that kill the body but cannot kill the soul." However, that maxim is usually not the relevant one by which to guide one's behavior. Rather, it is St Paul's: "Servants obey your masters in all things" and "The scribes and pharisees [the legitimate rulers of the Jews at that time, according to Hobbes] sit in Moses' chair, all therefore they shall say, that observe and do." Understanding what the essence of Christianity is will show people how difficult it is for the commands of the sovereign to conflict with those of God; put positively, God virtually always commands that people obey the sovereign.

Let's now discuss the two elements that constitute the essence of Christianity.

(1) Obedience to God. If people were perfect, obedience would be sufficient for salvation. But they are not. Everyone is "guilty of disobedience to God's law" in Adam and in addition has her own personal sins (*L* 43.3; *DC* 18.2). Hobbes is on strong theological ground here. It is unfortunate for his own purposes that he did not explicate the story of the first sin in Genesis, because it is clear that the author was conveying the idea that disobedience is the essence of sin. Eating the fruit was incidental to Adam and Eve's disobedience.

Because of disobedience, human beings need to repent. Mercifully, God accepts the will or the intention to do something as equivalent to the actual performance of the act. What is required is "not the fact, but the will and desire wherewith we purpose and endeavour as much as we can to obey for the future" (*DC* 18.3; *L* 43.4). Since repentance is all that God requires by the law, repentance is identical with obedience, according to Hobbes. That is why the Bible often uses the word "repentance" when it means obedience (*DC* 18.4).

Hobbes's equation of repentance with obedience gives him some additional latitude in defending his position that obedience to God is one of the two things essential to Christianity. Hobbes thinks it is legitimate to use as evidence that the Bible is teaching that the people ought to obey God any biblical passage that urges repentance. There is at least this much sense in Hobbes's position: repentance is one of the things that God commands in the Bible, and every descendant of Adam, swimming against the tide of sin, can make it to the shore of salvation only through repentance. According to Hobbes, repentance is also expressed by the word "righteousness" (*L* 43.4). So, his claim that obedience is one of the two essential elements of Christianity is tantamount to the claim that obedience, repentance, and righteousness are essential. By broadening his claim in this way, he makes it more plausible while preserving at the same time the apparent simplicity of the formula "Obey God." What is implausible is that "obedience," "repentance," and "righteousness" actually mean the same thing in the Bible.

Obedience requires adherence to law. What laws are these for a Christian? They cannot be the laws of Moses since they were superseded by the coming of Jesus. They cannot be any laws of Jesus since he did not give any. While he was on earth, Jesus only gave human beings counsel, not commands; he gave advice, not laws. (*See* CHRIST, OFFICES OF.) The only laws remaining then are the laws of nature (*L* 43.5). As Hobbes interprets the laws of nature in this context, they seem to overlap at least in spirit with the second essential element of Christianity, faith in Jesus. He says that the principal law of nature is "that we should not violate our faith, that is, a commandment to obey our civil sovereigns" (*L* 43.5).

In fact, starting from the requirement of obedience to God, one always arrives by Hobbes's reasoning at the requirement to obey one's sovereign. Consider the connection of obedience with divine and moral laws. Everyone who loves God will want to obey the divine laws; and everyone who loves her neighbor will want to obey the moral laws. Of course, the divine laws or laws of nature are identical with the moral laws. And what do the laws of nature enjoin if not obedience to the civil sovereign? Hobbes says, "The obedience therefore which is necessarily required to salvation is nothing else but the will or endeavour to obey; that is to say, of doing according to the laws of God; that is, the moral laws, which are the same to all men, and the civil laws; that is to say, the commands of sovereigns in temporal matters, and the ecclesiastical laws in spiritual" (*DC* 18.3).

(2) Faith in Jesus. As already indicated, the second essential component of Christianity is often explained as related to the first. Because of sin, obedience itself requires forgiveness or "remission of sin," and remission of sin is one of the rewards of FAITH.

Understood in its own right, the second component is faith in Christ or the belief that Jesus is the Messiah. Sometimes Hobbes gives the impression that these alternatives are in fact the same, as when he says that "to believe in Jesus and to believe that Jesus is the Christ is all one" (*L* 43.15; see also 34.13, 36.20, 43.11, 43.12, 43.16, 43.19, 43.22, 43.34). And they could be the same if a Christian trusted in Jesus and heard him say that he was the Messiah. As a matter of fact, it turns out that, although the belief that Jesus is the Messiah is essential to Christianity, that belief immediately rests not upon trust in Christ but upon trust in the Christian's civil sovereign. Trust in Jesus is the remote source of Christianity. All of this requires some explanation.

According to Hobbes, one can believe only a person whom one has heard. He says that Abraham, Isaac, Jacob, and Moses heard God and believed Him. The apostles and disciples heard Jesus and believed him. But most post-apostolic Christians cannot believe God or Jesus, because they do not hear either of them. Rather, they believe their sovereign, who

61

is the one who determines that the Bible rather than some other book expresses the propositions upon which the doctrine of their religious faith is based (*L* 43.6). In short, Hobbes holds that the basis for modern-day Christianity is the trust that believers have in their sovereign. The believers themselves are probably not conscious of this fact. That does not invalidate the point; it merely means that it is a discovery for the philosophy of religion.

Within the context of discussing the essence of Christianity, Hobbes does not press this point. He is more concerned with explicating and defending what he avers is the proposition that is central to Christianity, namely, that Jesus is the Christ (Messiah). He also describes it as "the only article of faith" (*L* 43.11; *DC* 18.5, 18.9–11). (While obedience to God and to his laws is an essential component of salvation, obedience is not itself an article or proposition.) Hobbes supports the claim that "Jesus is the Christ" is the single most important proposition of Christianity with four arguments, each of which involves an interpretation of the New Testament. The first is that the "scope" of the gospels is evidence of it. Hobbes gives a fair précis of the gospel of Matthew with the upshot that it summarizes the claim that Jesus is the Messiah (*L* 43.12). The second argument is "taken from the subject of the sermons of the apostles" both before and after the ascension of Jesus (*L* 43.13; *DC* 18.7). The main thrust of these sermons is that "the kingdom of heaven is at hand," and Hobbes interprets this as meaning that Jesus is the Christ. The third argument is that Jesus said that his yoke is easy and his burden light. This could be true only if the proposition that Christianity rests upon is simple and intelligible. The simplicity of the proposition is attested to by the fact that the good thief was able to learn enough about Christianity to be saved while hanging on a cross (*L* 43.14; *EL* 2.6.8). A full discussion of Hobbes's evidence for his interpretation of Christianity is not appropriate here. Suffice it to say that his case is plausible and has been affirmed by twentieth-century theologians, not thinking at all of Hobbes. They, like Hobbes, rely on such remarks as the following by the author of John's gospel, "These things are written that ye may know that Jesus is the Christ, the Son of the living God" (*L* 43.12; *DC* 18.6; referring to John 20:31). His fourth argument for the claim that the proposition that Jesus is the Christ is the only necessary article of faith is that the Old Testament scriptures point to Jesus as their fulfillment (*L* 43.15). Hobbes's treatment of this material is standard for his time. Hobbes follows his claim that the proposition that Jesus is the Christ is necessary for salvation with fairly conventional arguments that it is also sufficient (*L* 43.15–16). In *De Cive*, he claims that when a biblical text giving the essence of Christianity mentions only one of the two essential components, either obedience (aka repentance and righteousness) or faith, the other is left implicit (*DC* 17.8). Of course, this begs the question against anyone who would dispute that obedience and faith are both necessary to Christianity.

Two objections have been raised against Hobbes's position. The first is that the proposition that Jesus is the Christ is too simple to express Christian doctrine. This objection attacks then the simplicity of Hobbes's view. Hobbes's reply to this objection has in effect already been given, and I think it is decisive: Jesus's own words: "My yoke is easy and my burden light." If Christian doctrine were difficult or abstruse, then Jesus would have been mistaken about his own message. Also, if what needed to be believed were extensive or difficult, the good thief would not have been able to master it while hanging on the cross. He learned enough of Christian doctrine to enter heaven on that day (*DC* 18.8).

The second objection is related to the first. If the essence of Christian doctrine is the proposition that Jesus is the Christ, what is to be made of the other propositions that go to make up the Christian creeds? The creeds are supposed to state the essence of orthodoxy, and some of them run for two pages. Hobbes's reply is two-fold. He begins by saying that professing the creeds belongs not to faith but to the profession of faith. Recitations of the creeds are required by obedience to sovereigns. This would seem to imply that the propositions of the creed are logically unrelated to "Jesus is the Christ." But his second reply seems to contradict this. He says that the essential proposition of Christianity does "signify that Jesus was . . . the Son of God, the creator of heaven and earth, born of a virgin, dying for the sins of them who should believe in him," and so on. That is, he repeats the credal formulations, which he had just seemed to declare necessary only as professions of faith and not as inwardly believed propositions (*DC* 18.6 note, 18.11). In *The Elements of Law*, he had pointed out that the proposition that Jesus is "the begotten son of God" is denied by Arians; yet he considered it to be part of the explication of the formula that Jesus is the Christ and hence necessary to Christianity (*EL* 2.6.6). Hobbes seems to interpret the idea of faith in Christ narrowly or broadly, as it suits his purposes. Understood narrowly, the doctrine that Jesus is the Christ is weak enough to gain assent from Christians of any denomination. Thus, sectarian divisiveness is forestalled. Understood broadly, the doctrine entails the credal doctrines that traditionally constituted orthodoxy. Thus, Christianity remains robust.

Hobbes was often unfairly attacked for watering down the content of Christianity by reducing its essence to two items. The charge is unfair if he is measured against the same standard that is typically applied to respectable figures in the Church of England in the late seventeenth century. Latitudinarians prided themselves on just the sort of doctrinal looseness that Hobbes was advocating. Of course, they did not relate their views to his, because he had a bad reputation.

Hobbes's understanding of Christianity as consisting primarily in obedience to God and faith in Christ correlates strictly with the main doctrine of covenant theology, which was popular in England in the late sixteenth and early seventeenth century, namely, that God made two covenants with human beings, a covenant of works and a covenant of grace. The terms of the covenant of works were that human beings were to obey the commands of God. Adam and Eve soon violated that covenant, and God promised a second covenant, the covenant of grace, according to which people could be saved by the grace of God, which was given by having faith in Christ.

church (*ecclesia*) In *Leviathan*, Hobbes's preferred sense of "church" is defined as follows: "A company of men professing Christian religion, united in the person of one sovereign, at whose command they ought to assemble and without whose authority they ought not to assemble" (*L* 39.4; *OL* 3:337, 566). Before getting to this definition, Hobbes reports multitudinous uses of the word just as he did or would do for a cluster of other words relating to religious issues, such as "spirit," "angel," and "prophet." Hobbes gives similar treatments to the idea of a church in both *Leviathan* and *De Cive*, but not in *The Elements of Law*, which contains no catalog of the uses of "church." As used by the ancient Greeks and Romans, "church" referred to any assembly, not necessarily a religious one (*L* 39.2). But Hobbes focuses on its usage by Christians. They first used it to refer to themselves, gathered together in an assembly whether it was in a building or not. Later, "church" was sometimes used to refer to the building itself in which they assembled (*L* 39.1). Sometimes it was used to refer to them when they were not gathered together. Sometimes it meant all people who are baptized; sometimes it meant only those who inwardly believe in Christianity and not those who feign belief. Sometimes it referred only to "the elect," that is, only those who will go to heaven (*DC* 17.19; *L* 39.3). When it is used to refer to those who gather to judge others, it is the same as a church council or synod (*DC* 17.19).

In the sense that Hobbes favors insofar as it bears upon political philosophy, a church is an assembly that can have "actions attributed to it." It is not merely uniformity of doctrine that makes a church. Many people may have the same opinions without being a church. Rather, there must be some authority that can call its members together lawfully and impose obligations on them. In this sense, the church is an artificial PERSON (*DC* 17.20). It follows that "a city [state] of Christian men and a Church is altogether the same thing" (*DC* 17.21, 18.10, 18.13; *L* 33.24, 39.5). Both contain the same "matter," namely, the individual people, and the same "form," namely, the sovereign (*DC* 17.21). It follows that each Christian state (*civitas*) is a separate church (*DC* 18.10, 18.13). There is no universal Christian church. Consequently, "church" and "commonwealth" refer to the same thing in the sense in which a church has the authority "to command, to judge, to absolve, condemn, or do any other act" (*L* 39.5; *DC* 17.22).

Roman Catholic political theory distinguished between "temporal and spiritual government." It asserted that, while secular sovereigns controlled temporal governments, the pope controlled the spiritual government of all mankind and that spiritual government was superior to temporal government. Hobbes rejects the Roman Catholic theory completely. It is built upon a distinction without a difference. The head of the temporal government is also the head of the spiritual government in all cases. Where more than one government is acknowledged, "there must needs follow faction and civil war in the commonwealth, between the church and state, between spiritualists and temporalists, between the sword of justice and the shield of faith, and (which is more) in every Christian man's own breast, between the Christian and the man" (*L* 39.5). Hobbes is here not so much explicating the concept of a church as he is commenting on the causes of the English Civil War.

A further attack on Roman Catholic doctrine comes in the form of drawing a consequence about excommunication from the discovery that the church is identical with the state. It is impossible to excommunicate a state, because a state cannot excommunicate itself. An entire state could be excommunicated only if there were some universal church which had the unity and authority of a person. But, *pace* Roman Catholic doctrine, there is no such universal church. Similarly, a sovereign cannot be excommunicated since no private person within the state and no person or state outside of it has the authority to do so. (Although Hobbes does not mention the cases by name, he must have had in mind the supposed excommunication of various sovereigns such as Henry VIII and Elizabeth I by the Roman Catholic Church (*DC* 17.26).) A further consequence of identifying Christian states with Christian churches is that each state must interpret the Bible for itself (*DC* 17.27). There is no one interpretation that holds for every state. Excommunication originally meant expulsion from the synagogue and was used against lepers, who were considered unclean (*L* 42.20). In the early Christian church, before it became a state religion, excommunication was used only to correct unacceptable behavior and not "errors in opinion" (*L* 42.24–5).

In supporting national churches, Hobbes happens to be on the side of the Presbyterians and opposed to the Independents, even though in fact he had no use for the former and came to give qualified support for the latter in *Leviathan* (*L* 47.20). (*See* CATHOLICS AND PRESBYTERIANS.) In explaining the nature of the church, Hobbes also argues in favor of the office of bishop in the early church as separate from the office of presbyter, in contradiction to the Presbyterian history of the early church (*DC* 17.24).

A final note on ecclesiastical power is appropriate. Since the Christian church has no authority independent of the secular authority, it has no independent authority to make laws or issue commands. The function of its ministers is to teach: "the apostles and other ministers of the gospel are our schoolmasters and not our commanders, and their precepts not laws, but wholesome counsels" (*L* 42.5). (*See* COMMAND AND COUNSEL.) What ministers ought to teach is obedience to secular authority and faith in Jesus Christ (*L* 42.9). Hobbes is quite correct to point out that there are many passages in the New Testament that enjoin Christians to be obedient to the existing authorities: "Children obey your parents in all things," "Servants obey in all things your masters according to the flesh," "Submit yourselves to every ordinance of man, for the Lord's sake," and "Obey magistrates" (*L* 42.10). If Jesus, St Paul, and St Peter urged Christians to obey heathen princes, how much more should they obey Christian princes? Hobbes says, "It is therefore manifest that Christ has not left to his ministers in this world, unless they be also endued with civil authority, any authority to command other men" (*L* 42.10).

circle One way to know something is to be able to construct it. For human beings, this is the surest way. Knowing a circle by generating it from a line is one of Hobbes's favorite examples of such generative or synthetic knowledge. A circle is the result of holding one point of a straight line fixed and marking out a curved ("crooked") line by moving the line until it returns to its original position. The unmoved point of the circle is its center; the curved line is its perimeter; the straight line is its radius; and any straight line passing through the center and touching two points of the perimeter is the diameter (*DCo* 6.13, 14.4). Although it cannot be known that an object is a circle simply by looking at it, it can be known by generating it (*DCo* 1.5).

The description of physically generating a circle may seem inconsistent with the abstract character of GEOMETRY. But it is not for Hobbes, because he thinks of all geometrical entities as physical objects, and all except for a point are generated by motion (*DCo* 15.1). Thus, every geometrical object has a size, even a point, although the actual size of a point is ignored for the purposes of geometry; and every line has an actual breadth although it likewise is ignored.

Hobbes's position is not as odd as one might today think. Even in the twentieth century, mathematicians used to distinguish between physical or practical geometry and abstract or rational geometry. Within physical geometry, which began with the Egyptians, who needed a way of identifying fields that had the same area, points were small objects of "scarcely perceptible and practically negligible dimensions," as one mathematician described it. Lines were objects of small and negligible thickness, and so on. In contrast, abstract or rational geometry construed points, lines, and other figures as ideal objects that were never instantiated within the physical world. The seventeenth century was a period of transition from the dominance of physical geometry to its supplantation by abstract geometry. Hobbes was conservative in this, as in some other areas; Descartes, Fermat, and Wallis were progressives. Hobbes never adequately appreciated their work.

Hobbes did not see the benefit of analytic geometry, and denigrated the advantage of symbolizing mathematical problems. He takes the astounding view that symbolically represented formulas not only are not easier to understand than the corresponding sentence in English, but actually require more calculation: "symbols, though they shorten the writing, yet they do not make the reader understand it [the formula] sooner than if it were written in words" (*EW* 7:329, 187–8). The reason is that the formula has to be translated into words before it is understood: "For the conception of the lines and figures (without which a man learns nothing) must proceed from words either spoken or thought upon. So that there is a double labour of the mind, one to reduce your symbols to words, . . . another to attend to the ideas which they signify" (*EW* 7:329).

In antiquity, the problem of squaring the circle was the problem of constructing a square that has exactly the same area as a given circle. Constructing such a square would be a project of physical geometry, in which the construction would need to be done using only a straightedge and compass according to the three rules of construction: (1) that a straight line may be extended (by using the straightedge); (2) that another line may be drawn from a point on a line (by using the straightedge and compass); and (3) that a circle may be drawn (by using the compass). Now, it is possible by this method to construct a square with an area that so closely approximates the area of the given circle that it seems to be exactly the same. Hobbes thought that this appearance of identity was identity. But it is not.

Hobbes's attempt to solve the problem of squaring the circle by construction rather than algebraically is due, I would suggest, to at least three factors. One is his belief, already explained, that for human beings the surest way to know something is to be able to construct it. A second is his belief that geometry deals with the physical world, and that abstract entities do not exist. A third is his belief that all science ought to have practical benefits and not merely theoretical value. With regard to this last point, Hobbes denigrates the work of Ludovicus Van Cullen and Willebrordus Snellius (Snell), who found a slightly more precise value for π, on the grounds that the added precision has no practical value (*DCo* 20.1). His language suggests that part of his negative attitude is based on the fact that they achieved their calculation arithmetically:

> This [their results] is the furthest progress that has been made by the way of numbers; and they that have proceeded thus far deserve the praise of industry. Nevertheless, if we consider the benefit which is the scope at which all speculation should aim, the improvement they have made has been little or none. For any ordinary man may much sooner and more accurately find a straight line equal to the perimeter of a circle, and consequently square the circle, by winding a small thread about a given cylinder, than any geometrician shall do the same by dividing the radius into 10,000,000 equal parts. (*DCo* 20.1).

The last sentence of this quotation alludes to an alternative way of squaring the circle, namely, "the rectification of the circle." This is the problem of constructing a straight line that has the same length as the circumference of a given circle. If this construction could be done, then the problem of squaring the circle would also be solved since Archimedes had proved that the area of a circle is equal to the area of a right-angled triangle with a height equal to the radius of the circle and a base equal to its circumference. Given this right-angled triangle, it would be possible to construct from it a square that has the same area.

But Hobbes had a problem that he was not aware of. It was proved in the late nineteenth century that it is impossible either to construct a straight line equal to the circumference of a circle using only straightedge and compass or to square the circle. But in the seventeenth century, mathematicians did not know this, and both the attempt to rectify a circle and the attempt to square it were respectable mathematical projects.

Something should be said about how Hobbes presented his treatments of squaring the circle. (The word "treatment" is used advisedly.) In chapter 20 of the Latin version of *De Corpore* of 1655, Hobbes gave what he thought was a demonstration. It was almost immediately criticized by Wallis. For the English translation of 1656, Hobbes reworked the proof; so chapter 20 is in fact not a translation of the corresponding chapter of the Latin edition. Also, the English version introduces an important hedge in the text. Hobbes no longer refers to his proofs as demonstrations, but only as "attempts" (*DCo* 20.1, 20.3, 20.4). He does not explain what status an "attempt" has in mathematics. Later, in *Six Lessons to the Professors of Mathematics . . . in the University of Oxford*, Hobbes denied that he had ever asserted that he had succeeded in squaring the circle. He explained that he had sometimes said that he was looking for the solution to the problem and at one point said he thought that he had it, but never asserted it categorically (*EW* 7:333–4). He says that he calls his proofs "aggressions." My conjecture is that he is exploiting the etymology of the Latin "adgredi" (a proposal) or "adgressio" (the introduction to a speech); so by "aggression," he seems to mean a first attempt. He explains that he wrote the text as if he were asserting that the aggressions were demonstrations, because he was afraid that if he used the phrase "it seems to me," then his opponents would say that "it seems not to me" (*EW* 7:186). Hobbes hoped that his aggressions would inspire other mathematicians to improve upon his work. In fact what happened was that Hobbes was drawn into a long acrimonious debate with John Wallis about geometry, which sometimes spilled over into political differences and personal abuse.

civil law (*leges civiles*)   Every civil law consists of those rules for subjects that the sovereign has commanded, by either words or actions, that distinguish right from wrong (*L* 26.3; *DC* 6.9). Civil law, like law in general, is command. (*See* COMMAND AND COUNSEL.) Also, most cases of justice and injustice depend upon civil law. For injustice is breaking a covenant, and all civil laws are built upon a sovereign-making covenant (cf. *L* 26.4).

In *Leviathan*, Hobbes draws four consequences from the above understanding of civil law. (1) Only the sovereign can make laws (*L* 26.5). Implicitly, Hobbes is attacking parliament for having claimed the power to make laws. Shortly later he attacks the pre-Civil War views of those who hold that parliament has jurisdiction over the common law, and that, while the king has power, the parliament controls justice (*L* 26.10).

(2) The sovereign is not subject to any law. Since the sovereign is the lawgiver, he could change any law that might seem to apply to him (*L* 26.6). Every apparently universal law actually should be understood as beginning, "All except the sovereign." The doctrine that the sovereign is above the laws (*solutus legibus*) was hotly contested in the seventeenth century. It was defended by supporters of absolute sovereignty and attacked by all others.

(3) Custom or long practice does not make something a law. If it did, then longstanding bad practices would also be laws; and that is absurd. Hobbes is criticizing the views of Edward Coke, who at various times opposed James I's claims to absolute sovereignty (*L* 26.7, 26.9, 26.11).

(4) The civil laws and the laws of nature are "of equal extent" (*L* 26.8). This fourth point calls for a more extended discussion than the first three. On the face of it, it seems to mean that the civil laws and the laws of nature deal with the same subject-matter. Part of what Hobbes says here

confirms this interpretation: the laws of nature are not properly laws, but become laws when they are commanded by a sovereign. His point seems to be that the laws of nature are identical with, not the civil law as a whole, which includes the command of the sovereign, but the content of the civil laws. This would mean that if the sovereign commanded a subject to do something against the law of nature, such as to kill herself, then the utterance would not in fact be a civil law even though it may have the form of one (*L* 26.11, 14.29).

There are at least three problems for Hobbes if he holds this view. First, in the same chapter, he implies that only some civil laws are laws of nature (*L* 26.13, 26.15). Later he divides the civil laws into natural and positive laws; civil laws cannot coincide with the laws of nature unless there were no positive laws at all (*L* 26.36). The second problem is that the idea that the laws of nature are not in themselves laws does not fit well with what he says in other parts of *Leviathan*, where they seem to be laws commanded by God. (It does fit his account of the laws of nature in *The Elements of Law* and *De Cive* well enough.) The third is that, after seemingly identifying the laws of nature with the content of the civil laws, Hobbes says that, "the civil law is a part of the dictates of nature" (*L* 26.8), which must be the laws of nature. But if the laws of nature are the content of the civil laws, the civil laws cannot be part of the laws of nature, because being a proper part of something is an asymmetrical relation.

In *De Cive*, Hobbes's definition of civil law comes at the end of an attack on Aristotle's definition of LAW. He criticizes Aristotle's definition for being both too narrow and too broad. It is too narrow because it does not cover divine law and the laws of nature. It is too broad because it includes covenants; and covenants are not laws. Covenants impose obligations but they do not compel fulfillment of the obligation. Laws, and in particular, civil laws, do compel fulfillment, because they are backed by an irresistible or overwhelming power. Thus, Hobbes defines civil laws as "command of him, whether man or court of men, who is endued with supreme power in the city, concerning the future actions of his subjects" (*DC* 14.2).

command and counsel (*imperatum et consilium*) Many people confuse commands and counsels. One reason for this is that the same form of words can be used for either. Whether the sentence, "Close the door" is a command or counsel depends upon who is saying it and with what intention. In a command, the speaker has authority over the addressee and intends the addressee to satisfy her desire simply because she wants it. Since, according to Hobbes, something is good just in case it is desired, a speaker who commands something acts for her own good. In contrast, a speaker who is counseling someone acts as if she intends only the good

70

of that person (*L* 25.1–3). I say "acts as if" because it is possible that the purported counselor is in fact recommending what is good only for her own sake.

Exhortation and dehortation are simply counsel presented vehemently. The vehemence indicates that the counselor is in fact pressing her own good and not the good of the counselee (*L* 25.6–7). Although every counselor desires at least her own good since everyone always acts out of her own desires, the counselor does not intend to convey to the counselee that the recommended action satisfies her own good. In addition to their own good, people sometimes desire good for other people, and counseling is an instance of this.

The definitions of command and counsel in *De Cive* make it clear that they both belong to the genus of "precept" (*praeceptum*). A counsel is "a precept, in which the reason of my obeying it is taken from the thing itself which is advised" (*praeceptum, in quo ratio, quare paremus, sumitur ab ipsa re quae praecipitur*). In contrast, a command is "a precept, in which the cause of my obedience depends on the will of the commander" (*praeceptum, in quo parendi ratio sumitur a voluntate praecipientis*) (*DC* 14.1).

Hobbes's discusses the difference between command and counsel in all three of his political works. It is given little attention in *The Elements of Law* (*EL* 2.10.4). It has more, but not a great deal of, importance in *De Cive*; it occurs at the beginning of chapter 14, which is devoted to laws and ways of breaking the law, after chapters on the causes of the destruction of a commonwealth and the duties of a sovereign. It receives most attention in *Leviathan*, where it occurs as part of his general discussion of the nature of a commonwealth. Chapter 25 of that work begins with the contrast between command and counsel and then devotes the rest (and larger part) of the chapter to the nature of counsel. Chapter 26 discusses the nature of civil laws, which are a kind of command. Hobbes is more interested in commands than counsels because he is especially interested in law. Chapter 25, then, is a kind of prelude to chapter 26.

Hobbes lists there three differences between commands and counsels:

(1) A command is directed to a speaker's own benefit; a counsel is directed to the addressee's benefit.
(2) A command may impose an obligation on the addressee; a counsel never imposes an obligation.
(3) No one has a right to counsel another, because it is the counselee's good, not the counselor's, that is essential (*L* 25.4).

This third difference is subject to misinterpretation. Hobbes's use of "right" here does not fit with his theoretical view, according to which a person has

71

a right to everything, unless it is laid down. Hobbes is using "right" in this context in the ordinary sense, according to which, if a person has a right to something, she has a claim to it, and others have some obligation to her to meet that claim. What Hobbes means then is that no counselor can legitimately impose her opinion (proposition) on the counselee. If a person can legitimately impose her opinion (proposition) on another person, then the opinion is a command.

Anyone who requests counsel should be considered the AUTHOR of it. Certainly no one should be punished for giving counsel that is requested of her (L 25.5, 27.27–8). Hobbes is probably thinking of the fate of Lord Strafford, who was executed for the counsel that he gave Charles I. (Parliament initiated the charge of treason but Charles finally acquiesced in the punishment.) Hobbes mentions Strafford's case several times in *Behemoth*, and it is one of the few things for which Hobbes criticizes Charles (*B*, pp. 65–7). Hobbes also gives practical advice about who should be counselors and under what conditions. For example, they should be experienced people who do not have something to gain by giving a certain piece of advice; and it is better that they give it in private rather than in public (L 25.11–16).

While Hobbes is primarily concerned with the possibility of confusing counsel with command, he also warns against the related mistake of confusing counsel with law. Law belongs to whoever has power over others; counsel belongs to those who have no power. People have a duty (*officium*) to fulfill a law. Although in other places he claims that the phrase is a contradiction, Hobbes in one place seems to say that people follow a counsel through their "free will" (*arbitrium*) (*DC* 14.1). (This un-Hobbesian occurrence of "free will" may be one piece of evidence for those who contend that Hobbes is not the translator of *De Cive* into English. Also, see below for another example.) Law is intended for the good of the one who gives it; counsel is intended for the good of the one who receives it. Law is given even to those who do not want it; counsel is given only to those who want it (*DC* 14.1).

In addition to its use in clarifying the relationship between the king, his counselors, and parliament, the distinction between command and counsel also has two theologico-political uses. The first concerns the role of Jesus. According to Hobbes, Jesus will not reign as king until the end of the world (L 41.3). Thus, his precepts cannot be commands; they are counsels. This means that it is illegitimate for people to appeal to the teaching of Jesus to justify their rebellious behavior. Hobbes only came to see that the distinction between command and counsel could be used in this way by the time he wrote *Leviathan*. Before then, when he was writing *De Cive*, for example, although he denied that Jesus issued commands, he

72

did not take the next step and categorize them as counsels. He says that rather than giving human beings any new laws, Jesus simply endorsed the laws of nature and the Mosaic law. Such precepts as "Repent" and "Be baptized," "Keep the Commandments," and "Give to the poor" are, according to Hobbes, "not laws, but a calling of us to the faith" (DC 17.8–9).

There is a mistake at this point in the translation of De Cive in the English version, *Philosophical Rudiments Concerning Government and Society.* The English version says, "It follows therefore that by those laws, 'Thou shalt not kill' . . . 'Honour thy father and mother', nothing else was commanded, but that subjects and citizens should absolutely obey their princes in all questions." But Jesus commands nothing. The word translated as "commanded" should be "advised" (*praecepisse*). The Latin is: "Sequitur ergo legibus illis, *non occides*, . . . *parentes honorabis*, nihil aliud praecepisse quam ut cives et subditi suis principibus et summis imperantibus in quaestionibus omnibus" (DC 17.10).

For further evidence that Christ's precepts cannot be commands, Hobbes goes through the Ten Commandments and shows that each is inadequate as it stands to give people all the information they need in order to follow it. Each commandment needs to be interpreted and filled out, a task that can be accomplished only by the sovereign (DC 17.10, 17.18). Presumably, Hobbes's point is that, since Christ's precepts are vaguer than the Ten Commandments, they lack the requisite specificity to be commands.

The second theologico-political use of the distinction between command and counsel occurs as part of Hobbes's argument that the role of Christian ministers is to teach (counsel), not rule (command). After presenting a schematic history of the early church, Hobbes summarizes his point:

> now it should appear that there is no coercive power left them [ministers] by our saviour, but only a power to proclaim the kingdom of Christ, and to persuade men to submit themselves thereunto, and by precepts and good counsel to teach them that have submitted what they are to do that they may be received into the KINGDOM OF GOD when it comes, and that the apostles and other ministers of the gospel are our schoolmasters and not our commanders, and their precepts not laws, but wholesome counsels . . . (L 42.5)

Hobbes distinguishes two periods in the church. The first goes from the ascension until the conversion of Constantine in about 325; the second goes from the conversion of Constantine until the second coming (L 42.1). During the first period, Christianity was not sanctioned to be taught at all. During the second period, it was sanctioned to be taught by the secular sovereigns.

commonwealth (*civitas*)   About half of all of Hobbes's uses of "commonwealth" occur in *Leviathan*. Hobbes equates commonwealth, civil state, and *civitas*. This was one acceptable use of the term; and John Locke's use conforms to it (Locke, *Two Treatises of Government*, 2.133). Not all theorists equated commonwealth and *civitas*. Robert Filmer in *Observations Concerning the Originall of Government* (1652) criticized Hobbes's use of "commonwealth," because he thought that that term designated only a democracy. He prefers the term "commonweal," to signify any government (p. 186). George Lawson, one of Hobbes's earliest critics and a possible influence on Locke, in *Politica Sacra et Civilis* (1660) distinguished a community (*civitas*), in which there is no system of subjection and obedience, from a commonwealth (*respublica*), in which there is (pp. 24–5). In the act abolishing the monarchy on March 17, 1649, the new government was called a "Commonwealth." In mid-seventeenth-century England, "commonwealth" could be used broadly to refer to any civil state or narrowly to refer only to representative governments. It is possible that Hobbes adopted the word "commonwealth" for use in *Leviathan* both because the successful revolutionary parliamentarians had and because his theory of the origins (though not the exercise) of political authority is democratic.

According to Hobbes, only within a commonwealth (civil state) can people live a peaceful and commodious life, under the protection of the sovereign; it is a refuge from the STATE OF NATURE, which is a war of all against all. The nature and origin of sovereignty are discussed below in SOVEREIGN and SOVEREIGNTY BY INSTITUTION AND SOVEREIGNTY BY ACQUISITION. The rest of this entry is devoted to Hobbes's accounts of how a commonwealth is destroyed from within. Hobbes has no theoretical interest in a commonwealth being destroyed in war by a foreign invader (*EL* 2.8.1).

Hobbes's discussions of how commonwealths are destroyed by internal defects occur in all three of his political works. They follow his explanations for how the commonwealth is established by a covenant, the ways it is established by explicit agreement or conquest, and the three forms of government, namely, monarchy, aristocracy, and democracy. Some of these ideas are repeated in the chapters that immediately follow where he discusses the goals and duties of a sovereign. The duplication is understandable. If the goals and duties of a sovereign are not fulfilled, then the commonwealth will be destroyed. Putting the explanation of how a government is destroyed first gives it the appearance of a cautionary tale.

Since discussion of the causes of the dissolution of a commonwealth in *De Cive* and *Leviathan* are variations on the account given in *The Elements of Law* and not necessarily improvements upon it, the numbering below of the causes of destruction follows the one in the *Elements*. Hobbes says there that three things are necessary for the sedition that destroys a

74

commonwealth: (1) discontent, (2) a justification for rebellion ("pretence of right"), and (3) "hope of success" (*EL* 2.8.1).

(1) There are two kinds of discontent: bodily and mental. Concerning bodily discontent, it is not the presence of pain that causes discontent but the fear of having pain. What Hobbes has in mind is that there are many people who have a bad lot in life and suffer extensively who nonetheless are not disposed to rebel. The reason is that they are willing to live with their pain and are not afraid of it. Explaining political discontent in terms of fear of pain is probably also an oblique way of attributing cowardice to rebels. While Hobbes was not ashamed to admit his own timidity, he may have been exploiting the fact that rebels would have loathed the accusation.

In addition to bodily discontent, there is a mental discontent that leads to rebellion, namely, a sense of one's lack of power or honor, because all joy and grief depends upon comparing oneself with others. Many people in a commonwealth regard themselves as slaves and want freedom, not realizing that "liberty in a commonwealth is nothing but government and rule" (*EL* 2.8.3). The desire to receive greater honors than one already has is most likely to threaten a monarchy and least likely to threaten a democracy, where everyone is supposed to be equal.

(2) The kinds of discontents just discussed are not sufficient for rebellion, because a person may be dissatisfied with her lot but believe that nothing ought to be done about it. The second element leading to dissolution then provides some justification for rebellion. Hobbes lists six justifications in *The Elements of Law* and most of these reappear in *De Cive* and *Leviathan* within a similar context.

The first is the belief that a subject may disobey a sovereign if the sovereign commands something that contradicts the conscience of the subject. This justification is usually used by clerics and it is taught in the universities. In *Leviathan*, the appeal to conscience is traced back to the assumption that each person is the judge of good and evil. This is true for a person in the state of nature but not in a civil state. In transferring one's rights to the sovereign one has authorized him to make those decisions that the potential rebel is calling judgements of conscience. The law is "the public conscience" (*L* 29.7, 30.14). If each person followed her own conscience in a commonwealth, the diversity of judgements would undermine its stability. Part of the reason that people find the argument from conscience compelling is that they falsely think that conscience is some sort of spiritual entity mediating between God and human beings, when in fact "conscience" is just another name for "judgement" (*L* 29.7). Another problem with the argument from conscience is that it does not square with Christianity at all. Jesus, Peter, and Paul each gave clear instructions for subjects to obey their sovereigns (*EL* 2.8.5; *DC* 12.2).

In *De Cive*, Hobbes uses his doctrine of authorization to argue that a person can engage in behavior which would be a sin if it were her own act, but is not a sin if the behavior is actually the act of someone else. For example, a soldier must wage a war that her sovereign commands her to wage even if she thinks the war is unjust. For her to refuse to wage the war would be for her to arrogate to herself "the knowledge of what is just and unjust," which properly belongs only to the sovereign. Anyone who thinks she must follow her private conscience against her sovereign's commands is doomed to sin: for if she obeys her sovereign, she sins by violating her conscience; and if she follows her private conscience, then she sins by disobeying her sovereign (*DC* 12.2). Hobbes's argument here is fatally flawed. When he introduced the doctrine of AUTHORIZATION, he claimed that when a person engages in a sovereign-making covenant, the sovereign comes to act for the subject. He makes this claim in order to undercut the possibility of a subject complaining about what the sovereign does. It is not the sovereign acting, according to Hobbes, but the subject herself acting through the authorized behavior of the sovereign. But, when he wants to downplay the claims of conscience, Hobbes describes the commands of the sovereign as the sovereign's own actions and not those of the subject. He cannot have it both ways.

The second way of justifying rebellion is through the belief that the sovereign is obliged to obey his own laws. In *The Elements of Law*, Hobbes's explanation of why this justification fails is that the belief is inconsistent with sovereignty itself: "How can he or they be said to be subject to the laws which they may abrogate at their pleasure, or break without fear of punishment?" (*EL* 2.8.6). Since the sovereign is the only person that has the power to punish and would be unwilling to punish himself, he cannot be subject to his own laws. In *De Cive*, the argument is weaker, it seems to me. Hobbes says that a city (sovereign) cannot be bound to itself, because obligation always requires another person to whom the obligation is held. In other words, obligation is irreflexive. A city cannot be bound to a citizen for a similar reason. A citizen is part of the city and thus lacks the requisite otherness (*DC* 12.4). In *Leviathan*, Hobbes argues that to hold that the sovereign is subject to the civil laws is to set up a judge over him. But the sovereign is the supreme judge in the commonwealth; so no one and nothing is above him (*L* 29.9, 30.3). In both *The Elements of Law* and *Leviathan*, Hobbes acknowledges that the sovereign is subject to the laws of nature "because such laws be divine and cannot by any man or commonwealth be abrogated" (*L* 29.9; *EL* 2.9.1), but the point is more prominent in *Leviathan*.

The third way of justifying rebellion is through the belief that sovereignty may be divided. According to Hobbes, sometimes monarchs try to give away some of their power; when they do so, they must eventually fall even though it often takes some time because monarchy is such an inherently stable form of government. When a sovereign seems to try to divest himself of some of his power, it is better to hold that despite appearances the sovereign fails to give any of it away; for such an attempted grant contradicts his sovereignty, and when a person seems to contradict himself, a good interpretive strategy is to attribute to the person only a proposition that makes more sense (*EL* 2.8.7). Hobbes's words were prophetic; they were written before Charles in fact gave up much of his power for the sake of conciliation during the early part of the Long Parliament. In *De Cive*, Hobbes says that some people try to divide sovereignty by assigning secular functions to one entity and religious functions to another. Hobbes deconstructs the secular/religious distinction by saying that nothing is more important to salvation than justice, and justice belongs to the secular ruler (*DC* 12.5). Hobbes's example was topical. He was attacking the Presbyterians, who wanted the church to be able to make decisions independent of the secular sovereign yet to have authority over him in religious matters. In *Leviathan*, he says that it is the lawyers who are charged with promulgating the false belief that sovereignty can be divided. He is thinking primarily of Edward Coke, the distinguished theorist of common law (*L* 29.12, 30.14). The dangerous belief that sovereignty can be divided recurs as one of the false doctrines taught in the universities. In this context, the nature of the division is different. The teachers ("doctors") teach that, for each element of the secular commonwealth, there is a corresponding spiritual authority: "Supremacy against the sovereignty; canons against laws; and a ghostly authority against the civil" (*L* 29.15). Hobbes may be thinking of the views of the Roman Catholic Church, which claimed that the pope is supreme, called its laws canons, and appealled to a spiritual ("ghostly") authority. In any case, wherever there are two authorities, there are two commonwealths; and commonwealths, being in the state of nature with respect to each other, must be enemies. If a person were a member of two commonwealths, then she would have divided loyalties. Hobbes's judgement of this situation is biblical: a kingdom divided against itself cannot stand (*L* 29.15). If the secular and religious ministers are different, then one must be subordinate to the other. If the commonwealth is analogized as a human being, then the disease that subversive religious ministers cause in it can be compared to epilepsy, which the ancient Jews took to be caused by being possessed by evil spirits (*L* 29.15). Hobbes also mentions that dividing the sovereignty between one entity that has the power to tax and another authority that has the power to legislate is disastrous. For laws require money to enforce them. If laws are enacted and money is not provided for their enforcement, then

77

the law is useless (*L* 29.16, 30.3). Hobbes is thinking here of the tension between the English monarch, who had the power to make policy, and parliament, which had the sole power to vote taxes for his use.

Hobbes briefly mentions some other causes of dissolution, causes which are obviously related to events of the 1640s, such as a sovereign being unable to raise sufficient funds to wage a war, a private subject having too much political influence, and the dangers of having a city of "immoderate greatness" (*L* 29.18, 29.20–1). Hobbes ends this discussion in *Leviathan* by explaining when it is that a subject is freed from her obligation to a sovereign. It ends with the death of the sovereign, who is the soul of the commonwealth (*L* 29.23). Hobbes is referring no doubt to the death of Charles in 1649 and presenting for his royalist friends an ideological defense of his own impending return to England under the government of the Commonwealth in 1652.

The fourth justification for rebellion relies on the belief that property rights do not depend upon the sovereign. According to Hobbes, property rights are not absolute but only relative to claims that may be made against other subjects. To make a sovereign respect absolutely the property of subjects would interfere with his ability to perform his functions, such as defending the commonwealth against foreign enemies. Hobbes's references are no doubt to the issues of the Forced Loan and the Ship Money cases that preceded the English Civil War (*EL* 2.8.8; *DC* 12.7; *L* 29.10, 30.14).

The fifth justification for rebellion depends upon the belief that "the people" is an entity distinct from the sovereign (*EL* 2.8.9). (A classic presentation of this view is in John Locke's *Two Treatises of Government.*) In fact, "the people rules in all governments" (*DC* 12.8), because, according to Hobbes's theory of AUTHORIZATION, the sovereign represents all the people, who are united in his person. Even in a monarchy, what should be said is that "the king is the people" (*DC* 12.8). If a distinction is to be made between the people and something else, then the second term should be "the multitude." The multitude consists of the subjects without any principle of unity and with no political standing. If the subjects rebel against the sovereign, then the correct description of what is happening, according to Hobbes, is that the multitude is rebelling against the people (*DC* 12.8). This fifth cause of dissolution is not discussed in *Leviathan*.

The sixth justification for rebellion depends upon the belief that tyrannicide is lawful (*EL* 2.8.10). Since a tyrant is a person who has the right of sovereignty, the belief must be false. In *Leviathan*, Hobbes points out that "tyrannicide" is another name for "regicide," because a tyrant is simply a monarch that one does not like (*L* 29.14, 30.14, 46.35). In *The Elements of Law*, Hobbes briefly places the blame for this doctrine on the ancient Greeks and Romans, whom, he says, hated kings (*EL* 2.8.10). In

De Cive, the attack on the Greeks and Romans is more expansive, and one gets the sense that Hobbes is reacting to the impending Civil War, which began the year he published the first edition. He even resorts to appealing in effect to the divine right of kings as part of his attack on those who call kings tyrants, as the anti-royalist forces did in England: "For why dost thou call him a tyrant, whom God hath made a king"? It is even prophetic: "But how pernicious is this opinion to all governments, but especially to that which is monarchical, we may hence discern; namely, that by it every king, whether good or ill, stands exposed to be condemned by the judgement, and slain by the hand, of every murderous villain" (*DC* 12.3). In *Leviathan*, the rhetorical order of tyrannicide and the books of the ancient authors is reversed. Now, the evil that leads to the dissolution of the commonwealth is the reading of those books. Tyrannicide is simply one of the pernicious doctrines that are taught in them. Other seditious doctrines include the opinion that subjects within a democracy enjoy liberty while those in a monarchy do not. Indeed, the ancient authors are accused of being particular threats to monarchies. To read their doctrines is like being bitten by a mad dog, and political hydrophobia is the disease, "a certain tyrannophobia" (*L* 29.14).

These are the six justifications for rebellion (or causes of dissolution of the commonwealth) that are given in *The Elements of Law*. There are some additional ones given in *De Cive* and *Leviathan*, which are probably inspired by the events that occurred in England after 1640. One of these, the first listed as a cause of dissolution in *Leviathan* and not mentioned in *De Cive*, is that the sovereign is sometimes content to rule with less power than is needed to get the job done. While Hobbes's examples of William Rufus and Henry II go back to the eleventh and twelfth centuries, his remark that sovereigns may give away some powers "out of a hope to recover the same again at their pleasure" may be a reference to the concessions Charles I made to parliament in 1641 and 1642 such as not to dissolve parliament without its consent and to exclude the bishops from the House of Lords (*L* 29.3).

The second cause of dissolution listed in *Leviathan* and the first in *De Cive* is the belief that "every private man is judge of good and evil actions" (*L* 29.6). This belief is true only of human beings in the state of nature. In forming a commonwealth, people give up this private right to decide what is good and evil to the sovereign, except where the sovereign allows it: "the measure of good and evil actions is the civil law" (*L* 29.6; *DC* 12.1). The next cause that is listed, which has been discussed above, naturally follows from this previous one, namely, the belief that a person sins if she obeys the law when it goes against her own conscience; for conscience is simply one's own judgement about good and evil.

79

The third cause of dissolution in *Leviathan* and second in *De Cive* that is not mentioned in *The Elements of Law* is the belief that faith and holiness are not acquired by study and reason but by supernatural inspiration (*L* 29.8; *DC* 12.6). Like the claim of conscience over law, Hobbes thinks that this cause stems from judging good and evil for oneself. In contrast to this seditious belief, Hobbes holds that faith and sanctity come from "education, discipline, correction, and other natural ways, by which God works them in his elect" (*L* 29.8). A fourth additional cause of dissolution, mentioned in *Leviathan* but not *De Cive*, is imitating a neighboring nation. Here are two of Hobbes's examples. The first is the Jews throwing off the sovereignty of God and taking Saul to be their king because they wanted to be ruled as other nations were. The second is the Englishmen during "the late troubles in England" who imitated events in "the Low Countries" (*L* 29.13). Implicit in this second example is a criticism not only of the English rebels but also of the Dutch, who had successfully rebelled against the Catholic king of Spain. For Hobbes, although Roman Catholicism was an evil, rebellion was a greater evil.

Two other causes are mentioned in *De Cive*: poverty and the desire for honor. Poverty is a cause of dissolution because poor people are unwilling to admit that their condition is due to their own "sloth and luxury" and instead attribute it to "evil government" (*DC* 12.9). Concerning honor, it is in the nature of human beings to desire it and, uncontrolled, that desire leads to anarchy (*DC* 12.10). Hobbes's views are an odd mixture of liberal and conservative sentiments. His comment about the poor sounds conservative; his comment about honor sounds liberal. Both aspects of him stem from his jaundiced view of human nature.

(3) Even with discontent and justifications for rebellion, the commonwealth would not be attacked unless subjects believed they had a good hope of succeeding. This is the third necessary condition for the dissolution of a commonwealth. Hobbes lists four elements that constitute this hope in *The Elements of Law* and *De Cive*. The lists are slightly different. In the earlier work, they are (a) that the discontented have mutual intelligence; (b) that they have sufficient number; (c) that they have weapons; (d) that they agree on a leader (*EL* 2.8.11). Only element (a) requires some explanation. It is not clear to me whether by it Hobbes means that the rebels must know of each other's existence or whether they must be equally stupid (since the chances of a successful rebellion are so small) (*EL* 2.8.13). In *De Cive*, elements (b), (c), and (d) are the same. The fourth element is, ironically, "mutual trust" (*DC* 12.11). The very thing that is made possible by the civil state can also be a source of its destruction.

We have seen that in *The Elements of Law*, Hobbes specifies three necessary and jointly sufficient conditions, namely, discontent, a justification for rebellion, and hope of success. In *De Cive*, there is also supposed to be a three-fold analysis of this matter, but the model Hobbes purports to follow comes from physics. The reason is probably that *De Cive* is presented as the third part of his trilogy *The Elements of Philosophy*, which he viewed as a scientific treatise in which all reality is reduced to motion. In introducing the subject of the dissolution of government, Hobbes says that three things are to be considered in every motion: the internal structure ("dispositions") of the object to be moved; the external object that affects the object to be moved; and the "action itself," which presumably is the motion itself. The first of these items is identical with the justifications for rebellion. The third is the faction formed against the government. It is not clear that Hobbes discusses the second at all. Overall, the application of the three-fold analysis of motion to the dissolution of government is unsuccessful. Concerning the first item, the justifications for rebellion are not aptly described as the structure or dispositions that undergo the change in a commonwealth. For example, believing that sovereignty can be divided is not a structure of the commonwealth. Concerning the second item, it is odd to talk about an external object of the dissolution of a commonwealth when what causes the dissolution are some of the subjects, who are internal parts of the commonwealth. Concerning the third item, even if a faction is a part of every dissolution, it is not clear how a faction can be a motion of dissolution. A stylistic problem with the structure of Hobbes's discussion in *De Cive* is that the "hope of overcoming" the sovereign, which is the third necessary condition in the account in *The Elements of Law*, is listed as an additional disposition to dissolution after Hobbes had already introduced the "last" one three paragraphs earlier (*DC* 12.8, 12.11).

conatus *See* ENDEAVOR

conscience (*conscientia*) Conscience is "a man's settled judgement and opinion" (*EL* 2.6.12; *L* 29.7). The point of this definition is to undercut the standard seventeenth-century belief that conscience was some quasi-supernatural or special faculty of knowing moral truths. To attribute a judgement to conscience is to maintain not that the judgement is definitely true, but only that the person's opinion is firm (*EL* 1.6.8; *L* 7.4).

In the state of nature, the only standard a person can go by is her own conscience; that is, her own opinion about what the laws of nature do and do not require. Thus, to go against one's conscience is to sin, because it means that one is acting in disregard for what one believes to be the law (*EL* 1.17.13; *DC* 12.2). Since the laws of nature are the divine laws and promulgated through reason, it is true to say that "the divine law is dictated

81

to the conscience" (*EL* 1.18.10). However, Hobbes holds that, while the laws of nature bind a person in conscience (*in foro interno*), they do not always do so in action. That is, a person should calculate what the laws of nature prescribe in themselves. But, when circumstances are adverse, as they typically are in the STATE OF NATURE, actual behavior need not be in apparent conformity to them (*DC* 3.27–9, 4.21).

The role of conscience is quite different once a person leaves the state of nature. When a person contracts to be part of a civil state, she thereby lays down her right to follow her personal conscience and agrees to follow the conscience of the sovereign. Since the sovereign makes the law, "the law is the public conscience" (*L* 29.7, 37.13). People often worry about this apparent loss of liberty, but Hobbes maintains that, since entering the civil state is a necessary condition for self-preservation, the loss is "really no inconvenience" (*EL* 2.5.2, 2.6.12; *L* 24.7). If everyone followed her own private conscience, peace would be fractured in "an hour." The reason people think that following their own conscience is desirable is that they are considering only their own conscience and not that of everyone else (*EL* 2.5.2).

Many of Charles I's enemies justified their rebelliousness on the grounds that his laws violated their conscience. Hobbes had no sympathy for this view and listed it as one of six special causes of rebellion (*EL* 2.8.4–5, 2.9.8). Human laws do not touch a person's conscience at all. They bind a person's behavior, not her conscience. A person is free to believe whatever she wants; the sovereign is concerned only with how subjects conduct themselves. Not even the apostles pretended to have control over the consciences of people. They depended only upon instruction and persuasion (*EL* 2.6.3–4). Each subject owes her sovereign obedience, even when the sovereign is an infidel (*EL* 2.6.4–5).

People who preach the ideology of conscience usually are interested not merely in freedom of belief, but in freedom of action; and they want not merely the freedom to act as they want, but control over the actions of others: "But the truth is apparent, by continual experience, that men seek not only liberty of conscience, but of their actions; nor that only, but a farther liberty of persuading others to their opinions; nor that only, for every man desires that the sovereign authority should admit no other opinions to be maintained but such as he himself holds" (*EL* 2.6.13).

contempt Contempt is indifference. For Hobbes, who defines this and other emotions and cognitions in terms of some kind of motion, contempt is an absence of motion; it is neither a desire towards nor an aversion away from – Hobbes says "hate" here – some object (*L* 6.5). Implicit, but not stated, is the idea that contempt is attributed to a person when some object that usually would generate a motion does not. Some of this comes out when he defines two specific forms of contempt. Contempt of one's good reputation is impudence; contempt of the suffering of other people is cruelty (*L* 6.45, 6.47).

contract   *See* COVENANT

courage   Courage is the fear that one will be injured by an object that one wants to avoid and the hope that one will avoid that injury through resistance (*L* 6.17). (Hobbes does not define "cowardice" (cf. *L* 21.16).) Notice that fear is a component of courage. In Hobbes's translation of *The Peloponnesian War*, the Spartan king says that soldiers who are afraid fight more fiercely and that his own soldiers ought to "make their preparations as if they were afraid" (*PW* 2.11). That self-induced fear will give them courage. Hobbes's translation is tendentious. Paul Woodruff translates the relevant passage as: "In every war we should advance with confidence in our strategy, but fear for the event should guide our preparations. That way, we will be most spirited in attacking the enemy, and, at the same time, most secure against their attempts." Woodruff says that the passage is not about courage at all.

Given that Hobbes is reading a conceptual relation between fear and courage into Thucydides' text, it is plausible that he was already thinking about such relationships on his own rather than being guided by Thucydides.

covenant (*pactum*)   A covenant is a contract in which one (or both) of the parties is to perform her part of the bargain after the contract is made. A contract is a "mutual transferring of right" (*L* 14.9; *DC* 2.9; *EL* 1.15.8–9). What Hobbes means is that each party to a contract incurs an obligation to transfer her right to something to another party because the other party has done the same. A contract should be contrasted with mutual gift-giving, in which each person may give something to the other person because each is receiving something, but no obligation is involved in the exchange even if things like social pressure or pride motivate the behavior of the givers.

Contracts can be made either expressly or by inference. Express contracts are those that are made explicit by words or actions. The paradigmatic form for an oral contract is in either the present or past tense, such as "I (hereby) give" or "I (hereby) grant" or "I have given" or "I have granted." They are not in the future tense. The phrases "I will give" and "I will grant" are expressions of intention and do not thereby obligate the speaker (*L* 14.13). Hobbes calls these expressions of intention "promises,"

83

in line with seventeenth-century legal usage, according to which promises are not enforceable, because they do not impose obligations (*L* 14.15; *DC* 2.9). To be more precise, Hobbes calls these "bare promises." Promises can be the vehicle for enacting a contract by inference under certain conditions. If someone who has already received some benefit from another party promises to do something in exchange, then she indirectly covenants: "in buying and selling and other acts of contract, a promise is equivalent to a covenant, and therefore obligatory" (*L* 14.16; *DC* 2.16).

Contracts by inference can be effected in various ways. Hobbes's categorization of these ways is mildly amusing. They can be effected either by doing something or by not doing something and either by saying something or by not saying something. That indeed covers the spectrum. Hobbes recognizes that a person's intentions may be determined in a variety of ways depending upon the circumstances. In some African communities marriages are transacted by having the couple jump over a broomstick. Couples not recognizing this ritual can jump over broomsticks with no momentous effects. Some contracts to buy an item are effected by taking an object and not returning it within a certain space of time. Verbal contracts need no comment. Concerning nonverbal ones, there is a Latin expression, *qui tacet consentit*, which means that a person who remains silent gives her consent. Suppose Adam, who owes a debt to Beth, says "I'll wash your car, if you will forget about the money I owe you." If Beth says nothing, then she has made a contract with Adam by her silence.

A covenant requires trust in the party who is to perform in the future. Such trust is tenuous in the state of nature, where there is no human authority who can enforce a broken covenant (*DC* 2.11). It is not completely clear whether Hobbes thinks that covenants in the state of nature are valid or not and, if so, under what conditions. Here is a plausible account of what he holds on this matter. Such covenants are valid, but dangerous (*L* 14.18). In international relations, covenants are made between nations even though there is no common authority to enforce them (*L* 14.27). Because no one can ever lay down her right to preserve her life, a covenant is void if some previously unforeseen mortal danger in performing what is owed becomes apparent after it was made (*L* 14.18, 14.20; *DC* 2.11). But if a person was aware of the danger before the covenant was made, then it is not a voiding condition (*L* 14.20). Hobbes needs to hold that covenants in the state of nature are valid, in order to explain the possibility of a sovereign-making covenant. All covenants in the state of nature are made under some fear and duress, but that does not void them (*DC* 2.16; *EL* 1.15.13).

Those who interpret Hobbes as not allowing covenants to be made in the state of nature sometimes suggest that the sovereign-making covenant occurs simultaneously with the institution of the sovereign and hence is not made in the state of nature. One objection to this suggestion is that it tries to have things both ways: the act of instituting a sovereign being the way out of the state of nature and that act being performed when the parties are already out of it. A second objection is that, since the sovereign-making covenant is the cause of the commonwealth and since a cause always precedes its effect, the sovereign-making covenant cannot be simultaneous with the origin of the commonwealth. A third objection is that Hobbes sometimes indicates that the sovereign-making covenant institutes a commonwealth before a sovereign is selected. This is a brief and transitional state, but nonetheless an identifiable one. In *The Elements of Law*, this has the consequence that Hobbes claims that every new civil state begins as a democracy (*EL* 2.2.1; see also *L* 18.1). For our purposes, what is important is that even if a sovereign-making covenant were simultaneous with the origin of the commonwealth, there would not be at that point a sovereign who could enforce it.

A sovereign-making covenant is the means by which people get out of the state of nature and establish a civil state. The only way to be saved from the dangers of the prepolitical situation is for the people to "confer all their power and strength upon one man or upon one assembly of men that may reduce all their wills, by plurality of voices, unto one will" (*L* 17.13). What a civil state provides subjects with is unity. In the state of nature, there is no community and no society, only a group of individuals, each of whom has conflicting interests. Hobbes sometimes considers the possibility of people coming together briefly in the state of nature for mutual assistance. He thinks this is possible but explains that it is not sufficient to protect people from the dangers of the state of nature because such alliances are fleeting. The security that people need can be achieved only through a covenant by which individuals transfer their power to a sovereign. One of the things that the sovereign provides is unity, one voice that speaks for all and one will that decides for all (*DC* 5.4, 5.6).

There are some matters about which a person cannot make a covenant. One cannot covenant not to defend oneself from force, and one cannot covenant to confess to a crime, because to do so would contradict the inalienable right to preserve oneself (*L* 14.29–30; *DC* 2.18–19).

Since covenants require the use of speech, they cannot be made with beasts. Since they require evidence of acceptance by the other party, they cannot be made with God except through his earthly representative, usually a sovereign (*L* 14.22–3; *DC* 2.12–13; *EL* 1.15.11).

One of the most important aspects of Hobbes's doctrine about the covenants that institute a sovereign is that the sovereign is not a contractual party but what is known in law as a "third-party beneficiary." The purpose of this is to prevent the sovereign from having any obligations to anyone other than God. Covenants create obligations for the contracting parties.

Hobbes does not remain true to his doctrine about sovereign-making covenants when he discusses the great covenants involving God and His prophets. He refers to the covenant that God "made with Abraham" by which God established a prophetical kingdom (*DC* 16.9; *L* 35.4). Since God is the sovereign, it should be impossible for Him to be a contracting party to such a thing. That God is a genuine contracting party is confirmed by Hobbes's remark in *De Cive* that God promised Abraham the land of Canaan when He could have got away with not promising anything (*DC* 16.4). In the next chapter of *De Cive*, Hobbes talks about what was required of human beings and then what was required of God by the covenant (*DC* 17.7). The same problem of having God be a contractual party to a sovereign-making covenant occurs in Hobbes's discussion of the "new covenant," of which Jesus is the mediator. Speaking of the KINGDOM OF GOD, Hobbes says that Jesus was sent "to make a covenant between him [God] and the people" (*DC* 17.4). It would be an unacceptable to stretch the meaning of "between him and the people" to understand "him" as the third-party beneficiary of a covenant made only by those persons designated by "the people."

Hobbes says that a person is freed from her obligations arising from a covenant in one of two ways: either by performing the required actions or by being relieved of the obligation by the other party or parties (*L* 14.26; *DC* 2.15; *EL* 1.15.12). Unless the second way is interpreted in an artificially broad sense, a third way ought to be mentioned, namely, the death or destruction of the person to whom an obligation is owed. This is particularly important when obligations are owed to a person whose sovereignty is destroyed by a war. Hobbes used this kind of example to justify to royalists his own formal allegiance to the Commonwealth during the Interregnum. (It would seem to follow, as Mark Bernstein has pointed out, that people have no obligations to the dead and people need not fulfill deathbed promises. I think that Hobbes would agree but would hold that sovereigns may require subjects to fulfill certain promises that were made to a person before that person died. But the obligation here is to the sovereign, not to the deceased.)

Hobbes separates the covenant itself from the power that enforces the covenant: "covenants without the sword are but words and of no strength to secure a man at all" (*L* 17.2); and "covenants being but words and breath have no force to oblige, contain, constrain, or protect any man, but what it has from the public sword" (*L* 18.4).

Chapter 14 of *De Cive* has the sentence "Pactum obligat per se; lex obligatum tenet virtute pacti universalis de praestanda obedientia" (*DC* 14.2). The corresponding section of *Philosophical Rudiments Concerning Government and Society*, the English translation of *De Cive*, says, "A contract obliges of itself; the law holds the party obliged by virtue of the universal contract of yielding obedience". The translation of "pactum" by "contract" is suspect. Earlier, in chapter 2, Hobbes had distinguished between a contract (*contractus*) and a covenant (*pactum*). So "pactum" in 14.21 ought to be translated as "covenant." Some scholars doubt that Hobbes himself translated *De Cive* into English, and this is one piece of evidence that supports that position.

crime   *See* EXCUSES

curiosity   Curiosity is the desire to know why and how things happen. Along with reason, it is one of the two defining characteristics of human beings. Beasts are so consumed by the desire for food and other sensible objects that they have no interest in figuring out the causes of things. Human beings do. They delight in "the continual and indefatigable generation of knowledge" (*L* 6.35). Curiosity is a "lust of the mind" (*L* 6.35) in contrast with natural lust, which is "Love of persons for pleasing the sense only" (*L* 6.31). For Hobbes, "lust" is a colorful term for love or desire.

Curiosity also gives rise to RELIGION. Because most people attribute the wrong cause to certain kinds of events for which the cause is not obvious, they are led to invent false religion, that is, superstition (*L* 11.25). This is not to deny that some religion is true.

D

De Cive (1642; second, expanded edition 1647) [6]   *De Cive* was written and published originally in Latin. It is customary to refer to the English translation by the Latin title, even though it was published under the title *Philosophical Rudiments Concerning Government and Society*. It has the publication date of 1651. A copy in the British Library has that date crossed out and replaced with, "March 12, 1650," written in a seventeenth-century hand. Since in England the new year was taken at that time to begin on March 25, the notation indicates that the book was published in the early part of 1651. According to Aubrey, Hobbes is the translator:

> I have heard him [Waller] say that he so much admired Mr. Thomas Hobbes' book *De Cive*, when it came forth, that he was very desirous to have it done into English, and Mr. Hobbes was most willing it should be done by Mr. Waller's hand, for that he was so great a master of our English language. Mr. Waller freely promised him to do it, but first he would desire Mr. Hobbes to make an essay; he (T.H.) did the first book, and did it so extremely well, that Mr. Waller would not meddle with it, for that nobody else could do it so well. (Aubrey, *Brief Lives* 2:277)

But there are good reasons to doubt that Hobbes in fact is the translator or at least more than the translator of the first part even though Howard Warrender in the critical edition of the Latin text thinks he is. An early edition of *Philosophical Rudiments* contains a dedicatory letter signed "C.C" and some stylistic elements suggest a translator other than Hobbes. There are also some errors that Hobbes would have been unlikely to have made. The word "arbitrium" ("choice") is translated as "free will" even though Hobbes thought that that phrase was self-contradictory; and "praecepisse" is translated as "commanded" instead of "advised" in a context in which the difference is crucial (*DC* 14.1, 17.10). (See also, Drummond, "Hobbes's *Philosophical Rudiments*" and Tuck, "Warrender's *De Cive*.") In most regards, the English translation is accurate.

   De Cive is one section of Hobbes's trilogy *The Elements of Philosophy* (*Elementa Philosophiae*), which was supposed to be a complete system of philosophy: *De Corpore* (1655); *De Homine* (1658); *De Cive* (1642; 1647). *De Corpore* covers the nature of philosophy, logic and language, scientific method, motion, geometry, and physics. *De Homine* covers optics and psychology. *De Cive* covers political theory. In the dedication to *De Cive*, Hobbes talks about the divisions of philosophy. There he divides it into geometry (the study of figures), physics (the study of motion), and morals (the study of right). This division does not neatly correspond to the books in his trilogy, but that scheme was set (*DC* "Author's Preface" 7) before the earlier "sections" were completed. Hobbes prefers to call each part of the trilogy a "section," and Richard Tuck exploits this preference to help date some of Hobbes's works (see Tuck, "Hobbes and Descartes").

Hobbes says in the "Author's Preface to the Reader," which was added to the second edition of 1647, that the reason that the third section of the trilogy was published first was that "questions concerning the rights of dominion and the obedience due from subjects" were being debated at the time and mistaken beliefs about those issues were leading to civil war.

What is the logical relation between the three sections of *The Elements of Philosophy*? On the one hand, Hobbes claims that philosophy or science is deductive, that given explicit definitions as the starting point, everything else follows. On the other hand, he says that the third section of the trilogy can stand on its own: "grounded on its own principles sufficiently known by experience, it would not stand in need of the former sections" (*DC* "Author's Preface" 9). Various positions have been taken on this issue. One suggestion is that what Hobbes explicitly says about philosophical method applies only to natural philosophy and that his actual practice in doing political philosophy is something different, and that Hobbes knows it (Sorell, *Hobbes*, pp. 22–3). Sorell claims that civil philosophy differs from natural philosophy in three respects: first, natural philosophy says how things are while civil philosophy says how they ought to be; second, natural philosophy deals only in efficient causes while civil philosophy depends upon a final cause, namely, the purpose for which the commonwealth was instituted; and third, natural philosophy requires knowledge of the kinds of motion while civil philosophy does not (p. 24). Sorell's position is helpful as a statement of what Hobbes might have said or how he might have put some of the things he said together. It is less plausible as a statement of what Hobbes seems to have had in mind when he explicitly talked about the matter.

My suggestion is that one must separate logical relatedness from epistemological relatedness. Logically, the principles in *De Corpore* entail, according to Hobbes, the doctrines of *De Homine*, and those entail the doctrines of *De Cive*. Epistemologically, the principles of *De Cive* can be known "by

89

experience," as Hobbes says, and thus explained even though they logically rest on more-basic principles.

A quite separate point, which relates to the dedication, may be inserted here. Addressing William Cavendish, third earl of Devonshire, Hobbes says, "homo homini deus, et homo homini lupus." What he means by the first clause is that, when human beings band together in a sovereign-making covenant, they create something, namely, the civil state, which, like God, has overwhelming power, judges what is good and evil, and saves people from death; in *Leviathan*, the civil state is called a "mortal god." What he means by the second clause is that one government is related to all other governments like one human being is related to others in the state of nature.

In *De Corpore* (1655), Hobbes declares that political philosophy begins with his *De Cive* (*DCo* "Epistle Dedicatory" 1). *De Cive* is divided into three parts: "Of Liberty" (*Libertas*), "Of Dominion" (*Imperium*), and "Of Religion" (*Religio*). It is easy to find fault with this division. Chapter 1 of "Of Liberty" contains a discussion of the state of nature, that is, the state of complete liberty. But the other three chapters of the first part discuss the laws of nature as dictates of reason and as the divine law. So there is more about law than about freedom in "Of Liberty." The second part, "Of Dominion," discusses what its title suggests: the causes and origin of government, the kinds of government, the nature of sovereignty, the causes of the dissolution of governments, the duties of sovereigns, and the nature of civil law. But it also contains material that arguably belongs in the third part, "Of Religion," namely, evidence from the Bible for Hobbes's doctrines and a discussion of the nature of sin. Also, most of the material in "Of Religion" properly belongs in the first two parts. For even people in the state of nature have a natural religion, which is based upon their conception of God; and people in the civil state have or should have a state religion, determined by the sovereign.

Waiving objections to the organization, let's now consider the contents of each part. "Of Liberty" presupposes the doctrines of *De Corpore* and *De Homine* even though they were published later. Hobbes begins by denying that human beings are naturally social, *pace* Aristotle and the western European tradition of political thought. What he means is that human beings are not naturally sociable. He does not doubt that children need and desire other people because they are incompetent to care for themselves. Nonetheless, children are by nature quarrelsome; it is one thing to need society and something else to be fit for it (*DC* 1.2, note). Children can become fit for society by being taught that it is to their benefit to cooperate with others. This cooperation needs to be sealed in covenants, which are artificial, not natural, bonds between people (*DC* 1.2 note).

Even united in a civil state, people enjoy each other's company, according to Hobbes, only to "receive some honour or profit from it" (*DC* 1.2). Hobbes appeals to experience: if one looks at how people behave, one will see that, in business transactions, everyone is trying to maximize her own profit; in pleasure and recreation, people enjoy laughing, and laughing is nothing but thinking that one's own character traits are superior to those of certain other people who are thought to be defective or handicapped. Often the humor is harmless, but sometimes "we wound the absent; their whole life, sayings, actions are examined, judged, condemned . . . And these are indeed the true delights of society, unto which we are carried by nature" (*DC* 1.2).

Not sociableness, but fear of other human beings is what motivates people to form governments. The fear is due to two factors: to the natural equality of human beings in the state of nature and to their tendency to want to hurt each other. The second tendency results from unavoidable competition over the same scarce goods; the desire of some people for the glory that comes from overpowering other people; and the necessity of defending oneself against those who are looking for glory (*DC* 1.4– 6).

Whatever is naturally desired is good, and what people desire most is to preserve their life. Further, since whoever has a right to the means has a right to the ends, everyone in the state of nature has the right to do whatever she thinks is necessary to preserve her own life. (*DC* 1.7–8). In effect, this means that everyone has a right to everything, according to Hobbes, because in the state of nature there is no one to judge what a person needs other than the individual herself (*DC* 1.10). Obviously, this mutual competitiveness and universal right to everything puts everyone in a condition of war against everyone else. Since war obviously threatens the very thing that people want most, their lives, reason dictates that people make peace (*DC* 1.12).

The laws of nature explain how peace can be achieved. These laws are not agreements among human beings; rather, all agreements presuppose the existence of these laws, which Hobbes equates with dictates of right reason (*DC* 2.1). When Hobbes talks about their nature in chapter 2, the laws of nature are treated as essentially propositions, which, if used for guidance, will get one out of the state of nature. They are not properly laws in the sense that they are the commands of someone in authority. In chapter 3, he says that they are also laws in the sense that God commanded them, as revealed in the Bible. This fact about their divine connection would not seem to change their essential character. In *Leviathan*, it is arguable that Hobbes's view about the nature of the LAW OF NATURE changes and that he there holds that the laws of nature are properly laws and essentially commands of God, although even there the evidence is somewhat ambiguous. (*See also* LAW OF NATURE, FUNDAMENTAL; LAWS OF NATURE.)

Hobbes says that the third part of *De Cive*, "Of Religion," is necessary because one must not obey a human law if it conflicts with a divine law, and the only way to know whether there is a conflict is to know what divine law is. This topic is motivated by timely concerns. Many of Charles's opponents thought that they were justified in disobeying him because of their duty to divine law. Hobbes's goal is to show that they are mistaken because it is virtually impossible for there to be a conflict between human and divine law.

The topic of divine law is preceded by a discussion of the KINGDOM OF GOD on the grounds that one cannot know what the laws of a kingdom are without knowing the kingdom itself (*DC* 15.1). The kingdom of God by nature is the kingdom of which the laws are the laws of nature. God reigns over all who are rational. Inanimate and irrational beings, which includes atheists, are excluded from the kingdom of God, because a subject must be capable of understanding a sovereign's commands and those who do not or cannot acknowledge God's existence lack the requisite capacity (*DC* 15.2). The right by which God reigns is His irresistible power. According to Hobbes, everyone in the state of nature has the right to rule over others; however, human beings give up their right because it is in their interest to do so. Since everyone in the state of nature is equal, the attempt to exercise the right of dominion would be ineffective and have the opposite of its intended effect. Anyone who tries to rule among equals is sure to die. God, in contrast, because of His irresistible power never gives up His right to dominion. In the case of God, might makes right (*DC* 16.2).

In addition to the kingdom of God by nature, there are prophetical kingdoms of God. The first prophetical kingdom seems to have begun with Abraham. Adam and Eve had been ruled by a divine covenant, but there was no kingdom of God involved, according to Hobbes, because the existence of that covenant was brief. Although Hobbes does not say more about it, and in fact has relatively little to say about Adam and Eve in his writings, God's rule over Adam and Eve presumably would have been something like the rule of a parent over a FAMILY in the state of nature. *See* (KINGDOM OF GOD, PROPHETIC.) Concerning Abraham, what is emphasized is that he was the interpreter of both the secular and religious laws: "it follows that Abraham's subjects could not sin in obeying him, provided that Abraham commanded them not to deny God's existence or providence, or to do somewhat expressly contrary to the honour of God." The same held for Isaac and Jacob. The order of command for the subjects of Jacob was as follows: they first submitted themselves to God; then to

Abraham; then to the God of Abraham; then to Isaac; then to the God of Isaac; then to Jacob; then to the God of Jacob (*DC* 16.7). The story of the patriarchs is the story of a chain of authority that alternates between the God that commands the laws of nature, a secular sovereign, and the god [*sic*] that that sovereign commands his subjects to worship. The moral of the story is that it is virtually impossible for there to be a conflict between the commands of the sovereign and the commands of God, and the showing of this, recall, was the purpose of the part "Of Religion." For good measure, Hobbes points out that to deny the god of the sovereign is treason (*DC* 16.7).

I take it that God had a prophetical kingdom in virtue of a covenant to which Abraham was a party. The preceding sentence is somewhat periphrastic because, according to Hobbes's doctrine of COVENANTS, a sovereign is not a contracting party to the covenant and yet Hobbes does say that God made the covenant "with Abraham" (*DC* 16.9). It is difficult or impossible to save Hobbes's explicit doctrine of sovereign-making covenants with God. It does not even help to torture the text and interpret it as meaning that God made Abraham make a covenant, because there is no one else for Abraham to make a covenant with. Abraham's family cannot be the covenanting parties, because Abraham was already their sovereign before the covenant under discussion was made. This mystery must stand.

De Corpore (1655) [16] *De Corpore* should be understood in relation to a trilogy, *The Elements of Philosophy*, which was supposed to provide a complete system of knowledge. However, the trilogy was never published as a unit, and the three "sections" appeared at different times and out of logical order. (On the importance of referring to the parts of the trilogy as "sections," see Tuck, "Hobbes and Descartes.") *De Corpore*, logically the first section of the trilogy, was the second of the three to appear in print. *De Homine* (1658), the second of the three sections, appeared in print last. *De Cive* (1642; expanded in 1647), the third of the three sections, appeared in print first. All three sections appeared originally in Latin. A translation of *De Corpore* purports to have been inspected and corrected by Hobbes. There is some doubt about this, and, in any case, this translation is flawed. A new translation of the first part of *De Corpore* appeared in 1981. (*See* Bibliography [16])

De Corpore contains four parts. The first part is called "Logic." It contains a theory of meaning, a simplified Aristotelian logic, and a scientific methodology indebted to the Paduan school. The second part is called "The First Grounds of Philosophy." It contains definitions for the most important scientific concepts. These include place and time, body and accident, cause and effect, power and act, identity and difference, and quantity.

This part also defines certain geometrical entities such as lines, planes, solids, and angles. The third part is called "The Proportions of Motions and Magnitudes." It is purportedly about geometry (*DCo* "Epistle to the Reader"), but contains as much physics (*DCo* 15.1). The fourth part is called "Physics, or the Phenomena of Nature." It contains Hobbes's most systematic and mature discussion of the nature of sensation and animal motion; light, heat, and color; the nature of the planets and stars; and gravity (though not in this order).

At the beginning of the book, Hobbes defines philosophy as the knowledge of effects or phenomena, acquired through correct reasoning. This knowledge can be achieved either by beginning with an effect and constructing hypotheses about what cause might have generated it; or by beginning with a cause and explaining how it generates an effect. The first method is called analytic; the second is called synthetic. Hobbes returns to this point in chapter 25, in the fourth part of the book. Starting from causes, a philosopher specifies possible effects; and starting from effects, she specifies possible causes. While geometry, treated in the third part, begins with causes, physics begins with effects. These effects are the things that appear to human beings, that is, phenomena. In short, physics begins with individual effects and hypothesizes necessary propositions that might explain them (*DCo* 25.1).

Whether analytic or synthetic, what underlies the method of philosophy is reasoning. Reasoning is defined as computation. It is the addition and subtraction of ideas (phantasms) (*DCo* 1.2, 7.1). The idea of a human being is the sum of the addition of the ideas of body, animate, and rational. The remainder of subtracting the idea of rational from the idea of a human being is the idea of an animal. Hobbes's view of meaning is an interesting combination of intentionalism and nominalism. Hobbes's logic is a simplified and nominalistic version of scholastic, Aristotelian logic. Although he often denigrated Aristotle, he did not wholly reject his philosophy in practice, especially in *De Corpore*. He preserves such Aristotelian principles as, "Everything that is moved is moved by another," and the ideas of an efficient cause and prime matter. He keeps the ideas of formal and material causes but only in a radically reinterpreted way.

De Corpore contains Hobbes's mature view of physics and the foundations of philosophy. Within the history of science, it is an important document in the transition from Aristotelian to modern science. An early version of some parts of *De Corpore* appeared in a manuscript, *Anti-White*, which was not published until 1973.

De Homine (1658) [19]   *De Homine* is the second section of Hobbes's trilogy *The Elements of Philosophy*, and the last to be published. Like the other two sections, it was published in Latin; but unlike the other two, it has not yet been completely translated into English. In 1972, a translation of the Dedication and the last six chapters was published. These are the only chapters of philosophical interest, and they are largely redundant. Hobbes's explanations in *Humane Nature* (1650) and *Leviathan* (1651) are typically at least as good as, and often more extensively treated, than those in *De Homine*. Moreover, it is the least successful of the three sections. More than half of it (chapters 2 through 9) consists of Hobbes's theory of optics, which is a shortened and translated version of *A Minute or First Draught of the Optiques*, a work that was unpublished until Molesworth included part of it in his edition of Hobbes's works. The first chapter of *De Homine* is a naturalistic treatment of the origin of human beings, their nutrition, death, and development in the womb.

One gets the impression that Hobbes published *De Homine* mostly out of a sense of duty, to complete his trilogy. By 1658, his interests had turned to mathematical, scientific, and religious topics.

definition For Aristotle, paradigmatic definitions present a genus and specific difference for the definiendum (that which is to be defined). Although Hobbes in fact follows Aristotle in many of his definitions, in theory he does not accept these constraints on definition (*EW* 7:218). For Hobbes, since only bodies exist and motion is the predominant state of bodies, in general good definitions state the kind of motion that is signified by a word. In particular, he distinguishes two kinds of definitions: those of words that signify things for which a cause of motion can be specified and those of words that signify things for which no cause of motion can be specified. Although Hobbes says that the definitions of the words "body" and "motion" belong to the first kind, he must be mistaken about this, for a cause must always specify some accident in virtue of which the effect occurs, but no special accident applies to body or motion in general. It is more plausible that the first kind of definition could be applied to phrases of the form "an X body" or "a body X," where the X marks a place where some quality must be specified, which is then defined. An example is that a circular body is one generated from the rotation of a straight line around a fixed point. According to Hobbes, the method of generating an object ought to be provided in the definition because the world consists of bodies in motion and definitions are the foundations for understanding the world. Concerning definitions of that for which no cause can be given, an example would seem to be the definition of motion as "the uninterrupted desertion of one place and the acquisition of another" (*DCo* 6.13). Since no particular accident is specified in the word "motion," no cause of motion can be given in the definition.

95

Earlier in *De Corpore*, Hobbes had discussed definition without distinguishing two kinds and without requiring that the definition specify the way in which the object is generated. There, the purpose of definition was said to be the explanation of one word by means of many words. His example was "Man is a rational, animate, body" (*DCo* 3.9). Such definitions are primary because reason uses them; but they are not susceptible to proof. Axioms and postulates are sometimes thought of as first principles, but they are not, because, according to Hobbes, they are susceptible to proof (*DCo* 3.9, 6.13).

Definitions are true by convention; that is, they are true because people choose to use the defined word in the way explained by the definiens (the defining expression). As such, they cannot be proven; they are either accepted or not (*DCo* 3.9, 6.15). Yet sometimes Hobbes talks about some definitions being right and others wrong (*L* 4.13). Words that have a compound meaning can be defined by resolving or analyzing the term into its component parts (*DCo* 6.14). So no such definition can consist of a single word (*DCo* 6.15). Moreover, definition must stop somewhere. A word that is not susceptible to definition is called a genus. Although it cannot strictly be defined, it can be explicated; that is, the way the word is used can be explained (*DCo* 6.14; *L* 4.12).

The teaching of philosophy begins with definitions, and definitions should be "compositive," that is, built up out of simpler objects. The simpler objects are those that occur in the definiens in contrast with the definiendum. This means that the words in the definiens are more basic than the definiendum (*DCo* 6.15). It also follows that the definiendum cannot occur in the definiens. Hobbes explains this as a consequence of the fact that the definition is supposed to resolve the whole into its parts and the whole is not a part of itself (*DCo* 6.15). A more standard explanation for the same point is that such definitions are circular; that is, definitions are supposed to explain the definiendum, and if the word to be defined occurs in the definiens, then one would already have to understand it in order to understand the definition; and that is absurd. (These remarks apply to reductive definitions. Definitions that are primarily elucidatory tolerate certain occurrences of the definiendum in the definiens. Being concerned only with reduction, Hobbes does not discuss this matter.)

deliberation Human beings have a constant stream of internal bodily motions; these are desires, in the broad sense of both appetites and aversions. The last desire before an action is an act of will. Prior to this, there is usually a series of alternating desires to do or not to do the act. These alternating desires may also have the character of hopes and fears. (*See*

EMOTIONS.) Whatever their precise character may be, this series of alternating desires is deliberation (*L* 6.49, 6.53; *AW*, pp. 448, 452).

Some of the consequences of this analysis of deliberation are that one can deliberate only about the future and only about things that one thinks are possible. Also, since beasts have alternating desires, they deliberate as much as do human beings; and since the will is the last desire before an action, they also have will (*L* 50–3; *AW*, p. 448). (*See* DESIRE.)

There is also a political consequence to Hobbes's treatment of deliberation. Since the will is the last desire before an action and since fear is a kind of desire, acts done out of fear, such as laying down one's rights and setting up a government, are voluntary actions (*L* 6.53). So sovereign-making covenants are coerced but nonetheless valid.

delight   Delight is the pleasure that comes from satisfying a desire and appears to enhance the vital motions of the person having it. Pleasure is the experience of good, that is, the experience of having what was desired. Displeasure is the experience of evil, that is, the experience of having what one desired not to have (*L* 6.10–11; *EL* 1.7.1).

demonstration (*demonstratio*)   A demonstration is a kind of proof, but not just any kind. A demonstration is a syllogism or series of syllogisms that consists of definitions or the consequences of definitions. Since every definition is a necessary proposition, the conclusion of the demonstration must be a necessary proposition (*DCo* 3.9, 6.15). (This point is obscured by a recent translation of the first part of *De Corpore*, which renders *demonstratio* as "proof" (see Bibliography [16], *Thomas Hobbes: Logica Sive Computatio* 6.16).)

Hobbes's use of "demonstration" as a technical term is important because it explains how his presentation of proofs for the existence of God in various places is consistent with his claim that it cannot be demonstrated. No proposition expressing a matter of fact, for example, that a certain marble is moving across a table, is susceptible to demonstration, because matters of fact are expressed by categorical sentences and demonstrations must be expressed in conditional sentences. (*See* PROPOSITIONS.) So it is no wonder that there cannot be a demonstration of the existence of God. But that does not mean that there cannot be proofs, based upon reasoning from the best available evidence and adequate to merit assent. Thus, belief in the existence of God is supported by reasoning without being demonstrative. Hobbes's view is similar to that of William of Ockham.

The term "demonstration" comes from Aristotle through scholastic philosophy. Hobbes adopts the central feature of Aristotle's conception. Demonstrations have necessary premises and conclusions. Also, like Aristotle,

Hobbes accepts that there are two types: *demonstratio quia* and *demonstratio propter quid*. In the first, the conclusion specifies a truth, but the premises do not express the cause for its truth. An example is,

> All stars twinkle.
> All things that twinkle are distant objects.
> Therefore, all stars are distant objects.

Although the conclusion is true, the premises do not explain why stars are distant; in particular, twinkling is not the cause of their remoteness. In *demonstratio propter quid*, the premises jointly give the reason for the truth of the conclusion, as in this one:

> All distant objects twinkle.
> All stars are distant objects.
> Therefore, all stars twinkle.

Stars twinkle because they are distant.

desire (*appetitus*) In a broad sense, desire is any ENDEAVOR toward or away from an object that causes that endeavor. An endeavor is any motion that is too small to be measured. It may appear that there is no movement at all in an animal that has a desire. Not observing any motion, scholastic philosophers have called desire "metaphorical motion." Hobbes says the term is absurd. Only words may be called metaphorical; motions cannot be. Hobbes holds that the appearance that desire is not a motion is deceptive. A desire for food may cause an animal to move a long distance to get it. Any motion over a great distance is composed of motions over very small distances, and every cause is itself in motion. Consequently, since desires are causes, they must be motions; and since they are usually not apparent, they are usually imperceptibly small (*L* 6.1–2).

In a narrow sense, desire is the same as appetite, and appetite is an endeavor towards an object. The correlative notion to appetite is aversion. Aversion is a desire (in the broad sense) away from the object that causes the desire. Hobbes sometimes identifies desire in the narrow sense (that is, appetite) with love and pleasure (*voluptas*), and aversion with hate or annoyance (*molestia*) (*L* 6.2; *EL* 1.7.5; *DH* 11.1). (*See also* EMOTION.)

Hobbes's definition of desire in terms of appetite and appetite in terms of endeavor is important for his mechanistic and reductionist project. Desire itself, he is indicating, is simply a very small motion of some body. Hobbes then proceeds to define other concepts, relating to cognition and emotion, in terms of desire in the broad sense. In short, they are reduced to bodies in motion. What these definitions are supposed to show is that there is no need to think of mental or emotional concepts or entities as anything other than bodies in motion and hence understandable by natural science.

The project is a good one but flawed. The desire for food is an example of what is wrong with Hobbes's analysis. A hungry person desires food, and in its presence the person, given certain beliefs, will move towards it; but the food does not necessarily cause the desire. A person may desire food when none is present, and this is often exactly the case. Also, in moving about in search of food, the person may unwittingly be moving away from it.

Some desires (in the broad sense) are natural, such as hunger; some are acquired from experience.

despair   Despair is the belief that one will not get what one desires (L 6.15). It is "absolute privation of hope" (*EL* 1.9.8). In *Leviathan*, constant despair is defined as "diffidence of ourselves"; in *The Elements of Law*, diffidence is merely a mild case of despair (L 6.20; *EL* 1.9.8). When this mild case of despair applies to every human being, as it does in the state of nature, Hobbes calls it "perpetual diffidence" (*EL* 1.14.11).

dreams   The most systematic treatment of dreams occurs in *De Corpore*, as part of Hobbes's explanation for how all human experience consists of motions, which appear as phantasms. Sensation is a certain kind of motion caused by a present external object. Dreams are the phantasms of sleeping human beings (*DCo* 25.9; see also L 2.5).

Experience, says Hobbes, teaches five things about dreams: (1) there is little order or coherence to them, because in sleep people do not focus on any goal or end; (2) dreams are about things "compounded and made up of the phantasms of sense past," because no new sensations are received during sleep; (3) they can begin either interspersed with sensation or during a deep sleep; (4) except for sensations, they are clearer than the phantasms people have when they are awake; (5) the emotion of admiration cannot occur in dreaming (*DCo* 25.9; see also *EL* 1.3.3).

Hobbes's views about dreaming may strike a post-Freudian culture as naive insofar as he denies any sort of ordering or goal-oriented aspect to dreams. Concerning (2), Hobbes claims that interior changes in body temperature, specifically, those in the heart, affect the content of dreams. In *Leviathan*, he had attributed dreams to interior bodily changes generally, but these seem to be caused by cold and warm conditions exterior to the body (L 2.5–6). Item (5) seems to make a logical point. He says that, since only things that are recognized as new can be admired and since recognition of the new requires remembering things past, dreams cannot contain admiration, because in them "all things appear as present." It is not clear to me that this last claim about dreams is true.

The most important applications of his views about dreams are religious ones. He uses dreams to explain the origin of beliefs about ghosts. The phantasms of dreams are mistakenly interpreted as incorporeal substances (*DCo* 25.9; *L* 2.7). Also, many false beliefs about alleged revelations occur in dreams that are mistaken for waking experiences. He says that people sometimes unwittingly fall asleep without knowing it, have a dream about God appearing to them, and then believe that God appeared to them. On other occasions, people know that they were asleep and yet take a dream about God to be veridical. The absurdity of this view is proven with a devastating turn of phrase. Hobbes says that "God appeared to me in a dream" means the same as "I dreamed that God appeared to me"; and the lack of evidential value of the latter sentence is patent (*L* 32.6.). If someone said, "Napoleon appeared to me in a dream," no one would think that Napoleon himself was present to that person; yet people tend not to see that the appearance of God in a dream is analogous. None of this is to say that it is impossible for God to reveal Himself to someone in a dream. It is not impossible; but the dream is not evidential. If someone believes that God appeared to her in a dream, it is believed on faith. (*See also* PROPHETS.)

Most of the pagan ("gentile") religions originated because people did not know how to distinguish dream experiences from visual sensations. Such dreams explain the origin of satyrs and nymphs among ancient people, and fairies, ghosts, and goblins among Hobbes's contemporaries (*L* 2.8). Schools ought to disabuse people of such fictitious entities, but instead the clerics who teach in them use the belief in ghosts for their own self-serving ends (*L* 2.9).

What is perhaps most significant about Hobbes's treatment of dreams insofar as the history of philosophy is concerned is how apparently little affected he was by Descartes's worries about dreams. Hobbes of course knew the *Meditations*, but he was not impressed by its methodological skepticism. In *Leviathan*, Hobbes says that, for his part, dreaming differs from waking in that in dreams he does not usually "think of the same persons, places, objects, and actions" as in his waking life, that dreams are not as coherent as waking experience, and that on waking he often sees the absurdity of his dreams but never dreams about the absurdity of his waking thoughts (*L* 2.5). His view begs the question of what is dream and what is real. By what right are certain sorts of experiences judged not to have the mark of reality? It is possible that reality is chaotic (what is usually taken as dreaming) and that in order to cope with it people go into long periods of dreaming, in which a false order is imposed on things (what is usually taken as waking). In his early *Elements of Law*, he had said that one could never know when one was dreaming, because there is no criterion by which to judge the matter (*EL* 1.3.8, 1.3.10). Hobbes's nonchalance in the face of these skeptical problems is revealed in his remark that, "I am well satisfied that being awake, I know I dream not; though when I dream, I think myself awake" (*L* 2.5). Hobbes is not gripped by the worry that his sanguine belief that he is awake may well be one of those dream experiences that he concedes cause him to think that he is awake.

Some scholars think that Hobbes was concerned with skepticism but solved the problem to his satisfaction by working to develop natural science. It should also be added that Hobbes thought that skeptical problems could be solved by authority: the sovereign declares which propositions count as true and which count as false. Although there is much to this, Hobbes's position would not silence a skeptic, who would ask, "How do you know that your science is correct?" "How do you know who the proper authority is?" and "How do you know what that authority said or what was meant by the words spoken?"

E

Elements of Law, Natural and Politic (1640) [4]   The history of the distribution and publication of *Elements of Law, Natural and Politic* is somewhat complicated. It was written in early 1640 and circulated in many manuscript copies. The work created some stir, and Hobbes reports that it might have brought him into some danger if the king had not dissolved the Short Parliament when he did (*EW* 4:414). As it was, the Long Parliament was called into session in November of that year, whereupon Hobbes fled to the Continent, where he stayed for eleven years.

The work was published in two books in London in 1650 without Hobbes's permission. The first book went under the title *Humane Nature*, and consisted of the first thirteen chapters of *The Elements of Law*. (*Humane Nature* should not be confused with *De Homine*, which is the second section of Hobbes's trilogy *The Elements of Philosophy*.) The second book went under the title *De Corpore Politico, or the Elements of Law, Moral and Politic*. The similarity of this title to the manuscript title is just one of the many confusing elements in its history. Further, this second book was divided into two parts. Part I consisted of chapters 14 through 19 of Part I of the manuscript version of *The Elements of Law*, but numbered one through six. Part II consisted of all of Part II of the manuscript.

Since Hobbes had published *De Cive* in 1642 (revised in 1647) and would soon publish *Leviathan* in 1651, there was no reason for him to bother about *The Elements of Law*, which was his earliest and shortest treatment of human nature and political theory. No complete edition of *The Elements of Law* appeared in print, in the form in which Hobbes wrote it, until in 1889 Ferdinand Tönnies published one based upon the best manuscripts known.

The content and doctrine of *The Elements of Law* are very similar to those of *De Cive*. Both works were generally favored by royalists in contrast with *Leviathan*, which drew substantial criticism from exiled royalists in the 1650s. Unlike Hobbes's other two political works, *The Elements of Law* contains very little about religion. Also, he says there that democracy is "the first in order of time" of the three forms of government, and "it must be so of necessity" because the other two forms require the election of an aristocracy or a monarchy and this requires a political action that can be performed only by all the people (*EL* 2.2.1). He later abandoned this view, and only the ghost of it remains in *Leviathan* 18.1.

emotions Emotions are certain motions of the "mind" that often interfere with thinking (*DH* 12.1). They originate inside the body of an animal and cause the animal to move either toward or away from an object. (*See also* DESIRE and ENDEAVOR.)

The most philosophically important aspect of Hobbes's treatment of emotions is his attempt to reduce all emotions to or explain them in terms of bodily motions that are too small to be measured. That is, Hobbes's view of emotions is purely naturalistic and mechanistic. Here is a sampling on how those analyses proceed.

All emotions are desires in a broad sense. Desires towards an object are called "appetites," but also "desires" in a narrow sense of the word. Desires away from an object are called "aversions." The emotion of love is the same as appetite or desire in the narrow sense. Hate is the same as aversion. The difference between "love" and "desire" is a matter of usage, according to Hobbes. "Love" tends to be used when the object is present; "desire" tends to be used when the object is not present (*L* 6.3; *DH* 11.1). Similar remarks apply to the usage of "hate" and "aversion" *mutatis mutandis* (cf. *DH* 12.2).

Hobbes's analysis of contempt must be understood in its seventeenth-century sense. Contempt is neither appetite nor aversion but stands midway between them in the sense that to have contempt for something is to be so indifferent towards the object that it does not move one at all, either towards or away from it (*L* 6.5). Today we have the expression "beneath contempt," which Hobbes would interpret as meaning "not worth even hating."

Delight is the sensation of appetite. Hobbes thinks that delight is "a corroboration of vital motion" and means by this that what causes delight enhances one's life (*L* 6.9–11). He did not seem to have a sense that some things that cause pleasure are actually damaging. (Perhaps Hobbes would always find a way to distinguish the cause of the pleasure from the cause of the damage.) Displeasure or "trouble of mind" is the sensation of aversion; and it interferes with the motion of life. Pleasure and pain are essentially the same as appetite and delight on the one hand and aversion and displeasure on the other.

The reason that there are different words for the same phenomenon is that each word has a different focus and orientation towards it. Hobbes mentions four dimensions that determine that there will be different words for the same thing and how those words will be used: (1) the likelihood of satisfying the desire; (2) the nature of the object desired; (3) the place of the emotion among other emotions; (4) the succession of motions that the emotion is (*L* 6.13).

Concerning (1), hope is an appetite that one expects to be satisfied, and despair is an appetite that one expects not to be satisfied. Concerning (2), fear is the belief that the object of aversion will injure one (cf. *DH* 12.3). Concerning (3), courage is a combination of hope and fear: it is the appetite for resistance by which one expects to avoid hurt from the object of aversion that one believes will otherwise injure one. Concerning (4), confidence is the repeated occurrence of hope, namely, the appetite of expecting to be satisfied. Diffidence is just the opposite; it is the repeated occurrence of despair, namely the appetite of expecting not to be satisfied (*L* 6.20). This explanation of diffidence may need some elucidation. Diffidence is distrust. What this means is that what one wants to trust or rely upon (the thing for which one has an appetite) is thought not to fulfill that desire.

The four dimensions just discussed fit into a larger aspect of Hobbes's thought, his reductionist tendencies. What he wants to show in many instances is that seemingly rich and deep phenomena are not genuinely independent of other things, but are reducible to simpler things and ultimately reducible to the motions of bodies. For example, benevolence was typically treated as a divine gift. Within Hobbes's scheme, it is merely a desire, namely, the desire that someone else receive something good (*L* 6.22). Conversely, covetousness was typically treated as a vice of the soul. For Hobbes, it is again a desire, namely, the desire to have riches, combined with the attitude of disapproving of the person who has them (*L* 6.23).

One of Hobbes's more interesting analyses is that of pity. Pity is usually thought of as a feeling of tenderness towards a person caused by that person's pain or distress; it seems to be essentially an other-directed emotion. Such a conception of pity does not fit neatly into Hobbes's egoism, according to which everyone acts for the sake of some good for herself; so he needs to reinterpret the nature of it. In *The Elements of Law*, he describes it as "imagination or fiction of future calamity to ourselves, proceeding from the sense of another man's present calamity" (*EL* 1.9.10). Hobbes seems to take the hard edge off this description in *Leviathan* when he defines "pity" as grief for the calamity of another; but it remains there when he explains that pity "arises from the imagination that the like calamity may befall himself" (*L* 6.46; *EW* 6:461–2). So, a person's pity is caused by the pain of another, but what she is concerned about is her own possible future pain. Philosophers have sometimes said that pity requires the ability to imagine the suffering of others and even the ability to imagine oneself suffering what the person pitied is suffering; but Hobbes's claim is different. Pity is one's own suffering caused by the pain of another; and one seeks the relief of one's own pain. One seeks the relief of the other's pain only as a means to that end. In *Anti-White*, Hobbes discusses the self-interested character of pity at greater length.

> Whoever thinks that men pity the poor out of a desire to act in accordance with a rational desire is insufficiently aware of the spirit in which men do so. Some do it out of compassion, that is, in order to lessen the sorrow they feel when they imagine a similar wretchedness in their own persons, for the nature of pity is this: it is a sorrow arising from the contemplation of someone else's misfortune. Others do it in order to avoid the solicitings of those who ask. Both these groups, therefore, do it in order to avoid sorrow, i.e. they do it from pleasure. Others, again, do it for vain-glory, namely so as to appear merciful or generous, i.e. for reputation's (*honor*) sake. Finally, others do it so as to merit the Divine Mercy themselves, this being to God the best motive (*finis*) but nonetheless a useful one. (*AW*, pp. 402–3)

Hobbes's analysis of envy in *Anti-White* is also interesting:

> Suppose it is true that the greatest and everlasting torments that await the wicked in a future age are none other than envy, covetousness, sadness, fear, and similar mental stresses. Without doubt there are a great many people who would rather endure them than endure non-existence, because associated with them are the good things that outweigh them: with envy, a pleasant expectation of the evil that can befall him whom we envy. (*AW*, p. 487)

Here are some brief examples of some of Hobbes's other reductive analyses:

Ambition is a desire for office or high rank.
Pusillanimity is a desire for things that are of little help to achieving one's ends and a fear of things that are of little hindrance.
Magnanimity is contempt (indifference) for little helps and hindrances.
Fortitude is magnanimity (contempt for little helps and hindrances) in matters relating to a danger of death or injury.
Kindness is a desire for persons for companionship (*L* 6.24–30).

endeavor (*conatus*) An endeavor is any motion that is too small to be measured. This makes the concept of endeavor, like many of Hobbes's concepts, relative. If the smallest unit of measurement is an inch, then a movement of half an inch is an endeavor, for it would not be measurable.

Something like this is a common occurrence in American football, where a yard is the smallest unit of measurement used for statistical purposes. If a ballcarrier begins at a yardmarker, say, the twenty, and moves the ball forward less than one yard, say, one half yard, his movement is recorded as "no gain" or zero yards. Suppose that on the next play the ball is advanced an additional half yard. Since the ball now rests on the twenty-one yard line, the ballcarrier is credited with a gain of one yard (that is, moving the ball one yard) even though his forward movement in absolute terms was the same as the movement that resulted in no gain (and no measured movement).

Hobbes sometimes defines endeavor as motion through the length of a point. This may sound paradoxical or contradictory unless one realizes that for Hobbes every geometrical object, even a point, is a body and thus has an extension. What makes something a point is the fact that its extension is not considered (*EW* 7:201). Thus, there can be a motion through the length of a point, which occupies a space smaller than any space that is measured. Unlike the motion of a football in the example above, endeavors are usually motions that are imperceptible. That there must be imperceptibly small motions, Hobbes is certain. Any body in motion over a long distance must travel over distances that are smaller than the whole. These distances can be divided indefinitely, even when they are no longer observable. Yet, the body must still move across them (*L* 6.1). It should be obvious from this discussion that the concept of endeavor is the basic concept of Hobbes's theory of motion since all other motions are divisible into endeavors.

His most explicit formulation of the concept of endeavor is near the beginning of Part Three of *De Corpore*, just as he is about to expound his theory of motion and geometry. He gives three supposedly equivalent definitions of it: (1) endeavor is "motion made in less space and time than can be given"; (2) endeavor is motion that is smaller than can be measured by the system of measurement that is being used; (3) endeavor is motion through the length of a point or in an instant of time.

The system of measurement that endeavors are defined in relation to can thus be temporal. If a clock is divided into segments no smaller than one second, then an endeavor, relative to that system of keeping time, would be any motion that takes less than one second. If another clock is divided into tenths of a second, then that motion is not an endeavor.

So far, endeavor has been discussed with respect to a fixed system of measurement. Let's now consider the matter with respect to what Hobbes calls "exposed quantity" (*DCo* 12.2). There are some motions that are too small to be detected either by vision or by touch. Such motions are endeavors. Some people have better vision or tactile sensation than others;

106

and a motion that is an endeavor to one person may not be an endeavor to another who has more-sensitive sensory equipment. One of the most significant aspects of modern science is its understanding that what happens in the world is the result of motions and bodies too small to be observed by the human senses unaided.

Endeavor also plays a key role in human psychology. In *Leviathan*, Hobbes says that, because all actions depend upon preceding motions, "it is evident" that some internal, unseen motion begins the entire chain: "And although unstudied men do not conceive any motion at all to be there, where the thing moved is invisible, or the space it is moved in is (for the shortness of it) insensible; yet that does not hinder but that such motions are" (*L* 6.1; *EL* 1.7.2). Acts of will are endeavors (*AW*, p. 447).

When an endeavor is in the direction of some object, it is called an appetite or DESIRE. When an endeavor is in the direction away from an object, it is called an aversion. Hunger and thirst are two appetitive endeavors; fear and hate are two aversive endeavors. Other psychological states, conditions, and emotions are given similar analyses, and many differ only in being more complex. Indeed, it is only the complexity of a motion that ultimately distinguishes one psychological state from another (*L* 6.3). Also, out of these psychological endeavors come the motions that generate the civil state. Thus, in answer to any question of the form "What causes motion *X* to exist?" Hobbes will say that it is some motion *Y*; if this question is repeated concerning *Y*, and so on, at some point Hobbes will answer, "It is motion all the way down," unless and until one gets to God; and then Hobbes does not know quite what to say because GOD is incomprehensible.

Endeavor in its Latin form, *conatus*, was picked up by both Spinoza and Leibniz as a key concept. Leibniz is usually credited with the idea that the effects of any cause are infinite. That idea is a generalization of Hobbes's view that the motion of an endeavor proceeds to infinity along its vector (*DCo* 15.7).

Hobbes uses the concept of endeavor to define several other concepts in physics. Resistance is the endeavor of one body contrary to another body in motion and contiguous to the first. (*DCo* 15.2). One object presses another just in case the endeavor of the first object moves the second from its place (*DCo* 15.2). Pressure is the endeavor of one object against another. The pressure is mutual when the endeavors are opposite (*DCo* 22.1).

There is a less helpful discussion of endeavor in *Anti-White* (*AW*, pp. 125, 148–50).

envy *See* JEALOUSY

equality According to Hobbes, everyone is equal in rights and the ability to survive in the state of nature. Within the state of nature, men have no more rights than women; if anything, women have a better claim to dominance over children than men do.

Hobbes's seemingly enlightened attitude is a two-edged sword. Although everyone is equal in the state of nature, the state of nature is a wretched condition to be in, and people should be willing to suffer almost anything, including domination under a tyrant, in order to escape it. Inequality, along with art, culture, science, technology, and every other human good, arises only by leaving the state of nature. Inequality is artificial, but it is part and parcel with a decent life.

Ability to survive is roughly equal in the state of nature if intelligence and physical strength are averaged out. If Hobbes considered that women are on the average physically weaker than men, then he would have held that women are on the average more intelligent than men. But there is no evidence that he considered that matter. Reason is not the same thing as native intelligence because reason is thinking with words (*L* 5.2). But they are obviously closely related, and Hobbes says that reason is the same in all people, for "who is so stupid as both to mistake in geometry and also to persist in it when another detects his error to him?" (*L* 5.16). The correct answer to Hobbes's rhetorical question is that he was so stupid. He persisted in defending his various proofs of squaring the circle even after the Oxford geometer John Wallis showed that his proofs were defective.

essence Essence is the same as formal cause (*DCo* 10.7). (*See* CAUSE AND EFFECT.)

evil *See* EVIL, PROBLEM OF; GOOD AND EVIL

evil, problem of Several different problems may be called "the problem of evil," only one of which interests Hobbes, namely, the question, "On the supposition that God is omnipotent, omniscient, and omnibenevolent, why do good people suffer (or why do they suffer disproportionately to their sins)?" Hobbes never questions the supposition, which is the easiest way to solve or dissolve the problem. Given the conception of God in the supposition, it seems to follow that a person prospers if and only if she is good, and suffers if and only if she is bad. This is the principle taught in the book of Deuteronomy and the moral of the history of Israel, taught in the Deuteronomic history narrated in the Old Testament. Hobbes upholds the tradition: "even in this life the good fare better than the bad, and there is no art of outstripping others in gaining of wealth or honours (or anything else in this life which may be more delightful than these) more effective than honesty" (*AW*, pp. 460–1).

People who doubt this out of the pain of their own suffering nonetheless think that they are being treated unjustly by God. Hobbes has two basic replies, an unsympathetic one and a logical one. The unsympathetic reply is that people for the most part exaggerate their own innocence: "Anyone you care to point to supposes he is good ... Undeniably the complaint [that the evil prosper] is a universal one; but its cause is that no one admits his own depravity, and that, out of jealousy, the virtues of those whom one envies for their goods one calls wickedness" (*AW*, pp. 461–2). The logical reply is that it is a category mistake to think that God can be literally just or unjust. Since to be just is to follow laws and to be unjust is to break laws, one must be subject to laws in order to be just or unjust. But God is not subject to any laws, certainly not civil laws and not the laws of nature either since He is their author. God can do anything He wants to do without compunction; God is able "to enrich or to raise to earthly honours either the good or the evil, or both of them indiscriminately, just as He has wished." Concerning justice, Hobbes says, "if it be examined either according to the laws of nature or against the promises contained in the Holy Scriptures, God has an obligation to His creatures no more than the potter to his clay" (*AW*, p. 461). To the extent that God needs to fulfill His promises to human beings, He can do that by rewarding them in a future world.

excuses   After discussing the nature of civil law and the ways in which it is broken, Hobbes discusses how behavior not in accord with the law can be excused or the blame attached to it mitigated. An excuse totally removes blame because it removes obligation to the law (*L* 27.21–2).

Among the ways in which an action may be excused are the following: by not having any way of knowing what the law is; by being in the power of an enemy; by being immediately threatened with death whether by the actions of another person or by something due to nature, such as starvation; by acting under the authority of someone else (*L* 27.23–7). Although Hobbes does not enumerate ways in which blame for an action may be mitigated, presumably they will be like those for excusing an action when the conditions are not as extreme. For example, having great difficulty in knowing what the law is would mitigate blame substantially; having some difficulty in knowing what the law is would mitigate blame slightly.

Excusing a crime or mitigating blame concerns the individual psychological condition of the criminal. Crimes themselves can be ranked as greater or lesser by considering four dimensions: (1) "the malignity of the source or cause" of the action; (2) the bad example that is given to other people; (3) the seriousness of the effects of the crime; (4) the times, places, and people involved (*L* 27.29).

Hobbes seems to explicate the meaning of dimension (1) with the following example. A crime committed by a person who does it because she thinks she has enough strength, riches, or friends to oppose the sovereign is worse than one committed by someone who hopes to get away with it undetected. The first kind of crime inspires the perpetrator to break the law again and undermines authority (L 27.30).

Hobbes seems to give five examples of (2): (a) a crime committed by one's own mistaken reasoning is worse than one committed because one was taught that it was lawful by a teacher; (b) a crime that is punished whenever it is committed is worse than one which often goes unpunished; (c) a premeditated crime is worse than a crime of passion, though passion never completely mitigates a crime, since the time between learning of a law and violating it out of passion can be considered a period during which there was time for deliberation leading to the reform of one's dispositions; (d) a crime that violates a law that is publicly and often discussed is worse than violating one that is not; (e) an action that violates the manifest intention of the law but which the sovereign tacitly approves of is a crime less serious than that same action performed without the sovereign's tacit approval. Hobbes gives dueling as an example of (e). Suppose that dueling is forbidden, but that a person who refuses a duel is subjected to "contempt and scorn" and disqualified by the sovereign from having a military assignment. Then, the penalty for accepting a duel should be reduced (L 27.31–5).

Hobbes next explicates dimension (3), by mentioning crimes that vary with the seriousness of their effects. A crime that damages many people is worse than one that damages few. Hobbes is thinking particularly of crimes that injure additional people as time goes on. But his examples are somewhat odd. He says that it is worse for a minister of God to hold a false religious doctrine than it is for a private person, and worse for a professor of law to hold a false legal theory than it is for a private person. These examples would seem to fit under the rubric of (1) or (2) and are just like (a) above. However, the reason that Hobbes gives for the wickedness of a minister's or lawyer's bad behavior makes the example relevant to the seriousness of the effects. A minister or lawyer typically comes into contact with many more people than a private person does and thus corrupts more (L 27.36).

Because crimes against the state injure everyone in the state, they are worse than crimes against individual people. Hobbes's first example is the noncontroversial one of revealing state secrets. His next example is surely a criticism of the parliamentarians who opposed Charles I: "all attempts upon the representative of the commonwealth be it a monarch or an assembly, and all endeavours by word or deed to diminish the authority

110

of the same" (*L* 27.37). Hobbes then lists several other crimes the consequences of which extend beyond the immediate victim: perjury undermines the judicial system; embezzlement of public money injures all subjects; committing crimes that have obvious deleterious effects such as murder, torture, and rape pains everyone (*L* 27.38–49).

Concerning (4), by whom, where, and when a crime is committed may make the crime greater or worse. It is worse to kill one's own parent than to kill someone else; it is worse to commit a crime in a church or palace than in another place; it is worse to commit a crime during a religious service than at another time (*L* 27.51–2).

experience Experience is the memory of many things, according to Hobbes's standard account (*L* 2.4; *EL* 1.4.6; *DCo* 25.8). In *The Answer to the Preface Before Gondibert*, Hobbes treats experience in a more sophisticated way: "Time and education beget experience; experience begets memory; memory begets judgement and fancy; judgement begets the strength and structure, and fancy begets the ornaments, of a poem" (*EW* 4:449). The link between memory (experience) and poetry explains why the ancients made Memory the mother of the Muses. (*See also* SENSATION.)

F

faction   A faction is a collection of subjects bound together by contracts or by the power of an individual when the sovereign does not approve of their association. A faction amounts to a government within a government (*DC* 13.13). Factions often begin in aristocracies (*L* 22.30), but they are also a danger to monarchies. The destabilizing potential of such an arrangement is obvious. Factions usually begin with people meeting in private with the ostensible goal of reforming the government. They conspire to stage-manage public meetings; and, once they are large enough to have a significant influence, they present their plans to the public (*DC* 12.13).

Factions are a principal cause of civil war (*DC* 10.12; *L* 39.5). Subjects who have a covenant with a foreign government constitute a faction. Hobbes is probably thinking of Roman Catholics, who are committed to the pope. Charismatic individuals who win the favor of uneducated people, and the rich who use their wealth as power, are leaders of factions (*DC* 13.13; *EL* 2.5.7; *L* 22.31). So factions can be started through either eloquence or wealth (*DC* 10.12). One of the duties of the sovereign is to put down factions (*DC* 13.13).

faith   The word "faith" is equivocal. Hobbes notes three meanings of it: (1) the content of a belief that is held because of trust in the person from whom it is learned or who has authority over the believer; typically these are propositions that define a religion, e.g. "I believe that Jesus is the Christ"; (2) a psychological attitude that accompanies the kind of propositions specified in (1); and (3) the keeping of a promise or a covenant (*EL* 1.5.7, 1.6.7; *L* 14.11).

The first two senses are especially relevant to difficult issues involving religion and are related to each other. Sense (1) signifies a proposition or set of propositions; sense (2) signifies the attitude that accompanies that proposition or set of propositions and in virtue of which those propositions are called "faith" in sense (1). The distinction between the two senses is reflected grammatically in a sentence like this: I have faith [sense (2)] that God is omnipotent [sense (1)]. Sense (3) is used only in connection with

112

the law of nature that enjoins one to keep a COVENANT. Nothing more will be said about (3).

(1) "Faith" can mean a proposition or set of propositions that defines a religion. The Christian faith in this sense is contained in the Apostles' Creed or the Nicene Creed. The Jewish faith is contained in the Shema: "Hear, O Israel, Yahweh our God, Yahweh is one." When "faith" is used in this sense, a proposition is accepted, not as an object of knowledge nor as an object of opinion, but on the basis of the authority of the person who asserts it, "the person propounding" (*DC* 18.4).

Hobbes does not accept any version of the theory of double truth, according to which some proposition can be true in religion or theology and false in some other domain, say, science. For him, propositions of faith can never contradict propositions that are proven to be true by sense experience or reason: "we are not to renounce our senses and experience; nor (that which is the undoubted word of God) our natural reason." Alluding to the parable in which servants are given money to invest in the most profitable way, Hobbes says that faith is supposed to be used similarly for "the purchase of justice, peace, and true religion" (*L* 32.2). Hobbes's view was quite conventional. The theologian John Preston wrote, "But you will say, faith is beyond sense and reason; it is true, it is beyond both, but it is not contrary to both [*sic*]; faith teaches nothing contrary to reason" (Preston, *The Cuppe of Blessing,* 1633, pp. 12–13). And William Chillingworth, whose views were very influential, especially among the later latitudinarians, wrote that he would "believe many mysteries but not impossibilities; many things above reason, but nothing against it" (Chillingworth, *The Religion of Protestants,* 1638, p. 377). According to Hobbes, if there is a proposition of faith that seems to be false, then one of three things must be the case: either the meaning of it is being misinterpreted or the evidence against the proposition is defective or the argument against it is unsound (*L* 32.2).

Since propositions of faith are determined by religion, they cannot belong to philosophy: people are not "to labour in sifting out a philosophical truth by logic of such mysteries as are not comprehensible" (*L* 32.3). Some of the language Hobbes uses to make this point may strike the modern-day reader as offensive. He says, for example, that "it is with the mysteries of our religion as with wholesome pills for the sick, which swallowed whole have the virtue to cure, but chewed are for the most part cast up again without effect" (*L* 32.3; *DC* 18.4). But such language was in tune with the sensibilities of the age. Metaphors about chewing and swallowing doctrines were common, and some figures of speech were even more earthy. The theologian John Cotton speaks of the "garments of our sanctification, the best whereof is like filthy rags and menstruous clothes . . . so bespotted and besmeared with much filthiness" (Cotton, *Gods Mercie Mixed with His Justice*, 1641, p. 41).

(2) Let's now turn from the propositions of faith and the basis upon which they rest to the psychological attitude of faith. The reason that propositions of faith form an interesting class is that the basis for believing them is not evidence but trust in the person who propounds them (*L* 7.5, 32.4). Early in *Leviathan*, Hobbes gives a grammatical treatment of various phrases related to the expression of faith. He points out that the phrase "faith in" signifies trust in the person from whom some proposition is learned. The same idea is expressed by the phrase "belief of (a man)." A different idea is expressed by the phrase "believe that." This phrase signifies that some proposition is held to be true. So, belief has two aspects. One can either have "belief of" a person (that is, have trust in her) or "believe that" a proposition is true. Each of these phrases is appropriate and not misleading. A problematic case is the phrase "believe in," which Hobbes claims occurs only in the Christian creeds. This phrase is misleading because it combines "believe" in the sense it has in the phrase "believe that" with the word "in" as it occurs in the phrase "faith in." The resulting confusion is that Christians end up having faith in (or trusting) propositions, when in fact their faith is, or should be, in the person who taught them the propositions that they believe (*L* 7.6). Hobbes is not clear in this paragraph about whether Christians actually have faith in propositions or only think that they do. But in the next paragraph, it is clear that Christian propositions logically rest upon faith in a certain person: "when we believe that the Scriptures are the word of God, having no immediate revelation from God himself, our belief, faith, and trust is in the church" (*L* 7.7). Later in *Leviathan*, Hobbes points out that the sovereign is in effect the church. For now, he draws an implication that undermines pagan religions. He says,

> For if I should not believe all that is written by historians of the glorious acts of Alexander or Caesar, I do not think the ghost of Alexander or Caesar had any just cause to be offended, or anybody else but the historian. If Livy says the Gods made once a cow speak and we believe it not, we distrust not God therein, but Livy. So that it is evident that whatsoever we believe upon no other reason than what is drawn from authority of men only and their writings, whether they be sent from God or not, is faith in men only. (*L* 7.7)

Many people have seen that the very same form of argument can be directed against Christianity by substituting, say, "the authors of the gospels" for "Livy" and "Jesus rose from the dead" for "the Gods made once a cow speak." Whether Hobbes realized this or not is disputed.

Hobbes ends his discussion of faith as trust here but resumes it near the end of *Leviathan* when he discusses what is necessary for salvation. He says that one can believe only a person whom one has heard. Abraham, Isaac, and Jacob believed God, because they heard Him. The apostles believed Jesus, because they heard him. Post-apostolic Christians first believed their pastors (that is, prior to the establishment of Christianity as a state religion) and then believed their "Christian sovereigns, who are . . . the only persons whom Christians now hear speak from God, except such as God speaks to in these days supernaturally" (*L* 43.6). Hobbes does not say that Christians today do not believe God or Jesus, but that is the clear implication of his doctrine. In contrast with *Leviathan*, Hobbes's treatment of the phrase "belief in Christ" in *De Cive* is conventional. He says, "when we say, *I believe in Christ*, we signify indeed whom, but not what we believe." He then argues that the proposition that defines the Christian faith is that Jesus is the Christ. (*See* CHRISTIANITY, ESSENCE OF.) And he concludes, "To believe in Christ therefore is nothing else but to believe Jesus himself, saying that he is the Christ" (*DC* 18.5). According to this analysis, the sentence "I believe in Christ" says that the speaker puts her trust in Christ and relies upon him as the guarantor of the truth of the proposition or propositions that define her faith (in sense (1), explained above).

Hobbes contrasts this trust in a person to supply the basis for the credibility of a proposition of faith with the grounds of KNOWLEDGE and opinion. Knowledge does not rely upon trust in a person. The basis for holding to be credible a proposition of knowledge is awareness of the unvarying application of the words to objects. A proposition of knowledge is always susceptible to analysis; in fact, breaking it down into its component parts makes it more intelligible. Propositions of faith cannot be broken down in any similar way (*DC* 18.4). Focusing on faith as a psychological attitude is supposed to help dispel a misapprehension that many people have, according to Hobbes. The psychological attitude of faith may be confused with the profession or expression of that attitude. Faith, in the sense being discussed here, is something internal; profession is something external. What a person professes is subject to the limitations that a sovereign places on her; profession is a kind of conduct, not a mental state. Conversely, the mental state of a person is not conduct and is thereby immune to governmental regulation. Hobbes holds to a literal but narrow understanding of freedom of CONSCIENCE. Everyone is free to believe what she likes, but no one is permitted to act on her beliefs without permission of the government (*DC* 18.6 note; *L* 42.43).

One supposed advantage to Hobbes's view is that it gives him an easy solution to conflicts between the demands of faith and the demands of political obedience. Since faith or belief is internal, no sovereign can sensibly order subjects to believe something against their will. But since subjects owe a sovereign obedience, they ought to say that they do believe if commanded to do so; for, as Hobbes says, "Profession with the tongue is but an external thing, and no more than any other gesture whereby we signify our obedience" (*L* 42.11, 42.43, 43.23). The content of a person's beliefs is controlled by the understanding, not by the will; one cannot help what one believes. But what one professes is a matter of will, according to Hobbes.

By placing a firm barrier between what a person believes and what she professes, Hobbes wants to protect the person against the logical disease of inconsistency. Professing propositions out of obedience to the sovereign does not commit one to the proposition itself, he maintains. Even if the sovereign were to command the subject to profess both that there is only one God and that there is more than one God, the subject would not be asserting something contradictory. The reason is that, according to Hobbes, when a subject obeys her sovereign, she is merely an actor and the sovereign is the AUTHOR of that behavior. What Hobbes conveniently forgets is that, by his theory of AUTHORIZATION, the subject is the author of the behavior of the sovereign. Thus, by transitivity, the subject is the author of her religious professions.

There is seemingly a worse problem. Earlier, Hobbes had been at pains to ground a subject's religious faith in the sovereign, who is the voice of the church and the person in whom she places her trust. But now he wants to segregate faith from the profession of faith or worship that is commanded by the sovereign. Hobbes could cogently reply, I believe, that his earlier discussion showed that there is little risk of a conflict between faith and worship. The later discussion showed that, where there is an apparent conflict, it can be resolved in the way he described.

Be this as it may, Hobbes has another way of defending his view that a subject may securely worship in the way that her sovereign commands. He appeals to the biblical story of Naaman, who converted to belief in Yahweh but was permitted by the prophet Elisha to bow before the idol Rimmon (2 Kings 5:17). Hobbes considers the objection that Jesus said that he will not acknowledge in heaven anyone who denies him on earth. His reply, as noted above, is to appeal to his theory of authorization: anything done as a matter of obedience to the sovereign is not the action of the person performing the behavior but the action of the one being obeyed. So, even though it is Naaman's body that is bowing to Rimmon, it is his master's act of worship (*L* 42.11, 43.23, 45.22).

To strengthen his position, Hobbes asks rhetorically whether his opponent thinks that a Muslim, living in a Christian country, ought to obey a command to attend a Christian service of worship . If the opponent says "no," then he is promoting civil disobedience. This would have been an untenable position for any gentleman to take in the seventeenth century, and all the more so in the 1650s when most Englishmen were especially dissatisfied with the results of the English Civil War. If the opponent says "yes," then, by parity of reasoning, a Christian ought to attend a Muslim service if commanded to do so. If the opponent holds that Muslims should obey a Christian sovereign but Christians do not have to obey a Muslim one, then Hobbes would point out that such special pleading violates a basic Christian maxim, which is also a law of nature, namely, to treat others exactly as you would like to be treated and not to demand things of others that you would not be willing to do yourself (L 42.11).

There is still another objection to Hobbes's position that a subject ought to obey an infidel sovereign, namely, that God has called some people to be MARTYRS and to die for their faith. Hobbes's reply is simply to concede the fact. Each person must decide for herself whether God is calling her to martyrdom.

Sometimes Hobbes says that faith is a divine gift and cannot be instilled by human beings (L 26.40, 43.7, 43.9). Sometimes he says that the job of ministers of Christ is to get people to have faith (L 42.9). This latter view seems to presuppose that it can be instilled.

It is appropriate to ask why people have faith. Hobbes answers that "The causes . . . are various" but they all originate with God: "For faith is the gift of God, and he works it in each several man, by such ways as it seems good unto himself" (L 43.7). One might say that Christians believe in Jesus because they "believe the Bible to be the word of God" (L 43.7). But one may legitimately ask why one believes that the Bible is the word of God. Some purport to answer the question "Why do we believe in Christianity?" as if it meant the same as "How do we know that Christianity is true?" Roman Catholics claim that the infallibility of the church yields knowledge, while many Protestants claim that each person's "own private spirit" does. Hobbes thinks that each answer rests upon a false presupposition, namely, that religious belief is a matter of knowledge, rather than belief or faith. Knowledge depends upon reason, but belief or faith does not. The proper question concerns the authority by which the Bible is "made law" (L 33.21, 43.7–8).

family An ordinary family within Hobbes's philosophy is like a mule in Aristotle's, neither donkey nor horse. Members of an ordinary family are neither completely in the state of nature nor completely out of it. To the extent that a parent exercises some sort of dominion over the children the family is out of the state of nature. To the extent that the family is not large enough to preserve itself against invaders, it is in the state of nature.

117

Two, three, four, and even more people banded together do not constitute a civil state, because their power in the state of nature is easily equaled by a similar number of people who are coordinating their behavior to attack the family. A civil state requires a critical mass of power that will ensure stability against external enemies over an extended period of time (*L* 20.15). In a family, one or both parents may dominate the other members of the family and have a covenant with them. There is even a rudimentary concept of property within a family in the sense that the dominant parent may assign some objects to one member and other objects to another. But this division of objects is not full-fledged property since anyone not a member of the family has the right to take it from the family member precisely because they are in the state of nature. The dominant member of the family may be either the father or the mother since everyone is equal in the state of nature.

As an ordinary family grows in size and strength, usually through parents becoming grandparents and grandchildren maturing, a transition may be made to a small kingdom. A grandfather – at this stage men typically dominate – becomes a minor sovereign because he is lord over the possessions of his children and his children's children are possessions. A large family may also include servants. Thus Hobbes can say that "a great family is a kingdom, and a little kingdom a family" (*DC* 8.1; *L* 20.8). However, as soon as a family is a kingdom, it is an artificial entity like any other commonwealth; the ties of parent and child have no significance. What binds them together is what binds every commonwealth, namely a covenant. A civil state that evolves from a parental government is called an "hereditary kingdom" (*DC* 9.10).

fancy and judgement (*phantasia et judicium*)   Fancy is sometimes equated with IMAGINATION and is then merely fading sensation and the first motion in the chain that begins a voluntary motion such as walking or talking (*L* 6.1).

Hobbes contrasts fancy and judgement. Good fancy is the ability to see likeness in things that are conspicuously dissimilar to each other. Since fancy is a kind of mental event, it is a motion within a human being (*DCo* 25.8; *L* 3.2). Good judgement is the ability to see differences in things that are conspicuously similar (*DCo* 25.8). Fancy is associated with mental quickness, while judgement is associated with deliberateness. This leads Hobbes to consider the possibility that fancy and judgement cannot exist in the same person. In *Leviathan*, he says that with education and discipline they can and mentions as an example Sidney Godolphin, a friend of his (and the brother of the dedicatee of *Leviathan*) who had been killed in the English Civil War (*L* "Review and Conclusion" 4).

fear (*metus*) Fear is the belief that one will be injured by what one desires not to have (*L* 6.16). It is one of the most important emotions because of the role it plays in getting people out of the state of nature. Fear of death is essential to motivating people to form a political covenant (*L* 13.14). Since fear is an unavoidable pre-condition to a political covenant, it cannot in general be an invalidating condition, contrary to the received view, that covenants made under fear are coerced and therefore invalid. Fear may be an invalidating condition for covenants made within a civil state, but that is only because the sovereign has decided that it should be so (*L* 20.2).

Fear not only motivates people to get out of the state of nature but is also the emotion that is least likely to cause them to break the law; indeed, it inclines them to follow the law. (It is plausible that Hobbes is thinking about himself.) In contrast, such emotions as lust and hate incline people to break the law (*L* 27.18–19).

freedom *See* LIBERTY AND NECESSITY; WILL

G

geometry Geometry is part of "natural philosophy," that is, one of the natural sciences, according to the table of science or philosophy in *Leviathan* (*L* 9.4). In *De Corpore*, Hobbes says that it deals with the consequences of motion and determinate quantities. Motion is essential to geometry because geometry is the science of lines and figures, and they are generated by motion. Indeed, all geometrical entities are generable except points, but points are necessary for the generation of every other geometrical entity. Geometry is the science of what a body produces "when we consider nothing in it besides its motion" (*DCo* 6.6, 15.1; *EW* 7:219). A point produces a line; a line produces a plane ("superficies"); a plane produces a solid figure. It may not be obvious what these theoretical generations have to do with bodies unless one understands that every geometrical object for Hobbes, including a point, is a body and has dimensions. What makes something a point is not the absence of width, breadth, and depth, but the fact that these dimensions of a body are not considered (*DCo* 8.12, 14.9; *EW* 7:201, 217). If a point had no quantity at all, it would be nothing (*EW* 7:200–1). Analogously, lines have an actual breadth which is ignored for the purpose of considering their length (*EW* 7:202).

I conjecture that there are two main reasons why Hobbes ties geometry more closely to bodies than do other theorists. First, as a nominalist, he rejects universals as anything other than general names. Hobbes would seem to think that if geometrical entities genuinely existed apart from bodies, then his nominalism would be threatened. Second, the physical world is the only reality for Hobbes. So geometry could not study genuinely nonphysical entities and still be a science.

His most systematic treatment of geometry is in *De Corpore*. In the "Epistle Dedicatory," Hobbes gives a brief history of science. Copernicus, Galileo, Harvey, and Hobbes himself are named as the only scientists. But at the beginning of Part Three of that work, geometry is described as the most ancient of the sciences, and the works of Euclid, Archimedes, and Apollonius are recommended as scientific treatments of it.

In *Six Lessons to the Professors of Mathematics . . . in the University of Oxford,* a polemical and mathematical work that resulted from criticisms of some of his geometrical proofs in *De Corpore,* Hobbes defines geometry differently: it is "the science of determining the quantity of anything not measured, by comparing it with some other quantity or quantities measured" (*EW* 7:191). The only thing that has quantity is body. For Hobbes, geometry does not concern abstract entities, in the sense of being disembodied or ideal; rather, geometry may ignore some physical features of geometrical objects, such as their width or breadth, in order to concentrate on others, such as their location or length (*EW* 7:192–3). It seems to me that implicit in this description of geometry is a prejudice in favor of solving problems by construction rather than through the use of analytic or algebraic geometry. This preference is relevant to understanding Hobbes's attempts to square the CIRCLE.

God (*Deus*)   God is a body. Hobbes holds this controversial opinion because he thinks it is entailed by two straightforward propositions: Everything that exists is a body; and God exists. There is another, similar syllogistic proof that God is a body: Everything that is a substance is a body; God is a substance; therefore God is a body. Since the phrase "material body" is pleonastic, it is enough to say that God is a body. Hobbes uses the terms "body" and "substance" interchangeably. He thinks that the phrase "immaterial substance" is self-contradictory. He points out that the phrase does not occur in the Bible and was imported into Christian theology from ancient Greek metaphysics. Ordinary people were duped into using the term because they thought of God's nature as analogous to that of the human soul and the human soul seemed to them to be like the things that appear in dreams, "aerial bodies" (*L* 12.7).

Hobbes's view of God is nonstandard but not unprecedented. Tertullian, as Hobbes points out several times, held the view; and we may add that Mormons do too (*BCL* pp. 305, 382; *HH*, pp. 397–8; *RLM*, p. 429; *OL* 3:561). Yet some scholars use Hobbes's view of God to argue that he was an atheist. An alternative interpretation is that Hobbes recognized that modern science, which explains everything in terms of the motion of bodies, challenged the standard understanding of Christianity, and that, in order to meet that challenge, it was necessary to reconceptualize many traditional Christian propositions.

Hobbes's belief that God is a body is implied as early as 1640, in his first philosophical work, *The Elements of Law.* There he says that a spirit is a body that is so subtle that it cannot be sensed by human beings and that God is a spirit. While he does not assert that God is a body, he points out that the Bible does not call spirits incorporeal; he also says that the word

121

"spirit" is applied to God "as a signification of our reverence" and in order to "abstract from him all corporeal grossness" (*EL* 1.11.4; 1.11.5). In a letter, now lost, to Descartes in 1641, Hobbes seems to have said or implied that God and the SOUL are material (*OL* 5:278–9; Brandt, *Thomas Hobbes' Mechanical Conception of Nature*, p. 111). The corporeality of God is also implied but not asserted in *Leviathan* when Hobbes says that the phrase "incorporeal substance" is a contradiction in terms (*L* 4.21). It is also implied when he says that "substance" and "body" mean the same, since God is a substance (*L* 34.2). Also, SPIRIT is a kind of substance or body and "spirit incorporeal" is a self-contradictory phrase (its use is acceptable however when employed as a term of praise (*L* 12.7)). The Bible itself indicates that God is a body. In Genesis 1:2, the spirit of God is said to move upon the face of the waters. Since only bodies move, it might be argued that God is a body. Hobbes does not push the argument. He thinks it is more sensible to interpret this passage of Genesis as figuratively expressing that God is causing something (*L* 34.5). In the Latin version of *Leviathan*, published in 1668, Hobbes has three dialogues as an appendix and in one of them one of the interlocutors asserts, as a comment on Hobbes's text, that God is a body ("Affirmat quidem Deum esse corpus") (*OL* 3:561). In his reply to Bishop Bramhall's book *The Catching of Leviathan*, Hobbes also asserted the corporeality of God: "I . . . maintain God's existence, and that he is a most pure and most simple corporeal spirit" (*BCL*, p. 306). He takes a strong position against those who disagree with him: "to say that God is an incorporeal substance is to say in effect that there is no God at all" (*BCL*, p. 305). That is, his opponents are logically committed to ATHEISM. He continued his vigorous defense of his position in *An Historical Narration Concerning Heresy, and the Punishment Thereof* (*HH*, p. 392) and *Considerations upon the Reputation, Loyalty, Manners, and Religion of Thomas Hobbes* (*RLM*, p. 426).

Notwithstanding the assertion that God is a body, Hobbes claims that human beings can have no idea of God. The reason is that all ideas are caused by sensations, and God cannot be sensed (*ODM*, pp. 127, 130, 133). This is not to say that human beings do not have an image in their mind when they think about spirits. When he thinks about an angel, for example, Hobbes has in his mind the image of a flame or a beautiful child with wings even though he knows that "this image has no likeness to an angel" (*ODM*, p. 127). Hobbes says, "In the same way we have no idea or image corresponding to the sacred name of God. And this is why we are forbidden to worship God in the form of an image; for otherwise we might think that we were conceiving of him who is incapable of being conceived" (*ODM*, p. 127). Hobbes seems to be requiring of an image of God that it resemble God. This seems to be an unreasonable requirement since he

122

holds that no mental image resembles the body that causes it; this is an essential part of his modernist epistemology.

The inability of human beings to have an idea of God is related to His incomprehensibility, and Hobbes predicates incomprehensibility of God more than anything else (e.g. *DC* 11.1, 11.2; *EL* 1.11.3; *L* 3.12, 12.7, 31.28, 34.4, 46.15, 46.23; *DCo* 1.8; *BCL*, p. 313; *RLM*, p. 426; *AW*, p. 417). This is by no means unique to him. To assert that God is incomprehensible is a standard Christian position, especially in the calvinist tradition. Later, we shall see that it is more helpful to say that God's nature is incomprehensible, but it is strictly correct to say that God is incomprehensible, and that was the usual formula. Among other things, what lies behind the doctrine of God's incomprehensibility is the desire to restrain human pride and the presumptuousness that comes from thinking that one can understand everything, even God. When Eve ate the fruit in the garden, she was motivated by the desire to eat of the tree of the knowledge of good and evil and to become like God. In fact, the consequence of disobeying God's command was ignorance and misery. Many people opposed the rise of modern science because it seemed to be motivated by the same excess of human assertiveness as the tower of Babel. To affirm the incomprehensibility of God then is an acknowledgment of certain limits to human inquiry and an act of piety and humility. These are dominant themes in both the Bible and Hobbes. Hobbes's view about the incomprehensibility of God should be understood against the biblical background.

Notwithstanding His incomprehensibility, there is much to be said about God, and Hobbes is not reluctant to say the standard things, such as that God is eternal, omnipotent, good, just, holy, merciful, the creator, and so on (e.g., *DC* 15.14; *L* 12.7, 31.28; *RLM*, p. 426; *ODM*, pp. 131–2; *B*, p. 47). However, as a philosopher, Hobbes is more interested in exploring the scope, justification, and nature of such talk. It is sensible to begin with the existence of God.

Hobbes presents several proofs for the existence of God, and all of them have something to do with either motion or causality. None of them is especially well developed or persuasive, but then neither are the so-called "Five Ways" that Thomas Aquinas presents in *Summa Theologiae*. Hobbes, like Aquinas, probably did not think it was necessary to give an elaborate presentation since there was no extensive philosophical literature arguing that God did not exist. His proofs are conventional in form.

The earliest presentation of a proof appears in *The Elements of Law*, after the discussion of the cognitive and affective qualities of human beings and before the discussion of politics. In line with a strong Christian tradition, emphasized by many Protestants, Hobbes asserts that God is incomprehensible and thus cannot be imagined by human beings. Nonetheless, they can prove that He exists, just as a blind person can know that fire exists even though she cannot know its nature. The general strategy employed by blind people with regard to fire and all people with regard to God is to come to know the existence of a certain sort of thing through its effects (*EL* 1.11.2; *ODM*, p. 127; *L* 11.25). The proof then is that when something occurs there must be a cause that has the power to produce the effect. Now this cause is either eternal or not. If it is eternal, then it is God. If it is not eternal, then it itself has some cause, which is either eternal or not. An infinite regress is unacceptable. At some point, one must reach a cause that is eternal; and this cause is God (*EL* 1.11.2).

In *Leviathan*, two brief and related proofs for the existence of God are given. The first one begins with a statement of its psychological roots, namely, curiosity:

> love of the knowledge of causes draws a man from consideration of the effect to seek the cause, and again the cause of that cause, till of necessity he must come to this thought at last, that there is some cause whereof there is no former cause, but is eternal, which is it men call God. So that it is impossible to make any profound enquiry into natural causes without being inclined thereby to believe there is one God Eternal . . . (*L* 11.25)

In contrast, people who are not curious about causes invent "several kinds of powers invisible" (*L* 11.26).

The second proof of the existence of God in *Leviathan* is similar. It is introduced as a consequence of the cause of true religion, namely, disinterested curiosity about what the causes of things are. Anyone who sees that an event is caused and looks for the cause of that cause will, after tracing back these causes for some time, eventually conclude "that there must be (as even the heathen philosophers confessed) one first mover" (*L* 12.6). Notice that Hobbes is not bothered by beginning with an investigation of causal relationships and ending with an assertion that there is a first mover. The reason is that motion and causality are more closely tied together for him than they were for Aristotelian philosophers. For Hobbes, the identity of the First Mover with the First Cause need not be proven. In *De Cive*, he says that "by the word *God* we understand the world's cause" (*DC* 15.14).

Some scholars have questioned the sincerity of Hobbes's commitment to these proofs. Two problems may be considered here. First, in a manuscript, *Anti-White*, that remained virtually unknown until it was published in 1973, Hobbes says that there can be no DEMONSTRATION of the existence of God. The objection is that Hobbes was more likely to express his sincere beliefs in a work he did not intend to publish than in one that he did, and since he says in such a work that he did not believe that the existence of God could be demonstrated, he must have believed it. So his perfunctory proofs in his other works were not sincerely presented. There are two problems with this objection. First, there is no evidence that Hobbes never intended to publish his manuscript, only that he did not. Second, the key word in Hobbes's statement is "demonstration" (*demonstratio*) and its meaning should not be conflated with that of "proof." Every demonstration is a proof, but not every proof is a demonstration. A demonstration is a proof that has only necessary propositions as its premises; and all necessary propositions are true in virtue of the meanings of their words:

> Hence "Man is an animal" is true, because the word "animal" embraces and includes whatever the word "man" really means. Further, they know that the proposition is demonstrated when, as has been said, by means of explanations or definitions of the terms it is made clear that the subject is contained within its predicate. Therefore demonstrable truth lies in logical inferences; and in every demonstration the term that forms the subject of the conclusion demonstrated is taken as the name, not of a thing that exists, but of one supposed to exist. A conclusion, therefore, has a force that is not categorical, but is merely hypothetical. (*AW*, p. 305)

In short, there can be no demonstration of the existence of anything, because every demonstration has a conclusion that is necessarily true and hypothetical (conditional) in form, and existential propositions are contingent and categorical (assertoric). For most of the objects that human beings believe to exist, the basis for those beliefs is sensation. That type of experience is not available to ground belief in God. But proofs of the sort already discussed can be given and are sufficient to make belief in God rational. Moreover, God is not the only object the existence of which is inferred. The existence of imperceptibly small objects and imperceptibly small motions is similarly deduced. (*See* ENDEAVOR.) So, good reasons that fall short of demonstration can be given for the existence of God.

The second reason some scholars have been skeptical of Hobbes's proofs is that each proof seems to entail or presuppose that the world had a beginning and is not eternal, but in *Anti-White* Hobbes says or implies that the issue is undecidable (*AW*, pp. 344–7, 307, 351). So he seems to be insincere in his presentation of the arguments for the existence of God. Two things may be said in reply. First, in both *De Cive* and *Leviathan*, he says that the world cannot be eternal. He says, "In like manner, they who maintain the world not to be created, but eternal; because there can be no cause of an eternal thing, in denying *the world to have a cause*, they deny also that *there is a God*" (*DC* 15.14). In *Leviathan*, he again asserts that the world cannot be eternal, although the assertion comes much later than the proofs for the existence of God, and he does not tie it to them (*L* 31.16). Yet, in other works, Hobbes says that no one can know whether the world is eternal or not. Second, it is plausible that he did not think he was faced with a contradiction. Even Thomas Aquinas both presented First Cause and First Mover proofs for the existence of God and thought that it was undecidable whether the world was eternal or not. Hobbes had certain goals that were in tension with each other. One was to present a rational explanation for everything possible for human beings, and this included proofs for the existence of God. Another was to recommend the teachings of the Bible for instruction on those things that could not be proven, one of which traditionally was thought to include the noneternity of the world. It is arguable then that Hobbes did not clearly see that a presupposition or consequence of his proofs for the existence of God (namely, that the world is not eternal) did not square with his appeal to the Bible as being the only way that one can know that the world is not eternal.

To prove that God exists is not to specify what His nature is. Scholastic philosophers often contrasted knowing that something exists with knowing what something is, and they always held that the first could be done without the second. Also, to hold that one cannot know the nature of God is not to hold that one can say nothing of God. The nature of an object is what makes that object to be what it is. According to Hobbes, the only things of which human beings know the nature are the things that they can define. Nonetheless, it is quite possible to have extensive knowledge of an object without knowing its nature. Hobbes certainly thinks that human beings know quite a bit but also holds that they do not know "the nature of the smallest creature living" (*L* 31.33). So it should not be surprising that they do not know the nature of God.

It has already been mentioned that Hobbes often says many of the same things that other Christian thinkers say about God: that He is good, merciful, just, almighty, and so on. But when he explicitly treats the nature of such talk, his account is very different from theirs. It is also more sophisticated and foreshadows some twentieth-century philosophy on the topic of religious language, such as Ian Ramsey's book *Religious Language: An Empirical Placing of Theological Phrases* (1957). Traditional logic distinguished between categorematic words ("dog," "tree," "human," "rational") and syncategorematic words ("is," "all," "some," "not"). It might appear that all categorematic words are descriptive and thus must be used descriptively. What Hobbes noticed is that the same word may be used descriptively in some contexts and with certain intentions and nondescriptively in other contexts and with other intentions. The nondescriptive use that Hobbes focuses on is the honorific one. Most philosophers think that God ought

126

to be described when Hobbes believes that the only appropriate attitude for human beings to take is that of WORSHIP. He writes, "it is our purpose not to philosophize about God but to honour Him" (*AW*, p. 417). Taking the idea that what human beings say about God should be guided by their duty to honor Him, Hobbes explains what should and should not be said about Him. First, God should be said to exist, since no one can honor what she thinks does not exist. This justification for saying that God exists seems to be independent of any proofs for the existence of God. If there is a proof for His existence, then it is descriptively true that God exists; but in the present context, God is said to exist, because it is the appropriate thing to say.

God should be said to govern the world, since to "take from him the care of mankind" is to take away "his honour . . . , men's love, and fear of him" (*L* 31.17). Further, God should be said to possess any great-making quality to an infinite degree (*L* 31.18). In one place, Hobbes says it is honorable to say that God is potential; and the term is used only honorifically, not literally. (*AW*, pp. 417–18, 398). Similarly, God must be said to have understanding and will even though He does not have them in any way similar to the way human beings do (*AW*, pp. 385–8).

There are a number of things that should not be said about God, because to say them would be dishonorable. God should not be said to be conceivable or imaginable, because whatever human beings conceive is finite, and that would imply the dishonorable quality of being finite (*L* 31.20). Again, there are proofs that God cannot be imagined, but the reasoning that applies in chapter 31 concerns what it is honorable to say about God and not what is descriptively true. (One proof that God cannot be imagined is this: Whatever human beings can imagine is finite; God is not finite; therefore, human beings cannot imagine (have an image of) God. Another proof is this: Everything that human beings can imagine was first sensed; God cannot be sensed; therefore, human beings cannot imagine God (*L* 3.12, 45.15; *DC* 15.14).)

One should not say that God has a figure, that He has parts or is a totality, that He is in some place, that He is either in motion or at rest, that He experiences such passions as grief, repentance, anger, mercy, appetite, hope, or desire (*L* 31.19, 31.21–3, 31.25). One reason that this list is interesting is that at least some of the terms that Hobbes does not want ascribed to God are literally true of Him. Consider the pair "in motion" and "at rest." One of these terms must apply to God since they are contradictories. Yet, one must not say either one of them of God. (Given that God causes things to move and every cause is itself in motion, Hobbes is logically committed to the proposition that God moves. But he will never say this, because of his religious scruples.) Hobbes says that

127

"figure" and "parts" are applied only to finite things. That is dubious, at least for "parts." Again, since God is a body, it would seem to be literally true that He has parts. Hobbes's view concerning what ought to be said is the same as that of the Vatican some decades ago when it could condemn certain statements that were strictly and literally true, solely on the grounds that to assert them was "offensive to pious ears."

good and evil (*bonum et malum*) Good is whatever is desired (*DH* 11.4). Since different people desire different things, and the same person desires different things at different times, what is good is relative to people and times (*DH* 11.4; *L* 6.7; *EL* 1.7.3, 1.7.8; *AW*, p. 462). Hobbes is often criticized for this definition. Although it is flawed, many of the objections to it seem to miss the mark. For example, one criticism is that it is relativistic. It is, but that does not make it pernicious. To take two arbitrary examples, being a parent and being generous are both relative to objects, but neither concept is pernicious. Perhaps, a better way to put this objection to Hobbes's definition is that the object that goodness is related to is variable. But that too is not in itself pernicious. Suppose that people varied in wanting to feed the hungry, to visit the sick, and to clothe the naked. That would be wonderful, not terrible. As a matter of fact, human desires often tend to be more self-centered. Nonetheless, there is one desire that is universal: the desire for self-preservation (*DH* 11.6). It is upon this desire that Hobbes will eventually construct part of his ethics and politics.

One may also try to object that Hobbes's definition is defective because "desired" cannot be substituted for "good" in every occurrence. For example, "Bread tastes good" cannot be paraphrased "Bread tastes desired." The objection is uncharitable. It is not difficult to accommodate what Hobbes has in mind: "Bread tastes good" means "The taste of bread is desired." To show the course of substitution more explicitly: "Bread tastes good" is short for "Bread has a taste x and x is good" and that means the same as "Bread has a taste x and x is desired." I am not denying that there are other reasons for denying that "good" means "desired." In any case, Hobbes is trying, not to describe the actual usage of the word "good," but to explicate it.

Perhaps one source for the dissatisfaction with Hobbes's definition is that for most people goodness is a central concept in their morality. That is not the case for Hobbes. For him, morality is LAW, and only a certain kind of goodness, namely, the desires of the sovereign, is related to morality and that only derivatively. The law specifies what obligations people have and the limits of obligation are the limits of morality. In short, one of the most significant features of Hobbes's theory of morality, in the modern sense of the term, is his divorce of goodness in general from morality.

Hobbes thinks that people ought not to do many of the things that are good to them, that is, desired by them. Many of these things ought to be forsworn in the state of nature, because they conflict with other goods or desires. In fact, Hobbes uses the fact that private goods lead to destruction to help motivate people to get out of the state of nature and to establish a civil state. In doing so, people renounce most of their private desires and take the desires of the sovereign as their goods.

Hobbes's relativistic definition of good does not prevent him from making the usual distinctions between short- and long-term goods, between apparent and real goods, and between private and public goods, and recommending the goods that the received morality does: riches acquired by honest work are good, as are wisdom, science, the arts, literature, work, and progress (*DH* 11.7–11).

Concerning short- and long-term goods, Hobbes often preached against the tendency of people to satisfy those desires that result only in short-term satisfactions and frustrate long-term satisfactions, and in favor of satisfying those desires that result in long-term satisfactions, such as peace and prosperity. Having desires that lead to long-term satisfactions often requires having additional desires that are acquired through education (*DH* 11.14).

Hobbes has two accounts of the distinction between apparent and real goods. In *Leviathan*, he says that, since appetites and aversions are aroused by what a person thinks the consequences of some event will be, whether something is seen as good or not depends upon how long a string of consequences the person foresees. To the extent that the desirable consequences seem to outweigh the undesirable consequences, "the whole chain" is what people call "apparent good," and to the extent that the undesirable consequences seem to outweigh the desirable ones, the whole chain is what people call "apparent evil" (*L* 6.57). The account in *De Homine* is similar, but the moral that Hobbes draws from it is stronger. He says that people ought to attend to the desirable and undesirable features of the entire chain and not to look at them selectively, as many people do: "When it happens that inexperienced men that do not look closely enough at the long-term consequences of things, accept what appears to be good, not seeing the evil annexed to it; afterwards they experience damage. And this is what is meant by those who distinguish good and evil as real and apparent" (*DH* 11.5). What is really good, presumably, is what actually has long-term desirable consequences.

The distinction between private and public goods is best understood within the distinction between the state of nature and the civil state. In the

129

state of nature, where there is no standard or law that governs what a person may desire, each person determines what is good for herself (*L* 46.32). The desires of people vary from person to person and from time to time (*DC* 3.31). These variations inevitably cause conflict and create a state of war. Since no one desires war, everyone agrees that war is bad and peace is good. Thus, people often disagree about present goods and agree about distant goods. Peace requires a common standard of good. In the civil state, there is a common standard of good. It is the desires of the sovereign, who represents the subjects and bears their person (*L* 6.7). Problems arise if a person in a civil state seeks to satisfy her own private desires when they conflict with the desires of the sovereign (*L* 46.32). To believe that each person in a civil state should be the judge of what is good "is a doctrine . . . pernicious to the public state" (*L* 46.32).

Although goodness is always relative to some person, the usual problems arising from subjectivity in values are avoided by the imposition of the sovereign's desires on all: "the measure of good and evil actions is the civil law; and the judge the legislator, who is always representative of the commonwealth" (*L* 29.6). Hobbes also says, "There being nothing simply and absolutely so [good or evil]; nor any common rule of good and evil, to be taken from the nature of the objects themselves, but from the person of the man (where there is no commonwealth) or (in a commonwealth) from the person that represents it; or from an arbitrator or judge, whom men disagreeing shall by consent set up, and make his sentence the rule thereof" (*L* 6.7).

A problem with Hobbes's discussion of good and evil arises for another reason. It is possible to distinguish between interests and preferences. An interest is something that genuinely benefits the person, and it is expressed in clauses like "It is in your best interest to *X*." A preference is something that the person desires, and is expressed in clauses like "I prefer *X*." Interests and preferences are not mutually exclusive; one's preferences may be one's interests also. But they obviously need not identical. Hobbes often seems to hold that they are. For him, a good is whatever a person desires. From this, he infers that whatever a person desires is a good to herself, and this seems to mean that whatever a person desires is good for her. In this step there seems to be a slide from good as a person's preference to good as a person's interest (*L* 14.8, 15.16, 25.2, 25.4). This slide is confirmed when he says that, since what is desired is a good to that person, it is thus done for her own benefit (*L* 25.2). Because a benefit seems to be an interest, Hobbes in effect is holding that every preference is an interest. This interpretation is also supported by his physiological account of pleasure. Pleasure, the result of satisfying a desire, strengthens the motions that give a being life ("corroboration of vital motion") (*L* 6.10). That is, things are not good simply because they are desired; when desires are satisfied there is a genuine enhancement of life, according to Hobbes.

Let's now turn to another aspect of Hobbes's views about good and evil. He points out that, in addition to *bonum* and *malum*, Latin has the terms *pulcrum* and *turpe*. *Pulcrum* is used to designate something that promises to be good; it is translated variously as "beautiful," "fair," "handsome," "gallant," and "honourable." *Turpe* is what promises to be evil; it is translated variously as "foul," "deformed," "ugly," and "base." Latin also has terms designating good and bad effects, *jucundum* ("delightful") and *molestum* ("unpleasant"), respectively. Finally, there is a pair of terms designating what is useful as a means to something desired (*utile*) and what is not (*inutile*) (*L* 6.8; *DH* 11.5). It has been claimed that Renaissance political and moral theorists worried about a Stoic distinction between what is *utile* (what is beneficial to oneself) and *honestum* (what is moral). Cicero's solution was to assert that "what was *honestum* was what was *utile* to human society" (Tuck, *Philosophy and Government, 1572–1651*, p. 7). Perhaps Hobbes thinks of himself as contributing to this tradition, but he does not define *honestum* (cf. *EW* 6:25).

Evil or badness is strictly analogous to goodness. People call bad what they desire not to have. In the state of nature, there is no common standard, and each person determines for herself what is bad. In the civil state the desires of the sovereign are the common standard, and he determines what is good and what is bad.

grace (*gratia*)   Grace is a gift or "free-gift" (*L* 14.12). In the ordinary, non-Hobbesian understanding, a gift is given with no strings attached. Hobbes rarely understands such a self-disinterested concept. Usually, he thinks that everyone acts out of her own self-interest. Thus, he says that an act of grace is the transferring of the right to something to another person either in the hope of getting that person as a friend, or in order to enhance one's reputation, or in the hope of getting to heaven (*L* 14.12; *EL* 1.16.6).

The identification of grace as a gift is unexceptionable; nonetheless Hobbes's definition has theological problems. It is all very well for him to explicate grace and gifts egoistically insofar as human beings are concerned. One may perhaps concede to him that people act only for the purpose of ultimately benefiting themselves. But this account of motivation cannot be transferred to God. God's grace is supposedly the paradigmatic form of gift-giving; yet He cannot give anything with the hope of benefiting from it. Hobbes holds the standard view that God is self-sufficient and needs nothing, especially not from human beings (*L* 25.10,

31.13). People gain the right to heaven by getting grace but grace is not given by God out of any self-serving motive.

Hobbes holds that people are saved by grace alone, but also that obedience and works are required. He has a way of handling this apparent contradiction. Grace is given to people who are obedient and do good works, but not because justice demands it of God. Concerning works, Hobbes subscribes to the position of Paul and the apostle James: faith without works is dead. The works referred to however are not external works or sacraments, as Roman Catholics hold, but "the justice and obedience of the inward man." The works that are required are the wills, endeavors, or intentions to obey the law, not actual behavior (*EL* 2.6.10). Also, the obedience that is required is to the laws of God, which are the laws of nature; and the laws of nature commit subjects to obedience to the civil laws. So Hobbes gets some political mileage out of this theological issue.

In *Leviathan,* the concept of grace is introduced immediately after that of COVENANT, probably with the purpose of clarifying the latter by serving as a term of contrast. While a covenant is a mutual transferring of right, grace is a unilateral transfer. Grace is sometimes said to be one kind of reward; it is reward without a contract. Salary is reward with a contract (*L* 28.24). The contrast between covenant (or contract) and grace is continued indirectly a bit later in chapter 14 in the course of explicating the difficult theological concepts of *meritum congrui* and *meritum condigni* (*L* 14.17). According to Hobbes, *meritum condigni* is the merit that results from fulfilling some contract or covenant. If a person merits something in this way, it is due or owed to her as a matter of justice. In contrast, *meritum congrui* is the merit that results from taking advantage of an opportunity that is given to one. If someone throws a prize to a crowd, the person who catches the prize deserves to have it, not because of any contract that has been enacted between her and the benefactor, but because she succeeded in her effort. It is appropriate (*congruus*) that she has the prize, but she has it because of the grace or gift of the giver.

Scholastic theologians argued about the precise meanings of *meritum congrui* and *meritum condigni* and how they applied to the work of Jesus in salvation and the works of human beings in gaining salvation. The issue is too complicated and not sufficiently relevant to be discussed here. Hobbes says,

> For God Almighty having promised Paradise to those men (hoodwinked with carnal desires) that can walk through this world according to the precepts and limits prescribed by him, they [scholastic theologians] say, he that shall so walk shall merit paradise *ex congruo.* But because no man can demand

a right to it by his own righteousness or any other power in himself, but by the free grace of God only, they say no man can merit paradise *ex condigno*. This I say I think is the meaning of that distinction . . . (*L* 14.18)

Bishop Bramhall thought that Hobbes's treatment of these concepts was one of his "ignorant mistakes," but Bramhall does not give any exposition of them himself. Hobbes defended himself by denying that he had purported to give the correct statement of the problem and claiming only to have said what he thought it was: "For no man living can tell what a Schoolman means by his words" (*BCL*, pp. 380–1).

H

habit Habit is motion made easy "by perpetual endeavor" (*DCo* 22.20). (*See* ENDEAVOR.)

happiness Hobbes uses two English words to express the concept at issue here: "happiness" and "felicity." In Latin, he uses *felicitas* to convey "felicity," but several locutions to convey "happiness," such as *sanctus* and *salutas aeterna*, and *felicitas* (*LW* 3:94, 310, 324). "Happy" is sometimes translated as *beatus*. (My sense is that Hobbes thought that Latin did not have a true equivalent to the English "happiness," because sometimes the corresponding word that would translate it or the passage that contains the word "happiness" (or a cognate) does not occur in the Latin version.) He usually uses "happiness" in discussions of God's mental state, to speak loosely, and "felicity" in discussions of the human condition. "Delight" he defines as the experience of achieving one's goals or satisfying one's desires. The "real effect" of satisfying a desire, that is, "that which is really within us" is "only motion". What I have referred to as the "experience" of this motion Hobbes calls "the appearance or sense of that motion" (*L* 6.9; *EL* 1.7.7).

Most of what Hobbes has to say about happiness occurs in *The Elements of Law* and *Leviathan*. There are only passing mentions of happiness in *De Cive* and the word "felicity" or *felicitas* does not occur in it at all.

In *Anti-White*, Hobbes says, "Undeniably happiness consists in a life's being lived with pleasure, i.e. with the greatest delight; but the question remains: In what does this delight lie?" (*AW*, p. 468). It does not lie in sensual pleasures, or at least not in these alone. For beasts, happiness consists of nothing more than eating, resting, and copulating; but human beings need more (*L* 12.4). According to Hobbes, everyone knows that all sensual pleasures reach "satiety, and that they please no more than insofar as they are required by natural necessity." What constitutes happiness is "the gratifying thought of advancing from the enjoyment of one good thing to that of another" (*AW*, p. 468). Unlike the ancient Greeks and the scholastic philosophers, Hobbes does not think that there is any "ultimate end" or highest good for human beings. Happiness is a continual satisfaction of desires; so there is no rest for the happy (*L* 11.1). Felicity "(by which we mean continual delight) consists not in having prospered, but in prospering" (*EL* 1.7.7).

Hobbes's conception of happiness is directly opposed to the medieval and scholastic conception according to which happiness is a state and lack of motion. For them, motion indicates a defect, a lack of actuality, which the motion is supposed to remedy. For Hobbes, motion is good; without it, nothing is alive and nothing happens: "there is no such thing as perpetual tranquility of mind, while we live here; because life itself is but motion and can never be without desire" (*L* 6.58; *DH* 11.15).

Although Hobbes is explicitly against the use of metaphor in philosophy, he has an extended analogy that compares life to a race, according to which happiness is "Continually to out-go the next before," that is, continually to overtake the next person ahead of one (*EL* 1.9.21).

heaven *See* KINGDOM OF GOD

hell Just as the eternal life that will be enjoyed by the elect will be spent on earth, the punishment of the wicked will be on earth also (*L* 38.6). This place may be called hell, but hell should not be defined as a geographical location. Certain biblical texts suggest that hell is underground, others that it is under water, others that it is fire, and others that it is darkness (*L* 38.6–9). Not all of these can be true. So some other interpretation must be given to the texts that talk about the fate of the wicked. Usually, these ideas of hell come from some specific incident which talks about punishment in a metaphorical manner, which many people have mistakenly taken literally. This is especially true of the cases in which hell is described as fire (*L* 38.11). But since metaphors usually are based upon some factual ground, they can be used to work out what the literal truth about hell is. From all the descriptions of hell in the Bible, it seems clear that it is a place of torment. So it is better defined as the place where the damned are (*L* 38.6).

St Paul says that the wicked will die a "second death." So the wicked must be resurrected at the end of the world and then destroyed. They do not suffer eternally (*L* 38.14, 44.26, 44.29; *OL* 3:329–30, 466–7, 566). Without further argument, Hobbes simply asserts that the method of destruction will be fire (*L* 38.14). Thus, the descriptions of hell-fire are not merely metaphorical. Hobbes presents the doctrine that the damned burn in real flames as further evidence that SPIRITS must be bodies. For evil spirits are damned; the damned suffer by burning; and only bodies burn (*L* 46.20).

There are two reasons why the punishment of the wicked cannot be eternal. First, since they are thrown into real fire, they must be consumed in a finite amount of time. That is just part of the physics of human bodies and fires. Second, it is inconsistent with God's mercy that anyone should suffer for ever.

Given that each of the damned suffers for only a finite period of time, Hobbes thinks he has to come up with some explanation for how the fires of hell can be eternal, as the Bible says they are, this being the meaning of "eternal torments." His logically unsatisfactory solution in chapter 38 of *Leviathan* is that after one wicked person is consumed by the fires another will be thrown in, this process taking for ever. The problem is that, given a finite number of wicked persons and a finite amount of time for each to burn, eventually there will be no more fuel for hell (*L* 38.14). Hobbes does not seem to have thought of stoking hell with coal or wood after the wicked had burned. He must have given further thought to this problem, because in chapter 44, in which he examines various doctrines of the kingdom of darkness, he implies that the stock of human beings to be burned in the fires of hell will be infinite because the wicked, in contrast with the elect, will reproduce after the resurrection and presumably give birth to wicked children, who will eventually help keep hell stoked for eternity (*L* 44.29). (In my opinion, the imagination of the generally humane Hobbes failed him here.)

The biblical doctrine of hell was distorted by the ancient Greek and Roman mythology that was imported into Christian beliefs. In particular, hell cannot be a bottomless pit since the earth is finite; it cannot even be twice as deep as the stars are high, *pace* Vergil in the *Aeneid* (*L* 38.6).

heresy Originally heresy was any "taking of anything, and particularly the taking of an opinion," independently of whether the opinion was true or false (*HH*, p. 387). The term "heresy" was applied to "different sects of the old philosophers, Academicians, Peripatetics, Epicureans, Stoics." Hobbes's mentioning "Peripatetics," that is, Aristotelians, here suggests either that being a heretic is not inherently bad or that many of his enemies are heretics (*B*, p. 9; *DCL*, pp. 98–9; *OL* 3:540, 550). In one place, Hobbes denies that heresy in itself denotes something good or bad, true or false, legal or illegal (*OL* 3:540; cf. 552). A heretic is a person who teaches her own private opinion (*L* 11.19). "Heretic" did not become a term of abuse until the Christian church used it that way even though Christianity itself was originally called heresy (*OL* 3:541).

Within Christianity, "heresy" is "a sinful opposition" to a religious authority. Thus, heresy is to religion as rebellion is to secular authority (*B*. p. 9). According to Hobbes, it is important for heresy to be specified in a law, because the Bible is difficult to understand and a person may unintentionally come up with the wrong interpretation of it. To make a mistake should not in itself be a crime (*OL* 3:547). For something to be a crime and worthy of punishment, it needs to threaten the civil government.

Heresy originally entered the church when pagan philosophers converted to Christianity but retained some of their philosophical beliefs and used texts from the Bible to support them (*HH*, pp. 288–9; *OL* 3:542). The resulting diversity of beliefs within the Christian community scandalized nonbelievers, according to Hobbes. Consequently, the church leaders met periodically to determine which opinions would be approved and which would not.

Before Constantine, no Christian institution had the right to punish a Christian heresy. When he converted, it became possible to punish Christian heretics. At first, only clerics, not their lay followers, were punished by being deprived of their churches. But no bodily punishment was connected with persisting in one's opinions since only the civil power held that right (*HH*, p. 389; cf. p. 400; *OL* 3:542–3). Later, punishments were imposed only on clerics who refused to conform. Constantine called a general council of the church to decide the controversy between Arius and Alexander on the nature of Jesus and promised to enforce whatever decision the council made (*HH*, pp. 390–2; *OL* 3:543–4). Hobbes's point in reporting this first ecumenical council was to establish that ecclesiastical affairs were under the control of the civil sovereign and that uniformity of doctrine was more important than the truth: "he [Constantine] had for his end, in the calling of the synod, not so much the truth, as the uniformity of the doctrine, and peace of his people that depended on it" (*HH*, p. 393). Hobbes held, not that "princes make doctrines true or false, but that kings can prohibit any doctrine from being publicly taught, whether true or false" (*BCL*, p. 329).

After the first four ecumenical councils, the emperors grew lax and the Roman church grew in power and imposed further doctrines on Christians: "to an ingenuous and serious Christian, there was nothing so dangerous as to enquire concerning his own salvation of the Holy Scripture; the careless cold Christian was safe and the skilful hypocrite a saint" (*HH*, p. 403). The burning of heretics began with the pontificate of Alexander III (1159–81). Even then, heretics were given ample opportunity to recant and escape execution (*OL* 3:552–3).

In England, the first laws against heresy were enacted against the Lollards, followers of John Wycliffe. Later, during the reign of Edward VI, all laws against heresy were revoked. The Roman Catholic monarch Mary I reinstated them. As part of the reaction against the cruel intolerance of Mary I, Queen Elizabeth made it quite difficult to be convicted of heresy. She established the High Commission, which was to judge something to be heretical according to the following criterion: heresies were only those doctrines that had been condemned in the first four councils of the church, namely, Nicaea, Constantinople, Ephesus, and Chalcedon, or those propositions specified by parliament to be heretical (*B*, p. 10; *DCL*, pp. 103–6; *HH*, pp. 403–7; *L* 42.130; *OL* 3:546, 553). Hobbes most likely was aware of the irony of this procedure, for parliament had abolished the High Commission, and it had not been reconstituted at the Restoration. So, Hobbes could not be a heretic between 1641 and 1668. And if a person were a heretic, excommunication from the church and what follows from it could be the only penalties (*OL* 3:556–7, 560). Excommunication is not even required. St Paul advised his followers simply to leave alone people who had nonstandard views (*L* 42.25; *OL* 3:371).

In his *Historical Narration Concerning Heresy, and the Punishment Thereof*, Hobbes ends his history by describing the place occupied by *Leviathan*:

> And in this time it was, that a book called *Leviathan* was written in defence of the King's power, temporal and spiritual, without any word against episcopacy, or against any bishop, or against the public doctrine of the church. . . . But then both the one [the bishops] and the other [the Presbyterians] accused in Parliament this book of heresy when neither the bishops before the war had declared what was heresy . . . So fierce are men for the most part in dispute where either their learning or power is debated that they never think of the laws but as soon as they are offended they cry out, *crucifige* ["crucify"]. (*HH*, p. 407)

Hobbes's interest in heresy grew over the decades between 1650 and 1670. His treatment of the topic is relatively brief in *Leviathan* but is the theme of *An Historical Narration Concerning Heresy*, and one of the chapters of the appendix to the Latin version of *Leviathan* is devoted to the topic. Early in *Leviathan*, Hobbes says that "heresy" and "opinion" apply to the same thing or have the same meaning but differ in their connotation. An opinion is a belief that a person approves of; a heresy is a belief that a person disapproves of (*L* 11.19; *DCL*, p. 97). An analogous claim is made about the difference between "religion" and "superstition." Religion is approved of; superstition is not.

In chapter 42 of *Leviathan*, "Of Power Ecclesiastical," Hobbes discusses heresy after discussing excommunication. It is part of a long argument against Robert Bellarmine's defense of the Roman Catholic Church. According to Bellarmine, a Christian subject has the obligation to depose an heretical sovereign. Hobbes replies that, since the church is identical with the commonwealth and the sovereign of the commonwealth determines what is church doctrine, a sovereign cannot be a heretic (*L* 42.130–1,

44.6). The church, then, has no authority independent of the sovereign; its purpose is to teach obedience to the sovereign and the belief that Jesus is the Messiah (*L* 42.25). Excommunication on the church's own authority could have been effected only prior to the establishment of Christianity as a state religion, and a heretic proclaimed so by the church is simply a person who holds an opinion different from one approved by the church.

It is not surprising that Hobbes's interest in heresy increased after 1666, the year in which some ministers of the church brought charges in parliament against him for heresy. The action was part of the attempt by some overzealous preachers to purge and reform England after the twin disasters of the plague of 1665 and the Great Fire of London in 1666, which to them signaled God's judgement. Even though nothing came of the charges, one can imagine that Hobbes investigated the history of heresy in order to defend himself if that should have become necessary.

History of the Peloponnesian War   See PELOPONNESIAN WAR BY THUCYDIDES

honor (*honor*)   Honor, "to speak properly, is nothing else but an opinion of another's power joined with goodness" (*DC* 15.9). That is, to honor a person is to recognize and approve of that person's power. Since to honor someone is to think highly of her, honor resides in the person bestowing it and not in the person honored (*DC* 15.9). It is essentially "secret and internal in the heart" (*L* 45.12). Since everyone in the state of nature is equal, there is no genuine honor in that condition even though some people do seek glory for themselves. Moreover, titles of honor depend upon the existence of a civil state. The sovereign dispenses such titles as he will (*L* 10.52, 18.15). This applies to religious titles, such as "bishop," "priest," and "presbyter," as much as to secular ones. Hobbes does not believe that bishops have their jurisdiction over Christians *jure divino* as most of the Laudian clergy did. Rather, they have their jurisdiction *jure civili*, by the grace of the sovereign (*L* 42.80).

Three emotions are entailed by honor: love, fear, and hope. If a person honors someone, then she loves him in virtue of his goodness, she fears him in virtue of his power, and she hopes to avoid suffering harm from that power. In *Leviathan*, the connection of these emotions with the honor of God is made explicit (*L* 31.8–9; cf. *DC* 15.8).

"Honor" is sometimes used loosely to indicate public recognition of the power of another person. When used in this extended sense, honor is conflated with WORSHIP (*cultus*) (*DC* 15.9). There is good reason to keep separate the inward act of honoring someone from the outward act of worshipping someone. Worship is due to whomever the sovereign says is to be worshipped. A Christian who is the subject of, say, an Islamic sovereign must perform the ceremonies of worship commanded of her, just as a Muslim who is the subject of a Christian sovereign must perform the ceremonies of worship commanded of her (*L* 43.22). (*See* FAITH.)

Parents typically release their children from their control when the children are old enough to take care of themselves; but when they do so, they are not indicating that they think that their children are equal to them. Implied in the release is the requirement that the children continue to show that the parents are superior to them. This is how Hobbes explains why children ought to honor their parents (*DC* 9.8). A weak point in the explanation is that it works best for parents and children in the state of nature, where parents are sovereigns over their children. In the civil state, the parent is only a subject and does not retain natural parental rights. Technically, the parents have to raise their children as the sovereign commands them to do. The child then technically owes the sovereign honor, not the parents.

Given the self-oriented psychology of most people, it is easy to think that not all people who deserve honor, especially oneself, get it. Hobbes is not like that. He thinks that honor is pretty fairly distributed:

> The reason why others, I myself included, are without honour is either that we are neither craftsmen nor of the best, or that if we are *excellent* we are not recognized as such. However, one must not expect those civil honours, which are connected with public business, to be conferred on philosophers: it would be unjust to the human race to withdraw from their studies for public responsibility those minds that strive for the good and the honour not only of one country alone but of the entire human species. (*AW*, p. 474)

This was written about 1643, before he had become widely known.

hope Hope is an appetite that one expects to be satisfied (*L* 6.14). The hope of avoiding injury by resisting the object that poses the danger is courage (*L* 6.17). Constant hope is confidence (*L* 6.19). Hope is one of the key factors that lead people out of the state of nature. Fear of death, a desire for a comfortable life, and "a hope by their industry to obtain them" are the passions that motivate people to leave the state of nature. Reason shows how this can be done (*L* 13.14).

ideas Ideas, often referred to by Hobbes as "phantasms," are the experiences that beasts and human beings have when bodies affect their sense organs. That means that ideas are ultimately only motions even though animals experience these motions as ideas. Although ideas are usually thought of by Hobbes as iconic or pictorial, in fact for him each sense has its own kind of idea (*L* 4.17; *DCo* 7.3, 25.2).

Since all ideas come from sense and are of what is finite, and since God cannot be sensed and is infinite, human beings cannot have any idea of God (*L* 3.12, 31.20; *DC* 15.14). Sometimes Hobbes qualifies this claim by saying that human beings cannot have any idea of God "answerable to his nature" (*L* 11.25). This at least means that God does not directly stimulate human sense organs as other bodies do. What Hobbes says suggests that he thinks that some bodies do produce in human beings ideas that are answerable to their nature. But he does not really hold this view. A central element of Hobbes's philosophy is that human ideas or experiences do not literally re-present the objects that they sense (*DCo* 6.8). This is a large part of the reason that human beings do not know the nature of even the smallest living creature (*L* 31.33). The basis for belief in God is like the basis that the blind have for belief in fire. They feel the heat and infer that there must be fire (*L* 11.25).

There is some ambivalence in Hobbes about the limits of human rationality and the role of ideas. On the one hand, he recognizes that scientists can use words to reason about objects so small that they cannot have an idea of them. On the other hand, because he worries about the absurdity that results when human beings reason about things for which they have no idea – sometimes he says that there is no idea corresponding to "infinity" and "eternal" – he sometimes suggests that it is impossible for them to reason about things of which they have no idea (*DCo* 26.1).

There is no difference in kind between ideas as they are in the IMAGINATION and ideas as they are in the UNDERSTANDING, because all of them are reducible to motions within the subject that has them. Unlike Plato's ideas, Hobbes's are all individuals and only refer to individuals (*DCo* 2.14, 5.8). (*See* NAMES.)

Compared to Locke, Berkeley, and Hume, Hobbes has very little to say about ideas. This is partly due, I believe, to his desire to establish his materialism.

identity Identity is sameness, and difference is its opposite. Being identical with something and being different from something are common to every object. Hobbes discusses these issues in Part II of *De Corpore* just before discussing the various things that differentiate one thing from another, such as quantity.

A standard way of conveying what is characteristic of identity is the Principle of the Identity of Indiscernibles: If an object *O* has all the properties that an object *P* has, then *O* is identical with *P*. Leibniz is famous for, among other things, explicitly formulating it. A related principle may be called the Principle of the Nonidentity of Discernibles: If an object *O* has a property that an object *P* does not have, then *O* is not identical with *P*. It is just as good at the first principle for conveying what is characteristic of identity. Hobbes holds a linguistic version of the latter principle: "two bodies are said to differ from one another, when something may be said [truly] of one of them, which cannot be said [truly] of the other at the same time" (*DCo* 11.1).

It would be a mistake to think that identity is some (relational) property of an object in addition to its other properties. Rather, identity supervenes upon the other properties that the body has. To put this point in terms of a lack of identity, if *O* differs from *P*, it is because there is some property (other than identity or difference) that *O* has and that *P* does not have. It is this discrepancy between the objects that accounts for the difference. Objects are not identical because of identity, and they are not different because of difference.

Hobbes extends this point to relations in general. There is no relational property whiter-than or heavier-than in addition to whiteness and heaviness. If *O* is whiter than *P*, it is only because of the whiteness of *O* and not because of any additional property of *O*. In short, all relational properties supervene on nonrelational properties (*DCo* 11.7).

Philosophers have sometimes distinguished between the problems of identity and individuation. The problem of identity is the problem of explaining what makes something one or a unity. This can be discussed without bringing in the considerations of whether the object is an individual (in contrast with being a universal) and whether it persists through time. The problem of individuation brings in one or both of these considerations. Since all objects for Hobbes are individuals, the problem of individuation for him amounts to the problem of understanding what makes an individual at one time to be the same as or different from an individual at another time.

Hobbes says that there are three philosophical views on this problem. According to the first, individuation depends upon "the unity of matter." O is the same object as P if the matter of O is the same as the matter of P. A cubical lump of wax is the same body as a spherical lump of wax if the piece of wax is the same. One devastating objection to this view is that, according to it, the human being that gets punished for a crime after it is committed is not the same as the human being that sinned, because the matter in the human being is constantly changing (DCo 11.7). After seven years none of the original matter remains. According to the second philosophical view, individuation depends upon sameness of form. An infant is the same object as an adult if the form of the infant and the adult remains the same. Hobbes's formulation of the objection that he raises to this second view has entered the philosophical literature as one of its classical problems, although Hobbes attributes it to the ancient sophists. Suppose that the ship of Theseus is repaired over a period of time. It seems that, each time a plank is removed and replaced by a new plank, the ship remains the same because it retains the same form, even though its matter is changing. At some point, all of the planks, and hence all the matter, have been replaced. This would perhaps not appear problematical if it were not possible for someone to have saved all the original planks and, by putting them together in the same order, to have constructed a ship which would not only also thus have the form of the ship of Theseus but its matter too, making it "without doubt" also the same ship. In such a case, there would it seems be "two ships numerically the same, which is absurd." According to the third philosophical view, individuation depends upon having all the same properties. This view has nothing to recommend it. Nothing would survive any change whatsoever. A sitting person would lose her identity when she stood up. Water in a jug would not be the same after it was poured.

Hobbes's alternative view is that identity is always relative to some name, and the name is always connected with either the matter or form of the object. Consider Socrates. He is the same *human being* as an adult that he was as an infant because the name "human being" is connected with his form and his form has remained the same. But he is not the same *body* as an adult that he was as an infant, because the name "body" is connected with matter, and the quantity of it, Hobbes says, has changed.

If the name of something depends upon an accident, then the identity of the object depends upon its matter, since a change of matter is a change of accidents. Hobbes then gives his solution to the identity of the ship of Theseus: "a ship, which signifies matter so figured, will be the same as long as the matter remains the same; but if no part of the matter be the same, then it is numerically another ship; and if part of the matter remain and part be changed, then the ship will be partly the same, and partly not the same" (*DCo* 11.7).

As good as Hobbes's solution is, it does not seem to solve all problems concerning identity, especially problems raised about personal identity, which were first raised by John Locke. If the consciousnesses of a prince and a cobbler were switched, the identity of each person would be determined by the possession of the consciousness and not by the possession of the human body. If the consciousness of the prince is in the body of the cobbler, then the prince is where the cobbler's body is. (See Locke, *An Essay Concerning Human Understanding* book 2, chapter 27, and Yolton, *A Locke Dictionary*, pp. 163–6.) Many other, more complicated and puzzling problems concerning identity have been invented in the twentieth century of which neither Hobbes nor Locke conceived.

idolatry   *See* SUPERSTITION; WORSHIP

imagination (*imaginatio*)   Imagination is decaying sense (*EL* 1.3.1; *L* 2.2). Since many animals other than human beings have sensation, they also have imagination. Although, etymologically, "imagination" means an image and thus is named after the kind of sensation that results from seeing something, imagination applies to each of the senses. There are non-pictorial images for hearing, smelling, tasting, and touching. Also, imagination occurs both when people are asleep and when they are awake: "The imaginations of them that sleep are those we call DREAMS" (*L* 2.5).

To hold that imagination is a kind of decay is not to hold that the motion of the sensation runs down or exhausts itself. Hobbes is devoted to the principle of inertia, according to which an object in motion remains in that same motion unless it is acted upon by another object. Since sensation is a motion, it continues in existence until it is acted upon. Since sensations are continuously received, the motions of the later ones affect the earlier ones until they no longer affect the agent. This is one explanation that Hobbes gives. But he also gives the impression that the mechanism is different. It is not that the motion of a later sensation interferes with the motion of an earlier one, but that the earlier motions are obscured by later ones in the way that the light of a star is obscured by the light of the sun. The light of the stars is not negated but overwhelmed (*L* 2.3).

Imagination and memory are the same thing. The apparent difference between them is semantic. The word "imagination" focuses on or emphasizes the sensuous content of the experience and the fact that that experience is decaying is left in the background. The word "memory" focuses on the fact that the experience is decaying and the fact that the experience is sensuous is left in the background (*L* 2.3; *DCo* 25.8). Memory is the perception that one has perceived. It is the means by which human beings know how they acquire knowledge about the world (*DCo* 25.1). Experience is the memory of many things (*L* 2.4). (*See also* SENSATION.)

Imagination is also the source of understanding, of which there are two kinds. In a general way, understanding is imagination caused by a voluntary sign. Beasts have this sort of imagination, because a dog will respond to the call of its master (*L* 2.10). Contemporary linguists who believe that chimpanzees can use a finite number of signs to signal for food, and to express certain other things, would readily agree with Hobbes. But this kind of symbol manipulation is not the same as having a language. So, in a narrower way, understanding is imagination that is caused by words; and it is peculiar to human beings (*L* 2.10, 4.22). What is distinctive about language is that words are concatenated or strung together to form statements ("affirmations" and "negations"). Hobbes seems to have an inchoate grasp of the feature that philosophers of language now refer to as compositionality (*DCo* 2.4). (*See also* LANGUAGE AND SPEECH.)

infinity Although he does not explicitly say it, Hobbes, like the ancient Greeks, is biased in favor of finitude: all human thinking originates in sensation; all objects of sensation are finite; so human beings cannot think of anything that is infinite (*L* 3.12). The word "infinite" and its cognates have a use, but not as a name of a thing. "Infinite" signifies that a person is "not able to conceive the ends and bounds of the thing named" (*L* 3.12; *DC* 15.14). Hobbes's view contrasts sharply with that of Descartes, who claims that human beings have a positive concept of infinity. In the *Meditations*, Descartes needs such a concept in order to prove that God exists. Hobbes prefers to prove the existence of God by arguing from some empirical fact, such as motion or causation, to a first mover or first cause, respectively.

Infinity and its contradictory, finitude, are discussed in three contexts: (1) the nature of number; (2) the nature of the universe; and (3) the nature of God.

(1) As regards number, Hobbes defines finitude and infinity not in terms of the way things are, but in terms of how human beings imagine things to be. Something that is imagined to have boundaries or limits in every way is finite. Something that is imagined without limits being set to it is infinite. In *De Corpore*, he wrote that, because numbers are composed of unities, to say that a number is infinite is to say that no number is designated (*DCo* 7.11). To put the point grammatically, the word "infinite"

is an indefinite name, that is, a word "of uncertain signification, because the hearer knows not what thing it is the speaker would have him conceive" (*DCo* 2.11). Earlier, in *Anti-White*, he had written that "infinite in size" means "cannot be counted using number that is finite in size" (*AW*, p. 357). Hobbes would have no patience with the idea of an infinite, much less a transfinite, number. To say that numbers are infinite is to say that, given any number, another one can be added to it. But no number is itself infinite.

Hobbes's view that what is infinite cannot be imagined does not seem to fit neatly with the fact that space and time can be divided infinitely. He stipulates a way to understand that fact: "whatsoever is divided is divided into such parts as may again be divided" (*DCo* 7.13). Since this stipulation does not say anything about the parts being imagined, it is not immediately clear how he can accommodate both doctrines consistently. What he means is that, given words that have a meaning connected with something that can be imagined, it is possible to use those words to calculate correctly about things that are too small to be imagined.

(2) As regards the extent of the world, Hobbes seems to have changed his mind or at least the way he wanted to express his view. In *Anti-White*, Hobbes says that the world is either finite or infinite, depending upon how those words are defined (*AW*, pp. 28–9). Like Aquinas, Hobbes held that philosophers are not able to prove that it is one or the other: "But the existence of no body depends on our mind or thought; therefore even if we conceive of bodies unendingly added to bodies, it does not follow that these bodies exist in the things of nature." Neither can the definition of "world," that is, "the aggregate of all the bodies which exist," tell us whether or not another body can be added to the world. That knowledge is therefore to be derived from a knowledge of God's will, namely by asking, "Was it His will to create the world finite or to make it infinite?" The proposition "The world is finite," is therefore a dogma, not of science but of faith, and neither physical nor metaphysical reasons can determine it. In *De Corpore*, he writes that to ask whether the world is finite or infinite is to have "nothing in our mind answering to the name *world*." When people ask such a question, what they have in mind is whether the number or quantity of bodies that God has made exceeds our ability to imagine spaces for them (*DCo* 7.12). The numerical and the cosmological ideas of infinity overlap in the question of whether the world could be infinite. Hobbes holds that to say that a distance, power, or time is infinite is simply not to have a number big enough for it; from that it does not follow that there is no number big enough. Any distance conceived to be infinite is in fact finite (*DCo* 7.12).

Although Hobbes is quite skeptical about the idea of infinity in most contexts, he does think that some things are infinitely small; there are "quantities so small even that it eludes every sense and imagination" (*AW*, p. 30).

(3) It is appropriate then to say that GOD is infinite since He is "incomprehensible" (*L* 3.12). People who say that they can conceive God do Him no honor; yet to honor Him is the only appropriate reason for talking about God (*L* 3.12; *DC* 15.14; *EL* 1.11.3).

injury (*injuria*) An injury is harm or damage that is suffered due to an injustice. A sovereign can harm or damage a subject but cannot not injure her, for two reasons. First, the sovereign does not stand in the kind of relation to a subject that could generate an injustice. All injustice is the violation of some covenant; but a sovereign does not make any COVENANT with his subjects. Second, a subject authorizes the sovereign to act for her. Thus, any action performed by the sovereign is actually caused by the subject. A subject who has been harmed by a sovereign is suffering from a self-inflicted wound, according to Hobbes: "If therefore they style it injury, they but accuse themselves. And it is against reason for the same man, both to do and complain" (*EL* 2.2.3; *L* 14.7, 15.12; *OL* 3:104). Sometimes Hobbes says that a sovereign can commit "iniquity, but not injustice or injury in the proper signification" (*L* 18.6). (*See also* JUST AND UNJUST.)

interpretation (*interpretatio*) For Hobbes, the literal interpretation of a text is the meaning that the author intended. A distinction is sometimes made between the letter of the law and what it means (its "sentence"). If "the letter of the law" means the bare significations of the words themselves, then the distinction makes sense. But if "the letter of the law" means its literal meaning (what the author intended), then there is no difference between the letter of the law and its intention (*L* 26.26). According to Hobbes, the actual meaning of a law is the meaning intended by the legislator:

> But that is not always the law which is signified by *grammatical* construction of the letter, but that which the legislature thereby intended should be in force; which intention, I confess, is a very hard matter many times to pick out of the words of the statute, and requires great ability of understanding, and greater meditations and consideration of such conjuncture of occasions and incommodities as needed a new law for a remedy. For there is scarce anything so clearly written, that when the cause thereof is forgotten, may not be wrested by an ignorant grammarian, or a cavilling logician, to the injury, oppression, or perhaps destruction of an honest man. (*DCL*, p. 64)

Although Hobbes does not have a theory of interpretation, he articulated sensible principles for it on a number of occasions. One is that an

147

interpretation of a text should not be based narrowly on what its words seem to mean but be based on the intention of the writer, and this intention can be understood only by taking the entire work into account: "For it is not the bare words, but the scope [purpose] of the writer that gives the true light, by which any writing is to be interpreted; and they that insist upon single texts, without considering the main design, can derive no thing from them clearly" (*L* 43.24). Another principle is that, if an author explicitly says one thing that contradicts something else that is only implied by what he says somewhere else, then the view to be attributed to the author is the one that is explicit (*EL* 1.13.9).

All laws require interpretation. Unwritten laws, like common law, need it because people who are involved in a dispute are intellectually blinded by their passions and self-interest. Written laws need interpretation because, whether the law is simple or complex, a word may have more than one meaning, and its proper meaning in that context must be decided by someone (*L* 26.21; *OL* 3:202). According to Hobbes, only the sovereign is competent to make such judgements. He specifically rejects the view of the great common law theorist Edward Coke according to which legal interpretation requires "an artificial perfection of reason" acquired by long study. What Coke means is that lawyers are the proper interpreters of law. Hobbes counters that, since lawyers are simply private persons, they will each come to a different opinion and so nothing will be settled; also "long study may increase and confirm erroneous sentences [opinions]: and where men build on false grounds, the more they build, the greater is the ruin" (*L* 26.11). Similarly, commentators on the law are not official interpreters of it (*L* 26.25). Not artificial reason but the artificial man (the sovereign) must be the interpreter.

In addition to secular laws, the interpretation of the Bible belongs to the sovereign. If each person had the right to interpret it for herself, religious conflicts would arise that would destroy the government just as surely as secular ones would (*DC* 17.27). History and his own experience supported Hobbes's view. If a person does not rely upon the sovereign's power and authority to impose an interpretation on the audience, but relies upon reason to persuade them, then she is the interpreter (*L* 42.32).

The discipline of hermeneutics (the theory of interpretation) arose in the nineteenth century, primarily in response to scholarly questions over the proper way to interpret the Bible. The standard way of defining why hermeneutics is problematic is to say that, in nonhermeneutic understanding, the intentions or meaning of the speaker is evident in the speech situation; the speaker's demeanor and other elements of the context make the situation intelligible; and if there is any question about what the speaker means, she can be asked for a clarification. In contrast, written speech, especially that of ancient works, lacks all such clues. Hobbes made the same observation:

> For such is the nature of speech in general that although it deserve the chief place among those signs whereby we declare our conceptions to others, yet cannot it perform that office alone without the help of many circumstances. For the living voice hath its interpreters present, to wit, time, place, countenance, gesture, the counsel of the speaker, and himself unfolding his own meaning in other words as oft as need is. To recall these aids of interpretation so much desired in the writings of old time is neither the part of an ordinary wit, nor yet of the quaintest, without great learning and very much skill in antiquity. (*DC* 17.18)

J

jealousy   Jealousy is the combination of a desire for one person exclusively and the fear that that person does not have an exclusive desire for oneself (L 6.33). In contrast, the passion of love is a desire for one person exclusively without the fear that that desire is not reciprocated (L 6.33).

Hobbes is apparently thinking about one's being jealous for a person and not about one's being jealous of a person or her belongings. We would call being jealous of a person or her belongings "envy." For Hobbes, envy is the combination of "grief for the success of a competitor in wealth, honour, or other good" and the "endeavour to supplant or hinder a competitor" (L 6.48). I do not know why Hobbes thinks that a person can be jealous for only one person. It seems to me that a person may be jealous for several people, expecting each of those people to desire only her.

Jesus   According to Hobbes, Jesus is the Messiah and the second PERSON of the Trinity. Jesus represents the person of God the Son just as Moses represents the person of God the Father, and the apostles and their pastoral successors represent the person of the Holy Spirit (L 41.8, 42.3). Jesus differs from Moses and the apostles and their successors in that Jesus does not merely represent or personate God; he also is God (L 42.3).

In part three of *Leviathan*, Hobbes has a fairly extensive comparison between Jesus and Moses. Following Deuteronomy 18:18, Hobbes says that Jesus is also similar to Moses in that, when Jesus reigns at the end of the world, he will be God's "vicegerent" just as Moses had been. Also, just as Moses chose twelve princes to help him rule, Jesus chose twelve apostles; Moses chose seventy elders, and Jesus had seventy disciples (L 41.7). Each had two sacraments: Moses had circumcision as the sacrament of initiation and the passover meal as the sacrament of commemoration; Jesus had baptism as the sacrament of initiation and the eucharistic meal as the sacrament of commemoration (L 41.8). Hobbes conjectures that the ritualistic washing in baptism is inspired by the Mosaic law governing lepers, who were excluded from the community until judged by a priest to be clean and solemnly washed: "And this may therefore be a type of the washing in baptism, wherein such men as are cleansed of the leprosy of sin by faith are received into the Church with the solemnity of baptism" (*L* 41.8).

It may well be that Hobbes compares Jesus to Moses partly to take the wind out of the sails of those who, like Theodore Beza, thought that Jesus was already king and should be obeyed over the commands of the king. Hobbes emphasizes the subordination of both Moses and Jesus to God the Father: "Seeing therefore the authority of Moses was but subordinate and he but a lieutenant to God, it follows that Christ, whose authority, as man, was to be like that of Moses, was no more but subordinate to the authority of his Father. The same is more expressly signified by that that he teaches us to pray, 'Our Father, let thy kingdom come'" (*L* 41.8). This theme is a corollary of Hobbes's discussion of Jesus's office of messiah.

Following Reformation theology, Hobbes emphasizes the three roles or offices that Jesus has as Messiah: (1) redeemer or savior; (2) pastor or counselor or teacher; and (3) king. Three times correspond to these three roles. The first time is the death of Jesus on the cross. The second began with his death, continues now, and will end with his second coming. The third will begin with his second coming and will last for eternity (*L* 41.1). This three-fold division of time overlaps with the third and fourth epochs discussed in the entry KINGDOM OF GOD. (*See also* CHRIST, OFFICES OF.)

Hobbes's discussion of the salvific work of the redeemer is conventionally pious. (*See also* SALVATION.) The death of Jesus was prefigured in the Old Testament by the near sacrifice of Isaac and the ritual of the scapegoat (*L* 41.2). Beyond piety, Hobbes's point in explaining Jesus's role of redeemer is to argue that he was not king when he first lived on earth. This is the first of a two-stage argument to prove that Jesus does not become king until his second coming at the end of the world (*L* 41.3). The second stage of the argument is that Jesus was not king after his death and is still not king. The role that Jesus plays from his death until the end of this world is that of counselor, pastor, and teacher. That is, he, through his ministers, gives human beings the information and advice that they need in order to become reconciled to God. Jesus gives counsel not commands because he has not yet assumed the authority of a king (*L* 41.4). (*See* COMMAND AND COUNSEL.) Jesus himself taught that his followers ought to obey the existing rulers. For the Jews of his time, this meant the high priests and Roman authorities: "He allowed them to give Caesar his tribute and refused to take upon himself to be a judge" (*L* 41.5).

joy and grief (*gaudium et dolor*) Joy is mental pleasure; grief is mental displeasure (*L* 6.12; *EL* 1.7.9; cf. *DH* 12.2).

just and unjust (*justum et injustum*)   Since the time of Thrasymachus, there have been moral skeptics, that is, people who have claimed that justice is nothing but a word. Hobbes rejects such skepticism. The fact that the principles of justice had not been formulated as adequately as they should have been before Hobbes did it, is no proof that they did not exist, no more than the absence of durable buildings among "the savage people of America" would be proof that there are not architectural principles that would allow a house to stand as long as its materials endure (*L* 30.5).

Hobbes's treatment of the nature of justice and its relation to injustice is difficult to render consistent without some interpretive intervention. What that intervention should look like is controversial. There are two basic views: one is that there is no justice or injustice without a covenant; the other is that there is. If one holds that there are no covenants in the state of nature, then one is also committed to the view that there is no justice or injustice in the state of nature. For the most part, Hobbes holds that justice and injustice depend upon the existence of a covenant; but there are important exceptions to this position. Before discussing these issues further, something needs to be said about the different meanings of "just" and "unjust."

In his earliest treatment of the meaning of the words "just" and "unjust," Hobbes says that the words are equivocal. They can be used to refer either to actions or to people. When the words are applied to actions, "unjust" means causing INJURY, that is, breaking a covenant. As a consequence, injury gets its name from the fact that the injurer is acting without the right (*ius*) that she laid down in making a covenant (*EL* 1.16.2). It is the doctrine of *The Elements of Law* that there can be no injustice where there is no covenant (*EL* 1.16.2, 1.16.5). When there is an injustice, the injured person is the other party to the covenant. "Just" is the contradictory of "unjust" and not merely its contrary. Thus "just" should be defined as what is not unjust (*L* 15.2). It is worth noting here that Hobbes is taking "unjust" as the primary term and defining "just" in terms of it, just as he takes "WAR" as the primary term and defines "peace" ("not war") in terms of it. However, a more important point is that, taken strictly, justice should then not depend upon the existence of covenants at all, because, when no covenants exist, no covenant is broken; so no action is unjust; and hence every action is just. But it seems to be Hobbes's intention to restrict the use of "just" and "unjust" to those universes of discourse that contain covenants.

Let's now consider how "justice" and "injustice" apply to people. In such uses, "just" means having the tendency to do just actions, and "unjust" means not having the tendency to do just actions. Anyone who commits an unjust act is guilty, but is not thereby an unjust person. To be an unjust

152

person, one must typically commit a number of unjust actions. Since "just" and "unjust person" are defined in terms of certain kinds of actions, actions are primarily just and unjust, and persons are derivatively so. A person is just if and only if she does many just actions and few or no unjust actions; a person is unjust if and only if she is not just. Given these definitions, it is possible for a just person to do an unjust act and an unjust person to do a just act; even most of the acts of an unjust person may be just (*EL* 1.16.4, 1.17.14; *L* 15.10–12).

That justice and injustice require a covenant in *The Elements of Law* is confirmed shortly later. Endorsing the proverb *inter arma silent leges* (the laws are silent in warfare), Hobbes says that nonetheless the laws of nature do not justify cruel behavior, where cruelty is any action that inflicts suffering that does not improve the chances of one's own survival. To act cruelly, then, breaks a law of nature; but since injustice requires the violation of a covenant and none is violated in warfare, to be cruel is to act dishonorably, not unjustly (*EL* 1.19.2).

Being a virtuous person is related to being just but is not identical with it. To be virtuous is "to be sociable with them that will be sociable, and formidable to them that will not," and such behavior is "the sum of the LAW OF NATURE," which at this time in Hobbes's philosophy meant making peace whenever possible and otherwise making war (*EL* 1.17.15).

In the first edition of *De Cive*, Hobbes's treatment of "just" and "unjust" is the same as it is in *The Elements of Law*. To act justly is to act with right (*jure factum*); and to act unjustly is to cause injury (*injuria*), and injury always requires the breaking of a covenant, in which one has laid down a certain right (*DC* 3.3–6). In the second edition of *De Cive*, a slight change in Hobbes's position is introduced. In an explanatory footnote, he says that injustice always relates to some law, injury both to a law and to a person ("Injustitia nomen significat relative ad legem; injuriae, tum ad legem, tum ad personam certam") (*DC* 3.4 note). A wedge is being inserted between injustice and injury. What is unjust is unjust to everyone, even to those who are not injured by the action. Moreover, on this new view, sometimes the sovereign is the injured party, even though the sovereign is never a party to a covenant, and sometimes God, when the laws of nature are broken, even though they have force independently of any covenant. Also, Hobbes says that sometimes no private person is injured by an unjust act, even though only private persons are the subjects of the covenant. This new position of the second edition is inconsistent with the earlier view according to which only parties to a covenant can be injured. The new position suggests, without asserting it, that it is unjust to break the first law of nature, Seek peace and defend yourself, which does not depend upon the existence of any covenant. (*See* LAW OF NATURE, FUNDAMENTAL.)

In an earlier explanatory footnote, Hobbes maintains that no one can injure another human being in the state of nature when no covenant has been broken, but a person may sin against God in that state ("in tali statu peccare in Deum") if she breaks a law of nature, which does not require the violation of a covenant. For example, gratuitously harming a person breaks the first law of nature. While he says that the person sins and that no human injustice occurs in such a situation, Hobbes is silent about whether the perpetrator is guilty of an injustice against God or not (*DC* 1.10 note).

The dominant idea of his first two political works, that justice and injustice require the existence of a covenant, is also present in *Leviathan*: "the definition of injustice is no other than the not performance of a covenant" (*L* 15.2). It would appear then that the existence of a covenant is a necessary condition for a human being to be just. That interpretation does not seem to survive Hobbes's discussion of the kind of constraint the laws of nature impose on people. His view is that they "oblige *in foro interno*," that is, in the interior forum or in conscience. They do not always oblige "*in foro externo*", that is, one's behavior does not always need to appear to be in conformity with them. Given a dangerous situation, behavior that would otherwise break the laws of nature that forbid "ingratitude, arrogance, pride, iniquity, acception of persons" is permissible (*L* 15.36–9). Such behavior does not in fact violate any law of nature, because they restrict behavior only in conditions of perceived security; "for he that should be modest, and tractable, and perform all he promises in such time and place where no man else should do so should but make himself a prey to others and procure his own certain ruin, contrary to the ground of all laws of nature, which tend to nature's preservation" (*L* 15.36). (Hobbes sometimes speaks imprecisely and says such behavior does break the law (*L* 15.38).) Because the laws of nature "oblige only to a desire and endeavour," they are easily fulfilled, and anyone who "fulfills the law is just" (*L* 15.39). Here is a striking claim that is inconsistent with the doctrine he had earlier promoted. But it strikes me as the more sensible position. A person who tries to make peace and who, within the conditions imposed by the state of nature, is sociable, forgiving, equitable, impartial, and truthful certainly deserves the title "just" whether or not any covenant has been made. The apparent inconsistency in Hobbes's view can easily be dissolved. If a distinction is drawn between civil (artificial) and noncivil (natural) justice, then one can say that there is no civil justice without a covenant, but there can be natural justice.

Where does Hobbes's idea that desiring or intending to fulfill a law constitutes just behavior come from? My suggestion is that it comes from Protestant theology. Secular justice requires bodily action. In contrast, when the religious idea of justice is the topic, the mere desire to keep God's law, the law of nature, is sufficient for having justice (or righteousness) attributed to one; actual performance is not required. The circumlocution "having justice attributed" is necessary since Hobbes believes that no one is genuinely just in the eyes of God. Theologically, a person is just if she has good intentions: "the good intentions of the mind" (EL 2.6.10). The Kantian sound of this position is due to the fact that Kant himself was influenced by Protestant theology. Justice "is called righteousness by God, that takes the will for the deed" (EL 2.6.10; L 43.21). (The use of "will" is somewhat anomalous, because Hobbes defines will to be the last desire before a bodily action; yet no such action is necessary in these cases.)

It would seem that Hobbes would not accept the idea that human beings are saved by good works. Yet he does. The reason is that the Church of England affirmed it. The theology of the Church of England is a hybrid of calvinism and Roman Catholicism. Insofar as it was calvinist it was opposed to the idea that a human being merited salvation on the basis of good works. But because it also retained Roman Catholic elements, it accepted as canonical the Epistle of James, which preached the importance of good works. (In the early 1990s, I believe, the canons of Westminster Abbey debated the true name of their church and finally decided that it was "the Reformed Catholic Church of England.") In order to reconcile these two aspects of Anglican theology, Hobbes reinterpreted the idea of good works: "if by righteousness be understood the justice of the works themselves, there is no man that can be saved; for there is none that has not transgressed the law of God" (L 43.20). That position is fundamental Protestantism. So there is only one alternative: "And therefore when we are said to be justified by works, it is to be understood of the will, which God does always accept for the work itself, as well in good as in evil men. And in this sense only it is, that a man is called just, or unjust; and that his justice justifies him, that is, gives him the title, in God's acceptation, of just . . ." (L 43.20, 43.21; cf. 15.39; EL 2.6.10; LN, p. 252). In other words, theologically, "good works" does not mean good works but the intention to do good works. Hobbes's interpretation of the Bible may seem defective or insincere; but if it is, it is defective or insincere with the purpose of saving the biblical doctrine itself, which is inconsistent.

Traditionally, a distinction is drawn between commutative and distributive justice. Commutative justice is the justice that holds between private individuals concerning the exchange of goods and the keeping of contracts. Distributive justice concerns the allotment of duties, responsibilities, and rewards. Hobbes does not accept the distinction as theoretically sound (EL 1.16.5; DC 3.6; L 15.14). He understands the distinction to depend upon whether goods are distributed in "arithmetical" or "geometrical"

155

proportion, and he thinks such notions are irrelevant to justice: "But what is all this to justice?" (*DC* 3.6). Justice concerns whether people keep their covenants or not. It has nothing to do with the value of the goods exchanged, *pace* the notion of commutative justice. There is nothing unjust about selling something for more than one paid for it, says Hobbes. Although he thinks that the idea of commutative justice is defective, he nonetheless supplies an alternative definition of it: "To speak properly, commutative justice is the justice of a contractor; that is, a performance of covenant, in buying and selling . . . and other acts of contract" (*L* 15.14). Also, justice has nothing to do with the merits of the people receiving goods, *pace* the standard notion of distributive justice. If one person gets more than she deserves, it is a matter of grace or charity and has nothing to do with justice.

Although Hobbes does not say anything like this, my conjecture is that behind his objections to the distinction between two kinds of justice is his abhorrence for the idea that there may be a private realm (commutative justice) that does not depend upon the public realm (distributive justice). Since Hobbes does not believe that there are any property rights prior to the establishment of the civil state, he would be reluctant to recognize commutative justice, which might be used as the basis for natural property rights.

justice, divine The root of all obligation is irresistible power: "Power irresistible justifies all actions really and properly in whomsoever it be found; less power does not" (*LN*, p. 250; *QLNC*, p. 143). Hobbes's view is not an instance of the ordinary attitude that might makes right, because for Hobbes only the power of God, which is irresistible power, makes right. In the state of nature, all human beings have roughly equal power, so no one can dominate many people or even a few for a very long time. And in a civil state, the overwhelming power of the sovereign is legitimized by the consent of the people in the sovereign-making covenant. It is given to the sovereign by the subjects, not taken from them. Even if a person or persons are overcome by an enemy army, the actions of the army do not thereby become morally right, according to Hobbes. To be morally right is to be just, and to be just is to keep one's covenants. (*See* JUST AND UNJUST.)

That the irresistible power of God justifies any action of His is Hobbes's considered view: "the *power* of God alone without other helps is sufficient *justification* of any action he does. . . . That which he does, is made just by his doing it . . ." (*LN*, p. 249). One of the reasons that the book of Job is favored by Hobbes is its strong assertion of the divine prerogative.

The position that whatever God does is just ought to considered in connection with another position, one which has a strong claim to being a part of standard Christian doctrine: that God is the cause of everything (*B*, p. 42). It may seem that, if whatever God does is just and if God causes everything, then there can be no sin. Hobbes denies the consequent. To sin is to disobey a law. Human beings disobey laws, but God cannot, because, being supreme, He is not subject to any law (*LN*, pp. 250–1).

Hobbes would also not accept the following, related proposition: If God causes everything and sins are caused, then God is culpable for sin. The consequent is again false. Causation is a transitive relation; that is, if x causes y and y causes z, then x causes z. But being culpable for something is not inherited from causation. Xavier may do something y that causes Zeppo to do something bad; but that does not mean that Xavier has done something bad. For example, Xavier may collect a legitimate debt from Zeppo, which causes Zeppo to rob a bank. Thus, although God causes people to sin, He is not culpable for their sins since He has not violated any law and could not violate any law since He is above all law.

K

kingdom of darkness (*regnum tenebrarum*)   The kingdom of darkness is any "confederacy of deceivers, that to obtain dominion over men in this present world, endeavour by dark, and erroneous doctrines, to extinguish in them the light both of nature and of the gospel, and so to disprepare them for the kingdom of God to come" (*L* 44.1). As this definition indicates, the kingdom of darkness is correlative with the KINGDOM OF GOD. The principal deception is the proposition that the kingdom of God exists now. According to Hobbes, God had a prophetic kingdom from the time of Abraham (or Moses) until the inauguration of Saul as king, and will not establish a new kingdom until Jesus returns to earth. Hobbes is particularly exercised about this error because it undermines the authority of the secular sovereign (*L* 44.4–5). (*See* KINGDOM OF GOD, PROPHETIC.)

Members of the kingdom of darkness are not apocalyptic figures. Anyone who teaches falsehoods that interfere with another person's salvation is a member of the kingdom of darkness. Both CATHOLICS AND PRESBYTERIANS are consequently members of it; but the pope is not the Antichrist, and Catholics do not belong to the darkest part of the kingdom of darkness. That part of the realm is inhabited by those who do not believe that Jesus is the Christ (*L* 44.2). Members of the kingdom of darkness are sometimes called "children of darkness" in contrast with members of the kingdom of God, who are called "children of the light" (*L* 44.1). The New Testament sometimes calls Satan the leader of the kingdom of darkness, but Hobbes does not make anything of that locution. Alternative names for the kingdom of darkness, names which occur in the New Testament, are the following: "the rulers of the darkness of this world," "the kingdom of Satan," and "the principality of Beelzebub over demons" (*L* 44.1).

Hobbes's *ex professo* account of the kingdom of darkness occurs in part four of *Leviathan*, which bears that title. He categorizes the errors taught by members of the kingdom of darkness into four categories: (1) those involving an incorrect interpretation of the Bible (chapter 44); (2) those involving the retention of pagan mythology ("demonology") in Christian

158

doctrine (chapter 45); (3) those involving the use of Greek philosophy in Christian doctrine (chapter 46); and (4) those involving false traditions within Christianity, often mingling them with mythology and philosophy (chapter 46, para. 41). These topics are covered in the first three chapters of part four. The fourth and last chapter of that part explains who benefits from these false doctrines.

(1) Hobbes thinks that "the greatest and main abuse of Scripture, and to which almost all the rest are either consequent or subservient, is the wresting of it, to prove that the kingdom of God, mentioned so often in the Scripture, is the present Church, or multitude of Christian men now living . . ." (*L* 44.4). Hobbes explicitly says that he is thinking primarily of the doctrine of Catholics and Presbyterians (*L* 47.4). He refers specifically to the pope and then to "assemblies of the pastors" of "particular commonwealths" (*L* 44.5). The reason that pastors and other Christian ministers, especially the pope, teach this doctrine is that they try to benefit from it (*L* 47.2). They argue that the kingdom of heaven exists now, and they are its magistrates.

A second abuse of the Bible is the transmogrifying of "consecration into conjuration." According to Roman Catholics, when the priest consecrates the eucharistic bread, it is transformed into the body of Jesus. The substance of the bread is annihilated and replaced by the substance of Jesus even though all the sensible qualities of the bread remain unchanged (*L* 44.11). This is the doctrine of TRANSUBSTANTIATION. In the Middle Ages, the doctrine was interpreted so literally that Berengar of Tours, who denied the doctrine, was forced to affirm, as part of his reconciliation with the church, that in receiving the eucharist, the communicant "crushes with his teeth the true body of Jesus Christ." According to Hobbes, the doctrine was unknown before the papacy of Innocent III in the early thirteenth century. His history is a bit off here. Berengar lived in the eleventh century. Hobbes thinks that the doctrine of transubstantiation makes the commemoration of Jesus's last meal with his apostles magical. The deception of the Roman Catholic theory is worse than that of the Pharaoh's priests when they seemed to turn their staffs into snakes and water into blood. They at least were clever enough to effect a change that could be observed. In contrast, Roman Catholic priests get people to believe that bread is human flesh when there has been no visible change at all in the bread (*L* 44.11). According to Hobbes, following one Reformation view, consecration is a ceremony that makes something holy by extracting it from its normal, secular use and employing it for religious purposes. Jesus's words of consecration, "This is my body," should be interpreted as an "ordinary figure of speech" (*L* 44.11, 45.24). Hobbes also objects to Roman Catholic "incantations" involving some of the materials and ceremonies

159

of baptism, matrimony, anointing of the sick ("extreme unction"), and consecration of churches and cemeteries (*L* 44.12–13).

The third abuse of the Bible is the misinterpretation of such phrases as "eternal life" and "everlasting death." Combined with certain doctrines of Greek philosophy, it gives rise to a cluster of false beliefs. One is that the soul is immortal (*L* 44.14–15). This belief tends to diminish the importance of the resurrection. It also gives rise to the false belief that the wicked suffer "eternal torments," a doctrine that Hobbes thinks is inconsistent with the mercy of God. (*See* HELL.) The doctrine of purgatory and the rituals of exorcism and "conjuration of phantasms" also evolve from it (*L* 44.16). Of these, purgatory receives an extended discussion (*L* 44.17–40). Hobbes focuses on Robert Bellarmine's defense of it. The discussion can be considered an extension of the attack on Bellarmine's defense of the Roman Catholic Church in chapter 42 (paras. 81–135). In brief, the doctrine is that the souls of people who are destined for heaven suffer for a period of time in purgatory in order to make up for those sins that were not serious enough to send the person to hell but not forgiven while the person was alive on earth. One of Hobbes's objections to the doctrine is that it motivates belief in an independently existing soul. It is worth mentioning as a sidenote that Hobbes's friend, the heterodox Roman Catholic priest, theologian, and philosopher Thomas White also denied the doctrine of purgatory.

(2) The second category of false doctrines promulgated by the kingdom of darkness concerns demonology. Hobbes attributes the belief in demons to the ancient Greeks, whose culture influenced the post-exilic Jews (*L* 45.4). Almost all of the New Testament texts that refer to demons and SPIRITS can be straightforwardly interpreted as employing figurative language. When "spirit" is used literally, it refers to a material object. Belief in demons gives rise to idolatry, the worship of nonexistent objects that are represented by physical objects. Idolatry is condemned, implicitly by the first commandment: Thou shalt not take strange gods (*alienos deos*), that is, the gods of other nations, and explicitly by the second: Thou shalt not make to thyself any image to worship of thine own invention (*L* 45.10).

Hobbes emphasizes that idolatry is not the result of misinterpreting the Bible and was not imported from a pagan culture. Rather, it arose within Christianity because the idolatrous worship of pagan converts was not excised. Hobbes claims that these converts did not want to give up their expensive and finely crafted statues of such gods as Venus, Cupid, Jupiter, and Mercury. So they simply renamed them the Blessed Virgin, Infant Jesus, Barnabas, and Paul, respectively (*L* 45.33). The practice of the canonization of saints is a pagan ritual that was adapted to Christian liturgy. The first person canonized was Romulus during the age of pagan

Rome. The canonization of Julius Caesar and other emperors followed (*L* 45.34). Additional pagan rituals and paraphernalia transmuted into Christian rites and sacramentals include the following: *aqua lustralis* / holy water; saturnalia / carnivals; processions of Priapus / erection of maypoles (*L* 45.38). In true Reformation spirit, Hobbes predicts the eventual demise of these pagan elements (*L* 45.38).

(3) The third category of false doctrines promulgated by the kingdom of darkness concerns those imported from Greek philosophy. Plato required his students to know GEOMETRY before they entered his school. Hobbes gives the impression that he thought that geometry should have been the main subject of study in the schools. For Hobbes, geometry is the study of motion, and "nature works by motion" (*L* 46.11). In fact, Greek philosophy contributed virtually nothing to human knowledge: "To conclude, there is nothing so absurd that the old philosophers ... have not some of them maintained. And I believe that scarce anything can be more absurdly said in natural philosophy than that which now is called Aristotle's *Metaphysics*; nor more repugnant to government than much of that he has said in his *Politics*; nor more ignorantly than a great part of his *Ethics*" (*L* 46.11). Slightly later, Hobbes says," the writings of school divines are nothing else for the most part but insignificant trains of strange and barbarous words or words otherwise used than in the common use of the Latin tongue" (*L* 46.40). Jewish scholars, who originally were supposed to interpret the Mosaic law, were influenced by Greek philosophy for the worse (*L* 46.12). The stock-in-trade of false philosophy is unintelligible language (*L* 46.16–17). By getting people to buy into the incoherence of scholastic theories such as that the soul of a dead person can walk or that something that looks, tastes, and smells like bread is not bread, priests gain control over the beliefs of laymen and can manipulate them to engage in subversive practices (*L* 46.18). As Hobbes says, "who will not obey a priest that can make God, rather than his sovereign, nay than God himself?"

The converse of teaching false philosophy is the suppression of true philosophy. Hobbes appeals to the sixteenth-century explorations of the globe as evidence that there are antipodes and that years and days are determined by the motions of the earth. Yet writers who have but discussed such possibilities – Hobbes must be thinking of Galileo–have been punished for it by clerical authorities. He is bewildered by this: "But what reason is there for it? Is it because such opinions are contrary to true religion? that cannot be, if they be true. Let therefore the truth be first examined by competent judges or confuted by them that pretend to know the contrary" (*L* 46.42).

(4) The fourth category of errors taught by the kingdom of darkness

161

are those that involve false traditions within philosophy, and this is the result of "false or uncertain history" (*L* 46.41). Fictitious accounts of miracles in the lives of the saints, stories about apparitions and ghosts, told by the Roman Catholic Church in order to bolster its doctrine about hell and purgatory, exorcisms, and any other tradition attributed to the "unwritten word of god" are nothing but "old wives' fables" (*L* 46.41). Hobbes urges people to take the evangelist John's advice to heart: "But do not trust any and every spirit, my friends; test the spirits, to see whether they are from God, for among those who have gone out into the world there are many prophets falsely inspired" (1 John 4:1).

In chapter 47, Hobbes explains who benefits from the false doctrines promulgated by the kingdom of darkness. He lists a dozen or so doctrines, chiefly Roman Catholic, but also some Presbyterian ones, that are designed to benefit priests and other ministers of Christ at the expense of the sovereign (*L* 47.2–16). They concern the following issues and doctrines: the kingdom of God, *jure divino* institution of bishops, benefit of clergy, power to make sacrifices, control of matrimony, auricular confession, canonization of saints, absolution, purgatory, demonology, and scholastic metaphysics, ethics, and politics.

Hobbes completes his account of the kingdom of darkness with an extended analogy between the kingdom of fairies and Roman Catholicism. The analogy is appropriate according to Hobbes because each deals in ghosts and spirits. Indeed, the papacy is "the ghost of the deceased Roman Empire, sitting crowned upon the grave thereof" (*L* 47.21). Further, the official language of Roman Catholicism, Latin, is the ghost of a language. The fairies have one king, Oberon, although the Bible calls him "Beelzebub, prince of demons," while Roman Catholics have the pope. Fairies are spirits and priests are spiritual men; fairies have enchanted castles, and priests have churches; fairies cannot be captured, and priests have benefit of clergy, which protects them from being tried in secular courts . . . The *coup de grâce* is this: "The fairies marry not, but there be amongst them incubi that have copulation with flesh and blood. The priests also marry not" (*L* 47.30).

kingdom of God (*regnum dei*) A kingdom of God is any kingdom in which God reigns. There are two such kingdoms, a natural kingdom and a prophetical one (*DC* 15.4; *L* 31.4). (*See* KINGDOM OF GOD, PROPHETIC.) What distinguishes the two kingdoms is the mode by which God's laws are promulgated. The laws of the natural kingdom of God are promulgated through human reason, which allows a person to know the laws of nature. The laws of a prophetic kingdom of God are promulgated through prophets. Hobbes distinguishes a third mode by which God speaks to people, namely, through revelation, but, without explaining why, he claims that laws are never promulgated by revelation (*L* 31.3). It is easy to guess his reason. He does not want a private person claiming to have received a revelation about what the law ought to be. Only a civil sovereign can make civil law.

The natural kingdom, often referred to by Hobbes as "the kingdom of God by nature," is the one under which those human beings who "acknowledge his providence" are governed by the laws of nature, construed as the commands of God. Excluded from the natural kingdom of God are inanimate things, beasts and plants, young children, idiots, and atheists. All of these beings are excluded because they lack the ability to reason correctly. God "governs" everything in virtue of His power, but "reigning" properly requires that the subject acknowledge the authority of the ruler. The excluded groups lack the ability to recognize the authority of God (*L* 31.2).

One complication of interpreting Hobbes's views about the kingdom of God is the result of Hobbes's ambivalence about whether the laws of nature are genuine laws or not. For the purposes of this entry, it will be assumed that the laws of nature are genuine laws, because it would not seem to make sense for God to be a king and have no laws. (However, at one point Hobbes claims that there will be no laws in the kingdom of God that is set up at the second coming of Jesus, because laws are made to get people to heaven, and are not needed when people are in it (*DC* 17.8).) The controversial issue of the logical character of the laws of nature is discussed in the entry LAW OF NATURE.

In *De Cive* and *Leviathan*, Hobbes is concerned with the issue of the nature of the kingdom of God for expressly political purposes. During the 1640s and early 1650s, many of the king's opponents thought that his civil laws violated the laws of nature or some more-specific laws of God's kingdom. Thus, Hobbes was concerned to show that obedience to the king was consistent with both the natural kingdom of God and any prophetic kingdoms that God might have established. Hobbes assumes what would have been uncontroversial in the seventeenth century, that the civil sovereign ought to be obeyed unless his commands conflict with the commandments of God (*DC* 15.1; *L* 31.1). Hobbes does not explain whether obedience to God takes precedence over obedience to the civil sovereign because God is the greater power or because His punishment is greater.

The phrase "the kingdom of God" does not occur in *The Elements of Law*, but is often used in Hobbes's other two political treatises. In *De Cive*, the chapter "Of the Kingdom of God by Nature" is the first one of the third part of the book, "Of Religion." There he equates the word of God with the laws of nature and explains that the basis of God's natural sovereignty is His overwhelming power. The following two chapters, "Of the Kingdom of God under the Old Covenant" and "Of the Kingdom of God by the New Covenant," treat of the prophetic kingdom.

In *Leviathan*, Hobbes discusses the nature of God's natural kingdom in the last chapter of part two, "Of Commonwealth." It forms a kind of transition to part three, "Of a Christian Commonwealth," in which the prophetic kingdom of God is treated in three chapters. The first of these three discussions is in chapter 35, "Of the Signification in Scripture of Kingdom of God, of Holy, Sacred, and Sacrament," with most of the space being devoted to the first topic. It occurs after the chapter on the nature of spirits, angels, and inspiration, and before a chapter on prophets and a succeeding one on miracles. In each of these chapters and some further on, Hobbes is conscientious about surveying the various ordinary uses and meanings of these words before he renders his own opinion on the subject. He pays particular attention to the phrase "the kingdom of God" as used by theologians in sermons and devotional treatises. Hobbes says that they sometimes use it to mean eternal happiness in heaven, which they also call the kingdom of glory, and sometimes for sanctification, which they also call the kingdom of grace. But they never use the term in its proper, literal sense, namely, to signify the monarchy or sovereign power of God, which sovereignty is established by the consent of the people (*L* 35.1, 35.13). This is especially unfortunate, according to Hobbes, because the Old Testament always uses the term in its proper, literal sense; and the New Testament uses it only in the figurative sense of "dominion over sin" (*L* 35.2). In other words, theologians distort the true doctrine of the kingdom of God by misusing the term. As a general proposition, Hobbes thinks that much needless controversy is the result of equivocal uses of words; and one of his requirements on a scientific treatment of a subject is a fixed, clear meaning for the words expressing it.

The second discussion of the meaning of "the kingdom of heaven" is in chapter 38 as part of Hobbes's explanation of a cluster of related terms: "eternal life," "hell," "salvation," "the world to come," and "redemption." Concerning the meaning of "the kingdom of heaven," Hobbes maintains that it is the place where the elect will have eternal life, and that that place is earth (*L* 38.3). Since all human beings die, having lost eternal life in paradise because of the sin of Adam, and since all human beings will be made alive because of the death of Jesus, it is appropriate for eternal life to be on earth (*L* 38.3). There are numerous biblical passages to support this interpretation. For example, the evangelist John says that the new Jerusalem will come down from heaven. It would be pointless for it to be established on earth if no one will be living there. Also, there will be no marriage for those who have eternal life. It is plausible that the reason is that they would overpopulate the earth given an eternity of human reproduction and no death (*L* 38.3). In contrast, there are no good biblical texts to support the view that the elect will live on remote planets ("stars") in the universe (*L* 38.4). The phrase "the kingdom of heaven" merely means the kingdom of the king who lives in heaven; it does not designate the location of the subjects.

The idea that heaven will be on earth is fairly standard among Christians in the twentieth century; but it was something of a scandal in the seventeenth century. Part of Hobbes's reason for holding the view is that he wants to increase the value that people put on earth and earthly things. This involves increasing the value of political life and seeing in life on earth something of the eternal.

The third discussion of the prophetic kingdom of God is in chapter 40, "Of the Rights of the Kingdom of God, in Abraham, Moses, the High Priests, and the Kings of Judah." (*See* KINGDOM OF GOD, PROPHETIC.)

kingdom of God, prophetic   Hobbes is interested in the general concept of the kingdom of God insofar as it concerns a possible conflict between obeying the laws of God and obeying the laws of man. So his interest in the topic was political as much as religious. Political arguments in the seventeenth century often rested upon historical premises; and that is the case with respect to the prophetic kingdom of God. During the seventeenth century, like many other centuries, Christians believed that the end of the world was imminent. Theologians differed over whether that very kingdom was already established or would only be established at the end of the world. The evidence for the disagreement is complex and need not be reviewed here except to say that passages from the gospels can be used to favor each side.

Hobbes wanted to achieve two goals in his treatment of the kingdom of God. One was to affirm the orthodox view that there was a kingdom of God. The other was to be sure that the orthodox view was not politically destabilizing. Hobbes was able to achieve both goals by constructing a plausible, biblically based, history of mankind's relation to God. Four different epochs can be distinguished:

(1)   From Adam and Eve to Abraham (or Moses): No kingdom of God
(2)   From Abraham (or Moses) to Saul: A kingdom of God
(3)   From Saul until the end of the world: No kingdom of God
(4)   From the end of the present world for all eternity: A kingdom of God.

The biblical foundation of Hobbes's schema is evident. The schema has the added merit of being symmetrical. Symmetry was considered important

165

for any philosophy of history since God directs history and He would not do anything in a disorderly fashion. Concerning its political dimension, positing a kingdom of God that will come about at the end of the present age achieves two goals for Hobbes. First, he forestalls its possible use to destabilize a government by putting off its next occurrence to the indefinite, indeterminable, and presumably remote future. Second, to the extent that the concept can be used at all for political purposes, Hobbes shows that, under the kingdom of God, subjects ought to obey their sovereign, whoever he is.

(1) Let's now consider the first epoch. When he first introduces the concept of prophetical kingdoms in *De Cive*, Hobbes implies that they occur whenever God gives laws to "his peculiar people and some certain men elected by him" (*DC* 15.4). The "peculiar people" are the Jews; but who are the ones "elected by him"? It appears that Adam and Eve form the first group of elect, because he says that God "reigned ... by way of covenant" over them (*DC* 16.2). Yet he also says that, "because this covenant was made void, nor ever after renewed," God's kingdom is not taken to begin with them (*DC* 16.2). The covenant made with Adam to which Hobbes is referring was typically referred to as "the covenant of works" in the seventeenth century. The so-called "covenant theologians" emphasized how it ended with the first sin and was replaced by the covenant of grace, by which people are saved through the mercy of God and not in virtue of any good works that they have performed.

The same problem of the status of the covenant involving Adam appears in *Leviathan*. Hobbes initially gives the impression that the first and so far only prophetic kingdom of God comprised the Jews (*L* 31.4). But later he gives the impression that Adam and Eve are subjects of what must be a prophetic kingdom since he says that they are not merely subjects of God in a natural kingdom but also his "peculiar subjects." Further, Noah and his family are subjects of the same kingdom (*L* 35.3).

It is not clear how to resolve or understand the discrepancy. Here is a suggestion as to how to understand, if not to resolve, the problem. It is possible that Hobbes was misled by his distinction concerning natural/prophetic kingdoms of God. The terms of the distinction are supposed to be both exhaustive and mutually exclusive, but in fact they are not. They may be mutually exclusive, but they are not exhaustive. The proper contrast to "natural kingdom" is "nonnatural kingdom," not "prophetic kingdom." The third term then is the problematic one. On the one hand, the first kingdom to be established by a prophet in the ordinary sense of "prophet" is the one in which Abraham (or Moses) played a major role. (Hobbes is not always clear about with whom this COVENANT begins. See the discussion below.) This would incline him to think of Israel as the first prophetic kingdom of God. On the other hand, God's reign over Adam and Eve and the other patriarchs is not merely the natural reign that God has over all human beings who acknowledge His providence. Since the only alternative to the natural kingdom is the prophetic kingdom, according to Hobbes's terms, he thinks of the prophetic kingdom of God as beginning with them. He may suspect that something is awry with his view, because he does not use the term "prophetic kingdom of God" when he is talking about Adam and Eve (L 35.3).

(2) Let's now consider the second epoch. While Hobbes sometimes indicates that the first prophetic kingdom of God begins with Moses (e.g., L 44.4, 44.17), he usually says that it begins with Abraham (DC 16.2; L 35.4, 40.1). Since this latter view seems to be his dominant one, that is the one I shall adopt. Concerning Abraham, Hobbes says in De Cive that the covenant is to be for ever, that Abraham "shall submit himself to be governed" by God, and that God will give Canaan to Abraham (DC 16.3). Hobbes emphasizes that Abraham is committing himself, not to the God that every human being can come to believe in by using reason, but to the God who revealed Himself in the appearance of the three mysterious strangers, in a vision, and in a dream (DC 16.6). Two features of this covenant seem to impress Hobbes particularly. One is that God did not impose any laws upon Abraham in addition to the laws of nature (DC 16.5). The rite of circumcision is instituted as a sign of the covenant, perhaps to compensate for the absence of new laws (cf. DC 16.10). The second feature that impresses Hobbes is that Abraham and God are the only parties to the covenant. (On the oddity of having God be a party to a sovereign-making covenant, see COVENANT.) Neither of these features is part of the Mosaic covenant.

In Leviathan, Hobbes's views are somewhat different. Here he emphasizes that God's sovereignty constitutes a genuine kingdom, even though that word is not used in the biblical account, and that Abraham commits himself to "God's positive law," although Hobbes does not specify what these laws might be and continues to hold that the practice of circumcision is only a memorial of the covenant and not a law (L 35.4, 40.1). God's kingdom is an instance of sovereignty by institution ("an institution by pact") in contrast with sovereignty by acquisition (L 35.4). Hobbes derives three points from the Abrahamic covenant. One is that Abraham bound his family and all of his descendants to the covenant that he made with God. That is, people who do not receive an immediate revelation from God are supposed to do what their sovereign commands them to do (L 40.2). A second consequence is that, just as Abraham had the right to punish anyone who claimed to have a private revelation that he deemed illicit and who persisted in holding to it, any other sovereign has the same right (*L* 40.3). A third consequence is that Abraham had the sole right to interpret God's word, as does any sovereign (*L* 40.4, 40.7).

There is nothing odd about having God be both the king of all peoples and also king of a particular people. It is strictly analogous to a general who is both the commander-in-chief of all the armed forces and also general of a particular constituent army (*L* 12.22).

The covenant made with Abraham is "renewed" with Moses (*L* 35.5; *DC* 16.8). What is different about the Mosaic covenant is that all the Hebrew people are parties to it (cf. *L* 40.5). In *De Cive*, Hobbes says that "the covenant made at Mt. Sinai" was made with "the consent of each man" and in virtue of which "there becomes an institutive kingdom of God over them" (*DC* 16.9). Moses is not mentioned here and does not seem to be a privileged party to this covenant. Hobbes emphasizes Moses' initial lack of authority in order to emphasize the point that the authority of Moses, like the authority of every sovereign, depends upon "the consent of the people" (*L* 40.6). This democratic origin of the monarchical reign of Moses suits Hobbes's purposes in two ways. First, it shows that a democratic origin of a government does not guarantee that the government will be a democracy. (*See* MONARCHY, ARISTOCRACY, AND DEMOCRACY.) Second, since Moses alone was chosen to be God's lieutenant, the priests had no independent authority. Hobbes discusses Aaron's subordinate role at some length: "Therefore neither Aaron nor the people nor any aristocracy of the chief princes of the people but Moses alone had next under God the sovereignty over the Israelites; and that not only in causes of civil policy but also of religion" (*L* 40.7). The implication is that what is good enough for God's chosen people is good enough for England.

The Mosaic covenant originates a sovereignty by institution. In *Leviathan*, the point is made by saying that "by the kingdom of God is properly meant a commonwealth, instituted (by the consent of those which were to be subject thereto) for their civil government..." (*L* 35.7). In contrast with the Abrahamic covenant, as described in *De Cive*, laws are imposed on the Jews: the decalogue and the Mosaic judicial and ceremonial laws (*DC* 16.10). Also, God does not seem to be a contracting party of the covenant. Hobbes points out that this is the first time that the phrase "kingdom" is used in the Bible (*DC* 16.9).

After the assembly of the Israelites at the foot of Mount Sinai chose God to be their sovereign, Moses as God's viceroy had the sole authority to decide both religious and nonreligious controversies. Hobbes quotes extensively from the Bible to prove that no private person, no high priest (a criticism of Roman Catholicism), no assembly of priests (a criticism of presbyterianism) had authority (*DC* 16.13). During the time of Joshua, Eleazar, who "had not only the priesthood but also the sovereignty," had

full authority because he was the designated successor to Moses in accordance with the terms that the people had agreed to in their covenant at
Mount Sinai (*DC* 16.14; *L* 40.9). The moral is that "even in Joshua's time
the supreme power [of sovereignty] and authority of interpreting the
word of God were both in one person" (*DC* 16.14; *L* 40.9). During the
period of the Judges, the right of sovereignty continued to be in the high
priest although the exercise of it was in the prophets. To those who think
this situation proves the separability of sovereignty and religious administration, Hobbes has two answers. The first is that Moses had predicted that
the people would corrupt themselves in this way (Deut 31:29). The second
is that the prophets in fact exercised both secular and religious authority
and thus "these two powers continued inseparable" (*DC* 16.15; *L* 40.10).

(3) The theocratic epoch serves Hobbes's purpose of showing that secular and religious authority are united. But there can be too much of a
good thing. In order to avoid the arguments widely presented during the
late 1640s and early 1650s of those disruptive Englishmen who thought
that the kingdom of God still existed, Hobbes needed to find an event
that would terminate God's reign and reinitiate a purely secular sovereignty (the beginning of the third epoch). His preferred event is the
selection of Saul as king, which God Himself declares to be a renunciation
of His kingship. Once Saul was inaugurated, the priests became subordinate to the king. One piece of evidence of the power of kings over priests
is the episode in which Solomon removed Abiathar from the high priesthood (*L* 40.11, 42.118). Also, Solomon dedicated the Temple and blessed
the people himself. Later, when the book of Deuteronomy was redis-
covered in the Temple, the priests studied it "by the commandment of
Josiah," not on their own initiative: "The authority therefore of admitting
books for the word of God belonged to the king; and thus that book of
the law [Deuteronomy] was approved and received again by the authority
of king Josiah" (*DC* 16.16; *L* 40.11). Hobbes summarizes his position about
the third epoch in this way: "from the institution of God's kingdom to the
Captivity, the supremacy of religion was in the same hand with that of the
civil sovereignty; and the priest's office after the election of Saul was not
magisterial but ministerial" (*L* 40.11).

In *De Cive*, and sometimes in *Leviathan*, Hobbes says that the sovereignty
of the Jews returned to the high priests after the Babylonian Captivity
(*DC* 16.17; *L* 42.41). This is an odd position for him to take, for two
reasons. The first and less important one is that the Jews were no longer
an independent nation. Their liberation was the work of Cyrus, king of
Persia, and they remained a vassal state of Persia. The second and more
important reason is that, if the Jews re-established a theocracy, then it
would appear that God's kingdom was re-established and thus people may

169

appeal to the laws of God to disobey the secular sovereign; and this is precisely the kind of position that Hobbes wanted to avoid. He obscures the matter by saying that the political situation in Judaea was so troubled that the information we have today is insufficient to determine where the sovereign authority resided exactly; perhaps it remained with the high priests and perhaps it was transferred to "foreign princes." Nonetheless, he is confident that "the power of interpreting God's word was not severed from the supreme civil power" (*DC* 16.17). Hobbes's position here begs the question against those who think that there was a split between the secular authority and the religious authority. If Hobbes is not sure how secular and religious authority were distributed after the Babylonian Captivity, he should have realized that his opponents would be. Most clergymen of the Church of England and all presbyterians would have separated the ultimate religious authority from the secular authority.

In *Leviathan*, Hobbes takes a position that is historically accurate. He says that there was no commonwealth during the Captivity and that the renewal of the covenant with Esdras (Ezra) did not include any promise of political obedience. Unfortunately, this, given his other views, has the logical consequence that the religious authority of Judaism was in the Persian king; but Hobbes does not take notice of this consequence. He also says that the Jews eventually became subject to the Greeks, whose influence tended to corrupt their religion (*L* 40.14).

In any case, Hobbes seems to assume that the prophetical kingdom of God no longer exists by the time Jesus is born; otherwise his account of the mission of Jesus would make no sense in either *De Cive* or *Leviathan*. In *De Cive*, Jesus is supposed to serve as a mediator between God and human beings, in order to institute the covenant that will establish the new kingdom of God when Jesus returns to earth at the second coming (*DC* 17.5). The most important point here is that the kingdom of God that Jesus is to establish is "a real, not a metaphorical kingdom." It follows that it will be established "by force of our covenant, not by the right of God's power" (*L* 35.11).

Jesus himself in his role as Christ (Messiah) is neither the equal of God the Father nor a king. His role is similar to that of Moses when he mediated the covenant made by the Israelites at the foot of Mount Sinai. Jesus is the equal of God the Father as king, but that kingdom will come to exist only in the future (*DC* 17.3). Hobbes defends his interpretation of Jesus's mission with regard to the kingdom of God with extensive biblical quotations, only a few of which need to be mentioned here. One is the famous imprecation of the Lord's Prayer: "thy kingdom come" (*DC* 17.5; *L* 35.11). Theodore Beza, Calvin's successor at Geneva, believed that the kingdom of Jesus was already established. Hobbes calls him to task for not giving an adequate explanation for why Jesus would have urged us to speak of his future kingdom if it already existed (*L* 44.17–18). Another biblical passage supporting Hobbes's view is from the gospel of Matthew: "When the Son of man shall come in his glory, and all the angels with him, then shall he sit upon the throne of his glory." It would be pointless for Christ to come at the end of the world if he were already reigning. Jesus himself said, "My kingdom is not of this world" (*DC* 17.5).

(4) Concerning the history of the fourth epoch, there is, of course, nothing to say since it does not yet exist, and, as the gospels say, no man knows the hour or the day when Jesus will return to earth to inaugurate it. The New Testament books sometimes call the fourth epoch "the kingdom of heaven" and "the kingdom of glory" (*DC* 17.7; *L* 35.13). The phrase "the kingdom of heaven" gives the false impression that God's kingdom will be somewhere other than on earth. But that is not correct. The phrase "the kingdom of heaven" does not mean the kingdom that is located in heaven, but the kingdom of the king who lives in heaven (*L* 38.4). The New Testament makes clear that the kingdom of God will be on earth (*L* 38.3, 38.5, 38.17, 38.23). Hobbes has overwhelming biblical evidence for his view. Everlasting life is to be in Zion; Zion is in Jerusalem; and Jerusalem is on earth. Also, in Revelation, God is said to allow the elect to eat of the tree of life; and that tree is in the garden of Eden. And so on (*L* 38.3, 38.23). The reason that people will not marry after the general resurrection at the end of the world (Matt 22:30) is that the earth would soon become overcrowded if that were allowed (*L* 38.3).

For the most part, Hobbes does not engage in the kind of mythic thinking that sees symmetries in human history. His views about the epochs of human history are one exception. Another is his idea that, since Adam did not die immediately after disobeying God (even though God said that on that very day Adam would die), it is appropriate that his descendants remain dead for a time before their resurrection at the end of the world (*L* 38.3).

Hobbes says that "the kingdom of Christ is not of this world" (*L* 42.6); yet the second prophetic kingdom of God, which will be inaugurated at the second coming of Jesus, will be on earth. Hobbes's position has the advantages of simultaneously allowing him to affirm the traditional Christian view that Jesus is a king and yet make his kingship irrelevant to the contemporary political situation. Although the second prophetic kingdom of God will not be established until the end of the world, the covenant by which it is promised does have implications for how people should live their lives in the meantime, for there is a proper way to be led to it. Hobbes's views about how to travel that road are intended as an alternative to the anti-royalist millenarians of the 1640s who thought the road

171

was paved by revolution. According to Hobbes, Jesus came to earth as a teacher, not a ruler, and what he taught was a doctrine of SALVATION that had two components: obedience to God and faith in Jesus as the Messiah. (*See* CHRISTIANITY, ESSENCE OF.)

knowledge (*cognitio*)   There are two kinds of knowledge (*cognitio*): "knowledge of fact" and science. The latter is knowledge in the proper sense (*scientia*). When it is written down, it is usually referred to as philosophy. Let's consider it first. Hobbes explains it as "knowledge of the consequence of one affirmation to another" (*L* 9.1; *LW* 3:66). These consequences are formulated in conditional or hypothetical propositions; that is, they have the form "if *p*, then *q*," and are necessarily true (analytic) propositions. They are those necessary propositions that are true in virtue of the meaning of their words. He has various accounts of what this amounts to. Like most philosophers before the twentieth century, he discussed what made a proposition truth or false primarily with regard to subject-predicate PROPOSITIONS. In *De Corpore*, which should be considered his official account, Hobbes says that a true proposition is one "in which the predicate contains the subject within itself, or in which the predicate is the name of each and every thing of which the subject is the name" (*DCo* 3.7). "Contain" is a metaphor, and perhaps Hobbes intends the second disjunct to explain what it means. Using the standard philosophical example, "Man is an animal," he says that that is true because "animal" is the name of everything that "man" is. *Leviathan* contains a different explication. There he says that true propositions are those in which the meaning of the predicate is a consequence of the meaning of the subject. The proposition "Every man is an animal" is true because being an animal is a consequence of being a man (*L* 46.16).

When the name of something that has a cause is being defined, the definition ought to state the cause of that thing or the way in which that thing can be generated. For example, "circle" should be defined as a plane figure "generated from the rotation of a straight line in a plane" (*DCo* 6.13; *EW* 7:211–12). The reason is that "the goal of proof is the scientific knowledge of causes and the generation of things; and if this scientific knowledge is not in the definitions it cannot be in the conclusions of the syllogism which is first built up from the definitions; and if it is not found in the first conclusion, it will not be found in any later conclusion" (*DCo* 6.13; *EW* 7:205).

Every scientific proposition is a definition or follows from one or more definitions (*DC* 18.4). Hobbes's favored examples of a scientific proposition are those involving geometry, especially circles: "If the figure shown be a circle, then any straight line through the center shall divide it into two equal parts" (*L* 9.1; *DCo* 3.9). Notice that this sentence is hypothetical. It does not assert that the figure is a circle; one can never have scientific knowledge about individual objects. All one knows is that something is the case on the assumption that something else is the case. The knowledge is necessarily true and certain, but empirically vacuous. This is an odd doctrine and is consequently difficult to categorize. On the one hand, if a rationalist is one who holds that scientific propositions are not empirical, then Hobbes is a rationalist. On the other hand, if a rationalist is one who holds that scientific knowledge is substantive or synthetic, then Hobbes is not a rationalist.

If he is not a rationalist, is he an empiricist? There is at least this much empiricism in him. Every meaningful categorematic word must refer to a body, and all bodies are known either directly or indirectly through sensation. So all scientific knowledge is about empirical or physical objects, even if the content of that knowledge is analytic. Perhaps Hobbes's connection with empiricism can be made stronger. Even if scientific knowledge does not consist of substantive propositions, it originates in experience "all manner of sciences, which, comprehended under the title of philosophy . . . is to be learnt from reasoning; that is to say, by making necessary consequences, having first taken the beginning from experience" (*DC* 17.12).

There is an infallible sign of scientific knowledge. It is the ability to "demonstrate" propositions so clearly that anyone can understand them (*L* 5.22). There is a famous division of the sciences at the end of chapter 9 of *Leviathan*, in which science or philosophy is divided into natural philosophy and civil philosophy; ethics, poetry, rhetoric, logic, and the science of the just and unjust all belong to natural philosophy; only politics belongs to civil philosophy; and theology belongs to neither. (*See* PHILOSOPHY.)

Knowledge of fact (*cognitio facti*) can be treated more briefly. It is "nothing else but sense and memory" (*L* 9.1). (*See* SENSATION.) Hobbes calls it "absolute" in contrast with the conditional knowledge of science. There are two kinds of knowledge of fact. First, natural history consists of those facts that do not depend upon the human will in any way. Second, civil history consists of the story of "the voluntary actions of men in commonwealths" (*L* 9.2).

173

L

language and speech For Hobbes, either language or speech is the concatenation of words, and words are arbitrary signs devised by human beings to signify their thoughts. Expressed words are the verbalizations of individual ideas, and speech is the verbalization of mental discourse. The general purpose of speech is "to transfer our mental discourse into verbal" (*L* 4.3). This sounds as if the general purpose of speech is communication, in a broad sense. Also, speech piggybacks on language that is used to help people remember their thoughts. According to Hobbes, words were first invented as items to help people remember things, and only later used to communicate thoughts to other people (*DCo* 2.3; *L* 4.3). Only human beings have language; beasts use signs to communicate but they do not devise sounds or other things with the conscious purpose of having them signify ideas. Beasts use signs because of "the necessity of nature" (*DH* 10.1). Since Hobbes is a determinist, it is not clear how human beings would not also, in his view, have to use signs because of the necessity of nature.

It is difficult to know whether Hobbes draws a sharp distinction between language (which is a formal entity, consisting of sentences) and speech (which is a use of language), and, if so, how he does it. He discusses the nature of words and how they are concatenated to form sentences. He also discusses uses of sentences and explicitly refers to these uses as speech. What he does not have is an explicit contrast between language and speech. On the one hand, the concatenation of words is described as the origin of speech (*DCo* 3.1); and in *Leviathan*, his discussion of the various kinds of NAMES, a topic that is part of his discussion of the nature of language in *De Corpore*, is embedded in chapter four, "Of Speech." On the other hand, in *De Corpore*, the speech acts of questioning, requesting, commanding, and so on are mentioned in his chapter on PROPOSITIONS, which are treated as those *orationes* (speeches) that consist of two names, of which the second is supposed to name everything that the first names.

Hobbes has two significant discussions of language, one in *Leviathan* and one in *De Corpore*, with a lesser but still interesting discussion in *De Homine*. Language is discussed in *Leviathan* because human beings make

174

up the civil state, and language is characteristic of human beings; it is discussed in *De Corpore* because that work explains what science is and science consists of necessarily true propositions.

In *Leviathan*, Hobbes combines the mnemonic and expressive uses of language, mentioned at the beginning of this article, and comes up with four special uses and their correlative abuses. The first use is to register for oneself what the causes and powers of things are; its abuse is not to use words always with the same meaning, so that one mistakes what one has thought. The second use is to communicate beliefs to others; its abuse is to use words metaphorically and thereby deceive others. (Hobbes is quite opposed to the use of METAPHOR on theoretical grounds, notwithstanding his own brilliant use of it. He thinks that metaphors deceive people.) The third use is to express what one wants to do or what one wants done; its abuse is to say that one wants something when in fact one does not. The fourth use is for enjoyment and amusement; its abuse is to make people unhappy, unless someone in authority does it in order to improve the conduct of a subordinate (*L* 4.3–4).

Hobbes has an inchoate theory of speech acts. But what he says about the topic is motivated by the exigencies of his political theory and not as an area of intrinsic interest. He recognizes that the same form of words, for example, "Study hard," can be either command or counsel depending upon the intention and status of the speaker, and the person who is supposed to benefit from the act. (*See* COMMAND AND COUNSEL.) Hobbes cares about this distinction because he wants to maintain that the sovereign commands while a parliament merely counsels even when the form of words used by both is the same. Hobbes also sharply distinguishes between contractual speech acts, having a form such as "I hereby give *X*," and promises, in the seventeenth-century sense of being an expression of an intention that does not legally obligate a person. The simple subject and verb used for an express contractual speech act have a performative form in J. L. Austin's sense ("I give" or "I promise"), or the verb can be in the past tense ("I have given" or "I promised") (*L* 14.13). The performative form expresses that the action is being performed there and then; the past tense expresses that the action has already been performed.

There are other places too in which Hobbes shows a level of linguistic sensitivity unusual by seventeenth-century standards. Questions signify the speaker's desire for knowledge. Requests signify the speaker's desire to have something. Promises, threats, and commands signify other mental attitudes. In philosophy, he maintains, there is only one kind of speech act and that is what is sometimes called statement, assertion, or proposition (*dictum, enuntio, propositio*). A proposition is what is asserted or denied and is true or false (*DCo* 3.1, 5.1; *L* 4.11; *EL* 1.5.9–10; *DC* 18.4).

In general, language is an important topic for Hobbes both because he is interested in the methodology of science, for which language is the principal instrument, and because he thinks that the misuse of language, especially by scholastic philosophers, has prevented progress in science. Yet he does not have an especially sophisticated idea of language. He does not mention that natural languages contain an infinite number of sentences. He also does not have an appreciation for what Noam Chomsky has called the creative aspect of language, that is, its resources for expressing new kinds of thoughts. Still, he does emphasize the conventionality of meaning (*DH* 10.2), and he does think that the use of language represents a great intellectual leap over the kind of thinking that can be achieved only by rearranging sensed objects. He thinks that by having one word stand for many things – having "triangle" stand for any triangle – people are able to generalize their thoughts. Without language one may be able to work out that the interior angles of some particular triangle are equal to the interior angles of two given right angles, but only language allows one to see that this fact holds for every triangle and every pair of right angles. Language "makes that which was found true here and now to be true in all times and places" (*L* 4.9; *DH* 10.3). Hobbes seems to be interested less in discussing the nature of language for its own sake than in helping people avoid misusing it. Reasoning is calculation, and words are the units of calculation. But people are more likely to miscalculate with words than they are with numbers: "words are wise men's counters, they do but reckon by them; but they are the money of fools, that value them by the authority of an Aristotle, a Cicero, or a Thomas, or any other doctor whatsoever, if but a man" (*L* 4.13).

laughter (*risus*)   Laughter is the "grimaces" given rise to by sudden glory; that is, the sudden joy that arises from imagining one's own power and ability. Often the power and ability are measured against those of someone or something that is deformed; people with few talents often laugh, because they "are forced to keep themselves in their own favour by observing the imperfections of other men" (*L* 6.42; *DC* 1.2, 3.12). Laughter is inoffensive when it is abstracted from individual persons. Novelty is required for laughter, but not wit, because there is no wit in recognizing "mischances and indecencies" (*EL* 1.9.13).

law (*lex*)   Law is by far the most important concept in Hobbes's philosophical work. In addition to this entry, there are six others that are directly related to the topic: CIVIL LAW; LAW, COMMON; LAW OF NATURE; LAW OF NATURE, FUNDAMENTAL; LAWS, DIVISION OF; and LAWS OF NATURE.

A law is "the command of that person, whether man or court, whose precept contains in it the reason of obedience" (*mandatum ejus personae, sive hominis sive curiae, cujus praeceptum continet obedientiae rationem*) (*DC* 14.1, 14.13; *L* 26.2, 26.11). Definitions to the same effect are presented in other contexts: for example, that a law is "the command of him or them that have the sovereign power, given to those that be his or their subjects, declaring publicly and plainly what every of them may do, and what they must forbear to do" (*DCL*, p. 26); and that laws are "commands or prohibitions, which ought to be obeyed, because assented to by submission" (*DCL*, p. 24). The proper understanding of law depends upon understanding the distinction between COMMAND AND COUNSEL. To state the distinction briefly, a command is something that the addressee ought to do because the speaker wants it done; a counsel is something that the addressee is supposed to do because doing it will benefit her.

A law contains two parts. Let's call these two parts the form and the content. The form is that part of the law that expresses the authority by which the law is made. The content is the part that expresses what is to be done (or not done). In the sentence, "I command that you treat each person equally," the phrase "I command that" is the form of the law that the sentence states and the rest of the sentence is its content. Some sentences are formally indeterminate in use between being a command and being a counsel. A sentence of the form "Do *X*" may be used for either one, and only the context can determine what kind of speech act is being performed. Hobbes only came to see this by the time he wrote *Leviathan*. In *The Elements of Law*, he says that all sentences of the form "Do *X*" are laws (*EL* 2.10.1).

In order for something to be a law, it must be promulgated. Human laws are promulgated by oral or written words. Divine laws are promulgated in one of three ways: by reason, by revelation, or by prophecy. The first method, which is supposed to be the method applicable to the laws of nature, yields "the tacit dictates of right reason" (*tacita rectae rationis dictamina*) (*DC* 15.3). This phrase is odd because the word "tacit" seems to neutralize the requirement of promulgation. Nothing is a law "unless it is perspicuously published" (*nisi quae perspicue promulgantur*) (*DC* 15.3). This oddity is due to Hobbes's ambivalence in *De Cive* about whether the laws of nature are genuinely laws. If reason yielded express dictates, they would certainly be laws; but since they are only tacit, their status is less clear. (*See* LAW OF NATURE.)

There is also an oddity in the second mode of divine promulgation. By "REVELATION," Hobbes means what he elsewhere calls "immediate revelation," that is, the direct communication of God with some human being. This is typically achieved by a supernatural voice or in a vision or dream; and Hobbes also calls this mode of promulgation "sensible" (*sensu*). What is odd is that this supposed mode by which God promulgates His laws is then said not ever to have been used by God to promulgate any: "neither have any laws of his kingdom been published on this manner unto any people" (*DC* 15.3). One way to explain the oddity is to hold that, when Hobbes first introduces the concept of the three ways in which "God's laws are declared," he means the three ways in which God's word has been delivered to human beings. Hobbes could then hold that God has spoken to individual human beings by immediate revelation in order to give certain kinds of information to them but not to promulgate laws by this means.

The third mode of divine promulgation is the least controversial from an interpretive point of view. God makes His laws known through His prophets, whose authority must be taken on "faith" (*fides*) (*DC* 15.3). There are then two kingdoms of God: God's natural kingdom, the laws of which are promulgated through the dictates of right reason, and His prophetical kingdom, the laws of which are promulgated through prophecy.

A law is by definition just (*QLNC*, p. 182). Sometimes Hobbes says that whatever a sovereign commands is a law (*L* 30.20), and at other times he says that nothing that violates a law of nature can be a civil law (*DC* 14.10). This latter claim seems to leave room for people to refuse to obey a command of a sovereign, on the grounds that it violates a law of nature. However, Hobbes seems to reason in the opposite direction. If the sovereign commands something, then it is a civil law, and thus *ipso facto* cannot violate the laws of nature. For Hobbes, the same behavior may violate a law of nature in one context (that is, under one set of civil laws) and not in another. For example, the laws of nature "forbid theft, adultery, &c.; yet if the civil law command us to invade anything, that invasion is not theft, adultery, &c." (*DC* 14.10). Hobbes follows up this analysis of behavior with the claim that what people need to know, relevant to "the essence of law," is who has "the supreme power, that is to say, the right of making laws" (*summam potestam, hoc est, legum ferendarum jus habet*) (*DC* 14.11).

While there is no difference between a law and a just law, there is one between a law and a good law. A good law is one that is needed for the good of all the people and is "perspicuous" (*L* 30.20). Some people think that laws are made only for the good of the sovereign, but that is not so, according to Hobbes. A sovereign is strong only so long as his subjects are strong; so it is in his own self-interest to make good laws (*L* 30.21). The logical gap that Hobbes's argument does not bridge is that, while it may be in the self-interest of a sovereign to make good laws, that does not mean that he will make them. Hobbes should realize this since he holds that the sovereign is in the state of nature, and that people in the state of nature often desire their immediate short-term good at the expense of their long-term good.

A perspicuous law is one that has its "causes and motives" explained. It should be briefly formulated, because words are ambiguous and the more words there are the greater the chance for ambiguity (*L* 30.22). Hobbes's endorsement of brevity is laudable, but he is mistaken about the relationship between brevity and ambiguity. Since the meaning assigned to each word of a sentence needs to cohere with the meanings of all the other words of the sentence, a longer formulation often eliminates an ambiguity. For example, "Carol went to the bank" is ambiguous; but "Carol went to the bank, that is, the financial institution" is not. Nevertheless, one can only agree with his summary: a sovereign ought to "make the reason perspicuous why the law was made; and the body of the law itself as short but in as proper and significant terms as may be" (*L* 30.22).

A law can also never be against reason. That is uncontroversial. The difficult issue involves deciding whose reason should be followed in law. Lawyers such as Edward Coke thought it should be the "artificial perfection of reason" that is achieved through long study of the law allied with observation and experience. Hobbes objects that different lawyers have different interpretations of the law. What is needed is unanimity. The only way to achieve this is by following the reason of the "artificial man of the commonwealth," because it is his command that makes law (*L* 26.11).

The difference between law and counsel has already been alluded to. The difference between a law and a COVENANT, which Hobbes discusses at some length in *The Elements of Law*, also needs to be noticed. Both covenants and laws express the will of the person who makes them. But a covenant imposes an obligation upon the person who makes it, while a law imposes an obligation, not on the one who makes the law, but on the one to whom the law is addressed. A covenant imposes an obligation because a person has promised to act in a certain way, but a law, according to Hobbes, depends upon an obligation of obedience in general. He says that in a covenant what is to be done is expressed prior to the acquisition of the obligation to do it, while in a law the obligation to obey precedes the specification of what is to be done (*EL* 2.10.2; *DC* 14.2). What he means is that, in order for a covenant to be made, a proposal is first made. This proposal can either be accepted or not. If it is accepted, then the obligation follows upon the specification of the terms of the covenant. In contrast, a subject already has an obligation to do what the sovereign commands; so the obligation to obey it precedes the content of the command. The political importance of the distinction between law and covenant for Hobbes is that it allows him to insist that the sovereign, not being a party to any covenant involving his subjects, has no obligations to them, whereas, because he controls what is the law, all his subjects already have an obligation to obey him.

179

In *De Cive*, the confusion between law and covenant (*pactum*) is attributed specifically to Aristotle, who defines a law as "a speech, limited according to the common consent of the city (*civitas*), declaring everything that we ought to do" (*DC* 14.2). One criticism that Hobbes has of this definition is that, to the extent that it is correct, it applies only to civil law and not to law in general, because it is relativized to what a city decides should be done. A city may decide to change what should be done, and hence its laws may change. But the laws of nature are eternal and unchanging (*DC* 14.2). (This criticism does not square with Hobbes's identification of the civil laws with the laws of nature (*L* 26.8).) Hobbes also objects that the definition does not extend to divine laws, which obviously have nothing to do with human consent. Even as a definition of civil laws, Aristotle's formulation is deficient. If the government is a monarchy, then the laws are made by one person and the term "common consent of the city" makes no sense. (Hobbes's criticism seems unfair. By his own theory of AUTHORIZATION, subjects are the authors of whatever the sovereign does.) Hobbes says that Aristotle's definition also leaves out the central aspect of a law, namely, that it is a command (*DC* 14.2).

At the bottom of Aristotle's defective definition, according to Hobbes, is a confusion of law and covenant. What Aristotle says about law in fact applies only to a covenant or contract in the STATE OF NATURE, which imposes an obligation but does not tie one to act in accordance with it. The point that Hobbes is making is important to the correct interpretation of his idea of the laws of nature in his entire philosophy, and scholars have been actively arguing about it for decades. In *Leviathan*, it is arguable that the laws of nature are genuine laws because they are the commands of God, and they are compelling because of His irresistible power. Hobbes's view in *De Cive* is different. In this earlier work, the laws of nature do not seem to be genuine laws, even though they do create obligations. They are not laws, because there is no human authority that has overwhelming power to compel obedience; that is, the obligation they impose is not constraining, because it is not backed up with physical power. Hobbes distinguishes between being obliged and being tied by an obligation. He says that we are obliged by a covenant but that we, being obliged, are held by a law ("Pacto obligamur; lege obligati tenemur") (*DC* 14.2). Hobbes's distinction is sometimes compared to one that H. L. A. Hart drew between having an obligation and being obliged. For Hart, one has an obligation if one is required to do something on moral grounds; but one may be obliged to do something that is not morally compelling. For example, one may be obliged by a gunman to hand over one's wallet without having any obligation to do it. The reason that Hart's distinction does not fit Hobbes's point very well is that for Hart moral obligation itself moves people to

180

action but for Hobbes it does not; and being obliged for Hart involves extra-moral and extra-legal coercion, but for Hobbes the law is coercive.

law, common Hobbes disdains the idea of common law as a set of normative propositions or PRECEPTS that allegedly impose obligations, independently of the will of the person in authority. Common law may be contrasted with statute law, which expressly is the command of some authority. Sometimes Hobbes gives a kind of lip-service to common law. In *A Dialogue between a Philosopher and a Student of the Common Laws of England*, which is a debate between a Philosopher (Hobbes) and a Lawyer, the Philosopher professes to subscribe to the common law, considered as "equity . . . that interprets and amends the law written, itself being unwritten, and consisting in nothing else but right reason" (*DCL*, p. 4). The problem with this view, according to Hobbes, is that it allows any man to claim that some action against him "is against reason, and thereupon to make a pretence for his disobedience" (*DCL*, p. 4).

The greatest proponent of the theory that the common law is superior to all other laws was Edward Coke (1552–1634), who served as chief justice under James I. In 1608, Coke implied that the law was superior to the king. James became enraged and approached Coke as if to strike him; Coke dropped to his hands and knees and begged for pardon. But he persisted in holding his views; two years later he again said that the common law was supreme. In November 1616, James dismissed Coke from the Court of Common Pleas as the result of his refusal to obey James's order not to interfere in a case. In effect, Hobbes's attack on the common law is an attack on the views of Edward Coke.

Coke thought that common law is superior to any other because it is custom, which through long study, observation, and experience has been perfected. Hobbes disagrees. Custom has nothing to do with law: "Now as to the authority you ascribe to custom, I deny that any custom of its own nature can amount to the authority of a law. For if the custom be unreasonable, you must, with all other lawyers, confess that it is no law, but ought to be abolished; and if the custom be reasonable, it is not the custom, but the equity that makes it law" (*DCL*, pp. 62–3). And concerning study, "long study may increase and confirm erroneous sentences [opinions]: and where men build on false grounds, the more they build, the greater is the ruin" (*L* 26.11; *DCL*, p. 4). Hobbes prefers reason and authority to experience and longevity. But the reason Hobbes has in mind is not wisdom, but the recognition that logic requires an authority to maintain civilized behavior among people: "It is not wisdom, but authority that makes a law. . . . That the law has been fined [i.e., found] by grave and learned men, meaning the professors of the law, is manifestly untrue;

181

for all the laws of England have been made by the kings of England" (*DCL*, p. 5).

law of nations (*jus gentium*) The law of nations is the same as the LAWS OF NATURE (*L* 30.30).

law of nature (*lex naturalis*) This entry deals only with the essence of a law of nature, that is, the definition of "law of nature." Two other articles deal with specific laws of nature: LAW OF NATURE, FUNDAMENTAL and LAWS OF NATURE.

Hobbes has two basic ideas of what a law of nature is. In *The Elements of Law* and *De Cive*, natural law seems to be identified with reason itself or right reason (*EL* 1.15.1; *DC* 2.1). Hobbes's claim is probably stronger than he would have wanted to assert upon reflection, since in other places he defines REASON as computation. All he needs to say is that reason provides the means by which the laws of nature are discovered. He holds in *De Cive* that the laws of nature are nothing but "dictates of reason" (*DC* 3.25). There is some reason to think that sometime between the publication of the revised edition of *De Cive* in 1647 and the writing of *Leviathan* in 1650–1, he altered his idea of a law of nature. In the earlier two works, God plays no essential role in making the laws of nature to be laws even though He also commands them and reveals them to people through the Bible (*DC* 3.33, 4.1; *EL* 1.17.12, 1.18.1). In *Leviathan*, God seems to be essential to the laws of nature. They would not properly be laws if God did not command them, or so some scholars have argued (e.g., Taylor, "The Ethical Doctrine of Hobbes"; Warrender, *The Political Philosophy of Hobbes*; Martinich, *The Two Gods of Leviathan*). Other scholars remain unconvinced. The dispute concerns the proper interpretation of Hobbes's definition of a law of nature. In general, the definition in *Leviathan* is more expansive, yet much more problematic to interpret. There he says that a law of nature is (1) a precept or general rule, (2) found out by reason, (3) by which a person is forbidden to do that which would destroy her life directly or indirectly (*L* 14.3). These three aspects of the definition need to be discussed.

(1) "Precept" is a vague or ambiguous term. Many commentators have taken "precept" to mean something other than law or command. They think that a precept is a prudential counsel, something that can guide a person in some behavior but does not impose an obligation. There are several strong objections to this interpretation. One is that the word was commonly used in the seventeenth century to mean law. This leads other scholars to hold that "precept" means law in this context. These latter scholars may also point to the phrase in apposition, "general rule," and suggest that Hobbes is apparently disambiguating the term in the direction

182

of having "precept" mean law. The upshot of this interpretation is that the laws of nature are genuine laws. Although this interpretation is more plausible than the first, it is not compelling. It assumes that "rule" is tantamount in meaning to law or command; and that may not be the case. It is possible that "precept" and "rule" mean any action-guiding proposition, not necessarily a law and not necessarily a prudential maxim.

There is a third interpretation of "precept or general rule" that allows the same result as the second, namely, that the laws of nature are genuine laws, but it interprets "precept" as just indicated, as any action-guiding proposition. Laws and prudential maxims would be two types of precepts. This definition fits both general seventeenth-century usage and Hobbes's own. He uses the phrase "precept or general rule of reason" to refer jointly to the right of nature and the fundamental law of nature (L 14.4). It is plausible that "precept" applies to the right of nature, which is not a law, and "general rule" to the fundamental law of nature. Also, much later, in the context of contrasting "law" and "counsel," Hobbes uses the word "precept" to apply to both (L 43.5). If "precept or general rule" means action-guiding proposition, then Hobbes is using the phrase to indicate the genus to which the laws of nature belong. Interpreting "precept or general rule" as having a generic sense is also confirmed by his use of the phrase shortly later. The laws of nature belong to that category of precepts that express what is "forbidden."

(2) The laws of nature are found out by reason. On the one hand, they are not the result of some special revelation by God; and on the other hand, they are not invented by human beings. There is an objective order in the universe, created by God, which human beings come to know by using their reason.

In *Leviathan*, Hobbes wants to emphasize the difference between the law of nature and the right of nature, and more generally, law and right. A right is a liberty; a law is a duty. A right is an open area of action; a law restricts an area: "law and right differ as much as obligation and liberty" (L 14.3). This much seems clear, but a problem emerges from his next claim, that a right and a law "in one and the same matter are inconsistent." It would seem, on the contrary, that parents have both a right and a duty to care for their children; that teachers have both a right and a duty to teach. Even for Hobbes, it is not clear how his claim here can be correct. He said in *Leviathan* 14.1 that people have a right to preserve their lives, and in 14.3 that there is a law that people preserve themselves. The law and the right of self-preservation seem to concern one and the same matter and not to be inconsistent with each other. If Hobbes is confused on this matter, it may explain the difficulty of interpreting what he calls "a precept or general rule of reason" (L 14.4).

183

(3) The word "forbidden" in the definition then specifies the kind of action-guiding proposition that a law of nature is: it is a law. If something is forbidden, then someone must forbid it. Whoever does the forbidding is the lawgiver, for only someone in authority can forbid anything. This raises the question of who the lawgiver is who does the forbidding. Hobbes often says that it is God (*L* 31.7, 31.34; *DC* 4.1, 15.8). But one may object that "forbidden" is not being used strictly in this context but in either a metaphorical or transferred sense, notwithstanding Hobbes's strong objections to using metaphor in philosophy. One reason for thinking that "forbidden" is being used metaphorically is that in the same context Hobbes says that "everyone is governed by his own reason" (*L* 14.4). If reason can govern people, then it is plausible that reason can forbid certain things.

If the laws of nature are only metaphorically forbidden, by reason, then they would seem to be not genuine laws, but either prudential maxims or hypothetical assertoric propositions. Some scholars support this interpretation by appealing to the final paragraph of chapter 15. They interpret Hobbes as saying there that the laws of nature are dictates of reason and are "improperly" called laws. But that is not what he says. Rather, he says that "These dictates of reason, men use to call by the name of laws; but improperly, for they are but conclusions or theorems concerning what conduces to the conservation and defence of themselves" (*L* 15.41). It would be odd for Hobbes to use the phrase "men use to call" to report his own use of "laws of nature" and even odder for him to be saying that his use is improper. If he were one of the "men" who use the word "law" improperly, he should have given some indication that he belonged to that group. It makes more sense of the language to understand Hobbes in this passage to be pointing the finger at others who use the term improperly when his use is proper. Further, he goes on to say that the dictates of reason, considered as the word of God, are "properly called laws" (*L* 15.41). Later, he says that God promulgates the laws of nature through reason (*L* 31.3). On purely interpretive grounds, it is more plausible to understand such language as contrasting the improper use of other people with the author's, that is, Hobbes's, proper use. Moreover, there is nothing in the above passage that requires one to identify a dictate of reason with an entire law of nature rather than with only a part. A law, according to Hobbes, has two parts: a form, which expresses the will of the lawgiver, and a content, which says what is to be done or not done. The "dictates of reason" that Hobbes refers to may be only the content of the laws and not the form. And this interpretation is consonant with saying that the use of "law" to refer to mere dictates of reason is improper. I do not want to suggest that this settles the problem of properly interpreting Hobbes's idea, which has vexed scholars for decades.

It is impossible to settle once and for all how Hobbes wants "forbidden" to be taken here.

The definition that Hobbes gives of "law of nature" is not itself a law of nature. The individual laws of nature follow from the definition plus the statement of the wretchedness of human beings in the STATE OF NATURE. The law of nature supplies human beings with the rational basis for setting up the normative machinery they need to get out of the state of nature. (The non-normative machinery needed is the fear of death, the desire for a comfortable life, and the hope that they can help themselves (*L* 13.14).) There is a similar discussion of the relation between the state of nature and the law of nature in *De Cive*, chapters 1 and 2.

law of nature, fundamental There are two formulations of the fundamental law of nature. The first formulation is the logically stronger one, and it occurs in both *The Elements of Law* (1640) and *De Cive* (1642). In that version, the first and fundamental law of nature is "that peace be sought after, where it may be found, and where not there to provide ourselves for helps of war" (*DC* 2.2). It has two parts then: (1) to seek peace; (2) to use self-defense (*EL* 1.15.1; *DC* 15.2).

In *Leviathan* (1651), the fundamental law of nature consists of the first element only: to seek peace. Elements (1) and (2) are still combined, but under the title of "a precept or general rule of reason." Element (1) is said to be the first law of nature, as I have just stated, and element (2) is said to be "the sum of the right of nature" (*L* 14.4). Renaming the earlier formulation of the fundamental law of nature as a precept or general rule of reason is Hobbes's attempt to make the concept of the right of nature do some work. (It should be noted that Hobbes used the idea of the right of nature as the foil for explaining the idea of the law of nature at the beginning of chapter 14.) But the right of nature is logically superfluous. To the extent that element (1) of the fundamental law of nature can be derived from Hobbes's principles, element (2) can also. Self-preservation entails that one should make war if that is necessary just as much as that one should seek peace.

From what then does the first or fundamental law of nature follow precisely? In *Leviathan*, the fundamental law of nature follows from the definition of a law of nature and from the natural condition of human beings. A law of nature is defined as a precept or general rule, found out by reason, by which a person is forbidden to do that which would destroy her life directly or indirectly (*L* 14.3). Since both not making peace and not defending oneself (in the natural condition) would destroy one's life, both are forbidden by the definition of the law of nature, and both seeking peace and defending oneself are commanded. The right of nature

185

does not enter into this line of reasoning at all. Indeed, in both *The Elements of Law* and *De Cive*, seeking peace and self-defense are both part of the fundamental law, as we have seen.

The derivation of the fundamental law of nature is slightly different in *The Elements of Law* and *De Cive*. Whoever has a right to some end (goal) has a right to the means to that end. Everyone has a right to self-preservation. Therefore, everyone has a right to the means to self-preservation. There are two means to self-preservation: to make peace and to defend oneself. Therefore, everyone has the right to these things as means. But how does one get from this right to a law? The crucial premise is that reason is the law of nature. That is, by its nature, reason dictates and governs the means one uses to achieve ends (*EL* 1.15.1). Thus, since there are two means to self-preservation, reason dictates these means, as formulated in the first or fundamental law of self-preservation. Hobbes also identifies a law of nature with a "dictate of right reason" (*DC* 2.1). One problem with this view is that in other places Hobbes insists that reason is mere calculation, and it does not make sense to hold that a calculation can dictate anything.

laws, division of Hobbes discusses ways of dividing laws in all three of his political treatises. The neatest division is the one presented in *Leviathan*:

(1)   Natural: the laws of nature
(2)   Positive:
    (a)   Divine: God's commands to particular people
    (b)   Human:
        (i)   Distributive: deal with the rights of subjects
        (ii)   Penal: deal with punishments (*L* 26.36–9).

Some people distinguish between fundamental and non-fundamental laws. Hobbes does not accept any of the justifications that are typically given for such a distinction, so he offers his own. A fundamental law is one which, if it is broken, destroys the commonwealth. A non-fundamental law is one which, if broken, does not (*L* 26.41–2).

While the ways in which Hobbes distinguishes laws are not as neat in the other two political treatises, they are in some ways more interesting. In *The Elements of Law*, Hobbes says that how one divides laws depends upon what one takes as the principle of division. He mentions three. First, if the lawgiver is taken as the principle, then laws can be divided into divine, natural, and civil. Second, if the method of promulgating the laws is taken as the principle, then they may be divided into written and unwritten. Third, if the people to whom the law is addressed are taken as the principle,

186

then they may be divided into (simply) laws and penal laws (*EL* 2.10.6). Laws *simpliciter* are addressed to all people; for example, "Do not kill." Penal laws are addressed to judges; they give instructions about how to dispose of criminals, such as, "If a person kills another, he must serve forty years in jail."

The three-fold division of divine, natural, and civil is misleading, because the natural law is identical with the divine law since God is the author of both of them (*EL* 2.10.7). The three-fold division sensibly disappears in *De Cive*, which divides laws by author into divine and human. The divine law is then divided into natural and positive law (*DC* 14.4). Natural divine law thereupon is identified with the moral law, which, Hobbes says, "in this whole book I have endeavoured to unfold" (*DC* 14.4). What makes this remark puzzling is that sometimes Hobbes says that the law of nature is a genuine law, and sometimes he says that it is not. When he says that it is, then God is the lawgiver (*DC* 4.1, 6.13). When he says that it is not, then it is merely a dictate of reason (*DC* 2.1). Hobbes is simply ambivalent. Hobbes had, I would suggest, both a conservative and an innovative streak that he could not reconcile. As a conservative, who favored an absolute monarchy and top-down government in general, Hobbes believed the traditional view that God is the author of the laws of nature and so arranged the world that people who disobeyed them would eventually be severely punished. On the other hand, as an innovative, modernist thinker, he saw that human beings had to take care of themselves and could not depend upon God to arrange their daily affairs. Thus, he did not want to recognize any law other than laws that human beings made. He wanted the state of nature to be as unpleasant and lawless as possible; and thus he was sometimes led to deny that the laws of nature are genuine laws. What I am offering is a conjecture; scholars are thoroughly divided in their interpretation of Hobbes on this point.

God's natural law goes by two names. When it applies to human beings as individuals, it is called the law of nature. When it applies to them as they are grouped in commonwealths, it is called the law of nations. It is the same law masquerading under two names. Worse, the law of nations is sometimes "vulgarly . . . termed the right of nations." Hobbes's objection to the term "right of nations" concerns his insistence that there is a difference between law and right, which most political theorists confuse (*DC* 14.4; *EL* 2.10.10). (*See* RIGHT OF NATURE).

Positive divine law is the law that God legislated to particular peoples at particular times "by the word of prophecy" (*DC* 14.4). The Jews are the only people mentioned as being governed by positive divine law.

Human law, the other term of the primary distinction of laws by author, is identical with civil law. In *De Cive*, it is subdivided into sacred and

187

secular law. Sacred civil law deals with matters of religion: "that is to say, to the ceremonies and worship of God: to wit, what persons, things, places, are to be consecrated and in what fashion; what opinions concerning the Deity are to be taught publicly; and with what words and in what order supplications are to be made" (*DC* 14.5). One of the principal causes of discontent under the early Stuarts concerned ceremonial issues, such as whether the communion table/altar – people fought over which it was – would be located in the center of the church or at the eastern end; whether the minister would wear a surplice or not; and whether the sign of the cross would be made during baptism. These were some of the main issues between puritan and non-puritan members of the Church of England. Eventually, these disputes contributed to some people joining the Presbyterian church in England and others becoming Independents. To Hobbes, who had a personal preference for the liturgically rich ceremonies, these matters were not part of the essence of religion. How people worship should be settled by the sovereign.

The other term of the sacred/secular division, secular civil law, is divided into distributive and penal laws. Penal laws (also referred to as "vindictive laws"), as explained above where they were discussed in *The Elements of Law*, give instructions to judges about what punishment should be assigned to a criminal. Penal laws and distributive laws are not two kinds of law but two parts of the law. They cannot be separated, because if they were, then violating a distributive law would have no punishment assigned to it; and that is impossible. Hobbes does not say that laws without punishments are not laws but says that they are "in vain," and his definition of LAW does not say anything about punishment. Laws do not bestow rights; they remove rights from others (*DC* 14.7–8). Distributive laws are rules that guarantee each person what is due to her, especially in the form of property laws (*DC* 14.6). Hobbes does not mention commutative justice in *De Cive*. In *Leviathan*, he denies the distinction between distributive and commutative justice, because the traditional explanation of commutative justice is incoherent. According to the tradition, it deals with giving and getting things of equal value. Hobbes's objection is that what something is worth depends upon how much a person desires it, and there is nothing morally objectionable about selling more dearly than one bought (*L* 15.14).

What is listed in *The Elements of Law* as the second principle used in dividing laws, namely, the method of promulgating them, is introduced in *De Cive* as part of a discussion of "the essence of law," a discussion that follows upon that of the various ways of dividing laws. Laws are again divided into written and unwritten. "Written law" is a misnomer according to Hobbes, because explicitly promulgated laws are as old as mankind and

188

thus precede the invention of writing. "Written law" is better understood as law that is backed by someone's voice (*vox*), because laws were articulated in order to help people remember them. Unwritten laws are identical with the laws of nature. Hobbes thinks that they are too obvious to need publication. He sidesteps the issue of the authority and character of the laws of nature by talking metonymically: the law of nature commands us (*DC* 14.14).

One difference between *The Elements of Law* and *De Cive* is that in the latter Hobbes spends some time on the epistemological issue of how subjects know whether the sovereign has passed a law or not. In a democracy, the problem is minimal, because the people as a whole pass the laws. And if a citizen is absent, she can rely upon the word of her fellow-citizens to inform her of new legislation. The problem is more difficult in monarchies and aristocracies. Few subjects or citizens are present when laws are made under these governments. In such cases, edicts and decrees must be relied upon. Hobbes's discussion of this matter was probably inspired by the disputes between the king and parliament during the early 1640s over who had the power of making laws. But his treatment of the issue would have been of no practical benefit to either party (*DC* 14.13).

laws of nature (*leges naturales*)   This entry deals with the specific laws of nature that Hobbes gives in various works. (For the definition of the concept, *see* LAW OF NATURE.)

The first law of nature, which is either to seek peace or to seek peace and, failing that, to use self-defense, is said in *Leviathan* to follow from the definition of "law of nature" and a statement of the natural condition of human beings. That is, "Every human being is to seek peace" follows from "Every human being is to preserve her life" and "The state of war tends to destroy life" (*L* 14.3–4). In *De Cive*, Hobbes argues that a person who has a right to an end (goal) has a right to the means to that end; people have a right to preserve their own life; peace and self-defense are the means to preserve one's own life; one therefore has a right to these as means; reason dictates the means to ends; one ought to do what reason dictates; therefore, one ought to seek peace and use self-defense. (*See* LAW OF NATURE, FUNDAMENTAL.)

Both *De Cive* and *Leviathan* contain twenty numbered laws of nature. The lists are very similar, but there are some notable variations. The difference between the two versions of the first or fundamental law of nature is discussed in LAW OF NATURE, FUNDAMENTAL. The second law, stated below as (2/1′), appears in both works, but in *De Cive*, while it is said to follow from the first, it is not given a separate number (cf. *EL* 1.15.2). In *Leviathan*, all the laws are presented in chapters 14 and 15 except for the last, "Every person is bound to protect the sovereign in a war," which is stated as something of an afterthought in the "Review and Conclusion." Its addition was probably motivated by the execution of Charles I. Historically it is significant. Hobbes is often portrayed as writing *Leviathan* in defense of the victorious anti-royalist cause in order to enhance his chances of resuming residence in England safely. Yet, *Leviathan* is filled with defenses of the royalist cause, of which the last law of nature is an example.

Leviathan is the *locus classicus* for the laws of nature and the numbering below reflects that fact. The numeral preceding the mark "/" is the one it has in *Leviathan*; the numeral after the mark is the one it has in *De Cive*. If a law appears in the one work but not the other, only one numeral is given. While the laws in *The Elements of Law* are similar to those in the other two works, there are some notable differences. The order is somewhat different. Also, the laws are not numbered and thus not numbered below. Three laws that appear in *The Elements of Law* do not appear in the other two works; they are listed below as "(*)," "(**)," and "(***)." Whenever convenient, a short title has been given to the law in order to aid the reader in finding a law on a particular topic.

(1/1)   Seek peace (*L* 14.4). (In *De Cive*, self-defense is a second component of the law (*DC* 2.2).)

(2/1′)   Lay down the right to all things to the extent that others are willing to do the same (*L* 14.5; *DC* 2.3; *EL* 1.15.2).

(3/2)   Fulfill contractual obligations (*L* 15.1; *DC* 3.1).

(4/3)   Gratitude: Do not give a person who has given you a gift reason to regret it (*L* 15.16; *DC* 3.8; *EL* 1.16.6–7).

(5/4)   Compliance: Try to accommodate yourself to others (*L* 15.17; *DC* 3.9; *EL* 1.16.8).

(6/5)   Forgiveness: Forgive people who repent and desire it (*L* 15.18; *DC* 3.10; *EL* 1.16.9).

(7/6)   Revenge should be taken only to the extent that good will seem to come of it (*L* 15.19; *DC* 3.11; *EL* 1.16.10).

(8/7)   "Contumely": Do not give any indication of hatred or contempt to others (*L* 15.20; *DC* 3.12; *EL* 1.16.11).

(9/8)   Equality: Acknowledge that each person is one's equal by nature (*L* 15.21; *DC* 3.13; *EL* 1.17.1). Violating this law is pride.

(10/9)   In a covenant establishing peace, the conditions for each party should be the same; one is not to try to keep a right that the other person is forced to give up (*L* 15.22; *DC* 3.14; *EL* 1.17.2).

(11/10) Equity: Judges should be impartial in rendering decisions and should not favor one party over the other (*L* 15.23; *DC* 3.15).

(12/11) What cannot be divided should be shared in common; what is practically unlimited should not be restricted in its use; what is limited should be shared proportionately (*L* 15.25; *DC* 3.16; *EL* 1.17.3).

(13/12) Lots: The distribution of what cannot be divided or shared is to be determined by lot (*L* 15.26; *DC* 3.17; *EL* 1.17.4).

(14/13) Some distributions of goods are to be determined by arbitrary lots, that is, with the method agreed upon by the principals, and some are to be determined by natural lots, such as primogeniture (*L* 15.27–8; *DC* 3.18; *EL* 1.17.5).

(15/14) Mediators of peace are to be allowed safe conduct (*L* 15.29; *DC* 3.19; *EL* 1.16.13).

(16/15) Arbitration: Those in dispute are to submit the issue to an arbitrator (*L* 15.30; *DC* 3.20; *EL* 1.17.6).

(17/16) Against self-judgement: No one may be the judge in a dispute that concerns her own interests or desires (*L* 15.31; *DC* 3.21; *EL* 1.17.7).

(18/17) No one may be a judge in a dispute if she will benefit from a particular decision (*L* 15.32; *DC* 3.22; *EL* 1.17.7).

(19/18) No witness is to be given more credence than any other all other things being equal (*L* 15.33; *DC* 3.23).

(/19) A judge cannot have any contractual relationship to any of the parties to a dispute (*DC* 3.24; *EL* 1.17.7).

(/20) Sobriety: Do not get drunk (*DC* 3.25). (In *Leviathan*, drunkenness is said to be against the law of nature, as are other excesses such as gluttony, but is not numerated, because it is not relevant to getting out of the state of nature (*L* 15.34; *DC* 3.32).)

(20/) Every person is bound to protect the sovereign in a war (*L* "Review and Conclusion" 5).

(*) Free trade: Men are to allow commerce and traffic equally to all (*EL* 1.16.12).

(**) Give advice only to people who want it (*EL* 1.17.8).

(***) Laws are not to be observed to our detriment if in our own judgement the harm would be caused by the failure of another person to observe the same laws (*EL* 1.17.10).

Hobbes says that some people may find his deductions of these laws of nature difficult. A more intuitive confirmation of their status may be derived from the use of the principle "Do not do unto others what you would not have them do unto you" (*L* 15.35, 27.4; *DC* 3.26; *EL* 1.17.9, 1.18.9). This is sometimes called the negative formulation of the Golden Rule and is the one that Hobbes typically uses although he does use the affirmative formulation on occasion: "Do unto others as you would have them do unto you" (*L* 17.2). (Hobbes does not use the name of the rule.) An alternative way of seeing the cogency of the laws of nature is to imagine oneself in the place of the other (*EL* 1.17.9; see also *L* 15.35).

Hobbes uses his discussion of law (***) to say that the laws of nature bind *in foro interno*, that is, in an internal forum, which is identified with a person's conscience, not *in foro externo*. Hobbes says that what this means is that a person should want them to regulate her behavior, but that they cannot always do so. It would be absurd for a person to keep her promises if no one else did, for that would ensure her own ruin, contrary to the purpose of the laws of nature (*EL* 1.17.10; *L* 15.36; *DC* 3.27). A related maxim is *inter arma silent leges* (among armaments the laws are silent) (*EL* 1.19.2; *DC* 5.2). However, certain laws cannot be broken under any circumstances, such as (7/6), which does not allow revenge to be exacted beyond what will produce good (*DC* 3.27 note). This does not mean that excessive damage done to a person is always a breach of that law. Since each person is her own judge in the state of nature, she may punish someone too harshly without guilt.

Most, but not all, of the laws are formulated with a verb in the indicative mood and do not use "ought" or "should" or cognate words. This raises the question that Hume asked explicitly about moral laws. How does one derive conclusions that contain the verb "ought" as the main verb from premises that do not? Hobbes in effect sidesteps the question by, for the most part, formulating the laws without the use of "ought" and "should." And those that do contain those words could be reworded in a way that would not contain them. For example, "the right of all men to all things ought not to be retained" could be paraphrased as "the right of all men to all things is not to be retained." Nonetheless, the obvious normative and prescriptive force of the original sentence seems to be retained in the paraphrase. So a second question can be added to the Humean one: In what sense are the laws of nature normative or prescriptive?

One standard answer that scholars have given to the second question is that the laws of nature, as Hobbes presents them, are not moral laws in the traditional sense. They are prudential maxims, which can be used to guide behavior but do not impose a moral obligation as philosophers have traditionally thought of it. They are what Kant would call hypothetical assertoric laws. That is, given a certain goal, such as wanting to preserve one's life, they specify how to achieve that goal. The answer to the Humean question then is either that there is no derivation from "is" to "ought" or that "ought" simply signifies a means to an end, *pace* the classical tradition of philosophy. On either answer, the laws of nature only say what is the case: what the means to the given end of self-preservation are. This interpretation works well for *The Elements of Law* and *De Cive*.

192

It does not work so well for *Leviathan*, even though Hobbes still formulates most of the laws of nature without using the words "ought" and "should." In *Leviathan*, the verbal formulas under discussion express only the content of the laws, that is, the part that is deducible by reason. The rest of the law consists of the phrase "I [God] command that," which expresses the authority by which the content becomes a law, in contrast, say, with a counsel. (*See further* LAW OF NATURE.)

The laws of nature are immutable and eternal in the sense that they do not change and are discovered by people using their reason; they are not artificial or invented. By definition, pride, ingratitude, breach of contract, and inhumanity are always unlawful. However, some behavior that is lawful in some circumstances may be unlawful in other circumstances (*L* 15.38; *DC* 3.29)

Hobbes is rather sanguine in his derivation of the laws of nature. In *Leviathan*, he takes on the skeptic who claims that justice is "but a word" and that, if laws of nature were genuinely deducible from reason, then someone would have done it before now. Hobbes begins his refutation of this position by arguing from analogy. The skeptic is just like a savage who denies that a durable house can be built, because she is unable to build one. Hobbes then gives an Enlightenment defense of progress in morality and politics:

> Time and industry produce every day new knowledge. And as the art of well building is derived from principles of reason observed by industrious men that had long studied the nature of materials and the diverse effects of figure and proportion long after mankind began (though poorly) to build: so, long time after men have begun to constitute commonwealths, imperfect and apt to relapse into disorder, there may principles of reason be found out by industrious meditation to make their constitution (excepting by external violence) everlasting. (*L* 30.5)

Leviathan (1651) [13]   *Leviathan* is Hobbes's *magnum opus*. It contains a theory of the natural world, of human beings, of politics, and of religion. Because of its importance and comprehensiveness, it has been called "a Bible for modern man" (Martinich, *The Two Gods of Leviathan*). It was written quickly in late 1650 and early 1651. A substantially different Latin version was published in Amsterdam in 1668.

The name "Leviathan" comes from biblical mythology. Leviathan is a principle of chaos and an enemy of Yahweh (Pss 74:13–14, 104:26; Job 3:8, 41:1–34). Although it is sometimes represented as a crocodile or whale, it is supposed to be a mythic creature. Many authors associated Leviathan, like Behemoth, with evil, but not all. Shakespeare uses "Leviathan" to express speed and to suggest strength. Marvell in "Anniversary of the Government under O.C." uses the term to refer to a large ship. And Milton uses it to refer to largeness (*Paradise Lost* 7:412–16). Hobbes's own use of the term would not make sense if he thought of Leviathan as evil. For him, Leviathan is the civil government, and the civil government is the earthly savior of human beings and the principle of order, which depends upon God to function: "Leviathan [is] . . . that mortal God, to which we owe under the immortal God, our peace and defence" (*L* 17.13). He associates the sovereign with Leviathan because human beings need government because their pride makes them uncooperative: "God having set forth the great power of Leviathan called him King of the Proud" (*L* 28.27).

Leviathan consists of four parts: I. Of Man; II. Of Commonwealth; III. Of a Christian Commonwealth; IV. Of the Kingdom of Darkness. The first two parts are supposed to deal quite generally with the nature of human beings and the nature of civil government. The last two parts deal with governments with Christian sovereigns and subjects.

The first part, "Of Man," may itself be seen to consist of two parts. The first dozen or so chapters give a naturalistic and mechanistic explanation of human cognitive and affective states and abilities. Human beings are made up of small bodies in motion, and motion explains everything about them. Life itself is a kind of motion, and when the motion stops, the human being is dead. SENSATION is caused by the motion of external bodies pressing on the sense organs. This causal action generates further motions that go from the sense organs along nerve paths to the brain and ultimately the heart, which is the center of thinking and emotion. The heart then generates a counterforce that proceeds towards the exterior of the body. It is this motion outward that gives human beings the impression that the causes of their sensations are outside of them. All human action depends upon desires, which are motions of bodies that are too small to be measured (*See* ENDEAVOR.) WILL is the last desire before an animal acts. (Both human beings and beasts have will.) Human beings are free if their actions are not forcibly caused by external objects. But the will is not free, and no one can will to will. The will is caused by other bodily motions or desires, which are caused by some preceding bodily motion, which is caused ultimately by some moving body outside the person.

The transitional chapter between the first and second parts of Part I is chapter 12, "Of Religion." RELIGION is characteristic of human beings and thus belongs with Hobbes's discussion of their cognitive and affective abilities. The natural causes of religion are a mixture of some good qualities, such as curiosity, and several bad ones, such as ignorance of causes. A large part of the chapter deals with SUPERSTITION and other abuses of religion.

Yet, religion is an essential component of the civil state, and thus is related to Hobbes's views about law and covenant.

Chapters 13–16 are preparatory to Part II, "Of Commonwealth." They deal with the natural condition of human beings, which is a condition of misery and wretchedness, with the LAWS OF NATURE, which prescribe that people make peace with each other and give them the wherewithall to do so, and with what a person is. They thus present the immediate foundations of Hobbes's political theory. Chapter 13 argues that without a government each human being is at war with every other. (*See* STATE OF NATURE.) Chapter 14 argues that, given that condition, human beings ought to try to establish peace and this requires that each person give up some of her rights. These are the first two laws of nature. In chapter 15, Hobbes explains how COVENANTS that will guarantee peace can be created on the basis of these first two laws. The rest of the chapter then deduces additional laws of nature.

The second part of *Leviathan*, "Of Commonwealth," begins with a chapter on the origin of the COMMONWEALTH. In succeeding chapters, Hobbes presents his views on such issues as the difference between a government instituted by people not immediately threatened with death and a government instituted by people at the brink of death (chapters 18–20), the conditions that cause a commonwealth to flourish and the conditions that destroy one (chapters 24 and 29), the nature of civil law (chapters 25 and 26), and the right of a sovereign to govern and his duty to God (chapter 30). The final chapter of this part, "Of the Kingdom of God by Nature," suggests that all government is founded in God's natural right to rule in virtue of His irresistible power. It forms a transition to the next part of the book.

The third part, "Of a Christian Commonwealth," contains the essence what is naturally called Hobbes's theology, even though he claims that theology is not part of science or philosophy. In several chapters, Hobbes gives a brilliant analysis of the composition of the BIBLE. He argues that most of the Old Testament was written long after the events described in it and by authors unknown to us. He was the first person to argue – one or two others may have implied it – that Moses could not have written the entire Pentateuch. The New Testament was written soon after the events described in it by witnesses to the events or by people closely associated with those witnesses.

Concerning certain concepts that are crucial to biblical religion, Hobbes argues that no one can know when REVELATION has occurred; that, when the word "SPIRIT" is used literally, it refers to a material object; that PROPHETS can deceive people and be deceived; that each Christian state is its own church; and that two things are required for SALVATION: FAITH and obedience.

195

The faith referred to is belief that Jesus is the Christ (Messiah); the obedience referred to is obedience to one's sovereign. Hobbes also argues that the KINGDOM OF GOD does not currently exist. There was a kingdom of God that lasted from Abraham (or Moses) until the selection of Saul, and there will be a second kingdom of God at the second coming of Jesus. But for the meantime God commands, through the laws of nature, that people obey their sovereign. The third part as a whole can be considered a treatise on the correct understanding of the kingdom of God. To complement it, it is appropriate to have a part on the kingdom of darkness.

The fourth part of *Leviathan* thus concerns the KINGDOM OF DARKNESS, which is defined as anything that interferes with a person's salvation. There are four categories of obstacles: misinterpreting the Bible (chapter 44); the influence of pagan demonology on Christianity (chapter 45); the influence of Greek philosophy on Christianity (chapter 46); and misrepresenting the history and traditions of Christianity, often by mingling demonology with Greek philosophy (chapter 46). Chapter 47, the final one, describes the aims of this obfuscation and who it is that benefits.

Leviathan ends with "A Review and Conclusion," which has sometimes been interpreted as defending a *de facto* theory of government, namely, the position that any entity that holds power over people is a legitimate government. That is not Hobbes's position. He holds that two things are required for sovereignty: overwhelming power to protect people; and their consent. Merely overpowering a person is VICTORY, not conquest. In *Considerations upon the Reputation . . . of Thomas Hobbes*, Hobbes claims that he wrote the "Review and Conclusion" in order to explain to the defeated royalists how they could behave honorably under the Commonwealth. His position was that once a person's sovereign is defeated she is free to covenant with others to establish another sovereign. A royalist's taking the Oath of Engagement actually hurt Charles II less than not taking it would have done, because those who did not take it had their entire estate forfeited to the parliamentary powers (*EW* 4:423–4). It is possible that Hobbes was indirectly defending the behavior of his patron, the third earl of Devonshire. After leaving England with other royalists during the Civil War, the earl returned to his estates in 1645 in order to avoid having them confiscated. The earl seems to have been shunned by Charles II and his court after the Restoration, and he rarely left his estates afterwards to go to London.

The Latin edition of *Leviathan* is part translation and part expansion and emendation. The body of the Latin text is often shorter than the corresponding passage in the English text. This suggests that at least part of the Latin text preceded the English one, although it is possible that Hobbes thought that it was enough for him to translate the gist of his thought. The Latin text also contains three appendices, which must have been written after the English text. All three deal with some aspect of religion; and Hobbes was in more danger for his religious views than his political ones. A committee of parliament was assigned to investigate his orthodoxy in 1666; so the appendices were probably written after that time. All three appendices are cast as dialogues between "*A*" and "*B*," with *B* being the more astute discussant. The first appendix is a commentary on the Nicene Creed. *B* explains what each of its articles means, although he sometimes admits to not being sure about the meaning. The second appendix in on HERESY. Like his other treatments of the topic, Hobbes leans on the etymology of "heresy" as the doctrine of a group outside the mainstream; and, through a history of its use, shows that subjects should not be punished for heretical views. The third appendix answers some theological objections that had been raised against the English version of *Leviathan* concerning Hobbes's view that spirits are material, that God was personated by Moses and the apostles, and that the wicked will be punished on earth.

liberty and necessity (*libertas et necessitas*)   Hobbes is a compatibilist: "liberty and necessity are consistent" (*L* 21.4; *QLNC*, p. 101). Human beings are free (or, as he would say, have liberty) but do not have free will. Every human action has a cause and is therefore necessary, because a cause makes its effect necessary, according to Hobbes. One piece of evidence that he offers for the view that freedom or liberty is compatible with necessity is the theological doctrine that God's actions are necessarily good; that is, they are both free and necessary (*LN*, p. 263). Hobbes discusses liberty and necessity in several works, including *Leviathan* and *De Corpore*. His most extended treatment occurs in his two polemical works against John Bramhall: *Of Liberty and Necessity* and *The Questions Concerning Liberty, Necessity, and Chance*.

Hobbes defines liberty as the absence of all obstacles to movement. According to this definition, even water moves freely or with liberty if it is not impeded by a dam (*LN*, p. 274; *L* 21.1; *DC* 9.9; *AW*, p. 407). Obstacles are understood to be either external objects that impede a movement, or something inside the organism that causes some behavior and that is not part of the natural mechanism for causing behavior (*LN*, p. 273; cf. *L* 21.1). Human beings are free or have liberty whenever the immediate cause of their action is an act of will. If a person is blown over by the wind, then she is not behaving freely. But acts that are compelled in a quite ordinary sense are still free acts of the agent, according to Hobbes. Being compelled to hand over one's money to an armed robber or to jettison goods in a storm is nonetheless a free act,

197

according to Hobbes, because it is caused by an act of will. The agent had the option of being shot or drowning, respectively (*LN*, pp. 264–5; *QLNC*, pp. 260–1, 290; *L* 21.3, 21.22).

Since the WILL and other desires are natural to beasts and human beings, no will or other desire interferes with their liberty. In particular, FEAR, which is a desire, does not interfere with a person's liberty (*L* 21.3). Hobbes needs to hold this position because of his political philosophy. The main desire (will) that leads people to covenant with others to create a civil state is the fear of death. If freedom were incompatible with fear, then sovereign-making covenants would not be valid. (*See* LIBERTY OF SUBJECTS for another political application of the idea of liberty.)

Determinism is a hard doctrine. Hobbes thinks that one obstacle to accepting it is the failure to distinguish between necessity and compulsion. Compulsion is a violent external force that causes some behavior; necessity is simply the causal chain that follows the physical laws of the universe: "thus all men that do anything for love, or revenge, or lust, are free from compulsion, and yet their actions may be as necessary as those that are done by compulsion . . . But free from necessitation, I say, no man can be, and it is that which his Lordship [Bramhall] undertook to disprove" (*LN*, pp. 261–2).

Hobbes has no compunction about speaking of "free agents" or "free men" (*LN*, pp. 259, 272; *L* 21.2). Human beings and beasts are free; but the will is not; it is merely the last desire an animal has before acting. He does not usually make it explicit but he means that the last desire is the one that is causally efficacious in producing an action. Each desire is caused by some prior event, possibly even another desire. Since each cause–effect sequence is necessary, the sequence consisting of the cause of a will (a desire) and the will itself (the last desire prior to an action) is necessary. People act "according to" their wills, but they do not will to will, the phrase "will to will" being absurd (*LN*, pp. 240, 269, 273). The phrase "free will" is also self-contradictory. The clauses "the will wills," "the will suspends itself," and "the will determines itself" are false at best (*QLNC*, p. 4; *ODM*, p. 125). They are false because they attribute self-causation to the will when in fact nothing causes itself, as even scholastic philosophers recognize. It is also incoherent to attribute freedom to anything other than bodies, since "free" applies to a kind of motion and bodies are the only things that move (*L* 21.2). To say that the road is free or that someone speaks freely is to say that someone is free to go along that road or that someone is free to speak (*L* 21.2).

Hobbes sometimes defines "necessity" as what is "unable not to be" (*AW*, p. 424). In *De Corpore*, not "necessity" but "necessary act" is defined: "that, the production whereof it is impossible to hinder; and therefore every act, that shall be produced, shall necessarily be produced . . ." (*DCo* 10.5). Whatever exists, necessarily exists, because what shall be shall be. Most people, especially logicians, would object to Hobbes's alleged proof here that everything is necessary. Attention needs to be paid to the scope of the necessity in whatever form it takes. In the sentence "Necessarily, if Beth is human, then Beth is mortal," "necessarily" has wide scope; that is, what is necessary is the entire proposition that follows it. And, in this case, the proposition is true. "Necessarily" can also have a narrow scope. In the sentence "If necessarily (there are an infinite number of natural numbers), then mathematics is difficult for Beth," the scope of "necessarily" extends only to the end of the first clause; its scope is narrow. The parentheses indicate the words governed by the word "necessarily." The sentence does not say that necessarily mathematics is difficult for Beth. Even though mathematics in fact is difficult for her, it is possible that it need not have been so. The issue is a bit more complicated because sentences like "If Socrates is walking, then he is necessarily moving" are ambiguous. In ordinary English, when "necessarily" is embedded in the predicate of the consequent, it may have either wide or narrow scope. Usually, such sentences are disambiguated by context or by the principle of interpreting sentences in such a way that they come out true rather than false *ceteris paribus*. If the sentence under discussion has large scope, then it is equivalent to "Necessarily, if Socrates is walking, then he is moving" and it is true. If the sentence has narrow scope, then it is equivalent to "If Socrates is walking, then necessarily (he is moving)" and it is false. (Parentheses have been inserted to emphasize that "necessarily" has narrow scope.) It is not necessary that Socrates is moving; he could have been sitting or asleep and thereby at rest. Hobbes does not recognize the distinction between wide and narrow scope or anything similar. He believes that Socrates' movement is necessary, because it is caused by earlier events which make it impossible for Socrates to be in any other state.

John Bramhall, accepting some medieval distinctions, distinguished absolute necessity from hypothetical necessity. This is not the same distinction as that of scope, but it does some of the same work in the present context. It is absolutely necessary that seven is greater than five. But it is only hypothetically necessary that mathematics is difficult for Beth, given the hypothesis (of the antecedent above) that there are an infinite number of natural numbers. Bramhall used the distinction to concede that hypothetical necessity was compatible with liberty, even though absolute necessity was not. That is, given that a person willed to walk (and all other conditions were satisfied), that person necessarily is moving. Hobbes would have no truck with absolute, hypothetical, or any other division of necessity: "I would have your Lordship take notice hereby, how easy and plain

199

a thing, but withal false, with the grave usage of such terms as 'hypothetical necessity,' and 'necessity upon supposition,' and such like terms of School-men, may be obscured and made to seem profound learning" (*LN*, p. 262).

Hobbes's refusal to countenance any distinctions with respect to necessity comes out most clearly when he considers the sentence:

(R)   It is necessary that it will rain tomorrow or it will not rain tomorrow.

The scholastic view was that (R) is true (and even necessarily true) be-cause the sentence "It will rain tomorrow or it will not rain tomorrow" is necessarily true, even though neither of (R)'s disjunctive components is necessarily true. Some scholastics even held that neither of the disjunctive components has a truth-value at all; each is "indeterminate." Hobbes thinks that this is impossible. A proposition is a sentence that has a truth-value, thus each disjunct must have a truth-value. The future is not indetermi-nate or open to more than one outcome, according to Hobbes: "All future events will necessarily take place because of the force of preceding ones . . . At the moment, therefore, those acts exist which at some time will produce that effect we declare to be a future one" (*AW*, pp. 421, 426). It is simply that human beings lack sufficient information to know what that predetermined outcome is. Hobbes believes that (R) is true because one of the disjuncts is necessarily true. Either "it is necessary that it will rain tomorrow" is true or "it is necessary that it will not rain tomorrow" is true. If this were not the case, according to Hobbes, there would be no place for (R)'s necessity to come from (*LN*, p. 277). For all of his bril-liance, Hobbes could be obtuse; this and his futile efforts to square the circle are two examples.

Although the problem of free will and necessity is a topic in metaphys-ics, that is, an issue about how the world is, it grips people because of its apparent ethical ramifications. Free will is necessary, according to its pro-ponents, in order to justify the practice of assigning praise and blame, reward and punishment. It seems that, if a person's will is determined by causes that that person cannot control, then it makes no sense to hold her accountable for her actions. As a compatibilist, Hobbes denies that con-trol in this sense is either intelligible or necessary for assigning responsi-bility. A praiseworthy act is one that is good, and a good action is one that either an individual, a commonwealth, or God wants to be done. A blame-worthy act is the opposite. A sin or crime should be punished not because it was done without necessity but because it was "noxious" (*LN*, p. 253).

Justice and injustice are treated similarly: "not the necessity, but the will to break the law, makes the action unjust, because the law regards the will, and no other precedent causes of action" (*LN*, p. 252). Recall that the will is caused and is the last desire an agent has before acting. Moreover, laws themselves cause and necessitate justice; so justice cannot be incompatible with necessity (*LN*, p. 253). It is quite possible that some people, especially bad people, will try to use the truth of determinism to excuse their behavior; that is a good reason for not publicizing it; but it does not diminish its truth (*LN*, pp. 252, 256–7; *QLNC* pp. 434–5).

A variation on the objection that praise and blame are impossible without free will is the claim that deliberation or planning is in vain without it. Hobbes's reply is that, given the necessity of all actions, it is not the case that a person will choose something whether or not she deliberates; rather, she will choose only what she had deliberated about. The necessity of the connection between deliberation and choice is essential for choice to occur (*LN*, pp. 254–5).

In *De Corpore*, Hobbes defines possibility and impossibility. An event that never occurs is impossible. An event that occurs at some time or other is possible. That is, if something is possible it either has occurred, is occurring, or will occur (*DCo* 10.4–5). Since George Washington never had a grandchild, it was impossible for him to have a grandchild.

So-called "contingent" events are necessary events of the causes of which someone is ignorant (*DCo* 10.5; *LN*, p. 259). Many would concede that past events are necessary, and yet they would say about something in the past of which they lack knowledge that it is possible that it did not happen. For example, suppose that Smith was forbidden to go to Soho but did. Jones, not knowing the facts and intending to defend her friend, may say, "It's possible that Smith did not go to Soho." What this example shows is that some necessary events are said possibly not to be so (*DCo* 10.5).

liberty of subjects Since all phenomena must ultimately be explained in terms of the motions of bodies, it should not be surprising that Hobbes relates the liberty that human beings have to the liberty of bodies. Just as every body has liberty when its motion is not obstructed by external objects, so a human being has liberty when her action is not obstructed. In addition to the natural bonds that restrict every body, human beings create artificial bonds or chains called "civil laws." Although the laws themselves are easy to break, they usually restrain human behavior because of the fear of the dire consequences of breaking them (*L* 21.4).

In the state of nature, human beings are restrained only by physical obstacles. In other words, physical obstacles being excluded, the state of nature is a state of complete liberty. Once human beings enter a civil state by covenanting with each other to lay down their right to all things, they lose that liberty. Hobbes gives two different accounts of what rights people retain. Sometimes he says they retain the right to any behavior that is not

201

prohibited by the civil laws (*L* 21.6, 21.18). Sometimes he implies that they retain only those rights that cannot be given up in any circumstances: the right to self-defense, the right to the use of food, medicine, air, and anything else needed to survive (*L* 21.12, 21.13, 21.15).

Most people think that a life of liberty is better than life under the law. Hobbes tries to disabuse them of that notion. If liberty is the absence of law, then every person has the right to kill every other person, and this is a wretched state in which to be (*L* 21.6, 21.8). (*See* STATE OF NATURE.) The false ideology of liberty is not innocuous. It is one of the chief causes of civil war and can be traced back directly to the ancient Greek and Roman thinkers (*L* 21.8–9; *DC* 10.8). Aristotle, for example, taught that people living in a democracy are commonly held to be freer than under any other form of government (*L* 21.9). Hobbes thought that this view was false, because the sovereign has the same power under any form of government; so subjects are equally constrained under any form of government. The fact that the city of Lucca had "Libertas" written on its turrets, does not mean that the people were freer there than in other cities. What is free is the commonwealth itself in relation to other commonwealths, because every one of them is in the state of nature with respect to the others (*L* 21.8).

In *The Elements of Law* and *De Cive*, Hobbes had taken a somewhat different line about the liberty of subjects. After explaining that there is essentially no difference in respect of liberty between a child, a servant, and a subject, Hobbes comments on the desire most people have to do whatever they please. He describes liberty as the ability to do whatever is possible without being blocked by physical impediments. In the state of nature, people want to do whatever is necessary to preserve their health or life, but they are often prevented from doing so because of the dangers inherent in that condition. The civil state protects people from precisely these dangers. Thus, for people to complain about having their behavior reined in by the laws is for them to complain of being "restrained from hurting" themselves (*DC* 9.9; *EL* 2.5.2).

love and hate (*amor et odium*)   Love is the same thing as DESIRE; the word "love" is commonly used when the object of desire is present. Hate is the same thing as aversion; the word "hate" is used when the object of aversion is present (*L* 6.3).

M

***

magnanimity (*magnanimitas*)   Magnanimity is CONTEMPT of little helps and hindrances; that is, indifference about whether one receives small helps or is obstructed with small hindrances (*L* 6.26).

martyr   A martyr in its etymological sense is a witness to an event (*L* 42.12). Hobbes exploits this etymology in order to undermine the idea that a martyr is essentially someone who dies for her religious beliefs; and he wants to undermine this idea because it tends to encourage people to oppose their sovereign in the name of religion. Within Christianity, a martyr, according to Hobbes, is strictly a person who witnessed the resurrection of Jesus, whether that person died under persecution or not (*L* 42.13). This restricts the class of genuine martyrs to those who lived during the first century AD (*L* 42.12).

Hobbes discusses martyrs in part three of *Leviathan* as part of his long chapter on the proper role of the church. That role is to teach obedience to the secular sovereign and to instill in people the faith that JESUS is the Messiah (*L* 42.8–9). Christian ministers have no political authority of their own; whatever authority they have depends upon the sovereign. This position is designed to prevent the possibility that a conflict could arise between religious and political authority. Hobbes considers several attempts to find such a conflict. One concerns the proper response of a Christian who is commanded to worship in some way that violates her FAITH. Hobbes holds that when a person is acting in obedience to a command, it is not the subordinate who acts but the superior. But, if a Christian ought to obey the sovereign in every situation except for the sake of self-preservation, what should be said about martyrs who died rather than obey the emperor? Hobbes's response can be considered as consisting of two parts. First, he narrows down the class of martyrs to those who were witnesses to the resurrection, as indicated above. Second, he simply concedes the God called some of them to die for their faith. This response maintains due respect for the early Christian martyrs without allowing them to be exploited to justify rebellion (*L* 42.12). People who defend their rebellious behavior by appealing to the principles of the martyrs are presumptuous and self-serving. Most of them take their stand on tenets that are not even essential to Christianity. There is only one fundamental article of faith, namely, Jesus is the Christ (*L* 42.13). (*See* CHRISTIANITY, ESSENCE OF.)

In *De Cive*, Hobbes had allowed latter-day martyrdom:

> Must we resist princes, when we cannot obey them? Truly, no; for this is contrary to our civil covenant. What must we do then? Go to Christ by martyrdom; which if it seems to any man to be a hard saying, most certain it is that he believes not with his whole heart, that Jesus is the Christ, the Son of the living God; for he would then desire to be dissolved, and to be with Christ; but he would by a feigned Christian faith elude that obedience, which he has contracted to yield unto the city. (*DC* 18.13)

It is plausible that Hobbes tightened up the conditions that permitted martyrdom after he wrote *De Cive* because of the execution of Charles I.

means and ends   A well-known principle is that she who wills the means wills the ends. Although Hobbes never expresses this principle, he implicitly relies upon it in espousing the principle that whoever has a right to an end has a right to the means to that end (*L* 18.8). He appeals to this principle to support his claim that, since everyone has a right to preserve her own life, everyone has a right to everything, even the lives of other people (*L* 14.4). He again appeals to it to justify absolute sovereignty. Since the sovereign has the job of maintaining peace and defending his subjects, he has the right to judge how to do this (*L* 18.8).

memory   *See* IMAGINATION

metaphor   Hobbes thought that the use of metaphor in scientific or philosophical writing was a great evil: "in reckoning, and seeking of truth, such speeches are not to be admitted" (*L* 5.14; *AW*, p. 25). The success of geometry is due to its absence of metaphors. Any science built on definitions as precise as geometrical ones, would be as certain as geometry (*AW*, pp. 256–7).

Metaphors are absurdities (*L* 5.20). Similes, in contrast with metaphors, are acceptable, because they are true and helpful: "In demonstration, in counsel, and all rigorous search of truth, judgement does all; except sometimes the understanding have need to be opened by some apt similitude; and then there is so much use of fancy. But for metaphors, they are in this case utterly excluded. For seeing they openly profess deceit, to admit them into counsel or reasoning were manifest folly" (*L* 8.8). Presumably, he would have thought that there was a big difference between "Laws are chains" and "Laws are like chains" (cf. *EW* 6:490).

One passage may give the misleading impression that metaphors, like other tropes, are not especially offensive. After emphasizing that misused words can never contribute to a cogent argument, Hobbes says, "No more can metaphors, and tropes of speech: but these are less dangerous, because they profess their inconstancy; which the other do not" (*L* 4.24). It may appear that the word "these" applies to the phrase "metaphors, and tropes of speech" while the phrase "which the other do not" applies to misused words; but the Latin makes it clear that "these" (*haec*) has the force of "the latter" and applies only to "tropes of speech." That is, Hobbes is saying that other tropes of speech are less dangerous than metaphors.

In non-technical discourse, the use of metaphors is acceptable, and their apt use is a sign of "good fancy," which is a facility for identifying similarities among things (*L* 8.3; see also *EW* 4:489). Metaphors may also be used in rhetoric (*AW*, p. 25). Later, Hobbes makes the astute observation that for all good metaphors "there is some real ground that may be expressed in proper words" (*L* 38.11). He might have said that doing philosophy is getting rid of the metaphors.

method, philosophical and scientific   Hobbes thinks that the lack of a proper philosophical method prevented progress in philosophy or science until the late sixteenth century. His emphasis on method makes him similar to Descartes although they had different ideas of what correct philosophical method is. The chief discussion of method is in *De Corpore*. It is appropriate for a discussion of methodology to appear near the beginning of a work that purports to present a complete scientific theory of knowledge.

There are two methods in philosophy: the analytic or resolutive and the synthetic or compositive. The analytic method is finding a possible cause for a given effect. The synthetic method is positing a possible effect for a given cause. Hobbes gets his terminology of methodology from the Paduan school of which Galileo was a part. His own account of scientific methodology mixes rationalistic and empiricist elements. Concerning the rationalistic element, when he explains how to determine a cause, he says that first, for some given effect, a possible cause should be thought of; next, parts of it are mentally subtracted from the cause; then the investigator thinks about whether the effect "is still possible to be understood" to exist; if the investigator "cannot conceive" the effect to exist in such a case, then the subtracted part is part of the cause (*DCo* 6.10). Concerning the empirical element, he writes in the same context that, in order to discover the cause of light, "we first examine external things." Hobbes concludes that scientific investigation should be partly analytic and partly synthetic (*DCo* 6.10).

The only things that are ultimately real for Hobbes are bodies. Thus, these are the things that are easiest to know. On the other hand, knowledge consists of propositions containing universals, and it is easier to know what the cause of a universal is than to know what the cause of an individual is. Hobbes also holds that the causes of a whole consist of the causes of its parts (*DCo* 6.2). This is in fact a way of expressing one of the central principles of modern science, namely, that macroscopic events are caused by microscopic events.

miracles   The only one of Hobbes's political treatises in which he discusses the nature of miracles is *Leviathan*, and there he devotes one chapter in part three, "Of a Christian Commonwealth," to the topic. The chapter follows ones devoted to the nature of spirits, angels, the kingdom of God, and prophets, and precedes chapters on eternal life, hell, salvation, and the church. Unlike his treatment of most of these topics, Hobbes does not begin with a survey of various uses of the relevant words. Instead, he presents two related definitions or explications of the concept of miracle.

The first explication occurs at the beginning of the chapter. He says that a miracle is (1) an admirable work (2) of God, (3) done for the most part to show that He is commanding something (*L* 37.1). The crucial elements of this analysis have been enumerated.

Element (1) is the most interesting. An event counts as admirable if it satisfies two conditions: (a) it must have previously occurred rarely or never before; and (b) one cannot imagine, when it occurs, that there is any natural explanation for it. Each of these two conditions is necessary. Concerning (a), even though no one, in Hobbes's day, had any idea of how human beings generate other human beings or how wood can (apparently) turn into stone, the mere fact that these events often occurred meant that they could not be miracles (*L* 37.2–3). Concerning (b), suppose that someone performs the first triple somersault: even though it is unprecedented, it is easy to imagine some natural cause for it; so it is not miraculous. Potentially miraculous events include a horse or cow talking.

Hobbes asserts that the rainbow that Noah saw after the flood that destroyed the world was a miracle (*L* 37.4). It was the first rainbow to have been observed; and although the seventeenth-century had a natural explanation for rainbows, it was a miracle, because Noah and his family did not. (Hobbes's rival, René Descartes, was the first person to understand the physics of rainbows.) The example of the rainbow is interesting because it illustrates how Hobbes was trying to reconcile religion with modern science. On the one hand, Hobbes wanted to preserve religion. On the other hand, he was committed to modern science and saw that there was a tension between the two. His reconciliation here is ingenious. Religion needs miracles only for its foundation; so it is sufficient for religion that miracles occurred only in the past. But science treats the universe as a closed system; it purports to explain everything in terms of other events within the world. Thus, even miracles would have a natural explanation if people knew enough about the world.

Although Hobbes wanted to safeguard religion, he did not want it to subvert the existing political order. If miracles still occurred, they could be used to introduce novelties, first into religion and then subsequently into the political structure as well. So, Hobbes's view about the potential universality of scientific explanation satisfies his desires about religion as well. The more science progresses and explains the world, the fewer the phenomena that could possibly be miracles. Hobbes relativizes this point: "the same thing may be a miracle to one and not to another" (*L* 37.5). It is a miracle to a person too ignorant to know or unable to imagine a natural cause for it, and not a miracle for a person intelligent enough to know or able to imagine one for it. Every observation of a miracle is at the same time a confession of ignorance: "And thence it is that ignorant and superstitious men make great wonders of those works, which other men, knowing to proceed from nature (which is not the immediate but the ordinary work of God) admire not at all" (*L* 37.5; 37.11).

Element (2) can be dealt with briefly. When Hobbes discussed the nature of a prophet earlier in *Leviathan*, he held that even false prophets can work miracles and supported the point with numerous biblical passages (*L* 32.7, 36.20). But in his *ex professo* account of miracles only God can perform miracles. Apparent miracles of false prophets are tricks of some sort (*L* 37.10–12).

Concerning element (3), a miracle is usually, but not necessarily, performed in order to show people that God is commanding them to do something. The first rainbow, as mentioned above, was miraculous, but did not have any commandments connected to it. But for that very reason it was often not called a miracle (*L* 37.6). Since God's special commands always come through a PROPHET, Hobbes sometimes explains element (3) as related to the means by which a prophet is known (*L* 37.6).

After completing his explanation of these three elements of a miracle, Hobbes then purports to summarize that discussion with a definition: "A miracle is a work of God (besides his operation by the way of nature, ordained in the creation) done for the making manifest to his elect, the mission of an extraordinary minister for their salvation" (*L* 37.7). This definition emphasizes what was referred to as element (2) above. Only God performs miracles. Neither prophets, nor angels, nor devils have the power to do so (*L* 37.9–11). Further, God must cause the miraculous event by His "immediate hand" and not through the regular course of nature (*L* 37.9, 37.13). This position seems to take back what Hobbes had said about the first rainbow, which could have been caused in the ordinary way, though it was not known to be.

Element (3) above is made stronger in Hobbes's second definition. Now the purpose of a miracle is said to be to make a prophet known to the people. There is no "for-the-most-part" qualification. This revised position, if taken strictly, would again exclude the first rainbow from being a miracle.

Concerning element (1), Hobbes no longer says that a miracle must be admirable, even though he could have used this condition to exclude certain events from being considered miraculous. Hobbes does not want the consecration of the bread and wine in the eucharistic ceremony to be thought of as involving a transformation of those substances into the body and blood of Jesus, as the Roman Catholics claim. First, such a view does not fit into the scientific view. Second and more importantly, if priests had such a power, a good case could be made that they could control one's salvation, and Hobbes is unwilling to take this power out of the hands of the sovereign. yet, in his discussion of miracles, instead of arguing that the eucharistic ceremony cannot be miraculous, because it happens too often, Hobbes takes a much weaker line and says that the sovereign should decide the issue. If the sovereign says that the bread and wine are not changed, then one should accept that they are not; and if the sovereign says that they are changed, then one should accept that they are (*L* 37.13). One might think that, for an ardent Protestant like Hobbes, this is a remarkable concession. But even more than a Protestant, Hobbes was a conventionalist:

> we are not every one to make our own private reason or conscience, but the public reason, that is, the reason of God's supreme lieutenant, judge . . . A private man has always the liberty (because thought is free) to believe or not believe in his heart, those acts that have been given out for miracles . . . But when it comes to confession of that faith, the private reason must submit to the public; that is to say, to God's lieutenant. (*L* 37.13)

In part four of *Leviathan*, "Of the Kingdom of Darkness," Hobbes does argue that the consecration of the eucharist cannot be a miracle because it happens too often (*L* 44.11).

Hobbes's conventionalism ties in with his skepticism that miracles still occur. He says that he does not know of one intelligent person who has ever claimed to have seen a miracle (*L* 37.13). He believes that miracles ceased with the death of the apostles. This was one standard Protestant view of his time. Typically, someone declared that miracles had ceased, when that person's opponent was claiming some miraculous event to bolster her case, such as Roman Catholics claiming that each consecration of the eucharist constituted the miracle of changing ordinary bread and wine into the body and blood of Jesus. Often, people bent on changing the status quo appealed to miracles to legitimize their cause, such as political radicals. This largely explains James I's assertion that God had worked miracles in the Old Testament but that, after the death of Christ, "there was a cessation" of them.

It is worth mentioning a decidedly calvinistic doctrine that Hobbes holds. He believes that the purpose of miracles is to "beget belief, not universally in all men, elect and reprobate, but in the elect only; that is to say, in such as God had determined should become his subjects" (L 37.6). Hobbes did not accept the Arminian and Roman Catholic view that God sought the salvation of every human being. For example, God did not intend Moses" miracle to convert Pharaoh. God had earlier told Moses that he would "harden the heart of Pharaoh" to prevent such a possibility (L 37.6). And Christ died not for all people but only for the elect.

monarchy, aristocracy, and democracy   Following Aristotle, Hobbes holds that there are exactly three kinds of government. A people may be governed by one person or more than one; if more than one, then either by part of the people or by all of the people. Monarchy is government by one person; aristocracy is government by part of the people; democracy is government by all of the people. Other apparent names for governments are misleading. Tyranny is not different from monarchy. The word "tyranny" is simply used for a monarchy that is not liked. Similarly, "oligarchy" is used for an aristocracy that is not liked, and "anarchy" is used for a democracy that is not liked (L 19.1–2, 46.35, "Review and Conclusion" 9; DC 7.2; EL 2.1.3).

Other misleading terms are "elective kingdoms" and "limited monarchy." A government that elects a so-called king is in fact usually a democracy and the elected official is a minister of the democracy. The phrase "limited monarchy" is a contradiction in terms since sovereignty must be unlimited or absolute. (See SOVEREIGN.) A so-called "limited monarch" is a minister of whoever in fact has the sovereign power, and this may be either an aristocracy or a democracy (L 19.10, 19.12; DC 7.4; EL 2.2.9).

In The Elements of Law and De Cive, Hobbes claims that aristocracy and monarchy are necessarily preceded by democracy. His argument is that aristocracy and monarchy originally require people to be nominated for those positions and to receive the general assent by a vote in which the majority preference determines the outcome. Since the processes of nomination and voting are political processes, some government must be in

209

effect; and since majority rule is the mark of a democracy, it must be the form of the government in question (*EL* 2.2.1; *DC* 7.5). In *Leviathan*, Hobbes does not mention any separate process of nomination; the election is determined by majority rule, but this election seems to follow an initial covenant to abide by the results of the election. So a vestige of the original theory remains (*L* 18.1).

In *The Elements of Law*, Hobbes says that an aristocracy usually arises when people get tired of participating in the administration of the government or live too far away to make their participation convenient. When the members of the ruling aristocracy are elected, a new covenant is made, which, of course, does not include those members as parties to the covenant (*EL* 2.2.6, 2.2.7). The process for forming a monarchy is the same except that Hobbes is insistent that the monarchy is not elective, and that the succession of the monarch must lie within the purview of the monarch herself. The monarchy cannot be elective, because the monarch is absolute and not obliged to any subject. She must be able to name her successor because otherwise the government would dissolve and the people would return to the state of nature (*EL* 2.2.9).

No matter what form of government is involved, sovereignty is indivisible. While this is obvious in a monarchy, it also holds for the other two forms of government. Sovereignty is not divided among each of the members of the aristocracy. If it were divided, then the power would be divided and the members of the aristocracy would return to a condition of war. And the same is true of democracy *mutatis mutandis* (*L* 19.3; *EL* 2.1.16).

Hobbes's own preference is for monarchy. In a paradigmatic use of pretermission, he says that he will not mention that God rules the world as a monarch, that all the ancients, by custom and theological belief, preferred monarchy, that the original paternal form of government that God established on earth was monarchy, and that other forms of government arise from monarchy because of the rebelliousness of human nature (*EL* 2.5.3; *DC* 10.3). Hobbes prefers it because he thinks that the private interest of the sovereign and the public interest are most closely united in that form. In aristocracies and democracies, the people who share the rule may seek their own private advantage to the detriment of the nation (*L* 19.4). To those who object to having one person have so much power, Hobbes responds that they may as well object to being ruled by God. When monarchy goes bad it is because of the unsociable passions of the individual monarch. But these same passions are in every human being and thus may corrupt any government. In an aristocracy, far from that form of government mitigating the problems that arise from these passions, they are multiplied because the individuals who make up the government tend to advance their own narrow self-interests and to fight with each other instead of conducting the business of the state (*EL* 2.5.4; *DC* 10.4).

Hobbes thinks that monarchies generally spend fewer public funds for their maintenance than other forms of government. He claims that a monarch's entourage is smaller than those in aristocracies, because only one person is sovereign (*DC* 10.6). It is difficult to understand how Hobbes could believe this in the light of the excesses of Charles I's court. He also implausibly maintains that people are generally safer in a monarchy because a monarch is severe only to those people who directly oppose him. Even Nero and Caligula only persecuted "courtiers and such as are remarkable for some eminent charge" (*DC* 10.7). He thinks that people who mind their own business are safe: "Whosoever therefore in a monarchy will lead a retired life, let him be what he will that reigns, he is out of danger" (*DC* 10.7). How could Hobbes not have acknowledged that a monarch can mark out entire groups or even the entire population for repressive practices?

One of the problems with democracies is that ruling requires knowledge of both domestic and foreign affairs. Most people do not have the time or interest to master these matters and thus are not competent to have opinions about them even though they would have the right to judge them (*DC* 10.10). Also, anyone who gives her opinion thinks she needs to deliver a long speech; and the essence of rhetoric is to make one's own opinion look better, more profitable, or more just than it actually is, "whence it happens that opinions are delivered not by right reason but by a certain violence of mind" (*DC* 10.11). Aristocracies and democracies also breed factions, and factions breed civil wars (*DC* 10.12). The greatest advantage of monarchy over other forms of government then is that it is less susceptible to civil war (*EL* 2.5.8).

One of the characteristics of sovereignty is stability. In theory, sovereignty should last for ever and not perish with the death of any person. There is no problem with succession in democracies. Since all the people are the sovereign, the death of a person does not diminish sovereignty, and the addition of a person does not increase it. Similarly, there is no problem with succession in aristocracies. The group elects whatever new members it requires in order to keep it in existence. A problem only arises in monarchies. A monarch must have the right to determine who will succeed her. If a person does not have that right, then she is not a monarch, no matter what she may be called. She is in fact a minister of the state and the form of government is a democracy if all the people decide on a successor and an aristocracy if only some do (*DC* 9.11–12; *EL* 2.4.11).

If a monarch dies without explicitly naming a successor, then the following reasoning applies. It must be assumed that the monarch intended to

211

fulfill her function as sovereign. Thus, she must have wanted the government to continue. Further, she must have preferred monarchy to any other form of government since that was the way she herself ruled. Next, everyone prefers those who give honor to her, and a person's children are more likely than anyone else to honor that person. Thus, a monarch would prefer her own child to succeed her over anyone else. I have been using the feminine form of the generic pronouns, but Hobbes is clearly thinking primarily of men. He says, "every man after death receives honour and glory from his children, sooner than from the power of any other men: hence we gather that a father intends better for his children than any other person's" (*DC* 9.15; *EL* 2.4.12). It is somewhat odd that he should skew the discussion in that direction, because earlier he had made quite a strong case that women are as apt to rule over children as men. It appears that Hobbes simply wants to derive the conventional position. He goes on to say that male children "carry the pre-eminence in the beginning perhaps because for the most part, although not always, they are fitter for the administration of greater matters, but especially of wars." This natural aptitude underlies the custom of making males heir to the throne before females (*DC* 9.16; *EL* 2.4.14). Other than his desire to justify current practice, there was no good reason why Hobbes should not have argued that, since all people prefer members of their own sex to replace them in their activities, queens prefer daughters to succeed them over sons.

According to Hobbes, the oldest male is considered "more worthy" and hence primogeniture is "natural" (*DC* 9.17; *EL* 2.4.15). If the monarch has no children, then the succession passes to his or her brothers first and then to the sisters, beginning with the eldest. If the first-born child of a monarch dies, then the succession passes to that child's children rather than to the monarch's brothers and sisters (*DC* 9.19; *EL* 2.4.17). Even the first-born's siblings are passed over.

moral law   The moral law is identical with the law of nature and divine law (*DC* 4.1). Their identity is established by the following argument. The law of nature is the way to establish peace. The way to establish peace, as that very law states, is to be modest, equitable, humane, merciful, and so on. These same qualities are called virtues. That is, to practice the virtues is to follow the law of nature (*DC* 3.31).

motion   Ancient Greek and medieval philosophers thought that rest was superior to motion. What was in motion was only potentially what it was striving to be by moving towards its goal, while what was at rest was fully actual and hence did not need to change. As part of His perfection, God was unmoved, even though He could cause motion. Hobbes and other modern philosophers generally rejected this world-view. For them, if motion is not the more perfect condition, then it does not make sense to attribute better or worse to motion and rest: "Whether rest is nobler than motion is a ridiculous question, for nobility is the renown of men [deriving] from lineage, riches, civil power, virtue, and the like" (*AW*, p. 321). Without motion, nothing would happen. Everything would be lifeless since life is a kind of motion. Hobbes is not even willing to define one in terms of the other: "Rest is no more a deprivation of motion than is motion a deprivation of rest" (*AW*, p. 320). Moreover, there is no way of determining whether or not rest precedes motion, nor whether all bodies were created with motion or all at rest (*AW*, pp. 320–1).

Motion is the continual leaving of one place and the arriving at another place (*DCo* 8.10; *AW*, pp. 56, 148). No motion is instantaneous. Every body in motion takes some amount of time to leave completely the place it is initially located at. There is both an argument that exploits the idea of space and an argument that exploits the idea of time for this position. The spatial argument is that in order to move from place A to place C, the body must first move to place B, which is partly between A and C. Hobbes does not explain why A and C are not immediately adjacent. Perhaps it is connected with his idea that "every part of a movement is motion" (*AW*, p. 148). The temporal argument is that, since time, by definition, is an idea of motion, every motion must take some time (*DCo* 8.10).

While Hobbes's metaphysics is often thought of primarily as materialism, motion is equally important. Nothing would happen if nothing moved, and the only things that move are bodies. All reality is built up from the movements of bodies of the smallest size. Life is a kind of motion; reasoning is a kind of motion; and the civil state is generated and preserved by various kinds of motion. In short, the motion of bodies can explain all changes in the world (*DCo* 9.6, 9.9; *AW*, p. 323). Hobbes recognizes that this is not always obvious and that that partially explains why Aristotle had divided change into three kinds: change in quality, quantity, and place. He opposes this three-fold division and reduces all three types to one: all change is the motion of bodies from one place to another. Qualitative change, as when a green apple turns red, is simply a rearrangement of the small bodies constituting a thing, or an addition of others to it, that causes a new sensation in an observer. Quantitative change is simply the movement of more bodies to a certain place (*AW*, p. 56).

There is another Aristotelian doctrine that Hobbes needs to refute in order to establish that the local motion of bodies (the movement of bodies from one place to another) can explain all change. Aristotle held that there are four kinds of causes: formal, final, efficient, and material. A

213

formal cause supposedly makes an object to be what it is. The form of felineness makes something to be a cat. One of Hobbes's objections to this alleged kind of causality is that a formal cause is supposed to act simultaneously with its effect. Something is a cat as soon as and no longer than it has the form of a cat. But Hobbes held that every cause must temporally precede its effect (*AW*, p. 315). As soon as the effect exists, it has no need of the cause; thus, no cause can be causing the effect when the effect exists. The idea that causes temporally precede their effect is one of the main differences between the modern and contemporary view of causality as against the medieval and ancient view of it. A final cause, for Aristotle, is what an object aims at; it is either an object of desire, a reason for acting, or simply a part of the nature of an object. Since a plan, a goal, or something desired exists prior to its realization, Hobbes's objection to formal causes does not apply here. Rather, he argues, as we shall see below, that every final cause in fact operates through the motion of bodies, even though this is often not obvious to a nonscientific person. Aristotelian efficient and material causes are not rejected by Hobbes but reinterpreted to fit into his scheme. He says that in motion one body acts on another body. The acting body is called the efficient cause by Aristotle, and the body acted upon is called the material cause (*DCo* 9.1; *AW*, p. 315). He was even willing to use the term "prime matter" (*DCo* 8.24). (*See* BODIES AND ACCIDENTS.)

With some of the received Aristotelian doctrines removed or reformulated, it is easier for us to understand Hobbes's positive views. He asserts three theorems of motion. (1) Whatever is in motion has been moved ("quicquid movetur, motum esse"). For if the body were in the place where it had been, then it would be at rest. (2) Whatever is in motion will move ("quod movetur, motum iri adhuc"). The reason is that an object in motion is leaving the place it was at and must thus be moving to some other place. (3) Whatever is in motion is not at any one place during that time ("quod movetur non esse in uno loco"). For, by the definition of motion, it is continually leaving some place and arriving at another place (*DCo* 8.11).

Hobbes both expressed and tried to prove the principle of inertia in various formulations, sometimes by opposing motion with rest. Whatever is in motion remains in motion unless something causes it to be at rest ("quod movetur, semper moveri intelligitur, nisi aliud sit extra ipsum propter quod quiescit . . .") and whatever is at rest remains at rest unless something puts it into motion (*DCo* 8.19). Hobbes's argumentation for the first proposition contains an application of the principle of sufficient reason. If something is in motion, then there must be some reason for it not to remain in motion; this can only be something external to it since it itself is in motion. The reason that something at rest remains at rest unless moved by something outside of it, is that nothing causes itself to move (*DCo* 8.19). In other places, the principle of inertia is expressed in terms of unimpeded motion. Something that is moved remains in motion unless hindered by some other body (*DCo* 9.7, 15.3, 15.7, 22.14; *AW*, pp. 230–1, 324). (Descartes formulated the principle of inertia earlier than Hobbes: see *Principles of Philosophy*, part 2, sect. 36; Letter from Descartes to Mersenne, April 26, 1643.)

Many of the themes in *De Corpore* were explored in a preliminary way in Hobbes's critique of Thomas White's book *De Mundo*. The critique, which is now generally referred to as *Anti-White*, was probably written in about 1643 and remained unnoticed in manuscript for centuries until it was published in 1973. (See [7] in the Bibliography.) Therein Hobbes expresses his view about motion in quasi-Aristotelian terms. His view can be summarized in three propositions. The Nonidentity Principle: Whatever is moved by something is moved by something other than itself. The Causal Principle: Whatever is in motion was moved by something. The Principle of Moving Causes: Whatever moves something is itself in motion.

The Nonidentity Principle is in effect a consequence of another Aristotelian principle that Hobbes also accepted, namely, that nothing moves itself. Nothing can move itself, because if it could then it would be both actually in motion (by being the object causing the motion) and not actually in motion (by being the object caused to have that motion). And this purported simultaneous having and not having of a motion would violate the principle of noncontradiction: nothing can both have and not have the same property at the same time in the same way (*AW*, pp. 230, 317, 318; *DCo* 22.17; and Aristotle, *Physics*, book 3, chapter 1 (201a 10)).

The Causal Principle is a rejection of what may be called "brute motion." Brute motion is motion that exists without any explanation for its existence. Such motion was unthinkable until at least the middle of the eighteenth century. Hobbes, like earlier scientists and philosophers, thought that brute motion was impossible: every motion must have some cause. As Newton said, "By this principle alone [the principle of inertia] there never could have been any motion in the world. Some other principle was necessary for putting bodies into motion" (*Opticks*, book 3, part 1, query 31). This is what is asserted by the Causal Principle. The idea that the motion of individual bodies cannot explain itself or be in existence without some other thing having caused it forms the intuitive basis for a standard argument for the existence of God. The world, it seems, cannot just have motion in it without there being something that caused that motion. To my knowledge, Hume was the first philosopher to suggest the possibility of brute motion (*Dialogues Concerning Natural Religion*, part 8). It took a century or more for the idea to become assimilated into philosophy and science. Twentieth-century physicists no longer find the idea of brute motion difficult. It is now the standard scientific view.

The Principle of Moving Causes is in effect a corollary of Hobbes's view that the motion of bodies causes everything: "rest cannot be the cause of anything, nor can any action proceed from it; seeing neither motion nor mutation can be caused by it" (*DCo* 9.9). The Principle of Moving Causes in effect rejects Aristotle's notion of unmoved movers, of final causes. For Aristotle, things that are desired move objects to action without themselves moving. A beef steak, for example, seems to move a hungry dog to eat it without itself moving. Hobbes argues against this idea. He holds that there are tiny movements of tiny bodies from the meat, which enter the dog's nostrils and cause complex motions in the dog's heart and brain, part of which are the sensations of aroma, and these complex motions cause the dog to move to the meat and eat it (*AW*, p. 331). No movement, no cause.

N

names (*nomina*) Hobbes discusses names as part of his treatment of the nature of LANGUAGE AND SPEECH. There are two major uses of names: as marks and as signs. As marks, they help people remember their own ideas; as signs they are used for communicating one's ideas to other people. Thus, Hobbes defines "name" like this: "A name is a human vocal sound employed by a decision of man, so that there might be a mark by which a thought, similar to a previous thought, might be aroused in the mind, and which, ordered in speech and uttered to others, might be a sign to them that such a thought either previously occurred or did not occur in the speaker" (*DCo* 2.4). Of the two uses of names, the use as marks is logically prior, because an individual person could use names for this purpose that convey only to her the ideas they mark; while to use them as signs not only presupposes that the speaker remembers what idea she wishes to make known to another when she uses a particular name but also requires that that other person knows how she uses it (*DCo* 2.3). In short, Hobbes thinks that there can be private languages, *pace* Wittgenstein and some interpreters of Hobbes.

There are two major discussions of names, one in *Leviathan* and one in *De Corpore*. Names are discussed before PROPOSITIONS, because Hobbes thinks of names as the basic components of language. They are logically prior to propositions because the latter are built up out of the former.

The first name in a sentence is called the subject, antecedent, or contained of the sentence. The second name is called the predicate, consequent, or container. Some languages, such as English, have a grammatical requirement that the subject and predicate be joined by a copula, some form of the verb "to be." But the copula is not logically required and does not name anything. A propositional concatenation of names can be expressed by two names juxtaposed, as they can be in Latin for example (*DCo* 3.2).

Names, as mentioned above, are arbitrary marks and signs. A mark is an object used by an agent – it could be a beast or a human being – to remember something. A sign is an object used to make something known.

Because events succeed one another, they can be divided into antecedents and consequents. A sign can be either an antecedent of an event or a consequent of an event. An antecedent sign may cause the consequent event, as a cloud is the sign and cause of rain. A consequent sign may be caused by an antecedent thing or event, as the rain is a sign that there was a cloud, and the cloud causes the rain. But signs do not have to be causally related (*DCo* 2.1–4; *L* 3.8, 4.1, 4.3; *EL* 1.5.1–2). Perhaps Hobbes is indicating that one difference between linguistic and nonlinguistic signs is that linguistic signs are not causally related to what they are the signs of. But this is too strong. Since the object, say, a cloud, caused the person to have the idea of the cloud, which caused her to assign some name to it, namely, "cloud," the cloud and the word are causally related in this mediated fashion.

If words were used only as marks to aid our own memory, they would be much less useful than they in fact are. Any scientific discovery a person made would die with her, uncommunicated. By using words as signs, a person gets other people to think the same thoughts that she has had. These other people are then able to expand on the original discoveries and pass them on in turn: "scientific knowledge is able to increase in usefulness for the entire human race." The difference then between a mark and a sign is that marks are invented for one's own sake, while signs are invented "for the sake of others" (*DCo* 2.2).

A name is not a sign unless it functions within a sentence. An individual sound such as "man" might cause an audience to think of a man, but the audience has no way of knowing whether the utterer meant man or had not completed the utterance "manageable" (*DCo* 2.3). Hobbes, then, could subscribe to the present orthodoxy that the smallest unit of linguistic meaning is the sentence and the distinctively Fregean doctrine that a word has a sense only within the context of a sentence.

Since words are the signs of thoughts, there can be names of things that do not exist, such as those in the future, in dreams, and in hallucinations. Even nothing has a name: "nothing" (*DCo* 2.6).

Names are divided in several ways, for example, positive and negative. Positive names name things that are thought of as being similar to each other, e.g., dogs or trees. Negative names name things that are thought of as being dissimilar to each other; e.g., dogs and trees are both named by the negative name "nonmen". Positive names are logically prior to negative names, because the latter are formed from the former. The negative names "nonman" and "nonphilosopher" come from the positive names "man" and "philosopher" (*DCo* 2.7; *EL* 1.5.3; *L* 4.19, 46.16). Correlative positive and negative names are contradictories, since it is impossible for both of them to name the same thing at the same time (*DCo* 2.8; cf. 3.17; *AW*, p. 412).

218

Names are also divided into common and proper names. Common names can be the name of more than one thing. Universal names are common names prefixed with a universal quantifier, such as "every man". A universal itself is a name of a common noun. That is, "universal" is the name of "man," "dog," "chair," and every other word that can name more than one object (*DCo* 2.9; *L* 4.6–8; *EL* 1.5.5). This is a paradigmatic nominalist position. A "particular" name is a common name prefixed with an existential quantifier, such as "some man". A common name with no quantifier is an indefinite name and is, according to Hobbes, equivalent to a particular name (*DCo* 2.11; *L* 4.8).

Proper or individual names cannot name more than one thing. A proper name can be simple ("Socrates") or complex ("this tree" or "the man who wrote the *Iliad*") (*DCo* 2.9; *L* 4.6).

Although he does not define what a concrete name is, Hobbes thinks it is roughly the name of a body. Abstract names are names of the things that cause what concrete names name to be what they are. For example, the concrete name "hot" (which names every hot object) gets its name from a certain motion of the object it names; thus, the abstract names, "hotness" and "heat" name that motion that constitutes the hot object: "the causes of names are the same as the causes of our conceptions, namely some power or action, or disposition of the thing conceived or, as some say, its mode, what many call accidents" (*DCo* 3.3). Concrete names are logically prior to abstract ones, according to Hobbes, because the latter depend for their existence on propositions, while the former do not. Although the use of abstract names often results in absurdity, they are crucial for reasoning, which is nothing but calculation. For example, if one wanted to find the sum of the heat of one object plus the heat of another by adding one hot object to the other, the sum would be simply two hot objects, because "hot" names the object itself. In order to calculate the amount of heat in two hot objects, one must add the heat of the one, say 200°C, to the heat of the other, say 200°C, in order to get 400°C. This addition of heat to heat must use the abstract name "heat" in order to designate the right object (*DCo* 3.4). Absurdity results when people think that what the abstract name names can be separated from a body altogether. Bodies are hot and "heat" denotes a certain motion in them; so there can be no heat separated from all body. In particular, there are no essences and no "being" in general. There are only bodies in certain configurations or motions.

necessity *See* LIBERTY AND NECESSITY; PROPOSITIONS

O

---

oath (*juramentum*)   An oath is a promise with a phrase or clause stating that the oath-taker calls upon God to punish her if the oath is broken (*L* 14.31; *DC* 2.20; *EL* 1.15.15). There is an interesting change in Hobbes's treatment of oaths and covenants. In *The Elements of Law* and *De Cive*, the obligation to fulfill an oath is the same as the obligation to fulfill a covenant, but the origin of the obligation (however it is acquired) is independent of God. In an oath, God is supposed to enforce the obligation, but His existence is not stated as a necessary condition for the obligatoriness of the oath itself. (*DC* 2.22–3). In *Leviathan*, God both is supposed to enforce breaches of oaths and covenants and is a necessary condition for their existence; oaths and covenants bind "in the sight of God" (*L* 14.33). The reason that an oath does not obligate a person more than a covenant does is that God stands behind each equally. An oath merely makes explicit what is implicit in a covenant.

Of Liberty and Necessity (1654) [14]   During his voluntary exile from England, Hobbes was often in the company of the then marquis, later duke, of Newcastle. Hobbes and John Bramhall, an Arminian cleric, debated the issue of free will in front of Newcastle, in Paris in 1645. At Newcastle's request, Bramhall wrote up his views in a manuscript, which was then passed on to Hobbes, at Rouen. Hobbes wrote a manuscript in the form of a letter to Newcastle in the same year, 1645. There is some confusion about this date because, in the first publication of the debate, the date of Hobbes's letter is given as 1652 and Hobbes himself later wrote that it was 1646. But in order to make the best sense of all the facts, we must take it the initial manuscripts were written in 1645 (cf. *LN*, p. 278; *QLNC*, pp. 25–6). After some delay, Bramhall then wrote a reply to Hobbes's reply. There the matter rested for eight years. None of these manuscripts was published until 1654, when an unauthorized edition of Hobbes's work appeared in book form. The publication originated because Hobbes had consented to have his manuscript translated into French for a friend by a young Englishman, John Davys (Davies) (1627–97) (Macdonald and

Hargreaves, *Thomas Hobbes: A Bibliography*, p. 37). Davys made a copy of the original for himself and arranged for its publication, adding to it an introduction, "To the Sober and Discreet Reader." (For the above dating, see Bramhall, *Works*, 1:xxxi–ii, 4:19–24.)

Bramhall was incensed because he thought that Hobbes had approved of the publication, contrary to their agreement not to publish. Consequently, Bramhall published, the next year, his original manuscript, Hobbes's manuscript, and his reply to Hobbes. But instead of arranging them sequentially, he chopped the texts into small segments, which he interlaced, as if they were a record of the debate itself. In response to Bramhall's book, Hobbes published his own reply in 1656 under the title *The Questions Concerning Liberty, Necessity, and Chance*, which contains the complete text of all the previous works mentioned, plus Hobbes's responses listed in sections titled "Animadversions." Then, in 1657, Bramhall published one last response, *Castigations of Hobbes's Animadversions*. Fortunately no additional responses from either party were produced on this topic, although it might be mentioned that appended to an edition of Bramhall's *Castigations*, published in 1658, was his more important work, *The Catching of Leviathan or the Great Whale*. Although Hobbes never replied to the *Castigations*, his response to *The Catching of Leviathan* was published posthumously in 1682, *An Answer to Bishop Bramhall's Book, Called "The Catching of the Leviathan"*.

Bramhall's view is succinctly stated at the beginning of his first manuscript in what is essentially a constructive dilemma: "Either I am free to write this discourse for liberty against necessity, or I am not free. If I be free, I have obtained the cause, and ought not to suffer for the truth. If I be not free, yet I ought not to be blamed, since I do it not out of any voluntary election, but out of an inevitable necessity" (*LN*, p. 239; *QLNC*, p. 29). Hobbes defends his position by denying the second premise. He holds that a person who is free has still acted out of necessity; in other words, LIBERTY AND NECESSITY are compatible. Human beings are free even though there is no free will. Will, which is the last desire a person has before acting, causes an action, and ultimately there is some previous event, external to the human being, that is a cause of the will. Given that prior, external cause, it was necessary for the human being to act as she did. Hobbes's view may be summarized in these six propositions: (1) human beings are free, or have liberty; (2) human beings will things; (3) the will is not free; (4) the will is the last desire before an act is performed; (5) the will is caused by other events; (6) the events that cause the will are necessary.

Bramhall defends his position using a panoply of scholastic distinctions. Hobbes either denies the helpfulness of them or denies their intelligibility.

221

In regard to the philosophy of language, it is to Hobbes's discredit that he did not recognize the difference between sentences such as "Necessarily, if it is raining, then it is raining" and "If it is raining, then it is necessarily raining." Sometimes he indicated that he thought that every true proposition was necessarily true, and he thought that it was not important where the modal word "necessarily" was placed in a sentence. Considering the sentence "Necessarily, either there will be a sea-battle tomorrow or there will not be a sea battle tomorrow," Hobbes held that it was true because one of the disjunctive clauses was true, even though human beings did not know which. He thought that there was no other place for the necessity of the whole sentence to originate from.

A large part of *Of Liberty and Necessity* is devoted to explaining that the necessity of all action is compatible with such practices as assigning praise and blame, giving rewards and inflicting punishments, praying, and punishment for sin. Hobbes held that a person is praised for doing good, and that goodness is what an individual, commonwealth, or God desires; a person is blamed for doing bad, and badness is what an individual, commonwealth, or God wants not to be done. Necessity has nothing to do with it. Practices relating to rewards and punishments are treated analogously. It makes sense to pray even though prayers do not cause God to act as He does, because God in fact rewards those who pray. Finally, to sin is to break a law; so any sinner deserves to be punished. Although God causes a person to sin, He is not the author of sin and, being omnipotent, is not subject to any law; so God cannot sin.

P

paternal government   The nature of sovereignty is the same no matter how it is actually achieved. In particular, a parent does not have sovereignty over her children because she generated them, no more than God has sovereignty over His creatures because He created them. In these cases as in all others, sovereignty requires power over the subject. In the case of divine sovereignty, the power is sufficient because divine power is naturally and permanently overwhelming. In the case of parental sovereignty, power is a necessary but not a sufficient condition. The other condition is the implied consent of the children to obey the parent, in exchange for not being killed (*L* 20.4; *EL* 2.4.3). Of course, infants and young children are incapable of giving consent, but at some point before they acquire the strength to challenge the parent they can and do give their consent, if only implicitly, to one or both of their parents to rule them. The authority of parents is absolute: "they may alienate them [the children], that is, assign his or her dominion, by selling or giving them in adoption or servitude to others; or may pawn them for hostages, kill them for rebellion, or sacrifice them for peace, by the law of nature . . ." (*EL* 2.4.8). Hobbes is not being heartless. He is describing how things are in the state of nature, and there is no doubt that he thinks that it is good to get out of it.

Hobbes does not use the term "patriarchy." "Paternal government" and "paternal dominion" are his terms (*L* 20.4; *DC* 9). These are misnomers, since paternal government and paternal dominion for Hobbes are any governments exercised by a parent, and mothers not only are quite capable of governing, but also have a better claim to govern their children than fathers do: "it is manifest that he who is newly born is in the *mother's* power before any others; insomuch as she may rightly, and at her own will, either breed him up or adventure him to fortune" (*DC* 9.2–3; *L* 20.5; *EL* 2.4.7). The ordinary supposition is that a mother raises a child on the condition that the child obey her: "thus in the state of nature every woman that bears children becomes both a *mother* and a *lord*" (*DC* 9.3, 9.6). There are various ways in which a woman may lose her sovereignty over her children. She may abandon them, be taken prisoner, be the subject of another sovereign, or covenant with a man to have him be lord over the children (*EL* 2.4.3–4, 2.4.8). Nonetheless, if a woman is a sovereign and has children by a male subject, she, not the father, is the sovereign and lord of the children (*DC* 9.5).

Hobbes explicitly rejects the claim that men are superior to women: "But what some say, that in this case the *father*, by reason of the pre-eminence of sex, and not the *mother* becomes lord, signifies nothing. . . . [T]he inequality of their natural forces is not so great that the man could get the dominion over the woman without war" (*DC* 9.3; *L* 20.4). Hobbes points to the Amazons as an actual case in which women are rulers.

The textual evidence points to the conclusion that Hobbes was not a theoretical sexist. A cynical interpretation of Hobbes may however maintain that Hobbes defends the equality of women in the state of nature in order to add one more disadvantage to that condition: not only is the life of man there "solitary, poor, nasty, brutish, and short" but women are equals. All the more reason to get out of the state of nature.

Hobbes discusses paternal government in the context of explaining how governments can come to be in the actual circumstances of the state of nature. In *The Elements of Law*, Hobbes lists three ways: through an explicit covenant among people; through conquest; and through parental right (*EL* 2.3.2). In *De Cive*, the three ways are reduced to two: "institutive or framed government" corresponds to the first way described in *The Elements of Law*. The second way is a consolidation of the other two ways, and Hobbes calls it "natural" or "acquired" government. Natural government then arises either through conquest in war or through parental right (*DC* 8.1). In *Leviathan*, the same two-fold distinction is presented under the terms "sovereignty by institution" and "sovereignty by acquisition."

patriarchy *See* PATERNAL GOVERNMENT

Peloponnesian War **by Thucydides** (1629) [1] Before Hobbes's, the only English version of Thucydides' history of the Peloponnesian War was one based upon a French translation of a Latin translation by Laurentius Valla. Hobbes conveys some pride in reporting that his was based upon the Greek text of Aemilius Porta. Although it was written some time earlier, his translation was published in 1629, when he was forty years old; it was his first major publication. (His first great work, *De Cive*, was first published in 1642. So Hobbes was a late bloomer.) The book was dedicated to his former tutee, William Cavendish, the second earl of Devonshire, who had died the year before. But the dedication is addressed to his son, the third earl of Devonshire, also named William. Hobbes himself drew the map of Greece that precedes the text. He must have enjoyed the drafting since he reported in his verse autobiography that he loved to study maps in his youth.

One feature of Thucydides' writing that Hobbes admires is its narrative style; Thucydides eschews moralizing digressions and conjecture. He lets the events themselves suggest the moral (*PW* "To the Readers" 3, 1.22). Hobbes also praised Thucydides for "truth and elocution," truth being the soul of history and elocution being its body (*PW* "To the Readers" 8). The purpose of history, according to Hobbes, was to educate people about the past in order to allow them to conduct their lives "prudently in the present and providently in the future" (*PW* "To the Readers" 2). It is likely that he thought that the lessons offered by Thucydides would reduce the tension between the king and parliament. Charles's third parliament was meeting in 1628–9 and failing to satisfy his needs. Hobbes's efforts were to no avail. No parliament met for another eleven years, and when the next two parliaments met in 1640, they contributed to the outbreak of the English Civil War.

Thucydides' history consists of eight books. It is the story of the twenty-eight year war (431–404 BC) that pitted Athens and her allies against Sparta and its allies. The ostensible cause of the war was a dispute between Corinth and Athens, who had sided with the Corcyraeans (*PW* 1.24–49, 1.55). But the underlying cause, according to Thucydides – and Hobbes concurs – was Sparta's fear and jealousy of Athens' power and the possible consequences of her ambition (*PW* 1.23, 1.88, 1.90, "Of the Life and History" 18). The events of the war are too complex to be summarized here, and there are few striking parallels between either Sparta or Athens and England. Athens, like England, was a sea-power, but she was sometimes a democracy and sometimes an oligarchy, and never nominally a monarchy. There is no more reason why Athens should have reminded him of England than of Spain or the Netherlands. What Hobbes valued most in the history was the story of the decline of Athens because her citizens were swayed by the rhetoric of private persons who sought their own self-interested good while they represented themselves as being concerned with the good of the city-state. In *Leviathan*, Hobbes would describe this kind of activity as "dehortation." (*See* COMMAND AND COUNSEL.)

However, Hobbes was probably also impressed by some deeper features of the history. Thucydides, like Hobbes, has a pessimistic view of human nature and recognizes that nations typically make international policy based, not upon justice, but upon what they perceive to be their own self-interest. Although Thucydides, unlike Hobbes, was not a political theorist or philosopher, and although it is implausible that he shaped Hobbes's views, some of Thucydides' descriptions of the benefits of peace and the wretchedness of war could have been written by Hobbes himself and not just translated by him:

> And many and heinous things happened in the cities through this sedition, which though they have been before and shall be ever as long as human nature is the same, yet they are more calm and of different kinds according to the several conjunctures. For in peace and prosperity as well cities as private men are better minded because they be not plunged into necessity of doing anything against their will. But war, taking away the affluence of daily necessities, is a most violent master and conforms most men's passions to the present occasion. The received value of names imposed for significa-tion of things was changed into arbitrary. For inconsiderate boldness was counted true-hearted manliness; provident deliberation, a handsome fear; modesty, the cloak of cowardice; to be wise in everything, to be lazy in everything. A furious suddenness was reputed a point of valour. (*PW* 3.82)

In the account of the early history of Greece, Thucydides' description of the condition of the inhabitants foreshadows the famous description of the state of nature (*L* 13.9):

> For while traffic was not, nor mutual intercourse, but with fear, neither by sea nor land, and every man so husbanded the ground as but barely to live upon it without any stock of riches and planted nothing (because it was uncertain when another should invade them and carry all away, especially not having the defence of walls), but made account to be masters, in any place, of such necessary sustenance as might serve them from day to day, they made little difficulty to change their habitations. And for this cause they were of no ability at all, either for greatness of cities or other provision. (*PW* 1.2)

Thucydides explanation for Agamemnon's motives in leading the expedi-tion against Troy is also Hobbesian. Agamemnon was more powerful than his neighbors, and he wanted even more power (*PW* 1.9).

There are other incidental confirmations of Hobbes's later political theory in the text of Thucydides. Fear is the chief motivator for men in battle. When the Spartan king prepares his soldiers for the coming war with Athens, he tells them that soldiers who are afraid usually fight more fiercely than those who are not. He advises them to prepare "as if they were afraid," because that will give them "more courage to go upon the enemy" (*PW* 2.11). When an Athenian delegation to Sparta explains what motivated Athens to fight as fiercely and successfully as she did against the Persians, they say it was done "chiefly for fear, next for honour, and lastly for profit" (*PW* 1.75). These three motives correspond to the three causes of war in the state of nature. In *Leviathan*, Hobbes says that people must attack their neighbors out of fear of them; they must launch pre-emptive attacks to increase their power in order to protect themselves from attack (profit); and some people will choose to attack their neighbors for glory's sake (*L* 13.5–6). The Athenians then assert that a person in danger is justified in doing whatever is necessary to protect herself, and that "they that have the power to compel need not at all to go to law" (*PW* 1.77, 1.75–6).

The most famous episode in *The Peloponnesian War* is Pericles' speech in honor of the first soldiers killed in the war. It is a mixture of Hobbesian and anti-Hobbesian sentiments. Its main theme is anti-Hobbesian; it praises democracy. (Hobbes thinks that Thucydides disdained both democracy and aristocracy and actually preferred monarchy, for that is what the government of Pericles in fact was, even though it was called a democracy (*PW* "Of the Life and History" 5, 2.65).) Pericles says that, while all people are equal under the law, honor is extended to those who deserve it. The citizens are free within the city although they also obey their leaders and the laws (*PW* 2.37). Pericles claims that all the citizens, even laborers, know enough about public affairs to be able to make intelligent political decisions (*PW* 2.40). In contrast, Hobbes had claimed that one of the defects of democracy is that most people do not. Subjects are all equal only in the sense that the sovereign has all the power and the subjects have none of their own. But there are titles of honor among subjects, which are doled out by the sovereign however he sees fit. However, the amount of disagreement should not be exaggerated. For example, Hobbes said that subjects should not prefer the form of government of neighboring nations to that of their own (*L* 30.7), and Pericles praised the Athenians for not copying the laws of any other nation (*PW* 2.37).

In an appendix to the history, Hobbes provides a biography of Thucydides. He mentions that Thucydides was accused of being an atheist. Part of his explanation of the charge is that Thucydides was clever enough to recognize the absurdities of the pagan Greek religion. Hobbes's conclusion is that Thucydides "appears to be on the one side not superstitious, on the other side not an atheist" (*PW* "Of the Life and History" 2). The same should probably be said of Hobbes. In *De Cive*, Hobbes talks about the difficulty human beings have in thinking about religion correctly and says that it is "almost impossible for men, without the special assistance of God," to avoid both atheism and superstition (*DC* 16.1). Hobbes may have seen a resemblance between himself and Thucydides, as when he wrote that Thucydides led a private life because a person who gave good counsel in that commonwealth was likely to be vilified.

Concerning literary style, Hobbes defends Thucydides against the charge that he is obscure, by attributing any difficulty of comprehension to his

227

profundity. Hobbes believes that an author should speak her mind clearly: "a wise man should so write (though in words understood by all men) that wise men only should be able to commend him" (*PW* "Of the Life and History" 23).

person (*persona*)   For the sake of precision in this discussion, let's distinguish between behavior, which is any physical movement of a human being, and an action, which is something for which a human being is to be held responsible. Hobbes does not use the contrasting terminology of "behavior" and "action." He uses the word "action" indifferently to refer to what is done by both actors and authors. Nonetheless, he has the distinction. When he tries to determine who "owns" an action (in his general sense of "action"), he is trying to identity the person who is acting whether or not that person is exhibiting any physical behavior. In his terminology, an AUTHOR owns her actions while an actor does not. An actor may exhibit behavior in virtue of which an action is attributed to another person (the author).

A person is a being whose behavior counts as an action either (1) of herself or (2) of some other thing. There are thus two kinds of persons. A natural person is a being whose behavior counts as her own actions, and as such she is accountable for them. An artificial person is a being whose behavior counts as the actions of some other thing, called the thing personated (*L* 16.1–2). This "other thing" may, but need not, be animate, and often is not. A church, a hospital, or any other institution can have an artificial person represent it. In such a case, the behavior of the artificial person generates actions that are attributed to the institution by the authority given her by its owners or governors (cf. *L* 16.9). Even nonexistent things such as idols and pagan gods can be represented by persons (*L* 16.11).

For Hobbes, a person always has the potential at the same time to represent or bear the person of both herself, as a natural person, and another thing, which she artificially personates, though not by one and the same bit of behavior. If a person behaves for her own good, then she is a natural person and bears her own person. If she behaves for the sake of something else, then she is an artificial person and bears the person of the thing she represents (*L* 23.2).

Hobbes's treatment of the concept of person in *Leviathan* occurs in the last chapter of Part I, immediately following his chapters on the natural condition of human beings and the laws of nature. It prepares the way for the explanation of the nature and generation of the civil state. The head of a civil state is a sovereign, and the sovereign is an artificial person who represents his subjects. Hobbes is not interested in natural persons as a distinct philosophical topic. The issue of personal identity is discussed only briefly in the context of IDENTITY in general. Locke seems to have been the first philosopher to consider personal identity as a problem in its own right. It is the nature of artificial persons that exercises Hobbes.

An artificial person is an actor in contrast with an author. The theater offers a helpful analogy. An actor is not speaking for herself (not speaking *in propria persona*); she is only reciting the lines written for her by the author (*L* 16.3). It is the author who has responsibility for what is said. (For the purposes of explaining Hobbes's idea of an artificial person, it is not relevant to consider the quality of the way the actor recites the lines.) If an artificial person represents ("personates") an inanimate thing, then there is no author of the actions (*L* 16.9). In *Leviathan*, only animate, rational beings are persons, and inanimate objects that are represented by artificial persons are not themselves persons at all. In a relatively late work, Hobbes changed his terminology to fit the ordinary way of talking about such matters. He came to say that "an inanimate thing can be a person . . . and can act in law" (*DH* 15.4).

If a competent human being is represented – that is, not an idiot or a child – then she is the author of the action. One difference between a stage actor and an artificial person is that, while a stage actor is given her lines by the author, an artificial person may use her own reason and will to make decisions about what to do. Nonetheless, the behavior elicited by those decisions results in actions attributable to the author, if there is one, just as long as the artificial person is operating within her area of AUTHORIZATION (*L* 16.5). In short, an artificial person is an actor, whose behavior results in actions owned by an author, if there is one; and the author is the thing that owns the actions (*L* 16.4).

It may seem odd, but Hobbes says that the actor, rather than the author, has authority for what she does (*L* 16.4). The reason he does this is to be able to assert that the sovereign, who is an artificial person and hence an actor, has authority. In this way, Hobbes effects a kind of Hegelian reversal. He argues that, since a natural person authorizes someone to act for her, the person authorized has authority; therefore, the actor has authority over the natural person. The reasoning is specious. The move from "has authority" to "has authority over" turns on an equivocation. The actor (sovereign) who is subordinate to the author (the subjects) insofar as she needs to be authorized by the author ends up having authority over the author. (*See* AUTHORIZATION.)

According to Hobbes, an artificial person gives unity to a multitude of human beings. In the state of nature, there is disunity among the people. Unity is achieved when they unite by having one artificial person, the sovereign, represent them:

A multitude of men are made one person when they are by one man or one person represented; so that it be done with the consent of every one of the multitude in particular. For it is the unity of the representer, not the unity of the represented, that makes the person one. And it is the representer that bears the person, and but one person. And unity cannot otherwise be understood in multitude. (*L* 16.13, 16.14; *DC* 10.5)

The distinction between natural and artificial persons does not appear in *The Elements of Law*. Instead, there is a forerunner of the distinction. Hobbes says that the word "people" is ambiguous between any collection of human beings living within a certain geographical area and "a person civil," that is, one or more human beings who are united in one will. His example is the House of Commons, which is a people when it is in session, but which breaks up into a group of people in the first sense when it is dissolved (*EL* 2.2.11). His example surely has a political purpose. Parliament was disputing with the king over the location of sovereignty. Radicals held that sovereignty was solely in parliament; moderates held that it was partially in parliament. Hobbes, like the king, held that sovereignty was solely in the king. Hobbes's argument in effect is that no part of sovereignty can be in parliament since the sovereignty of England does not dissolve when parliament is dissolved.

In addition to its political use, Hobbes uses his view about artificial persons to explain the doctrine of the Trinity, namely, the doctrine that there is one God and that three persons are God. Hobbes asserts that the one God was represented ("personated") by three persons, Moses, Jesus, and the apostles and their successors: "For so God the Father, as represented by Moses, is one person, and as represented by his Son, another person, and as represented by the apostles and by the doctors that taught by authority from them derived is a third person, and yet every person here is the person of one and the same God" (*L* 42.3).

There are numerous problems with this theory of the Trinity. While most of them are theological, one philosophical problem should be mentioned. When he first introduced the notion, Hobbes made it clear that the artificial person is the thing that represents something. Thus, when an inanimate object such as a hospital is represented, the artificial person is whatever human being represents the hospital (*L* 16.9). This should have the consequence that Moses is the artificial person that represents God as Father; Jesus is the artificial person that represents God as Son; and the apostles and their successors are the artificial person that represents God as Holy Spirit. God is three persons in the sense that three artificial persons represent him: "God, who is always one and the same was the person represented by Moses, the person represented by his Son Incarnate, and the person represented by the apostles" (*L* 42.3). This may be a sense in which God is three persons, but it is not the right sense. What Hobbes needed to show was that God is three persons, not that three artificial persons represented Him.

At least three theological problems for Hobbes's theory of the Trinity should be mentioned. First, his view is clearly a form of Sabellianism, the heresy that overemphasizes the unity of God by not giving sufficient reality to the trinity of divine persons. Second, it has the consequence that the Trinity did not exist before the time of Moses, as his opponent John Bramhall was happy to point out (*BCL*, p. 315). Third, each person of the Trinity comes into and goes out of existence at various times. The person of the Father, represented by Moses, would seem to have ceased to exist when Moses died. There would seem to have been no artificial person representing God as either Father, Son, or Holy Spirit between the death of Moses and the birth of Jesus.

Hobbes came to see that his view had problems. In an appendix to the Latin version of *Leviathan*, Hobbes admitted that his view makes Moses a person of the Trinity. He tries to minimize the problem by saying that each problematic passage "can easily be corrected." But what he means by easily correcting a passage amounts to no longer applying his theory of persons to the Trinity but merely rehearsing the traditional formulas: "If he [Hobbes] had said that God, in his own person, created the world, that God, in the person of his Son, redeemed the human race, and that in the person of the Holy Spirit he sanctified the church, he would have said nothing but what was said in the catechism published by the church" (*OL* 3:563). That is true enough, but Moses and the apostles and their successors as representers of the Trinity have completely dropped out of the account.

It is important not to draw the wrong conclusion from Hobbes's flawed theory of the Trinity. There is no good evidence that Hobbes was trying to undermine the doctrine. Rather, he seems to have been doing his best to explain a doctrine that cannot be explained. This is a mark of a devoted Christian thinker. (Bernard Lonergan, a distinguished Catholic theologian, used to say this about the standard treatment of the doctrine of the Trinity: There are four relations, three persons, two generations, one God, and no explanation.) What Christian theologian has produced a theory of the Trinity that has no logical problems? Even though Hobbes's theory is heretical, to be a heretic, far from indicating any ill will or lack of ardor, indicates sincerity. Usually, it also means that the person has lost a religiopolitical battle over what will count as orthodoxy.

It may seem that Hobbes's problems with the interpretation of the Trinity also indicate a problem with his views about an artificial person in general.

Bramhall thought so. He said that a king would have as many persons as he has justices of the peace since each one of them represents and thus bears the person of the sovereign. Hobbes did not see that this was a problem and merely acknowledged the consequence (*BCL*, p. 315).

philosophy Hobbes identifies philosophy with science. It is a kind of KNOWLEDGE *DCo* 1.2; *EL* 1.6.4; *L* 46.1; *DH* 10.4; *AW*, p. 26). Today, science is usually thought of as some organized body of knowledge, and Hobbes emphasizes orderliness too. From definitions, various consequences follow because the meanings of the words are connected (*L* 5.17). But in his discussion of the nature of philosophy, Hobbes is much more interested in explaining what the method of discovering these consequences is than in specifying the definitions upon which they rest. In this respect, Hobbes's concern is like that of Francis Bacon and Descartes, although each of them had different accounts of what the correct philosophical or scientific methodology is.

In *Leviathan*, Hobbes emphasizes three aspects of philosophy or scientific knowledge. One is that it is the result of reasoning. Mere empirical experience, no matter how full or reliable, is not philosophy, both because "brute beasts" have experience as much as human beings do and because experience alone does not allow one to predict the future reliably (*L* 46.2). A second aspect is that philosophy explains how objects are produced or generated. This view is inspired by his belief that to know something is to know its cause, and that all causes are motions. A third aspect is the requirement that philosophy or science be practical. The effects that philosophy investigates are those that "human life requires" (*L* 46.1).

There are two methods for acquiring scientific knowledge. One is called analytic or the method of resolution (*resolutio*); the other is called synthetic or the method of composition (*compositio*) (*DCo* 6.7). The analytic method begins from some effect and hypothesizes some possible cause for it. The cause need not be the actual cause of the effect; it suffices if it presents a possible explanation for the effect until a better explanation comes along. The hypotheses are however necessary propositions, true by definition. Thus, a distinction needs to be made between the necessary truth of the scientific hypothesis and its being a true explanation of some effect. Because Hobbes does not always make this distinction clear, his view has often been misinterpreted.

Since causes make or produce their effect, to know a possible cause is to know a way in which an effect could be produced. Hobbes sometimes illustrated this idea by explaining that a circle is the possible effect of drawing a line around and equally distant from a fixed point. Given any particular object, it is necessary that, if it could have been generated in the way described, then it is a circle; but one cannot be sure whether that object is in fact a circle or, if it is, whether that was the way it was in fact constructed. The actual way in which it was constructed is, however, immaterial, because, however it was constructed, facts about a way in which it could have been constructed are sufficient to allow one to draw consequences about its actual properties (*DCo* 1.5, 6.13; *DH* 10.5).

The second method is the synthetic; it begins with a cause and reasons to some possible effect. The causes of course are expressed by necessary propositions, which can be the causes of some effect, but whether they are the actual cause of some effect is left open. (*See also* METHOD, PHILOSOPHICAL AND SCIENTIFIC.)

Both the analytic and synthetic methods are united by reasoning, where reason is understood literally as computation, that is, addition and subtraction (*DCo* 1.2). The necessary presence of reasoning in philosophy or science distinguishes it from imagination, memory, and prudence.

The goal of philosophy is practical; it is the good of human beings (*L* 46.1). The discovery of a truth that has no practical benefit is worthless. When Hobbes describes the discovery of a more precise value for π, he denigrates it by saying that there are practical methods for getting a result that is less precise but close enough for human purposes (*DCo* 20.1). Hobbes expresses a variant on a Baconian theme: knowledge is for the sake of power (*Scientia propter potentiam*). Some of the benefits of philosophy as practical knowledge are measurement, architectural construction, navigation, and cartography (*DCo* 1.6–7; *L* 5.20, 46.1). The practical benefits of philosophy include the knowledge of how to avoid civil war. It may appear incredible that human beings had lacked political science until Hobbes wrote *De Cive*, but he thinks it is true. Since knowledge is unified, ultimately, political philosophy rests on a correct physics, which Hobbes tries to give in *De Corpore*.

Philosophy excludes theology in the sense in which theology is the "doctrine of the nature and attributes of the eternal, ungenerable, and incomprehensible God, and in whom no composition and no division can be established and no generation can be understood" (*DCo* 1.8). Theology is also excluded because it is acquired by "supernatural revelation" and not by reasoning (*L* 46.4). This separation of philosophy and theology is sometimes interpreted as the expression of an antireligious streak in Hobbes. However, it can be fully explained as part of a long movement within western European philosophy, which begins in the fourteenth century, to either promote religion over philosophy or insulate religion from the criticisms of philosophy and science. It is a tradition that includes the two greatest Protestant reformers, Luther and Calvin. Moreover, natural and political history and literature are also excluded from philosophy, and Hobbes was certainly not opposed to them (*DCo* 1.7).

In *De Corpore*, Hobbes divides philosophy into two types, based upon how the kinds of bodies they treat of are generated. Natural philosophy deals with natural bodies; civil philosophy in a broad sense deals with things that are generated artificially by the human will. Civil philosophy in this broad sense is divided again into ethics and politics. Politics is also called civil philosophy in a narrow sense (*DCo* 1.9). These three parts of philosophy correspond to the three sections of Hobbes's *Elements of Philosophy*: *De Corpore* deals with natural bodies; *De Homine* deals with optics and human psychology; *De Cive* deals with politics. This division should be taken with a grain of salt, because there is much in *De Homine* that is not ethics, and there is as much ethics in *De Cive* as there is in *De Homine*.

In *Leviathan*, there is an alternative and less satisfying scheme of the parts of science. It begins with the same broad division of natural philosophy and civil philosophy. But it is natural philosophy which is divided into two branches, an unnamed science that deals with the consequences of the accidents common to all natural bodies, that is, of quantity and motion, and physics, which deals with the consequences of qualities. Moreover, ethics is merely one of over a dozen other sub-sciences. One of these is astrology, which is not considered a science in *De Corpore*; and another is the science of the just and unjust, which is thus separated from both ethics and civil philosophy (*L* 9.4).

Hobbes believed in the unity of science in the sense that everything is ultimately explainable in terms of the motions of tiny bits of matter. This holds for civil philosophy as much as for physics. And he gives some indication that the relationship between physics, ethics, and politics is deductive. Yet, he held that civil philosophy (in the narrow sense) can be done independently of the first two, and justified the publication of *De Cive* before *De Corpore* and *De Homine* on this ground (*DC* "Author's Preface" 9). The correct resolution to this problem is still debated. My suggestion is that, while the logical relationship between the sciences is deductive, civil philosophy can be done independently of the other two because its principles are known by experience independently of them. That is to say, the epistemic independence of the principles of civil philosophy allows it to be presented independently of the other sciences even though it is logically related to them.

False or vain philosophy, as one of the elements of the KINGDOM OF DARKNESS, is discussed in *Leviathan*, chapter 46.

power, irresistible   *See* JUSTICE, DIVINE

precept A precept is a proposition which guides behavior. COMMANDS AND COUNSELS and canons are types of precepts. A command is a precept that is to be obeyed because of the authority of the speaker; a counsel is a precept that is supposed to specify an action that is good for the audience. A canon is a precept that is a rule. Hobbes does not further explicate "rule" (*L* 42.36). A canon may also be a law, when a person is obliged to obey the canon (*L* 42.36).

predestination Predestination is the doctrine that God determines from all eternity the ultimate state of a human being. It seems to follow from the view that God is the cause of everything, which Hobbes holds (*QLNC*, pp. 9, 11). For, if God causes everything, then He causes some people to go to heaven and some to go to hell. Predestination is consonant with the doctrine that human beings are saved by grace alone, not works, and was held by most Protestants in the seventeenth century against the Roman Catholics and Arminians. Simple predestination is the doctrine that God determines from all eternity who will go to heaven. In contrast, the damned determine their own condition through sinning. Differentiating the causes for the fates of the elect and damned in this way is not logical, and Calvin plumped for the logical but hard doctrine of double predestination, that is, God alone determines from all eternity who goes to heaven and who goes to hell. Why God chooses as He does is inscrutable.

Hobbes holds the calvinist view, which he finds in the Epistle to the Romans (*LN*, p. 248; *QLNC*, p. 3). The view is also consonant with his scientific determinism. Nonetheless, Hobbes thinks that works are necessary for salvation, and he quotes approvingly from the epistle of James, which Luther had called "straw": "Even so the faith, if it have no works, is dead in itself" (*EL* 2.6.10). The reason that Hobbes holds both views is that they were both part of the Elizabethan and Jacobean tradition of the Church of England in which he was raised. Reformation and Roman Catholic elements stood together in a fragile equilibrium.

Although Hobbes subscribes to predestination, he does not think that it ought to be discussed, much less argued about. John Calvin felt about the same. In *The Elements of Law*, Hobbes pointed out that, if human beings have no idea of how God can see, hear, or speak, it is odd for any of them to think that they can work out "the manner of God's predestination" (*EL* 2.6.9). He thinks the attempt is an instance of the "philosophy and vain deceits" that Paul warns against and that the controversy over predestination and free will is not a distinctively Christian one. The Epicureans and Stoics engaged in it (*EL* 2.6.9). (*See also* LIBERTY AND NECESSITY.) Hobbes himself rarely mentions predestination explicitly. Even though it is mentioned in the long-title of *Of Liberty and Necessity*, he only alludes to it in the text. And he only briefly mentions it in *Behemoth* (*B*, p. 62).

proof   *See* DEMONSTRATION

property   There is no personal or real property (often spelled "propriety") in the state of nature (*L* 13.13, 15.3, 24.5; *DC* 6.15). Property comes to exist with the commonwealth, because only in a commonwealth does the stability exist to allow the owner to keep it securely in her possession or to transfer it in an orderly way. In fact, all property ultimately belongs to the sovereign. The relation between sovereign and subject is strictly analogous to that between master and servant. Just as a master has a "supreme power" over the servant, he has supreme power over all of the servant's possessions: "For he that can by right dispose of the person of a man may surely dispose of all those things which that person could dispose of. There is therefore nothing which the servant may retain as his own against the will of his lord" (*DC* 8.5).

Subjects only have property rights relative to other subjects. How property gets distributed is due solely to the sovereign's discretion (*L* 24.6). The sovereign can redistribute or take property at will in order to preserve the peace as he sees fit (*L* 24.7). Hobbes no doubt argues for this position in order to support the position of Charles I over the Forced Loan of 1626–7 and the Ship Money controversy of the 1630s. It is worth quoting some of Hobbes's numerous passages on this issue, both because he was adamant about it and because it was the source of much of the opposition to his political philosophy: "Propriety therefore being derived from the sovereign power is not to be pretended against the same" (*EL* 2.5.2); "seeing both the servant and all that is committed to him is the property of the master and every man may dispose of his own, and transfer the same at his pleasure, the master may therefore alienate his dominion over them or give the same by his last will to whom he list" (*EL* 2.3.5); and "The master of the servant is master also of all he has, and may exact the use thereof, that is to say, of his goods, of his labour, of his servants, and of his children" (*L* 20.13; see also *EL* 2.3.4, 2.5.2; and *DC* 8.5). Many of these remarks are in *The Elements of Law* because, at the time that it was being written, Charles's policies were still a live issue.

The use of gold and money in general is a convenient way of allowing people to consume the commodities (a form of property) that they have saved. The transfer of money from person to person is like the circulation of blood in a body and nourishes the whole (*L* 24.11). Hobbes extends the metaphor: tax collectors are the veins of the commonwealth while bursars are the arteries (*L* 24.13).

prophets The word "prophet" is used in various senses in the Bible, and Hobbes begins his discussion of the topic in *Leviathan* in characteristic fashion by enumerating some of these senses. Sometimes a prophet is someone who speaks from God to human beings, such as Moses, Samuel, and Elijah. Sometimes a prophet is one who speaks from human beings to God, such as Abraham. Sometimes a prophet is someone who foretells the future. Teachers are sometimes called prophets. Anyone who has the authority to say public prayers is properly termed a prophet. And women are prophets in one sense whenever they praise God. Even heathen poets are properly termed prophets (*L* 36.7). In the sense of predicting the future, even false prophets are prophets. And madmen and evil people have been prophets (*L* 36.8). Hobbes's purpose in this catalog of uses seems to be to deflate the importance of the term by allowing it to be used of almost any sincere Christian and many non-Christians as well. Hobbes shortly later further deflates the concept when he points out that some true prophets are not holy people or members of the elect; God sometimes speaks through ungodly beings, such as Baalam and the witch of Endor (*L* 36.20).

It is curious that Hobbes does not mention "the godly exercise of prophesying," which was the Elizabethan puritan practice of having clergy (and often laymen) gather together with two or more clerics preaching on the same topic, which was then discussed. The practice was extremely controversial during Elizabeth's reign. She sequestered the archbishop of Canterbury, Edmund Grindal, for supporting it.

In *De Cive*, Hobbes's definition of a prophet is unpolemical. He says that a prophet is someone "whom God recommends to the rest, as worthy of belief by the working of true miracles" (*DC* 15.3).

In the Old Testament, a person must satisfy two conditions in order to be a prophet: she must be able to work MIRACLES, and she must teach the established doctrine of the religion. These condition's are individually necessary and jointly sufficient (*L* 32.7). Hobbes points out that Deuteronomy 13:1–4 condemns people who work miracles but teach that something other than the God of Abraham is the true God (*DC* 16.11). In an epilogue to a story, discussed further below, about a true prophet who was misled by another prophet, Hobbes mentions that the Egyptian sorcerers worked miracles and were not true prophets. Also, Jesus warned that there would be false Christs and false prophets who would perform "wonders and miracles" so great that even the elect would be seduced by them, if that were possible. It follows then that false prophets have the power to perform miracles, and thus such a power cannot be a sufficient condition for a true prophet (*L* 32.7).

The second essential mark of a true prophet is that the doctrine that she teaches is the true one, as we saw. But again this is not a sufficient sign. Deuteronomy 18:21–2 condemns people whose seemingly miraculous predictions do not come true and Hobbes takes these to include those who "teach not false doctrine" but who here make evident their failure to show themselves to be prophets by not also working miracles (*L* 32.8; *DC* 16.11). The characteristic doctrine that false prophets teach is revolution. Hobbes claimed that to urge a revolt against the king was equivalent to urging a revolt against God, because the Jews had made God king at the foot of Mount Sinai (*L* 32.7). This works as a judgement about the Jews between the time of Moses and Saul, but not afterwards. Yet, it is fairly clear that Hobbes wants the point generalized to all times. In this context, Hobbes counted the proposition "Jesus is king" as true in order to use a text of St Paul as further evidence that to speak against a king is irreligious, even though in the chapter 35 it is important for Hobbes to insist that Jesus is not yet king but will be at the end of the world. (*See* KINGDOM OF GOD, PROPHETIC.)

Hobbes says that Moses was considered a prophet because of "his miracles and his faith." The first criterion is not problematic in this context. Miracles were performed that were intended to show Moses to have the approval of God. The meaning of "faith" is not quite so straightforward, because the word has many meanings. In this case, "faith" does not mean any gift that God gave to Moses or any particular mental state that he was in. Rather, "faith" refers to the propositions that God wanted to be taught about Him. That is, the faith of Moses was his teaching that the God who called the Hebrews out of Egypt was identical with the God of Abraham, Isaac, and Jacob (*DC* 16.11).

Suppose a person has both marks of a true prophet. Is there still a problem? Yes; even though the marks are individually necessary and jointly sufficient conditions of being a prophet, it may not be easy to recognize that the person has those marks. The two conditions may seem to provide a criterion by which a person can judge who is a true prophet and who is not, but in fact they do not. Interpretations of what a person means can differ and whether what that person has predicted has come true is open to doubt. How should one judge? Hobbes gives two basic answers. One is that people should judge "by the way of natural reason" (*DC* 16.11; *L* 36.20). The other answer is that the sovereign ought to judge (*DC* 16.13; *L* 36.20). The second answer is a special case of the first in the sense that natural reason dictates that, if each private individual judges the matter for herself, dissension and war are the inevitable outcome; therefore, in order to avoid such a state, some judge must be agreed upon to settle the issue; and the sovereign is the one who functions in just this way:

> For when Christian men take not their Christian sovereign for God's prophet, they must either take their own dreams for the prophecy they mean to be governed by, and the tumour of their own hearts for the spirit of God; or they must suffer themselves to be led by some strange prince; or by some of their fellow subjects that can bewitch them by slander of the government into rebellion without other miracle to confirm their calling than sometimes an extraordinary success and impunity; and by this means destroying all laws, both divine and human, reduce all order, government, and society to the first chaos of violence and civil war. (*L* 36.20)

What civil war he is talking about is obvious. If this reasoning does not seem sound or if reason in general does not seem reliable, then the position that the sovereign ought to be the judge of prophets can be justified by an appeal to the teaching of the Bible (*DC* 16.13).

So far, this discussion has centered on what the Old Testament says about the matter. In the New Testament, there was only one mark of a true prophet; it was to teach that Jesus is the Christ (*L* 36.20). Anyone preaching a different doctrine, even if she could work miracles, was a false prophet; and she that taught it was a true one. This claim is in keeping with Hobbes's effort to simplify Christianity. There is also a political dimension to Hobbes's view. False prophets are politically dangerous, as we have seen.

The term "(true) prophet" is a retrospective one, if one is employing the Old Testament criterion. One cannot determine who is a true prophet until after the predicted events have occurred. Sometimes the prediction may refer to the indefinite future, in which case it is not clear how long one should wait before a judgement is made about the person's status as a true or false prophet. Also, many people who eventually proved to be true prophets were taken for false prophets, condemned, and killed by their contemporaries. Hobbes's sanguine description of such cases is this: "peradventure it is, that the Jews esteemed the writings of those whom they slew when they prophesied, for prophetic afterward" (*DC* 16.12). Hobbes's advice is that any allegedly miraculous prediction that a supposed prophet makes ought to be specific and timely enough to be confirmed or disconfirmed by "an immediate or a not long deferred event" (*L* 32.8).

In *Leviathan*, Hobbes discusses prophets in the context of considering how one can determine whether an alleged REVELATION is genuine. No empirical evidence can be compelling, because anyone who claims to have had either a dream or a vision of God may be either lying or mistaken. One possibility to which Hobbes gives short shrift is that people can rely upon prophets to determine which alleged revelations are genuine. Numerous biblical stories show the problem with this suggestion. In the ninth century BC, Ahab, king of Israel, wanted to know whether he should ally himself with Jehoshaphat, the king of Judah, in order to go to war with Syria to take Ramoth-gilead. Four hundred of his prophets, predicting victory, urged him to go to war. Only one prophet, Micaiah, disagreed. But Ahab did not believe him. So he went to war and was killed. That is the story Hobbes tells (*L* 32.7). The moral of course is that even an overwhelming majority of prophets cannot be believed. There is more to the biblical account that makes his case even stronger. When Ahab first asked Micaiah for his opinion, he lied and said that Ahab would be victorious. It was only when Ahab persisted in interrogating Micaiah that he discovered that the prophet expected him to be defeated (1 Kings 22:13–28). So, even a true prophet may lie. God Himself has called prophets liars (*L* 36.19). Even when a prophet does tell the truth, there is no guarantee that people will act in accordance with her prophecy. The Jews often killed the prophets who told the truth and only honored them posthumously, as we indicated above (*DC* 16.12; *L* 36.19).

It is obvious that the general run of humanity cannot pick out true from false prophets. But it would not do ordinary people any good even if true prophets could pick out true from false prophets, since, as just mentioned, there is no way to determine who the true prophets are that are identifying other true prophets. Perhaps there would be some consolation if at least the true prophets themselves were able to recognize each other. But even that is not the case. Hobbes tells the story of the true and well-intentioned prophet who is ordered by God to condemn the altar that Jeroboam, king of Israel, set up at Bethel. The prophet does so and sets out to return home. Another prophet, hearing about what the first prophet has done, intercepts him and invites him to eat. The first prophet demurs on the grounds that God has told him to eat nothing before he returns home. The second prophet then assures the first that God, through an angel, has countermanded that order and wants him to eat. The first prophet takes the second at his word. He eats, resumes his journey, and is killed by a lion, sent by God to punish the prophet for disobeying Him. One might try to object that the first prophet was not a true prophet. But Hobbes will not accept that. The dead prophet had condemned the altar at Bethel as God had instructed him; and at least two and arguably three miracles are performed as verification of the prophet's character. The arm of a servant is withered when he tries to interfere with the prophet; it is restored when the prophet asks God to restore it; and the altar falls to pieces when the prophet declares that it will (*L* 32.7, referring to 1 Kings 13). (Hobbes does not comment at all on the apparent injustice of the death of first prophet – how could he have known that the second prophet was lying? – but one would not expect him to, because for Hobbes, God, being omnipotent, can do whatever He likes without injustice.)

Suppose that all the problems already discussed were solved. Suppose that true prophets could in principle be identified, could human beings now rely upon them to communicate what God wanted? No, because MIRACLES no longer occur (*L* 32.9).

propositions (*propositiones*) For Hobbes, names are the basic units of language. Propositions are constructed out of names by the concatenation of them (*contextu nominum*). Hobbes says, "A proposition is speech (*oratio*) consisting of two copulated names by which the one who is speaking signifies that he conceives the name which occurs second to be the name of the same thing as the name which occurs first" (*DCo* 3.2). The first name is the subject or antecedent; the second is the predicate or consequent. Hobbes's definition and terminology indicate the extent of his commitment to the categorical Aristotelian logic he was taught at Magdalen Hall. For Hobbes, "Mary walks" is reducible to "Mary is walking," or else "walks" is a name. The word "is" is not a name and is eliminable; many languages would say "Mary walking" where English requires "Mary is walking." Although "is" does not name anything, that is not to say that it does not have an important function. Two names simply juxtaposed would not be a proposition. A proposition consists of copulated names and what the copulation does is to induce "the thought of the cause on account of which those names were imposed." Thus, to say "A body is movable" is to intend to get the audience to think about why the named object is called a body and why it is called movable. While it may not be clear what this means exactly, such thinking about the name is the source for the belief in platonic entities, according to Hobbes.

Calling the subject and predicate the "antecedent" and "consequent," respectively, is proleptic, because Hobbes eventually wants to argue that scientific propositions that have the superficial form of a subject-predicate sentence are in fact conditional propositions. Before getting to that point, he presents a standard late-seventeenth-century type of taxonomy of propositions. There are universal ("Every man is an animal"), particular ("Some man is educated"), indefinite ("Man is educated"), and singular propositions ("Socrates is a philosopher" and "This man is black"), all based upon the "quantity" of the subject. There are also affirmative and negative propositions, based upon its "quality" (*DCo* 3.5–6). These distinctions are eventually used in Hobbes's treatment of syllogisms, which again is conventional for the period.

As we have seen, Hobbes defines all propositions as two copulated names of which the second purports to name everything that is named by the

241

first. This view works for sentences like "Man is an animal," but not for "No man is a dog." His definition of truth and falsity suffers from a strictly analogous mistake. He says that a true proposition is one in which the predicate is the name of everything that the subject names. Again this works for "Man is an animal" but not for "No man is a dog" (*DCo* 3.7; *L* 4.11). But Hobbes does not seem to be thinking of such examples here. He is in fact giving a standard seventeenth-century rendering of Aristotelian logic.

Hobbes departs from the terminological necessities of Aristotelian logic when he introduces the distinction between primary and nonprimary propositions. He does not explain what nonprimary propositions are, but presumably they are any propositions that are not primary. Primary propositions are the most basic kind used in scientific reasoning. They are definitions that explicate the name in the subject position by specifying in the predicate position names for the same thing. The sentence "Man is a rational, animate body" is such a definition, because everything named by "man" is also named by the compound name "rational, animate body" (*DCo* 3.9).

Hobbes's view is novel. He contrasts such definitions, which are the foundations of science, with axioms and postulates. He believes that propositions that go under the name "axioms" are actually provable from definitions, even though they typically are not proved by the geometers who use them, because of their obviousness. Postulates, such as "A straight line can be drawn between two points," are also not primary propositions, because they too are not definitions, and, it seems, not even provable, although Hobbes does not say this explicitly. What he says is that postulates are "principles of art or construction, but not of scientific knowledge or demonstration" (*DCo* 3.9).

Another distinction relevant to philosophy (science) is that between necessary and contingent propositions. Hobbes says, "A proposition is necessary when no thing can be conceived or imagined at any time, of which the subject is a name while the predicate is not" (*DCo* 3.10). This definition may be objectionable on two grounds. First, it uses psychological terms: "conceived or imagined." My guess is that Hobbes uses these terms because of his linguistic theory of science. Science consists of analytic propositions, which are true solely in virtue of their meanings; and all meaningful words have to name objects that can be imagined, in order to prevent the intrusion of absurdly metaphysical ideas. This at least explains his use of these notions if it does not justify them. Second, his definition uses "can" to define "necessary." But "can," which has the same meaning as "possible," stands in as much need of explication as "necessary" does. They are correlative words. This is especially problematic because, when

242

Hobbes explains necessity in another context, it turns out that every true proposition is necessarily true. This is best explained after his definition of "contingent" propositions is presented.

A contingent proposition, Hobbes says, is one that "can sometimes be true and sometimes be false" (*DCo* 3.10). This does not seem to have any psychological element connected to it. And it seems to get the right results. The sentence "Socrates is sitting" is obviously contingent on this account, and, more interestingly, so is "Every crow is black," according to Hobbes. What he means is that crows are not essentially black. If some climatic or dietary alteration caused crows to change color, they would nonetheless remain crows. This is not an odd explication of contingency; but it is not clear whether Hobbes has the right to espouse it. What is the basis for his position that "black" is not especially important to being a crow? Since the meanings of names are arbitrary for Hobbes, "black" is no more arbitrary a name when applied to "crow" than "bird" is. Since Hobbes cannot appeal to Aristotelian or any other sort of essence, it does not seem that he has any principled way of distinguishing between names that make a proposition necessary and those that make it contingent. He says that the predicate of a necessary proposition has to be "equivalent" (*equivalere*) to the subject or be part of an equivalent name. He says that, even if every man were a liar, "Every man is a liar" would not be a necessary proposition, because "liar" is "not part of a compounded name to which the name 'man' is equivalent" (*DCo* 3.10). But he does not say why here. Later he says that two propositions are equivalent just in case they can both be "reduced" (*reducantur*); but it is not clear what reducing a proposition means. It cannot mean that both are deducible from the same proposition, because "Every man is rational" and "Every man is animate" are both deducible from "Every man is a rational, animate body" yet they are not equivalent. And it cannot mean that both entail the same proposition, because "Every man is a rational body" and "Every man is an animate body" both entail "Every man is body" but, again, they are not equivalent.

A categorical proposition is one that is "pronounced simply or absolutely" (*simpliciter sive absolute pronuntiata est*), such as "Every man is an animal" or "No man is a tree." A hypothetical proposition is one that is pronounced "conditionally" (*conditionaliter*). A necessarily true categorical proposition (e.g. one of the form "Every *S* is *P*") entails its corresponding hypothetical proposition (e.g. "If anything is *S*, then it is *P*"). For example, "Every man is an animal" entails "If anything is a man, then it is an animal." The idea is easily extended to necessarily true negative categorical and hypothetical propositions: "No man is a tree" entails "If anything is a man, then it is not a tree" (*DCo* 3.11).

243

These examples should be contrasted with the proposition "Every crow is black," which is true but not necessarily true, as discussed above. Thus, it does not entail "If anything is a crow, then it is black." Hobbes apparently construes, "if . . . , then ———," as expressing entailment or strict implication, rather than material implication, as understood by modern logicians. He does not further explain or justify his position. What he asserts is: "therefore, whenever a hypothetical proposition is true, the categorical proposition answering to it is not only true, but necessarily true. I have thought that it should be noted for the sake of argument, that philosophers would reason more safely, for the most part, with hypothetical propositions than with categorical ones" (*DCo* 3.11). What Hobbes seems to envision is a science consisting of definitions, formulated as conditional propositions, with other propositions derived from them by hypothetical syllogism.

In addition to his account of necessary and contingent propositions, Hobbes has an account of necessary and contingent events. Although it is important not to confuse propositions, which are linguistic, with events that are not, it is relevant to explain his views of necessity and contingency here. Every event is necessary, according to him. Not only does every event have a cause, but the event is necessary in virtue of the cause. This is a metaphysical account of necessity. Hobbes's account of contingency is not metaphysical but epistemological. A contingent event is one of which the causes are unknown. To say that an event is contingent is to say that one does not know whether it did or did not, will or will not occur (*AW*, p. 427). This means that all contingent events are necessary, although not all necessary events are contingent.

Most of Hobbes's discussions of necessity and contingency occur in his polemical works on free will against Bishop Bramhall. In *Of Liberty and Necessity*, Hobbes maintains that every true proposition is necessary (even though this does not fit the account in *De Corpore*) because every event is necessary. For example, the sentence "It is necessary that tomorrow it will rain or tomorrow it will not rain" is necessary because one of the disjunctive component sentences is necessarily true. But, because we do not know which disjunct is true, we say that one of the disjuncts is contingently true and the other contingently false. That is to say, a sentence is contingent if one does not know whether it is true or false or, if true, know what caused the event that makes it true (*LN*, p. 276; *QLNC*, pp. 195, 222). (*See also* LIBERTY AND NECESSITY.)

A conflation of the sense in which propositions are necessary or contingent with the sense in which events are is evident in the following passage:

> Wherefore, all propositions concerning future things, contingent or not contingent, . . . are either necessarily true or false; whereas their verity

depends not upon our knowledge, but upon the foregoing of their causes. But there are some, who though they confess this whole proposition, *tomorrow it will either rain, or not rain*, to be true, yet they will not acknowledge the parts of it . . . to be either of them true by itself; because they say neither this nor that is true *determinately*. But what is this *determinately true*, but true upon our knowledge, or evidently true? And therefore they say no more but that it is not yet known whether it be true or no; but they say it more obscurely, and darken the evidence of the truth with the same words with which they endeavour to hide their own ignorance. (*DCo* 10.5; see also *LN*, pp. 259, 277; *QLNC*, pp. 121–3)

punishment   Hobbes discusses punishment in various contexts with various intentions. He divides punishment into two types: (1) human and (2) divine (*L* 28.14). This entry will consider each in turn.

(1) There are several kinds of human punishment: corporal punishment, capital punishment, pecuniary punishment, dishonour ("ignominy"), imprisonment, and exile (*L* 28.16–21). But we shall concentrate on what is common to all of these, the nature of human punishment.

Hobbes's best discussion of human or civil punishment occurs in *Leviathan*. There he defines it as an evil inflicted by a public authority on a person who in the judgement of that authority has done something forbidden or has failed to do something required by the law, and the authority's intention in inflicting it is to make people more inclined to obey the law (*L* 28.1). Five aspects of this definition deserve attention. (a) When Hobbes says that a punishment is an evil, he does not mean that it is wicked or unjust. In accordance with his definitions of good and evil, he means that a punishment is a harm; it is something that the victim does not want done to her.

(b) Punishment must be inflicted by the sovereign or his representative; an evil inflicted by a private person may be revenge but it cannot be punishment (*L* 28.3).

(c) In addition to administering the penalty (evil), the sovereign or his representative must be the one who judges the criminal to have violated the law. This judgement needs to be made in public and the act publicly declared to be a violation of the law (*L* 28.5). In other contexts, Hobbes emphasizes that the sovereign must state what the facts of the matter are and he says or implies that the facts are whatever the sovereign says they are. If the sovereign judges that someone has committed murder, then it is a fact that that person has committed a murder. These facts may be called institutional facts since they depend upon a procedure within an institution although Hobbes does not use the term. Institutional facts exist in many areas of life. If an umpire calls a runner out, then the runner is out no matter what the natural facts may be. However, in the context of discussing punishment, Hobbes does not mention the fact-making power of sovereigns. Rather, he says that harm done to an innocent subject is against the law of nature, "and therefore there can be no punishment of the innocent" (*L* 28.22). In fact, three laws of nature are violated by harming the innocent: the law that forbids revenge without a commensurate good, because no good to the state can come of harming the innocent; the law that forbids ingratitude, because the sovereign was given his authority by the subject in order to be protected if she obeyed the laws; and the law that commands equity. This is a firm defense by one who emphasizes the absoluteness of the sovereign's will of the rights of subjects to be treated fairly. Aspect (c), like (b), is an application of Hobbes's view about sovereignty that judicial decisions and power must be located in the same person. (*See* SOVEREIGNTY.)

(d) A person may merit punishment for commissions or omissions. Nothing more need be said about this.

(e) The purpose of punishment must be to produce something good, namely, more obedience to the laws. If a sovereign punished a person solely to inflict harm with no hope or intention of improving the behavior of the criminal or other subjects, then the harm inflicted would technically be not punishment but "hostility" (*L* 28.7; *DC* 13.16). Later Hobbes says that the purpose of punishment is to improve the behavior either of the criminal or of other people for whom the punishment of the criminal can serve as an example (*L* 30.23).

Three other points should be made about aspect (e). First, a penalty that is less than the benefit the criminal received by committing the crime is not punishment, according to Hobbes, but merely the "price" the criminal paid for what she got. Hobbes's thought is that a punishment is supposed to deter people from committing a crime. But if there is a net profit received by doing something criminal, then doing the act and suffering the punishment are a kind of business transaction (*L* 28.9; *DC* 13.6). (For similar reasons, Hobbes is opposed to the satisfaction theory of redemption, according to which there was a price to be paid for sin (*L* 38.25). *See* SALVATION.) Second, harm inflicted that is greater than the stated penalty for a crime is not punishment but hostility. The reason is the same as the one mentioned above. A penalty will not deter a person unless she knows about it. So, harm suffered beyond what was advertised for the offense could not have had a deterrent effect on that criminal (*L* 28.10; *DC* 13.16; *LN*, p. 253). Of course, one may argue that that penalty will deter other people in the future, although Hobbes does not. Hobbes is willing to accept laws that have no penalty specified. In such a case, people ought to know that they will deserve whatever they get (*L* 28.10; *DC* 13.16).

Third, retroactive laws are not permitted, because a person cannot disobey a command that has not been given (L 28.11).

Some crimes are worse than others because they pose a greater danger to the state and consequently ought to be punished more severely. Those that are motivated by contempt for justice, those that are most offensive to most people, and those which may seem to be authorized if they are not punished, such as those committed by friends of government officials, are examples of the worst sorts of crimes (L 30.23). Some crimes should be punished less harshly because the guilt connected with them is mitigated by EXCUSES, such as those done from great fear, out of great need, or in ignorance (L 30.23).

Two parts of Hobbes's discussion of the definition of punishment seem to be related to the trial and execution of Charles I. Hobbes says that harm inflicted by "judges without authority from the sovereign is not punishment, but an act of hostility," and Charles's main contention at his trial was that the court lacked authority. Charles was right about the legal point, but was nonetheless executed. Also, Hobbes says that harm inflicted on "the representative of the commonwealth is not punishment but an act of hostility" (L 28.6, 28.12).

Hobbes's definition of punishment as something inflicted by a public authority presupposes a sovereign-making covenant. Hobbes says that harm inflicted on a declared enemy of the state is not punishment, because enemies are in the state of nature with respect to each other and hence not under a common civil law (L 28.13, 28.23). Sometimes Hobbes says that whatever is done to an enemy is "lawful" in the sense of not violating any law; sometimes he puts limits on what is lawfully inflicted on people even in the state of nature.

Punishment is necessary because a covenant alone does not ensure security (DC 6.4). The right to punish is "the sword of justice" (DC 6.5). The sword of justice is the domestic correlate of the sword of war, which protects subjects from external enemies (DC 6.7). The power of punishment and the right of judging who is to be punished must be in the same entity, otherwise the right of judging would be ineffective (DC 6.8).

What justifies civil punishment? The question is a serious one because no one can ever give up the right to self-preservation and self-defense even when entering into a sovereign-making covenant; it follows that no one "gave any right to another to lay violent hands upon his person" (L 28.2); yet punishment is justifiably administered by the state. The answer is that what people gave up when they left the state of nature was the right to defend other people from punishment by the sovereign (DC 2.18), and that the sovereign did not get the right to punish from anyone, he already had the right to harm anyone he chose by the right of nature, which allows everyone to do whatever she thinks is necessary to preserve herself (*LN*, p. 254). While other people lay down their right to everything when they covenant with others, the sovereign, not being a party to it, does not. He remains in the state of nature. The reason that the sovereign has the strength to punish people is that in making the covenant everyone gives up her right to protect her fellows and agrees to help the sovereign satisfy his desires (*L* 28.2).

Sometimes, Hobbes uses his doctrine of AUTHORIZATION to justify the institution of punishment. He says that a person who is punished by a sovereign actually punishes herself, because, by the sovereign-making covenant, she authorized the sovereign to act for her; so she is the AUTHOR of her own punishment (*L* 18.3). This account is not consistent with Hobbes's principle that a person can never forfeit her right to life nor her right to resist punishment (*DC* 2.18).

(2) Concerning God's punishment, two kinds can be distinguished. There is punishment in this life and there is the punishment that awaits the wicked after death. Since human beings have no natural knowledge of what happens after death, they must rely upon their belief in revelation for their opinions about it. (*See* HELL.) The divine punishment in this life is the result of the natural order of things:

> There is no action of man in this life, that is not the beginning of so long a chain of consequences as no human providence is high enough to give a man a prospect to the end. And in this chain there are linked together both pleasing and unpleasing events, in such manner as he that will do anything for his pleasure must engage himself to suffer all the pains annexed to it; and these pains are the natural punishments of those actions which are the beginning of more harm than good. And hereby it comes to pass, that intemperance is naturally punished with diseases, rashness with mischances, injustice with the violence of enemies, pride with ruin, cowardice with oppression, negligent government of princes with rebellion, and rebellion with slaughter. For seeing punishments are consequences to the breach of laws, natural punishments must be naturally consequent to the breach of the laws of nature, and therefore follow them as their natural, not arbitrary effects. (*L* 31.40)

Q

***

Questions Concerning Liberty, Necessity, and Chance (1656) [15]   This is
Hobbes's reply to John Bramhall's *Defence of True Liberty from Antecedent and
Extrinsecal Necessity* (1655), which was his reply to the unauthorized pub-
lication of Hobbes's *Of Liberty and Necessity* (1654). (*See further* OF LIBERTY
AND NECESSITY.)

   Hobbes identifies his views with those of Luther and Calvin and associates Bramhall's views with those of the Arminians. Thus Hobbes in effect
claims to be a true Protestant in contrast with Bramhall, who takes the
Roman Catholic position. The consequences of this dispute were not purely
theological, according to Hobbes. The English Arminians, who were for the
most part the followers of Archbishop William Laud, offended the Presbyterians and Independents, often referred to as "puritans", and this dissension helped to cause the English Civil Wars (*QLNC*, p. 2). (Politically,
Hobbes sides with Laud against the Presbyterians and Independents.)

   In this work, Hobbes holds that a human being does not have the power
to choose to will; that chance produces nothing; that every event has a
cause; that every cause is necessary; and that God is the cause of everything.
According to Hobbes, Bramhall holds that God is not the cause of human
actions. He also says that both of them accept Scripture. The difference
between them is that Bramhall is a "learned School-divine" and Hobbes is
not (*QLNC* "To the Reader"). Hobbes defends his position by using both
biblical texts and philosophical argumentation. He begins with the biblical evidence by correctly claiming that St Paul, who discussed the sources
of human action, "never uses the term of *free will*" and does not hold an
equivalent doctrine but makes God the cause of all actions (*QLNC*, p. 1).
Later he quotes a large number of biblical passages, some of which support his position and some of which do not. He does not have the attitude
that the Bible is contradictory or useless in this area of debate; rather, he
does his best to give an interpretation of the opposed passages that is
consistent with his own.

   Aside from the preliminary materials, the book takes the following form.
Hobbes quotes the entirety of one of Bramhall's thirty-eight numbered

249

sections from the latter's *A Defence of True Liberty from Antecedent and Extrinsecal Necessity* and then criticizes it in a section with a title of the form "Animadversions upon *X*," and so on for all thirty-eight sections. The structure is a bit more confusing, because each of Bramhall's sections consists of interlaced passages from Hobbes's *Of Liberty and Necessity* and Bramhall's criticism of Hobbes's position. In short, most of Hobbes's book is a gloss on a gloss of Bramhall's view or his own.

R

reason (*ratio*) Reason is computation or reckoning for Hobbes. It is literally addition and subtraction, according to his mature view (*DCo* 1.2; *L* 5.1–2). Earlier, he had defined right reasoning as a kind of syllogism ("the correct combining of true propositions into a syllogism" (*AW*, p. 157)). But even at this time, he held that right reasoning depends upon "the correct coupling of terms, i.e. of the subject and predicate, in accordance with their proper and adequate meanings," which in turn depends upon "an efficient nomenclature of things" (*AW*, p. 157).

There are two major discussions of reason, of which the later one in *De Corpore* is simpler and more moderate than the earlier one in *Leviathan*. Theoretically the discussion of reason is also more crucial to *De Corpore* since it is the first section of Hobbes's complete system of scientific knowledge, *The Elements of Philosophy*. Hobbes thinks that if the foundations of a science are uncertain, then so are all of its results. It is no good doing some sophisticated calculation carefully if the given numbers have not been correctly obtained (*L* 5.4).

In both *Leviathan* and *De Corpore*, reasoning is said to be addition and subtraction. Hobbes illustrates the idea from arithmetic, geometry, and language. Mathematicians add and subtract numbers; geometricians add and subtract lines, figures, angles, and proportions; speakers add and subtract words. Concerning this last group, Hobbes holds that the addition of "rational," "animated," and "body" gives the sum "man." Also, a syllogism is the addition or subtraction of ideas which yields the conclusion (*DCo* 1.3; *L* 5.1). One can also begin with a conclusion, say "Socrates is mortal," subtract a premise, "Every man is mortal," and find the other premise as a remainder, "Socrates is a man."

Hobbes seems to equivocate on the ideas of addition and subtraction. He maintains that forming a sentence from words or forming a syllogism from three sentences is the same process of addition as arithmethical addition (*L* 5.1). But addition and subtraction in the arithmetical sense of finding a sum and a remainder are not the same as adding and subtracting words to form a sentence or sentences to form a syllogism. At best, a

251

sentence would seem to be a formula to be understood along the lines of "Socrates = a man" and a syllogism an arithmetical problem which requires adding or subtracting to determine its validity but not to construct it.

Let's now consider the relation between reason and right reason. It is plausible that reason and right reason are the same just as believing a proposition and believing it to be true are the same. But this does not seem to be correct. A distinction needs to be made between mere reason as calculation and reason itself. Since calculations can be correct or incorrect, mere reason can be correct or incorrect. So mere reason cannot be the same as reason itself, which can never be mistaken. The phrase "reason itself" indicates the same as "right reason."

Although right reason is infallible, there is no natural criterion for identifying it. Majority opinion certainly does not determine truth and hence cannot determine when a calculation has been done correctly. And the opinion of a private person is certainly no criterion. In fact, according to Hobbes, the phrase "right reason" is typically used by people who simply want their own opinion followed; it is a rhetorical term used for partisan purposes (L 5.3).

Hobbes's solution is conventionalistic. Someone must be designated as the judge and final arbiter of what is going to count as correct, in order to avoid controversy. There is only one sensible person to serve this role, the sovereign. (A distinguished philosopher once told me of his experience as an instructor in philosophy at West Point. He and his chairman (his commanding officer) were arguing about whether a certain proof was valid. Being unable to come to an agreement, the superior officer said to him, "Lieutenant D, that proof is valid. That is all." "Yes, sir," said Lieutenant D, saluting.) Hobbes's solution to the lack of a criterion for right reason is not skeptical or cynical. It is realistic. He does not deny that there is a true and false calculation of each matter. (In one place Hobbes calls reason "the undoubted word of God" (L 32.2) and in another the "soul of the law" (DCL, p. 4).) The issue is rather how to settle disputes.

Hobbes does not restrict the matters in which a judge must decide what counts as right reason. It applies to scientific and mathematical issues as well as religious and political ones. Sovereigns may rely upon experts for advice on technical matters, but they have the ultimate responsibility for deciding what will be taken as true beliefs (DC 16.16). When he is discussing who is to supervise the study of the land, seas, and stars, "the nature of all things . . . and all manner of sciences, which [includes] philosophy," Hobbes raises the issue of who is to decide the truth or falsity of disputed theories. He says that it is to be those who are appointed to that task by the sovereign. Since they are merely acting for the sovereign, it is in fact the sovereign himself who decides what is true and what is false, what inferences are valid and which are invalid, in matters of science (*DC* 17.12). He considers the problem of determining whether a being born of a human mother but having a monstrous shape is human or not. The issue, he says, cannot be decided using Aristotle's definition of a human being as a rational animal, or by any philosopher. Only the civil authorities are competent to decide the matter (*DC* 17.12; *EL* 2.10.8). In a letter to the Royal Society, Hobbes described a woman who allegedly lived without eating anything; instead of asserting that she was or was not a natural marvel, he left it to the proper authorities to decide. Hobbes's conventionalistic solution is also obviously politically motivated.

As early as *The Elements of Law* (1640), Hobbes pointed out that, in the state of nature, there is no way to determine right reason. It certainly cannot be identified with what some call "a common measure." Since there is no common measure, "the reason of some man or men" must serve as the standard by which disputes about what is correct and incorrect are settled (*EL* 2.10.8).

Hobbes calls a mistake in reasoning about individual events "error." It is an error to say "That bull is going to charge" when it is not going to (*DCo* 5.1; *L* 5.5). ABSURDITY is something else. In *Leviathan*, he takes the very strong position that any false general proposition is an "absurdity or senseless speech" (*L* 5.5). In *De Corpore*, his view is more moderate and he explains absurdities as category mistakes.

redemption   *See* SALVATION

religion   Hobbes discusses religion and religious issues from many perspectives and in many places. This entry will concentrate on his two significant attempts to define religion in *Leviathan* and *De Homine*. The definition in *Leviathan* (1651) occurs in a highly controversial context and will be discussed first. The definition in *De Homine* (1658) may indicate some desire at that time to reduce the animosity that had been directed against him to varying degrees since at least 1640. Later writings of his about religion are often polemical and inflammatory.

In Leviathan, religion is defined along with SUPERSTITION and true religion. It occurs inconspicuously among numerous definitions of emotions and affective properties in chapter 6, the ostensible point of which is to show that all human desires, along with cognitive and noncognitive functions, can be analyzed ultimately in terms of the motions of small bodies.

Religion is defined after curiosity, which is asserted to be the cause of religion. Curiosity is unique to human beings. It is the desire to know how and why things happen by tracing their causes back as far as possible

253

(*L* 6.35, 12.1–2). Religion itself is "Fear of power invisible, feigned by the mind or imagined from tales publicly allowed" (*L* 6.36; *OL* 3:45, 3:563). The genus of religion, fear of invisible power, is scarcely objectionable. The function of the remaining disjunctive phrase, "feigned by the mind or imagined from tales publicly allowed," is problematic. Is each disjunct supposed to supply the specific difference for one of what would seem to be the two species of religion, namely, superstition and true religion? This suggestive question would be at least partially helpful if Hobbes defined superstition as religion that is feigned by the mind. Instead, he takes the negation of the other disjunct as the specific difference: superstition is religion that is not permitted (*L* 6.36). The objectionable consequences of this definition were obvious to his contemporaries. According to it, Christianity was superstition in pre-Constantinian Rome, and was not superstition afterwards. Roman Catholicism was superstition in England in 1651 but was not superstition in Spain at the same time. One of the odd features of Hobbes's definition is that he had given an unobjectionable definition that some clerics might think incisive in *De Cive*. There he defined it as "the fear of invisible things, when it is severed from right reason" (*DC* 16.1). It is somewhat similar to ATHEISM, which he thinks arises from "fear without right reason."

There is no analogous problem with the definition of true religion. Again taking the negation of a disjunct that appears in his definition of religion, "feigned by the mind," Hobbes presents a non-relativistic, unobjectionable definition: true religion is religion such that "the power imagined is truly such as we imagine" (*L* 6.36). Nonetheless, this definition combined with the one for superstition has the consequence that something can be both a superstition and a true religion. Assume for the sake of the point that Christianity is a true religion; it was also superstition in pagan Rome.

Some explanation is appropriate for the oddity of Hobbes's definition of superstition, if only a conjectural one. My guess is that Hobbes's definition is the result of a linguistic insight: how people use a word is not always consonant with its meaning or cognitive content. The identification of meaning with use, which some philosophers in this century have promoted, is not correct in general. There is often a divergence between how people use a word and what the word means. People often use the word "know" as a way of expressing their certainty about some matter, but "know" does not mean that a person is certain. (In the ordinary sense, one can know something about which one is not certain; and one can know something without expressing one's certainty about it.) Similarly, Hobbes may have been calling attention to the fact that people often call "superstition" any religion with which they disagree, independently of the relationship that that religion has to the truth. Hobbes was fully aware of what had happened in sixteenth-century England when the religion changed from Roman Catholicism to the Church of England, back to Roman Catholicism, and then to a form of Protestantism. And he lived through the change from a calvinistic to an Arminian Church of England, the disputes between Presbyterians and Independents, and the Thirty Years' War. With each change of religion there were asseverations from members of the religion then established that the outlawed religion was superstitious.

The distinction between what a word means and how it is used can also be applied to what is left implicit in Hobbes's discussion of true religion. His definition of it, as we saw, was unexceptionable. What about how the word is used? For that, it is necessary to think of the second disjunct in the definition of religion, "imagined from tales publicly allowed," as suggesting how people use the term "true religion." As a matter of fact, people typically accept the religion that is presented to them as "allowed," that is, socially respectable, as the true religion, no matter how absurd it is. It also needs to be mentioned that Hobbes himself wanted the governmentally approved religion to be considered the true religion.

Let's now consider more closely the context within which Hobbes defines "religion." He holds that philosophy or science requires that one know what causes an object to exist. He tries to satisfy that requirement by defining religion immediately after defining curiosity, as mentioned above. Religion is caused by curiosity, and curiosity is the desire to know how and why things happen by tracing their causes back as far as possible (L 6.35, 12.2). Curiosity, along with reasoning with language, is one of the two properties characteristic of human beings (L 6.35, 12.1–2). It also gives rise to the standard argument for the existence of GOD. Because religion follows upon curiosity, and curiosity is inherent to human beings, Hobbes thinks that religion can never be eliminated (L 12.23). Since religion is often used for politically destabilizing purposes, it is all the more important for people to understand its proper nature and function.

Religion is the explicit topic of chapter 12 of *Leviathan*. That chapter can be considered as transitional from the earlier chapters, which are devoted to various aspects of human beings that are not saliently political, to the following chapters, which are. It occurs immediately prior to the chapter on the state of nature. Elaborating on his earlier remark that curiosity is the cause of religion, Hobbes speaks of three "seeds" of religion in chapter 12: curiosity about what happens, especially about the good and bad things that happen to oneself; curiosity about why something happened precisely when it did and not earlier or later; curiosity about the relationships between causes and effects, independently of any personal involvement (*L* 12.2–4). The first two produce anxiety and explain the origin of false religions (*L* 12.5); the third generates the authentic proof for the existence of God as a first mover (*L* 12.6).

Having just spoken of three seeds of religion, Hobbes then seems to give an alternative account of the same matter, four things that constitute the "natural seed of religion": (1) beliefs about the nature of spirits; (2) ignorance about "second causes," that is, causes other than God; (3) natural worship; (4) beliefs about prognostications or about how God reveals Himself to human beings (*L* 12.7–10). For the most part, Hobbes gives the impression that these four things depend upon false beliefs about causality (*L* 12.13–19), and many scholars think that Hobbes intends his discussion to undermine belief in religion. Yet he says that these seeds give rise to true religion (*L* 12.12). No doubt the debate about Hobbes's true intentions will continue. (For a careful study of this part of chapter 12, it is helpful to know that the following paragraphs are correlated: for (1) 7 with 13–16; for (2) 8 with 17; for (3) 9 with 18; and for (4) 10 with 19.

Let's now consider Hobbes's treatment of religion in *De Homine*. Hobbes there defines religion as the worship offered by human beings who sincerely honor God (*DH* 14.1). Implicit in this definition are an internal and an external aspect of religion. The internal aspect is the sincerity of the honor directed to God. This sincerity is the faith that God exists and that He governs all things. In the same context, he describes this faith as the belief that God exists, is omnipotent, and is omniscient (*DH* 14.1). This is a rather conventional explanation of what religion and faith are. Hobbes gives no indication that elsewhere he says that the only thing that can be known about God is that He exists and that all other talk about God is merely honorific. One potentially controversial element of his explanation is that virtually all propositions of faith are merely opinions, which depend for their force upon authority. A private individual who claims to teach some religious truth must be able to work miracles in order to have her message corroborated. Since miracles no longer occur, according to Hobbes, following one venerable Protestant tradition, religion depends upon the authority of the sovereign (*DH* 14.4, 14.12).

The external aspect of religion in the definition in *De Homine* is WORSHIP. It consists of all of those ceremonies and actions that express one's love of God. Worshipful behavior can be done either in private or in public (*DH* 14.8). Public worship is whatever worship is commanded by the sovereign. Private worship is all other worship. It follows that private worship can be performed either by one person alone or by a group of people (*DH* 14.9).

repentance Repentance is being glad of returning to the right way of doing things after having felt sad about having done something bad. For

Hobbes, writing in the context of his debate with Bishop Bramhall about free will, there is nothing odd about feeling sad for something that was necessarily done, and nothing odd about feeling glad about doing what is right even if one had to do it: "So that the necessity of the actions takes away neither of those parts of repentance, grief for the error, and joy for returning" (*LN*, p. 257).

resurrection Hobbes believed that at the end of the world all human beings who had previously been dead would be bodily resurrected. The elect, that is, those whom God chose to be saved, would enjoy eternal life and happiness on earth as part of the second prophetic KINGDOM OF GOD. The damned would be destroyed by the fires of HELL and suffer the second death that St Paul talked about.

Hobbes was a mortalist. He believed that although Adam would have lived for ever had he not sinned, he and all human beings became mortal after the first sin. That is, they must die. Since death is the destruction of a being, human beings do not exist after death until they are resurrected. The standard Christian belief was that the immaterial soul survived death and that the souls of the elect went immediately to heaven, according to Protestant belief. (Roman Catholics held that most good people spend a time in purgatory before going to heaven.) Hobbes did not think of souls as immaterial substances but as some crucial bit of matter that made people live. When a person died, the soul either decomposed or otherwise lost its effectiveness.

Hobbes believed that the elect would be immortal "not by a property consequent to the essence and nature of mankind, but by the will of God that was pleased of his mere grace, to bestow eternal life upon the faithful" (*L* 38.4). He correctly argues that the doctrine of the immortality of the soul is not biblical. To the contrary, chapter 14 of the book of Job presupposes that human beings do not survive death. Hobbes is mistaken however in thinking that there is a doctrine of resurrection in that book (*L* 38.4).

In *Leviathan*, the doctrine of the immortality of the soul is said to be one of the doctrines of the KINGDOM OF DARKNESS and a consequence of a mis-interpretation of the biblical phrases "eternal life," "everlasting death," and "second death." Hobbes thinks that the doctrine diminishes the salvific work of Jesus. If the human soul is already immortal, the resurrection, construed as the restoration of human life, is less awesome (*L* 44.14, 44.23–6). Some people may think that the immortality of the soul is required in order to preserve the identity of a person between death and resurrection. Hobbes does not think so: "cannot God that raised inanimated dust and clay into a living creature by his word, as easily raise a dead

257

carcass to life again and continue him alive for ever or make him die again by another word?" (*L* 44.15). Hobbes's position here is consonant with the one he took on the IDENTITY of substances in general. A ship that is dismantled plank by plank does not exist when it is dismantled; but that very ship resumes its existence if it is reassembled.

revelation Revelation is closely connected with two other concepts: MIRACLES and PROPHETS. Revelation comes through prophets, and in the Old Testament one essential mark of a prophet is the ability to work miracles. (The other is teaching nothing contrary to the true FAITH.) Hobbes's best discussion of the issue comes at the beginning of part three of *Leviathan* where he begins his discussion of those principles that must be understood in order to understand what a Christian commonwealth is.

There are two kinds of revelation: immediate and mediate. Immediate revelation occurs when God communicates with a human being without there being any intervening (mediating) human being through whom the message is transmitted. Immediate revelation does not exclude there being some medium through which the divine message comes. On the contrary, there is always some medium for the message if for no other reason than that God is invisible. The medium is usually a dream or a vision.

Mediate revelation occurs when God communicates with a human being through another human being. Virtually every person who receives a revelation receives a mediate revelation. Anyone who relies upon the Bible for her revelation is the recipient of a mediate revelation. The mediator is either the author of the Bible, or a prophet, or an apostle, or perhaps the church, which has endorsed the Bible as reliable (*L* 32.6). Of course, there could be many human beings between God and the person who receives the mediate revelation (*L* 32.5).

Hobbes never questions the possibility of there being revelation. He never raises the issue of how a god, invisible and, in other ways too, completely unlike human beings, can communicate with them. One reason for this is that, since GOD is material, according to Hobbes, and hence connected with the material universe, Hobbes would have had less of a problem explaining how God could communicate with human beings than have those theologians who maintain that God is immaterial and transcends the universe. If a distinction is drawn between the metaphysical issue of how revelation is possible and the epistemological issue of how people know when there has been a revelation, then Hobbes is sanguine about the metaphysical issue.

Concerning the epistemological issue, Hobbes raises serious questions. At first, he gives the impression that there is no problem with immediate revelation: "How God speaks to a man immediately, may be understood by those well enough to whom he has spoken" (*L* 32.5). The difficulty seems to reside in determining authentic cases of immediate revelation. Suppose someone claims to have received a supernatural, immediate revelation from God. How can the claim be proven? What reason should a person have to accept it? Hobbes says that he cannot think of any. He has a devastating argument expressed laconically: "To say he [God] has spoken to him a dream is no more than to say he dreamed that God spoke to him" (*L* 32.6). Hobbes's point is that, just as the proposition "Napoleon spoke to me in a dream" has no evidential value (even if sincerely asserted), because it means the same as "I dreamed that Napoleon spoke to me," the proposition "God appeared to me in a dream" has no evidential value. Most dreams have natural causes, and there is no criterion by which a person can differentiate between those and the supernaturally caused dreams. Most of the dreams that purport to contain a revelation are caused by "self-conceit, and foolish arrogance, and false opinion of a man's own godliness, or other virtue, by which he thinks he has merited the favour of extraordinary revelation" (*L* 32.6). But one can never be sure of the cause. So, while Hobbes does commit himself to the existence of genuine cases of revelation occurring in dreams, he claims that there is no empirical way of picking them out.

It might be objected that, even if Hobbes's point holds for alleged revelations that come through dreams, there are many instances of revelations that come in visions. Hobbes's reply is that people often dream in a state that is "between sleeping and waking." Being in that condition, a person is not competent to judge whether she is having a vision or a dream. People who claim to have had revelatory experiences often resort to saying that they speak by "supernatural inspiration," but that amounts to no more than their saying that they have "an ardent desire to speak" or some "strong opinion" of themselves for which they "can allege no natural and sufficient reason" (*L* 32.6).

If no evidence is compelling, on what basis should a person accept the claim of an immediate revelation? Hobbes's answer is that one should accept the word of one's sovereign, to whom one owes obedience in all things (*L* 32.5). Some might suggest that one should obey prophets or look for miracles. But Hobbes points out that there are epistemological problems about determining who is a true prophet and when a miracle occurs.

Although it is impossible to know when genuine immediate revelations occur, Hobbes believes that they have. He thus raises in chapter 36, after explaining what the word of God is and what prophets are, the question of the way in which God has revealed Himself. His approach is thoroughly biblical. The Bible does not say how God appeared to Adam and Eve or

259

how He appeared to Abraham before he left Haran (*L* 36.10). After Abraham arrived in Canaan, God revealed Himself in visions, in dreams, by the appearance of angels, and by voice. He appeared to Moses in a burning bush. But for the most part, dreams and visions are the standard mode of presentation (*L* 36.10). The same methods of revelation are used in the New Testament as well (*L* 36.18).

Since Moses is an extraordinary prophet, God spoke to him in an extraordinary way. The Bible describes it as the way in which "a man speaks to his friend" (*L* 36.11). Yet this description does not really explain the nature of the appearance. Some biblical passages suggest that the revelation was mediated by an angel or angels and "was therefore a vision, though a more clear vision than was given to other prophets" (*L* 36.11). In surveying a large number of biblical texts, Hobbes shows that, no matter how different the descriptions may initially seem to be and no matter how informative they may seem, in the end they all amount to saying that God reveals Himself to people in visions. And we do not know what these visions consisted of. Hobbes wants to preserve the mystery of revelation:

> To say God spoke or appeared as he is in his own nature is to deny his infiniteness, invisibility, incomprehensibility. To say he spoke by inspiration or infusion of the Holy Spirit, as the Holy Spirit signifies the deity, is to make Moses equal with Christ, in whom only the Godhead . . . dwells bodily. . . . Therefore in what manner God spoke to those sovereign prophets of the Old Testament, whose office it was to enquire of him, is not intelligible. (*L* 36.13–14)

Hobbes holds that God spoke supernaturally to Moses, the other sovereign prophets, and Jesus but that there is no compelling evidence to hold that He spoke supernaturally to any of the other prophets. Their messages can be interpreted adequately simply by thinking of their revelations as the result of God's normal method of instilling piety and righteousness in people (*L* 36.15–16). Because of the difficulty of discriminating between supernatural and natural revelations, "there is need of reason and judgement" to avoid making a mistake about which is which. The best policy is to follow the decision of one's sovereign (*L* 36.19).

Revelation is related to the idea of the word of God. In *De Cive*, Hobbes distinguishes three senses of this phrase: (1) what God Himself says; (2) what the Holy Spirit moves human beings to say about God in the Bible; (3) the doctrine of the Christian faith. In sense (3), "the word of God" is referred to by a large cluster of other terms, such as "the word of the kingdom of God," "the gospel of the kingdom of God," "the word of life," and "the word of truth." Sense (3) is contained within sense (2) since not everything in the Bible expresses the doctrine of the Christian faith (*DC* 17.15–16).

The purpose of this three-fold distinction is to serve Hobbes's political point that the sovereign is to be obeyed in questions of religion. Concerning sense (1), few people claim to have spoken to God directly. For those who have, Hobbes's comments about the difficulty of knowing when an alleged immediate revelation is genuine suffice. Since sense (3) is part of sense (2), the issue is reduced to deciding who is the proper interpreter of a text. If each person interpreted the text for herself, she would be in the state of nature. In getting out of the state of nature, each person transferred to the sovereign the right of interpretation, along with everything else that is necessary for peace. Since the sovereign is the proper interpreter of Scripture, and since "the word of an interpreter of Scriptures is the word of God" (*DC* 17.17), the sovereign's word is the word of God.

In *Leviathan*, the explication of "the word of God" is treated somewhat differently and is not overtly political, as it is in *De Cive*. In one sense, it means "the dictates of reason" (*L* 36.6). But Hobbes devotes more attention to its meanings for revealed religion. In this regard, "the word of God" means either what God Himself has said, which is sense (1) above, or what has been said about God (*L* 36.2–3). And what God Himself has said can be taken either literally or metaphorically. God literally spoke to His prophets but only metaphorically said "Let there be light" when He created the world (*L* 36.3). Some of the metaphorical things said about God are absurd. From the fact that the Bible calls Jesus the Word, some theologians have called him the Verb. This is absurd since a verb is nothing but a part of speech or a sound and not, says Hobbes, something substantial or corporeal, as Jesus is (*L* 36.4). The true explanation for why Jesus is called the Word is that he is the fulfillment of God's word, His spoken promise to send a redeemer (*L* 36.4).

It is odd for Hobbes to say that God literally speaks, since he usually criticizes anthropomorphizing in religion. Also, later in the same chapter, he denies that God may properly be said to have "voice and language" when He does not have "a tongue or other organs as a man" (*L* 36.9). Talk about God's words, vision, or hearing is figurative, according to Hobbes; it is meant to honor Him, not to describe Him (*L* 36.9). One reason to avoid anthropomorphic descriptions of God is that they would tend to dishonor Him. If God has a mouth, does He also have an esophagus? a stomach? intestines? If God had the same parts as human beings "many of them [would be] so uncomely, as it would be the greatest contumely in the world to ascribe them to him" (*L* 36.9).

The concept of revelation is related to the concept of inspiration, but since etymologically "inspiration" means putting a spirit into a person,

261

Hobbes discusses inspiration in *Leviathan* in the chapter on spirits and angels and not in the one on revelation. Given that SPIRITS are thin, imperceptible bodies, one might say that inspiration was the mechanism by which God gave life to Adam; He breathed life into him. In most of its uses, however, according to Hobbes, "inspiration" is used metaphorically to mean the cause by which God moves a prophet to give a revelation, where the revelation is the message or proposition expressed (*L* 34.25).

rhetoric   Hobbes generally had a low opinion of rhetoric. There is some irony in this: his own rhetorical skills are among the best that exist in philosophy, and he published the first translation of Aristotle's *Rhetoric* into English (in an abbreviated form; *see* Bibliography [3]) and thought it was among Aristotle's best work. The English translation was itself a translation of a Latin translation that Hobbes had prepared for his tutee the third earl of Devonshire. The English translation was published in 1637 but no doubt done many years earlier.

For Aristotle, the use of rhetoric is not an inherently degenerate activity; it is the art of persuading, primarily with proofs consisting of examples or enthymemes. Because the goal of rhetoric is persuasion, the rhetorician uses as premises propositions that are commonly believed, in particular, by the person to be persuaded (*EW* 6:423–5).

In his own writings, Hobbes contrasts rhetoric with logic. In *The Elements of Law*, Hobbes apologizes for its style on the grounds that "whilst I was writing I consulted more with logic than with rhetoric" (*EL* "Dedication"). In *De Cive*, Hobbes says that there are two kinds of eloquence. The kind that relates to logic is "an elegant and clear expression of the conceptions of the mind"; it depends in part on discovering the nature of things themselves and in part on using words properly (*DC* 12.12). The kind that relates to rhetoric is "a commotion of the passions of the mind"; it depends in part on commonly held opinions – the prejudices of the tribe, Bacon would have said – and in part on metaphorical uses of words. The goal of eloquence is "not truth (except by chance) but victory" (*DC* 10.11). Expressing it more specifically, Hobbes says that the goal of eloquence is "to make good and evil, profitable and unprofitable, honest and dishonest, appear to be more or less than indeed they are; and to make that seem just which is unjust, according as it shall best suit with his end that speaks; for this is to persuade" (*DC* 10.11; *EL* 2.8.13). Eloquence is often used for seditious purposes (*DC* 12.13; *EL* 2.8.12). Eloquence is "power because it is seeming prudence" (*L* 10.12); and people with power tend to have the ambition to overthrow governments (*L* 11.13).

These negative remarks about rhetoric and eloquence invite the objection that rationality and persuasiveness cannot exist together. Hobbes thinks that such co-existence is difficult but not impossible. Education and discipline are necessary in order to reconcile the rational and emotive aspects of human beings: "So also reason and eloquence (though not perhaps in the natural sciences, yet in the moral) may stand very well together" (*L* "Review and Conclusion" 4).

right of nature (*jus naturale*)   Hobbes gives two different versions of what the right of nature is. Sometimes he says that the right of nature is the right to everything that a person needs in order to preserve her life. Sometimes he drops the qualification about self-preservation and says that it is simply the right to everything. There is obviously a big difference between these two versions, but he ignores it. There is an explanation for how and why Hobbes begins with one and gets to the other. Before giving it, something needs to be said about the relationship between the right of nature, the state of nature, and the laws of nature.

The state of nature is the condition that human beings are in when there is no government. In such a condition, each person has the right of nature. In *De Cive*, Hobbes introduces the idea of the right of nature as a consequence of the state of nature. But when he introduces the idea of the laws of nature, he contrasts it with the state of nature. The phrase "the right of nature" does not occur at all in that discussion, and in fact, given the state of nature, the idea of the right of nature is superfluous. In *Leviathan*, Hobbes does not use the term "the state of nature" at all; instead he conveys that concept under the rubric of "the natural condition of mankind" and "the right of nature" is not mentioned in that context. (*See* STATE OF NATURE.) The right of nature appears in the following chapter, as the contrasting concept to the law of nature, which is the focal topic. The idea of the right of nature thus plays a more conspicuous part in *Leviathan* than it does in his two earlier political treatises.

In *Leviathan*, the concept of the right of nature begins chapter 14, "Of the first and second Natural Laws, and of Contracts." It is introduced, as just mentioned, as the correlative term to "law of nature" (*lex naturalis*) (*L* 14.1–3). Hobbes wants to forestall a confusion between right (*jus*) and law (*lex*), which he claims other, unnamed people have fallen into. Right is to law as liberty is to obligation (*L* 14.3): "law is a fetter, right is freedom; and they differ like contraries" (*lex enim vinculum, jus libertas est, differuntque ut contraria*) (*DC* 14.3). By right (in the condition of mankind before government), every person has the right to everything, including the bodies of other people. It is law that restricts what a person may do (*L* 14.4).

In *The Elements of Law* and *De Cive*, the contrast between right and law (*ius et lex*) is introduced after all the justifications and explanations of

263

government and its functions have been completed. Hobbes's doctrine about the terms is the same as that in *Leviathan*, but its use is different. In *The Elements of Law*, Hobbes's point is this. Since right is liberty and law is the absence of liberty, the phrase "civil right" must not mean something that civil law obliges others to respect or something that the law guarantees. Rights are natural and impose no civil obligations on anyone. In contrast, civil law is artificial and creates obligations. Analogously, the phrase "divine right" does not mean something that God obliges others to respect or something that He guarantees. The phrases "civil right" and "divine right" refer to those liberties that the civil law and God, respectively, have not prohibited. If some law prohibits a certain action, then that action "cannot be said to be [done] *iure* [by right]" (*EL* 2.10.5).

Divine right is broader than civil right. Hobbes explores the consequences of this idea in *De Cive*. Whatever God prohibits cannot be permitted by the civil law. But the civil law may prohibit actions that the divine law permits. Hobbes probably wants this proposition to undermine the view that divine law justifies something like rebellion (*DC* 14.3).

The change in the way that the concept of the right of nature is deployed by Hobbes in various works, namely, the prominence it assumes in *Leviathan*, as opposed to its incidental occurrence in *The Elements of Law* and *De Cive*, indicates some uncertainty in Hobbes's mind about it. It seems to me to be logically superfluous. If one begins with the state of nature (the natural condition of mankind), then it is obvious that one must do something to get out of that condition, because of its wretchedness. The laws of nature are essential to that process. Nothing needs to be said about the right of nature, which is a fifth wheel. As I have suggested above, its use in *Leviathan* is rhetorical. It is used as a term of contrast in order to explain the concept that Hobbes is more interested in, namely, "law of nature."

All of this notwithstanding, Hobbes in fact ties the right of nature to the state of nature and the laws of nature in an intriguing fashion. In *De Cive*, the conditions of the state of nature are such that everyone's life is in danger. Further, it is a matter of natural fact that everyone tries to avoid death. Since whoever has a right to an end has a right to the means to that end, it is a matter of right reason that a person has the right of nature (*DC* 1.7–8). In *De Cive* then, Hobbes mediates the state of nature and the right of nature by right reason. To this point, the right of nature is restricted to "all the actions without which . . . [a man] cannot preserve himself" (*DC* 1.8).

This is not an unlimited right to everything. If a person needs one fish to live and there are ten fish available, she has the right to only one fish. Further, if she mistakenly believes that she needs more than one and acts

264

on that belief, then she may violate the laws of nature and offend God (*DC* 1.10 note). Even though no one in the state of nature can authoritatively judge that she has violated a law of nature or punish her for it, she may nonetheless have broken such a law. (Someone in the state of nature may inflict harm on her for what she has done, but that harm does not count as PUNISHMENT.)

At this point, Hobbes broadens the scope of the right of nature by adding the premise that in the state of nature each person is the sole judge of what is necessary to her preservation. Thus, if she mistakenly believes that she needs two or all ten of the fish, then she has the right to them. This line of argument in *De Cive* about the limits of the right of nature is cogent. Hobbes's later discussion of the right of nature in *Leviathan* is not. Recall that the concept of the right of nature is introduced in a different way in *Leviathan*. "The right of nature" is used initially as a contrasting term for "the law of nature." The right of nature is to the law of nature as liberty is to obligation (*L* 14.3, 26.43). The right of nature is the liberty to do whatever in one's own judgement one thinks will preserve one's life (*L* 14.1). In order to get an unlimited form of the right of nature, that is, the right to everything without restriction, Hobbes says that everything a person can make use of may assist her in preserving her life (*L* 14.4). It follows that each person has a right to everything, including the bodies of every other person. The rhetorical point of this argument is to intensify the wretchedness of the state of nature and to make escape from it all the more urgent. Indeed, having attributed to each person the right to everything, Hobbes then uses that fact to insist that each person should try to seek peace.

Hobbes's argument seems to rest on a false premise. There are all sorts of things that people can use that in fact do not enhance their chances of survival. Some things are inherently dangerous, such as poison and explosives. If they pose a danger to the survival of someone, then that person does not have a right to them. Other things, not inherently dangerous, do not enhance one's survival if taken to excess, for example, food and drink. Thus, it does not seem correct to say that, by the right of nature as Hobbes defines it, a person has the right to everything; rather, she has the right to whatever enhances her survival, and this is always less than everything.

It would have been easy for Hobbes to have concocted a justification for an unlimited right of nature. He might have argued that, since only laws bind a person to act in a certain way, if there are no laws at all, then a person has the right to everything. Hobbes does not use this justification, as we have seen, for he wants to build his system on the desirability and hence the goodness of self-preservation.

265

rights, laying down A right is a liberty or the freedom to do something. To most people, rights sound like good things to have. In the United States, there is an enormous ideology about rights. Any defense of rights is prima facie a good thing. Hobbes held the opposite view. In the state of nature, everyone has the right to everything in order to survive and is miserable as a consequence. The only good hope for a decent life is to lay down this right to everything. Hobbes's purpose then in discussing the laying down of rights is to prepare the ground for his discussion of the establishing of a civil state, a state which will enhance each person's self-preservation.

To lay down a right is the same as alienating it, and to alienate something is to lose it in such a way that it cannot be regained simply by wanting it back or by one's own just actions. (A right may be regained unjustly by, for example, overthrowing the government.) In the language of "liberty," to lay down a right to something is to lose the liberty of preventing someone else from possessing it. To lay down a right does not increase the right of any other person. This is obvious in the condition of the state of nature, in which everyone already has a right to everything, and this is the only case that Hobbes discusses (L 14.6). According to Hobbes, the benefit that accrues to other people when someone abandons a right is indirect. It eliminates one obstacle to possessing that thing for oneself (L 14.6; DC 2.4).

There are two ways to lay down a right: to renounce it and to transfer it. To renounce a right is to lay it down without caring who benefits from the action (L 14.7). If there were a tree with one apple on it and ten people with a right to the apple, then if one of them renounces her right to the apple, she merely stands aside and does not help anyone to get it. Each of the remaining nine people benefits by having only eight competitors instead of nine. To transfer a right is to lay down a right with the intention of having one or more specific people benefit from the action (L 14.7). Since whoever wills the end wills the means, to intend someone to benefit from one's laying down a right to something is to intend that that person gets the thing. To return to the apple in the tree, to transfer a right to that apple is to intend that that person gets it, leading one perhaps to assist her, by boosting her up or by interfering with the efforts of the others to get it.

The term "transfer of right" is something of a misnomer since in the state of nature where everyone has a right to everything no one can get more rights than she already has. What then gets transferred? Power. This is easy to see in the most important kind of transfer of right, namely, the one that occurs in a sovereign-making covenant. To transfer the right of government to the sovereign is to agree to one's own strength being called upon to enable the sovereign achieve that goal: "he who submits his will to the will of another, conveys to that other the right of his strength and faculties" (*DC* 5.8, 5.11; *EL* 2.1.8). Hobbes sometimes obscures this point when he explains it like this: "because no man can transfer his power in a natural manner, [transfer] is nothing else than to have parted with his right of resisting" (*DC* 5.11). This explanation of transferring makes it sound just like renouncing a right. But that does not make any sense. If a subject merely stood out of the way of a sovereign and did not contribute her own power, the job of the sovereign would be impossible. He would have to defend all the lives under his charge with only his own strength, which in the state of nature is merely equal to that of every other person. The sovereign must get power from a transfer from the subjects. Such power is enormous but necessary (*DC* 5.9). So, the best way to make sense of the above passage is to interpret the idea of a person's parting with her right of resisting as meaning that she then does what the other person wants.

In *Leviathan*, Hobbes gives the impression that laying down a right gives rise to obligation and duty. When a person lays down a right, "then is he said to be obliged or bound . . . ; and that he ought, and it is his duty, not to make void that voluntary act of his own" (*L* 14.7). Perhaps the locution "is . . . said to be" is being used as a hedge ("Jones is said to be generous, but he's only looking for glory"). But Hobbes often uses this locution when he means "is" categorically, often when he is defining a term. It is not clear how "is . . . said to be" should be construed in this case. Even if laying down a right does introduce an obligation, one might wonder how or why this happens or what the obligation is. It appears that the words or actions that are required to lay down a right are themselves the "bonds" of the obligation. Since words have no intrinsic strength, the strength they do have is the result of the fear of the consequences of breaking them (*L* 14.7; *DC* 2.4; *EL* 1.15.3). (Laying down a right must be done by some word or deed, and transferring a right requires acceptance by the person to whom it is to be transferred (*L* 14.7).)

Transferring a right, rather than renouncing one, is the type of laying down that Hobbes is interested in. He holds that each person in the state of nature transfers her rights to the entity that is to be the sovereign – this will be one person in a monarchy, several people in an aristocracy, and the entire group in a democracy. In doing so, each person alienates those rights and they cannot be regained by any just action of the person. (They are recovered only by the dissolution of the civil state, which may occur either through civil war, external aggression, or abandonment by the sovereign.) Establishing a civil state by the transfer of rights makes for a stable government.

A different contrast is drawn for transferring a right in *A Dialogue between a Philosopher and a Student of the Common Laws of England*. In this work, the term of contrast is "committing" a right. To commit a right is to permit another person to exercise it in one's name and for one's own good. While a right that has been transferred has been alienated, a right that has been committed, far from being irretrievable, is never lost by that committal (*DCL*, p. 52). (*See* AUTHORIZATION.)

S

salvation (*salvatio*) "Salvation" means to be saved; and to be saved is to be protected from something that otherwise would injure one. A person can be protected from one or more specific threats to her safety or protected from all things. The latter is absolute salvation, and it is achieved by the "remission of SIN" (*L* 38.15). (Sin, presumably, injures a person by incurring the wrath of God.)

Salvation occurs on earth in two senses. First, Hobbes believes that the salvation promised by Christianity will come when the KINGDOM OF GOD is restored at the end of the world; and that this kingdom will be on earth (*L* 38.17, 38.23). Second, there is a salvation that is achieved during this life on earth. Although Hobbes does not put it in these terms, his views about this second kind constitute a doctrine of secular salvation. The state of nature is a condition in which human beings are in constant danger of death and of suffering every kind of misery. By entering a civil state, one is saved from these dangers. The sovereign, who is a human analog of God, has characteristics that are similar to divine attributes. Corresponding to God's omnipotence is the overwhelming and monopolistic power of the sovereign; corresponding to His omniscience is the sovereign's right to decide what will be counted as true and false when a dispute arises; corresponding to His omnibenevolence is the fact that what is good and evil in the civil state is whatever the sovereign wills; corresponding to His justice is the legislative and judicial power of the sovereign. Hobbes means quite seriously the claim that the sovereign is the "mortal god, to which we owe, under the immortal God, our peace and defence" (*L* 17.13).

Most of what Hobbes says about salvation is within a strictly theological context. He holds that two things are required for salvation: faith and obedience. (*See* CHRISTIANITY, ESSENCE OF.) Only one proposition of faith is necessary: that Jesus is the Christ (Messiah). The obedience that is required is obedience to the laws of God, and these are the laws of nature. Since the laws of nature commit subjects to obedience to the civil laws, civil obedience is half of salvation. Faith and obedience save one from the injury that is a consequence of sin.

269

Salvation is closely connected with redemption. To redeem something is to save it by paying a fee or a ransom, usually in order to eliminate a debt. The amount or character of the ransom is determined by the person to whom the debt is owed. In describing redemption in terms of ransom and a person offended, it is clear that Hobbes is thinking specifically of the Christian doctrine of redemption.

Of the traditional Christian theories of redemption, only two need to be explained here. One was the ransom theory, according to which, Jesus ransomed human beings. The theory is biblically based in the sense that the gospels talk about redemption in terms of ransom, even if the specifics of that ransom are not discussed. According to St Augustine of Hippo, who is credited with articulating the standard theory, Jesus ransomed human beings from the devil, who held them captive as the result of their sin. That is, Jesus had to die in order to release human beings from the control of the devil. Anselm of Canterbury decisively refuted this theory in *Cur Deus Homo* by pointing out that, although human beings were rightly punished for sinning, the devil had no right to punish them. The devil is merely a creature, and no creature can have spiritual control over another. Anselm substituted what is known as the satisfaction theory, which is the second of the traditional theories that needs to be explained. He argued that, since a human being had to pay the debt owed to God and since only God had the wherewithal to pay the debt, the redeemer had to be both God and human being. Thus, the incarnation was necessary.

Without mentioning Anselm, Hobbes obviously rejects the satisfaction theory and reinterprets the ransom theory. Hobbes's objection to the satisfaction theory is that it makes redemption consist of the payment of a debt. What is objectionable about this is that it makes sin something that can be bought and sold. It has the implication that one may sin as long as one is willing to pay the set price: "sin cannot be taken away by recompense; for that were to make the liberty to sin a thing vendible" (*L* 38.25). Another way to put this objection is to say that it makes the redemption of human beings a matter of justice and not mercy. According to the satisfaction theory, the death of Jesus is a just or fair price to pay for human sin. Hobbes, in contrast, believes that redemption is solely a matter of mercy. The death of Jesus was supposed to be not a satisfaction for sin but a sacrifice, in view of which God mercifully forgave human beings. It would not have been unjust of God to have punished sinners even though Jesus died (*L* 38.25, 41.2).

science *See* PHILOSOPHY

Scripture *See* BIBLE

sensation Sensation is a certain internal motion of animal bodies; it is a motion that is identical with having a phantasm or idea (*DCo* 25.2). Hobbes's most sophisticated treatment of this view is in the fourth part of *De Corpore*, where he applies to various topics many of the basic ideas about motion that he had developed in the third part of the book. The most important of these basic ideas is that all motion is generated by one body moving against another body. From this idea, Hobbes argues that the cause of sensation is a motion of an object (the sensed object) that moves objects in a medium (usually air), that move some external part of an animal (the sense organ), causing a motion of some internal parts of the animal (the sensation itself) (*DCo* 25.2).

In sensation, the internal part of the animal always puts up some resistance, which Hobbes had earlier defined as an ENDEAVOR (*conatus*), in reaction to an inward motion. Since this resistance is a movement towards the outside of the animal, the animal perceives the sensed object to be outside of itself. Although all sensation is a reaction, not all things that have reactions have sensations (*DCo* 25.5; *L* 1.4). The difference, according to Hobbes, is that the reactive motion in a sensation stays in the organ and this is not the case in non-sensing objects.

The subject of a sensation is the animal that has the sensation. The object of sensation is the body that originated the motion that results in the sensation. Hobbes thinks that these definitions make it evident that it is more correct to say that an animal sees than that its eye sees, and that it is the sun that is seen, not light or color (*DCo* 25.3; *L* 1.1). This position is somewhat analogous to his view that human beings are free even though there is no free will.

One of the most important consequences of Hobbes's view of sensation is that the qualitative properties of a sensed object (that is, how the object appears to a perceiver) are not in the object itself. The sensed object causes the qualitative property, which is the same as a phantasm or representation, but that phantasm is in the perceiver, not in the object itself (*L* 1.4). Hobbes argues that, if the qualitative properties were in the object itself, then it would not be possible to separate a color from an object by "glasses," echoes would not occur, and one could not generate colors by, for example, pressing against the eye.

While sensation is a certain motion caused by an object that is present, IMAGINATION is that same kind of motion when the object is absent. Alternatively, imagination is the motion of a sensation that is deteriorating in strength; the motion is decaying because the object that initiated the motion is no longer present and other motions are affecting it. An individual instance of imagination can be more intense than an instance of sensation if the perceiver is not receiving much external stimulation. Such a condition often occurs when a person is asleep. That is why dreams, which are a form of imagination, can be so intense (*DCo* 25.7; *L* 2.2).

Senses are differentiated both by the kinds of phantasms there are and partially by the organ needed to have a kind of phantasm (*DCo* 25.10). Five senses are usually distinguished: sight, hearing, smell, taste, and touch.

servants Hobbes sometimes refers to subjects as "servants," especially in chapter 20 of *Leviathan*, where he explains what sovereignty by acquisition is. (See also *DC* 8.3–7; *EL* 2.6.4.) One reason for using "servants" to refer to subjects is to emphasize the absolute subordination of subjects to the sovereign. Another reason is that he wishes to appeal to biblical evidence in support of his position, as in the second half of chapter 20; and he shows how the Bible often refers to people under a sovereign as servants. (*See further* SOVEREIGNTY BY INSTITUTION AND SOVEREIGNTY BY ACQUISITION.)

sin (*peccatum*) Hobbes has broader and narrower senses of sin. In *De Cive*, sin is given its broadest sense of being any "deed, word, and thought against right reason" (*factum, dictum, et volitum contra rectam rationem*) (*DC* 14.16). In this sense, sin stands to error as will stands to understanding. An error is a mistake of reasoning; sin is acting on that mistake (*DC* 14.16). This extremely broad sense is consonant with the Latin word "peccatum," which can mean any mistake.

In *De Cive*, the broadest sense of sin is then narrowed to "blameable" actions that break a law (*DC* 14.17). Sin has to be defined in terms of breaking a law and not in terms of doing something bad, because what is bad, according to Hobbes, is simply something that someone does not like, just as what is good is simply something that someone desires. The same action then can be GOOD AND EVIL relative to different people. If Smith and Jones both want the same apple, then Smith's getting it is good to her and evil to Jones. What follows from this understanding of good and evil is that the attempt by private persons to determine what individual actions are sin (*peccatum*) must result in conflicts since each person will be judging matters according to her own desires. The only way to avoid this kind of conflict is for each interested party to defer to the desires of the sovereign as they are formulated in laws. It is in this way that what is good and evil become objective in the only way that they can be (*DC* 14.17).

A fault (*culpa*) or sin is anything that goes against reason according to the judgement of the sovereign. According to this view of fault, a person may commit a sin unintentionally and still be blameable. In other words, Hobbes subscribes to strict liability. However, the goodness of the sinner is not diminished by these kinds of sins. Wicked people are those who

272

break laws without any regard for them. And they are wicked even when they are not sinning (*DC* 14.17–18). In another place, Hobbes includes an act of will as a necessary condition for sin: it is what proceeds from the human will and is against the law (*LN*, pp. 259–60).

In *Leviathan*, sin is defined as any contempt of a legislator or sovereign. The contempt can take the form of violating a law or simply being indifferent to it (*L* 27.1). In its narrowest sense, a sin is any contempt of God. A crime is a sin (in the broad sense of contempt of a legislator or sovereign) that consists of violating a law. It is thus either an action that is forbidden or the omission of an action that is required. So all crimes are sins (in the broad sense) but not all sins are crimes. Hobbes does not make it clear initially that crimes must be violations of civil laws, but that is the best way to make sense of what he says (*L* 27.2–3; *DCL*, p. 37).

By the narrower definitions of sin in both *Leviathan* and *De Cive*, there is no sin where there is no law. But since the laws of nature are eternal, it is always possible to commit a sin (*L* 27.3; *DC* 14.19). Although this view may seem conventional, Hobbes discussed a supposed consequence of it that got him embroiled in a controversy. He considered someone arguing to the effect that, since every law depends upon a lawgiver who has supreme power, and "no man has a supreme power which is not bestowed on him by our own consent," an atheist or anyone who denies that God governs the world cannot sin because such a person does not bestow this power on God (*DC* 14.19). The inference is a patent *non sequitur*. The second premise talks about bestowing supreme power on a human being. God obviously does not fall into that category. He has supreme power by nature. So, the fact that an atheist does not recognize God's supreme power is irrelevant, especially since Hobbes holds in *De Cive* and *Leviathan* that intent is not a necessary condition for sinning. Unfortunately, Hobbes does not criticize the argument in this straightforward way. Instead, he says that what the argument shows is that its proponents are guilty of sins of imprudence (*peccata imprudentiae*), and they should be punished for them. More generally, the justification for inflicting injury on atheists, even though they are not His subjects, is that they are enemies of God, because they do not acknowledge Him as their sovereign. (This treatment of the issue seems to imply that atheists are not genuinely subject to the natural laws of God, that is, the laws of nature. If this is correct, then the laws of nature require the command of God.)

Hobbes's position met with resistance. He reports the objection as follows: "Many find fault that I have referred atheism to imprudence, and not to injustice." In his reply, he still does not accuse atheists of injustice but emphasizes that he has taken a very strong stance against ATHEISM: "I show them to be enemies of God. But I conceive the name of an enemy to be somewhat sharper than that of an unjust man." That is true but irrelevant. It is not how strong a stance he is taking against atheism, but the justification of that stance, that his critic is questioning (*DC* 14.19 note).

From one perspective, it seems that Hobbes's critics are unfair. Why should it matter whether atheists are made to suffer because they are unjust or because they are enemies of God? From another perspective, it matters a great deal. I think that the intuition of Hobbes's opponents is that, if atheists were simply God's enemies, because they do not recognize that He exists, and were punished simply on the grounds that they are His enemies and not because of anything that they have done, then God's behavior would seem to be arbitrary and unjust, and perhaps even sinful. But Hobbes would not have had any worries along these lines. For him, God can do anything He wants to do and cannot sin. Everything He does is justified by His irresistible power:

> God cannot sin, because his doing a thing makes it just, and consequently, no sin; as also because whatsoever can sin, is subject to another's law, which God is not. And therefore it is blasphemy to say, God can sin; but to say, that God can so order the world, as a sin may be necessarily caused thereby in a man, I do not see how it is any dishonour to him. (*LN*, pp. 250–1; *QLNC*, p. 138)

It is appropriate to conclude a discussion of sin with some account of what it means to repent of sin. According to Hobbes, it is to confess the sin. Confession is acknowledgment, and where there is no confession there is no acknowledgment. Repentance then does not precede but follows confession. And to confess a sin presupposes that one knows that one has sinned (*DC* 17.25).

society Man is a social animal by nature, according to Aristotle, and few before Hobbes doubted it. Hobbes did. There is a difference between needing other people and being fit to live with them, Hobbes observed. Children need other people in order to survive, but they are not fit for society: "Unless you give children all they ask for, they are peevish and cry, aye, and strike their parents sometimes; and all this they have from nature" (*DC* "Preface" 3).

Hobbes is not denying that some people are sociable. In his "Dedication" to *Leviathan*, he praises the virtue of Sidney Godolphin as emanating from the "generous constitution of his nature." What he denies is that all or even most people are sociable or that being sociable is a defining feature of being human. (Because enough people are unsociable and one cannot easily identify them, everyone must engage in unsociable behavior in the STATE OF NATURE.) When he discusses the fifth law of nature, "complaisance," that is, that one strive to get along with others and not take more than one needs, he says that some people obey it naturally and others do not. Society is like a building; differently shaped stones are necessary for constructing it. But there are some stones that are too rough, hard, and irregularly shaped to be fitted into the building. Just as stonemasons throw these away, people who are incorrigible because of "the stubbornness of . . . [their] passions" ought to be "cast out of society, as cumbersome thereunto" (*L* 15.17).

People choose to be in society because they hope to "receive some honour or profit from it." In business, people try to establish a "market-friendship" and in leisure society people want to be entertained by others or to be honored by them: "All society therefore is either for gain or for glory; that is, not so much for love of our fellows as for the love of ourselves" (*DC* 1.2).

Some animals are social but not political. Ants, for example, work together for a common good, because each of them has the same desire. But they are not political animals, because they are not united by one will (*DC* 5.5). Six features differentiate human group behavior from that of ants, bees, and the like. (1) Human beings seek honor; social animals do not. (2) The desires of social animals serve the common good; human desires do not. (3) Social animals never believe that they see defects in the way their lives are run; human beings do. (4) Social animals do not talk about what is good and bad; human beings do. (5) Social animals cannot distinguish between injury (an injustice) and harm (any deprivation); human beings can. (6) The behavior of social animals is coordinated naturally; the coordination of human behavior is artificial; it requires the consent of the people through a covenant (*DC* 5.5).

Hobbes holds in *The Elements of Law* and *De Cive* that there can be society without government. It consists of many people "gathering themselves of their own free wills" (*DC* 6.1). In such a condition, people can make contracts with other individuals and cause them to think that they can distinguish between what belongs to one and what belongs to another. However, he holds that such a condition is still part of the state of nature and that there is no genuine property, because there is insufficient security to protect the possession of anything. This group of people also cannot call anything collectively its own and cannot act as one entity, because it does not possess its own will. Unity of will only arises when there is a SOVEREIGN (*EL* 2.1.2; *DC* 6.1). In *Leviathan*, this notion of a pre-political society is not raised.

soul "Soul" is not a technical term for Hobbes, and he uses it rather infrequently; it often occurs in analogies or when he is reporting the views

275

of other philosophers. On several occasions he says that the sovereign is the soul of the civil state (*L* "Introduction" 1, 29.15, 42.125). In another place, he says that spies or undercover agents are "like the beams of the sun to the human soul" (*DC* 13.7). As a materialist, Hobbes probably consciously avoided the term, and in many of its occurrences, it is not easy to tell what he precisely thinks about the soul. But he does not avoid it completely. When he says that God should not be said to be conceived by human understanding, imagination, "or any other faculty of our soul," he is using it in a completely non-controversial, but probably non-technical, way (*DC* 15.14). In his early work, *The Elements of Law*, he even includes belief in the immortality of the soul as something that follows from the fundamental Christian doctrine that Jesus is the Christ (*EL* 2.6.6).

Hobbes spends much time undermining belief in the natural immortality of the soul, principally on the ground that it is not a biblical view: "That the soul of man is in its own nature eternal, and a living creature independent on the body, or that any mere man is immortal, otherwise than by the resurrection in the last day, . . . is a doctrine not apparent in Scripture" (*L* 38.4, 44.15, 44.24). Hobbes shows that in the Bible the word "soul" usually means no more than the word "life" (*L* 38.4). His analysis is similar to that of "spirit." (*See* SPIRITS.)

One reason for opposing the doctrine of the immortality of the soul was that Roman Catholics used it to support the doctrine of purgatory. If something goes to heaven before the resurrection of the body, and if it needs to be purified before it goes there, as Roman Catholic theologians argued, then there must be some object, which exists on its own and is other than the body, that undergoes the purification and translation; this object is the immortal soul. Hobbes considered and refuted Robert Bellarmine's defense of this view (*L* 44.30–40). A second reason for opposing the idea of an immortal soul was that it was used to explain the appearances of ghosts, which clerics often used to frighten and manipulate superstitious people (*L* 46.41). A third reason for opposing the idea was that, if there were an immortal soul, then the damned would suffer for eternity, and Hobbes believed that such a fate is inconsistent with the mercy of God (*EW* 4:350). Hobbes believed that the wicked would be resurrected from the dead and destroyed in the finite amount of time it takes a fire to destroy a human body. A fourth reason is that political stability requires that people be more afraid of the sovereign than of anything else. A belief in the immortality of the soul seems to encourage a greater fear of what happens after this life than during it.

Traditionally, the soul has been thought of as an immaterial substance or spirit. Hobbes thinks that the phrase "immaterial substance" is a contradiction in terms, and he thinks that, when "spirit" denotes a substance, it always denotes something material. If "soul" means an immaterial substance with an independent existence, then every living being has one, since the Bible talks about the souls of creatures indifferently (*L* 44.15). Aristotelians would accept this last statement, as Hobbes formulated it. They would disagree among themselves about whether the human soul was immortal or not.

sovereign (*summa potestas*) For Hobbes "sovereign" is primarily the word for an institution. In a monarchy, the sovereign is an individual human being; but in an aristocracy it is a group of people; and in a democracy it is the entire population. So "sovereign" refers to an individual human being only in special circumstances.

Also, for Hobbes a sovereign must be what would ordinarily be considered an absolute sovereign (*L* 20.14, 22.5; *DC* 6.13); that is, his power must be unrestricted and monopolistic. It is unrestricted in the sense that he has, in principle, control over all areas of life and conduct. In *Behemoth*, Hobbes even argues that a child has the obligation to kill her own parent if commanded by the sovereign to do so (*B*, p. 51; cf. *DC* 6.13). As broad as the power of a sovereign is, it does not extend beyond behavior. A person's own beliefs are beyond the scope of political control. Hobbes, then, believes in a form of freedom of conscience, but it is not what normally goes by that name. (Freedom of conscience usually is taken to justify acting on certain sorts of beliefs and not just having them.)

The power of a sovereign is monopolistic in the sense that there cannot be any political power that competes with it (*L* 19.11–12, 20.18, 22.5; *DC* 6.18, 7.3; *EL* 2.1.13). If there were, then the sovereign could not perform his function of protecting subjects from domestic discord and foreign invasion. Hobbes believes that a mixed government, by which is meant a government in which more than one entity is a political force, or any system of government that involves checks and balances, is inherently unstable and does not have or display genuine sovereignty. He thinks that a belief in mixed government, specifically, the view that the king and parliament have separate authority, was one of the causes of the English Civil War. One of the charges against Charles I at his trial was that he had violated his "limited power to govern." Also, monopolistic power implies that it must be overwhelming. If a sovereign lacks a power great enough to crush any domestic disturbance with little effort or is not competitive in the international arena, then his sovereignty cannot long survive.

Two other features of the sovereign's power should be mentioned. The first, which has already been introduced, is that it is a unity. The unity of sovereignty should be contrasted with two envisioned multiplicities, one actual and one impossible. The actual multiplicity is the kind found in the

277

state of nature. There, any collection of human beings is a multiplicity. Each human being has her own will. Creating a civil state creates unity. Subjects within a civil state are united in the one will of the sovereign (*DC* 6.1). The impossible multiplicity is a sovereignty shared between two or more political entities. This is impossible, because whenever two or more political entities have power, they compete with each other and in effect are at war. If any political entity independent of the sovereign has its own power, it can challenge the sovereign and jeopardize his operation (*L* 18.16). Even in an aristocracy or a democracy the sovereignty is not divided. The natural persons who compose an aristocracy or a democracy do not have any individual sovereign power; each is part of the indivisible sovereignty.

The second additional feature of the sovereign's power is that it is irrevocable (*L* 18.3). This is required for stability. If people covenanted for specific purposes only, then once those goals were achieved, they would return to the wretchedness of the state of nature. In *De Cive*, Hobbes argues both that subjects cannot void their sovereign-making covenant even if all of them should jointly try to do so; and that in any case it would never happen that they should all try to do so (*DC* 6.19). The latter point is not a significant issue. Hobbes is almost certainly right that not everyone in a civil state would choose to void its covenant. The former point is more interesting. He is obviously afraid of allowing any justification for revolution; and he thinks that if the sovereign-making covenant could be voided under any conditions, then revolution would be justified. But Hobbes does not seem to be on solid ground here, to judge from what he had said about COVENANTS earlier, namely, that one can be freed from the obligation to fulfill a covenant in either of two ways: by performing, or by being relieved of the obligation to perform by the other party or parties (*DC* 2.15). It would seem then, *pace* Hobbes, that sovereign-making covenants theoretically could be voided if all the subjects released each other. Since the sovereign himself is not a party to the covenant, he could not legally prevent it. But Hobbes does not accept this. He rests his case on his peculiar idea of the sovereign-making covenant. According to him, it is an alienating AUTHORIZATION. That is, when people covenant to form a government, they irrevocably authorize the sovereign to act for them. From that time on, the sovereign alone has the competence to decide whether he should keep or give up his sovereignty (*DC* 6.20).

Hobbes's most elaborate and reflective discussion of the powers that a sovereign has occurs in *Leviathan*. One might have expected a full treatment of them in *De Cive*, especially since they came under attack in the Nineteen Propositions of June 1642. But the treatment of these powers there is inchoate; several of them are enumerated one after the other in a few sentences (*DC* 6.13, 6.18). In *Leviathan*, in contrast, Hobbes lists at some length twelve powers of sovereignty, in the context of explaining what sovereignty by institution is. (*See* SOVEREIGNTY BY INSTITUTION AND SOVEREIGNTY BY ACQUISITION.) The list is a thinly disguised commentary on the causes of the English Civil War (*L* 18.16) and more particularly on the official charges brought by parliament against Charles I and the sentence that was handed down by the High Court on him. A comparison of Hobbes's items below with the relevant documents is revealing.

(1) The subjects cannot revoke their authorization of the sovereign (*L* 18.3). Parliament pretended to do this in putting Charles on trial.

(2) The sovereign cannot forfeit his authority, because he cannot act unjustly towards his subjects. Injustice arises only from breaking a covenant with a person and the sovereign makes no covenant with his subjects (*L* 18.4).

(3) Anyone entering into a covenant must support the person or persons chosen by majority vote to be sovereign (*DC* 6.2; *L* 18.5). Hobbes is a radical democrat in his view of the origins of the civil state (*EL* 2.2.1). (*See also* MONARCHY, ARISTOCRACY, AND DEMOCRACY.)

(4) The sovereign cannot do an INJURY to a subject, for the reason given in (2) (*L* 18.6). Parliament said Charles had.

(5) The sovereign cannot be put to death justly or be otherwise punished by his subjects. Since the subject is the AUTHOR of the sovereign's actions, to harm the sovereign is to punish him for the subject's own actions (*L* 18.7; *EL* 2.1.19). This is Hobbes's judgement on the execution of Charles I. In the second edition of *De Cive*, written after Charles had been captured by the parliamentary army but before his execution, Hobbes had written that the sovereign "must not be punished" (*DC* 6.12).

(5′) The sovereign has the right to make all decisions concerning the means of achieving and maintaining peace and security for his subjects, because whoever has the right to an end has the right to the means and the sovereign, having by institution been charged with that end, has the RIGHT OF NATURE to the means (*L* 18.8; *DC* 6.18). (This item is numbered "6" in the marginal note in *Leviathan*, but in the text it is presented as a corollary to (5).)

(6) The sovereign has the right to declare what opinions are true and what false on any matter he chooses (*L* 18.9; *DC* 6.11). This includes opinion in religion and science (*DC* 6.11 note).

(7) The sovereign has the right to make all laws, including property laws; property comes into existence only with the sovereign (*L* 18.10; *DC* "Dedication," 6.18; *EL* 2.1.10). This was a sore point even for

279

royalists like Lord Clarendon, who believed that property rights were God given and independent of civil authority.

(8) The sovereign has the right of the judiciary (*L* 18.11; *DC* 6.18; *EL* 2.1.9). In English law, decisions of the king were susceptible to independent judgement by the High Court. A problematic case for Charles I was Hampden's refusal to pay ship money. The king's case was won by a narrow vote.

(9) The sovereign has the right to make war against whomever he pleases and to levy taxes on the subjects to pay for it (*L* 18.12; *DC* 6.18). Charles I's decisions to wage war on Scotland in 1639 and 1640 were frustrated by parliament's refusal to grant him the revenues he needed. He lost both wars. The Hampden case was similar.

(10) The sovereign has the right to choose his own counselors, ministers, and magistrates (*L* 18.13, 30.25; *DC* 6.11, 6.18; *EL* 2.1.19). In the Nineteen Propositions of 1642, parliament demanded the right to approve all of Charles's counselors and to administer an oath to them.

(11) The sovereign has the right to reward and punish whomever he pleases according to his laws (*L* 18.14; cf. 30.23–4).

(12) The sovereign has the right to distribute titles of honor and "order of place and dignity" to whomever he pleases (*L* 18.15, 18.19). This may be an allusion to James's and Charles's practice of selling knighthoods and their instituting the order of baronet, in order to increase revenues. Hobbes may also have had in mind the fact that Charles began to enforce in 1629 a law that allowed him to fine landowners worth annually at least £40 who had not presented themselves for knighthood. Again, Charles's motive was purely pecuniary.

Shortly before the Civil War broke out in open warfare in 1642, Charles made several disabling concessions to parliament, such as the requirements that a parliament be called every three years and that it could not be dissolved without its own consent. Hobbes says that such apparent concessions are void unless the sovereign explicitly renounces his sovereignty, which Charles had not done (*L* 18.17; *EL* 2.2.13).

Hobbes ends the chapter on the structure of sovereignty by saying that no matter how bad things appear to be under a sovereign, they would be much worse in a civil war or other form of the state of nature (*L* 18.20, 20.18). He apparently could not imagine such lives as were lived in National Socialist Germany and the Soviet Union under Stalin.

Let's now consider further the office of sovereign. To say that sovereignty is absolute and to say that the sovereign does not have any obligations to his subjects may give the impression that the sovereign can do nothing wrong and is subject to no law at all. Many scholars have interpreted Hobbes in this way. But to do so they have had to discount his own assertions. The first of these occurs in a chapter in which he is arguing that the only freedom that subjects have is the freedom that the sovereign allows them to have. He points out that this notwithstanding, a sovereign can sin, because he is a subject of God "and bound thereby to observe the laws of nature" (*L* 21.7). By sacrificing his daughter, Jeptha did not injure her; and by sending Uriah into battle where he would meet certain death, David did not injure him: but only because of the technical meaning of "injure," namely, to be unjust to a person. Each sinned against God by violating a law of nature (*L* 21.7). Hobbes's treatment of the sin of sovereigns should be compared with the problem with ATHEISM. Atheists do not technically sin, because one cannot break someone's law unless one acknowledges the existence of the lawgiver. Hobbes's theory requires him to give a nonstandard account of what is wrong both with being an atheist and with certain behavior of a sovereign; but he is careful to come up with the right result: atheists deserve to be destroyed (because they are the enemies of God) and sovereigns should curb their behavior (because they can be punished by God). It is commonplace for novel theories to give novel treatments to ordinary facts.

Hobbes's claim that a sovereign cannot with impunity break the laws of nature is not a matter of mere piety or a nod in the direction of conventional morality. The stability of the commonwealth depends upon it. In both *De Cive* and *Leviathan*, Hobbes has a chapter on what causes a commonwealth to be destroyed by internal problems, followed by a chapter on the goals and duties (*officia*) of a sovereign. The topics are related. If the sovereign does not achieve his goals and fulfill his duties, then the commonwealth cannot survive. And many of the causes of dissolution are explicitly mentioned as things to be prevented by the sovereign. But what can induce a sovereign to achieve his goals and fulfill his duties if he is not obliged to do so by any civil law? The answer is that only the laws of nature can obligate him.

In *Leviathan*, the reason given for setting up a sovereign is that he will secure "the safety of the people" (*L* 30.1). In *De Cive* and *The Elements of Law*, this topic is presented as a justification for the conventional wisdom that the safety of the people is the supreme law (*salus populi suprema lex*) (*DC* 13.2; *EL* 2.9.1). In earlier chapters of all three political works, when the safety of the people was discussed under the rubric of self-preservation, nothing was directly said about living comfortably or happily, although it was implicit insofar as the state of nature was described as a wretched condition and the civil state was supposed to remedy it. But now Hobbes makes the full benefits of the civil state clear when he explains that the safety of the people means not bare survival "but also all other contentments of life, which every man by lawful industry, without danger, or hurt to the commonwealth, shall acquire to himself" (*L* 30.1); and people formed a government not merely for survival (*conservatio*) but for a good life (*vita beata*) and in order to live happily (*jucundissime vivere*) (*DC* 13.4; *EL* 2.9.2–4).

In *De Cive*, the first duty of the sovereign is to ensure the eternal salvation of his subjects, and this requires imposing his religious views on them. Although Hobbes represents this action as a matter of conscience – it would not make sense for the sovereign to impose some beliefs that he himself did not hold – it is more plausible that Hobbes is merely rationalizing the existence of a state religion; for he often claims that religious diversity undermines the secular authority of a sovereign (*DC* 13.5). Writing this in 1642 makes sense since religious dissension was rapidly getting out of hand; by 1650, the issue was *passé* and imposing religious uniformity does not appear as a duty of the sovereign in *Leviathan*.

Rather, in that work the sovereign best ensures the safety of his subjects not by rescuing them when they are in imminent danger but by preventing such dangers from arising in the first place. Such foresightful government is achieved in two basic ways: by setting up good laws and by education (*L* 30.2). Within this context, Hobbes explicates the duty of setting up good laws negatively: the sovereign has a duty not to renounce any of his rights or transfer any of them to any other entity. The things that Hobbes mentions are just those that he had discussed earlier as the rights of a sovereign: not being subject to the civil law, the authority to make war, to levy taxes, to raise an army, to appoint ministers and teachers (*L* 30.3; cf. *L* 18).

More space is devoted to the second way of realizing a "general providence," that of educating the subjects. When they are ignorant of a sovereign's rights or misinformed about the grounds of those rights, they are susceptible to being induced to rebel (*L* 30.3). This duty cannot be discharged by passing a law. Hobbes says, somewhat surprisingly since in another place he says that the laws of nature and the civil laws are of equal extent (*L* 26.8), that a supposed civil law not to rebel does not thereby impose any obligation on a subject (*L* 30.4). What obliges a person not to rebel is the law of nature, which forbids a person to violate her faith. Since law cannot achieve the goal of preventing rebellious attitudes, education must. In *Behemoth*, one of the principal causes given for the English Civil War was the ignorance of the people of what their duty towards the king was (*B*, p. 4). This also explains why Hobbes thought the doctrine of *Leviathan* should have been taught in the universities (*L* "Review and Conclusion" 16; *EW* 7:335).

One would expect the universities to be the primary places where education would occur. Unfortunately, they have failed miserably, according to Hobbes, because they have been infected with false doctrine. Until the latter part of the reign of Henry VIII, most university teachers supported the pope against the sovereign (*L* 30.14). Even under the Stuarts, the universities were teaching false doctrines and nonsense (*DC* 13.9; *EL* 2.9.8).

The sovereign, then, can and ought to instruct and counsel his subjects about their responsibilities. Of course, it is not just his duty to instruct them; it is in his own self-interest, in order to protect himself "against the danger that may arrive to himself in his natural person from rebellion" (*L* 30.6; *EL* 2.9.8).

The sovereign has other duties in addition to the two main ones just discussed (setting up good laws and teaching his subjects what their duties are). One is to ensure equal treatment under the law. The "poor and obscure" are to be treated as well as the "rich and mighty." It is simply a matter of equity, which is a law of nature. The sovereign should not treat one person better than another, because before him all people are equal, just as they were in the state of nature. Differences in status are artificial and depend upon his own decisions about who to raise to a higher level (*L* 30.15–16). There is no contradiction between the insistence on equality before the law and the artificiality of rank. Justice requires equality; honor creates inequality.

Taxation should be considered the "wages" due to the sovereign for doing his job (*L* 30.17). This attitude towards taxation depends upon the authorization model of sovereignty, according to which the government is the agent for the subjects.

Hobbes's tax policy is regressive. Since the purpose of the civil state is to protect a person's life and since the life of the poor is protected as much as the life of the rich, rich and poor ought to pay the same taxes (*L* 30.17). Hobbes does not consider here an objection that might be raised against this policy based upon his own principles: the purpose of the government is to maintain the safety of the people, and safety requires more than simply the "bare preservation" of a person's life; it includes life's "other contentments" (*L* 30.1); since the rich enjoy more safety from the government than the poor do, they ought to pay more. Oddly, Hobbes had expressed this attitude in *De Cive*: "although all equally enjoy peace, yet the benefits springing from thence are not equal to all; for some get greater possessions, others less" (*DC* 13.11).

Although his tax policy in *Leviathan* is regressive, Hobbes does soften its effect by holding that the rich should pay the taxes for their servants since they benefit from their service. Hobbes himself would have benefited from this since he was a servant to the Cavendishes. He also holds that taxes

283

should be based upon consumption not wealth (*L* 30.17; *DC* 13.10). Here he is promoting the stereotypical puritan ethic of thriftiness.

Hobbes has a decent concern for the destitute. The sovereign has a duty to provide for the care of those who through no fault of their own cannot care for themselves (*L* 30.18). Those who can work but do not want to should be forced to work. When overpopulation threatens, the poor ought to be "transplanted into countries not sufficiently inhabited." They should not persecute the natives of those countries but cultivate the land so that it is used more efficiently. When the entire world is overpopulated, "the last remedy of all is war; which provides for every man by victory or death" (*L* 30.19).

The duties of the sovereign also include allotting PUNISHMENT, distributing rewards, and appointing wise counselors (*L* 30.23–6). As in *Behemoth*, Hobbes warns against thinking that good judgement is inherited. One should not assume that the child of a good counselor will herself be wise (*L* 30.25; *B*, p. 31).

In *De Cive*, Hobbes divides the benefits that the sovereign is to bestow on his subjects into four kinds: (1) protection against foreign enemies; (2) protection against domestic enemies; (3) their enrichment "as much as may consist with public security"; and (4) their enjoyment of a "harmless liberty" (*DC* 13.6).

Concerning (1), the job of protecting against foreign enemies is used to justify the use of spies, the maintenance of a standing army and navy, and well-supplied garrisons and forts (*DC* 13.7–8; *EL* 2.9.9). One of the complaints against Charles concerned his desire to maintain a standing army and navy, and Hobbes presents a clear defense of the king's policy of collecting ship money and a clear case against John Hampden, who refused to pay: "they who think it then seasonable enough to raise monies for the maintenance of soldiers and other charges of war when the danger begins to show itself, they consider not surely how difficult a matter it is to wring suddenly out of close-fisted men so vast a proportion of monies" (*DC* 13.8).

Concerning (2), Hobbes mentions false doctrines and poverty as the principal cause of sedition (*DC* 13.9–10). Since people are likely to complain about taxes, it is important for the sovereign to make the tax burden equal. Equality here does not mean equal payments by each subject, but a payment from each in proportion to the benefits that she receives (*DC* 13.11). A sovereign also has a duty to control the ambitions of people. The sovereign needs to reward those who help him and to punish those who do not, in order to show his subjects that the best way to succeed in the commonwealth is to support him (*DC* 13.12). Along the same lines, the sovereign ought to restrain FACTIONS, which are unauthorized groups that undermine his power (*DC* 13.13).

Concerning (3), Hobbes mentions three principal things that make people rich: "labour and thrift" (*labor et parsimonia*) and natural resources such as good soil and adequate water. The first two are essential. His example of "a city constituted in an island of the sea" (*civitas in insula maris constituta*) may be an allusion either to England or to the Athens of Thucydides. An army may be considered a means to riches; undoubtedly it helped to make Rome and Athens great (*DC* 13.14). But usually more harm than good comes from keeping an army; for winning a war involves a lot of luck, and most countries are damaged, not improved, by war. In light of this, the sovereign ought to promote the arts that take advantage of the first three resources (labor, thrift, and natural resources): agriculture and fishing, navigation, mechanics, mathematics (*DC* 13.14).

Concerning (4), subjects are permitted to do anything that is not forbidden, that is, anything that is not against the law (*DC* 13.15). Hobbes thinks that a sovereign can never legislate against most activities and claims that "it is necessary that there be infinite cases which are neither commanded nor prohibited, but every man may either do or not do them as he lists himself" (*DC* 13.15). This is another case where I think that Hobbes fails to show enough imagination about how restrictive the laws of a government can be. In chapter 14 of *Leviathan*, Hobbes says that, in order to establish a government, people must give up their right to all things. This injunction is ambiguous between (1) giving up some rights, that is, those necessary to establish a government, and keeping the rest; and (2) giving up every right (except the right to self-preservation against immediate threats). When he wants to establish the necessity of absolute sovereignty, he exploits (2). But in discussing the LIBERTY OF SUBJECTS in chapter 13 of *De Cive*, Hobbes exploits sense (1).

In *The Elements of Law*, Hobbes invites the reader to consider how difficult it is to be a sovereign: "The inconvenience arising from government in general to him that governs consists partly in the continual care and trouble about the business of other men that are his subjects, and partly in the danger of his person. For the head always is that part not only where the care resides but also against which the stroke of an enemy most commonly is directed" (*EL* 2.5.2). It is these difficulties that justify the honor and wealth that sovereigns usually control.

The analogy of a city and its citizens to a human being makes it tempting to think of the sovereign as analogous to the head of the human being; this may even be suggested by the famous illustrated title page of *Leviathan*, in which the sovereign wears the crown. But the analogy would be mistaken. The sovereign is the soul of a civil state; he is what gives it life (*DC* 6.19).

285

sovereignty by institution and sovereignty by acquisition The nature of sovereignty is the same no matter how a particular SOVEREIGN comes to power (*L* 20.2–3, 20.14). Nonetheless, Hobbes categorizes instances of sovereignty according to their origin. The point of the distinction may be pedagogical. The discussion of sovereignty by institution makes the logical structure of sovereignty clear, and the discussion of sovereignty by acquisition is supposed to be historically more likely.

Sovereignty by institution results from a COVENANT being made by each (natural) person with every other (natural) person to transfer her right to govern herself to a sovereign. Such a covenant is motivated by the fear that each person has of every other person in the state of nature and not by any immediate threat by a superior power. Sovereignty by institution has a distinctly democratic ring to it. Everyone votes in the choice of the sovereign, and the winner represents them and is authorized by the voters to act for them. (*L* 18.1). Of course, for Hobbes, the AUTHORIZATION is irrevocable. In his earliest formulation of his political philosophy, Hobbes thought that democracy indeed was the original form of government (*EL* 2.2.1). But, if people were wise, they reconstituted the commonwealth into an aristocracy or monarchy.

Sovereignty by acquisition results from a covenant being made by each (natural) person with every other (natural) person to transfer her right to govern herself to a superior power (an artificial person) when she is under immediate threat of death or great personal harm from that power (*L* 17.15, 20.1, "Review and Conclusion" 6–7). There are two broad categories of sovereignty by acquisition: sovereignty by virtue of the relationship between a parent and her children, namely, "being able to destroy them if they refuse," and sovereignty acquired by conquest in war (*L* 17.15; cf. *EL* 2.3.2). (For parental sovereignty by acquisition, *see* PATERNAL GOVERNMENT.) The sovereignty acquired by conquest in war is also called "despotical." It is the sovereignty that a lord or master has over his servant, and is the normal way that sovereignty is established, including the established sovereignty in seventeenth-century England, which began with William the Conqueror (*L* 20.10, "Review and Conclusion" 8).

There is an earlier version of the distinction between the ways that sovereignty arises. In *The Elements of Law* (1640), Hobbes distinguished between three ways in which sovereignty is established: by agreement ("voluntary offer of subjection"), by conquest ("yielding by compulsion"), and "upon the supposition of children begotten amongst them" (*EL* 2.3.2).

space and time Space and time are treated most reflectively at the beginning of the second part of *De Corpore*, although it should be noted that

Hobbes titles chapter 7 "Place and Time" ("De Loco et Tempore"). This chapter marks the proper beginning of the study of body since the first part had treated such preliminary topics as what philosophy is, the nature of reasoning, and proper scientific method.

Hobbes sometimes uses the phrase "real space," when he is propounding the views of other philosophers in order to refute them (*DCo* 8.5, 8.9). And in an earlier work, *Anti-White*, Hobbes had asserted the existence of real space and had identified it with body itself: "Next, it is impossible to admit the existence of any certain body without at the same time realizing that it possesses its own dimensions, or spaces. So this space which, when inherent in a body, as the accident in its subject, can be called 'real,' would certainly exist even if there were no being to imagine it" (*AW*, p. 41). But according to the doctrine of *De Corpore*, space (*spatium*) is simply the phantasm (that is, the image) of a body, absent its other properties, that has an existence outside of the mind: "space is the phantasm of a thing existing without the mind simply; that is to say, that phantasm, in which we consider no other accident, but only that it appears without us" (*DCo* 7.2). Since every body exists outside the mind, space is imagined as being external to the mind. But in fact space is only in the mind. Bodies are not literally in space.

Hobbes seems untroubled by an obvious problem with this. There can be phantasms and images only of sensed qualities, so the description of a phantasm that has no qualities would seem to be every bit as incoherent as he says that of "immaterial body" is. Be that as it may, what Hobbes wants to convey is that space is not an independently existing external object; it depends upon human imagination. Thus, a space does not move with an external body. He holds that when an external body moves out of a space, the space remains where it was. However, this too seems incoherent. Since space is mental and bodies are nonmental, how could a body be in a space to move out of it? At best, one might have an idea of some quality, say redness, mentally moving out of some space. At least one scholar has claimed that Hobbes's views as expressed here prove that he was a phenomenalist, not a materialist. My interpretation is that Hobbes was confused about these issues.

Nonetheless, Hobbes is confident about his position: "And this is of itself so manifest, that I should not think it needed any explaining at all, but that I find space to be falsely defined by certain philosophers, who infer from thence, one [of them, that is], that the world is infinite (for taking space to be the extension of bodies, and thinking extension may increase continually, he infers that bodies may be infinitely extended)" (*DCo* 7.2). Hobbes is obviously criticizing Descartes here. He thinks that it is equally easy to criticize philosophers who think that God could not create more than one world. Hobbes is probably thinking of his debating companion, Thomas White.

Shortly later, Hobbes gives a more coherent description of his view: "As a body leaves a phantasm of its magnitude in the mind, so also a moved body leaves a phantasm of its motion, namely, an idea of that body passing out of one space into another by continual succession" (*DCo* 7.3). This is the basis for the phantasm of time. Time is only a phantasm and not a real succession of bodies, because once a "real succession . . . has passed . . . [it] exists no more, because it has passed; and a future one does not yet exist, because it is a future one." Since things are measured by time, time must exist: "It remains, then, that time is not a motion in things themselves, outside the mind, but is mere imagination" (*AW*, p. 339). Time is the idea or phantasm of a body in motion; it includes within it the idea of before and after in motion, the notion of former and latter, and the notion of "succession in the motion of a body, in as much as it is first *here* then *there*" (*DCo* 7.3; see also *DCo* 14.4; *AW*, pp. 339–40). Here is one place where Hobbes cites his agreement with Aristotle.

From his analysis of space, Hobbes is able to explain what a part is. A part is always relative to some whole that contains it (*DCo* 7.4). "Whole" is defined correlatively: a whole is "*all the parts taken together*" (*DCo* 7.7). Thus every whole consists of parts; to hold that something lacks parts is to hold that it is not a whole. If the SOUL has no parts, then it is not a whole (*DCo* 7.9).

Space and time are never actually divided: to divide space or time is simply to consider some of it and not the whole: "the division is not made by the operation of the hands but of the mind" (*DCo* 7.5). From this, an explanation of oneness is given. To be one thing, is to be considered a separate or individuated item among other things of the same kind. If parts or segments of space or time were not distinguished from other parts or segments, then space or time would only be a mass object, that is, the kind of thing designated by mass terms, such as "wood" or "snow." The standard view, that to be one is to be undivided, is incoherent (*DCo* 7.6). Hobbes seems to reduce all numbers to collections of objects, each of which is one. For example, the number two is "*one* and *one*." The number three is "*one one* and *one*" (*DCo* 7.7; *AW*, p. 29). His point, I take it, is to give a nonplatonistic, wholly, materialistic account of mathematics.

spirits This entry is divided into three sections: (1) the nature of spirits; (2) the nature of angels; (3) demons.

(1) Spirits. Hobbes's method of discussing "spirit" is similar to his method of discussing "CHURCH" and "REVELATION." He notes that these terms are

288

used in many ways and that inattention to the diversity of their uses has led to many mistakes and pointless controversies. There are three general categories according to which the uses of "spirit" can be divided: the scientific use (*L* 34.2); the ordinary ("vulgar") uses (*L* 34.3); and the uses in the Bible (*L* 34.4).

In science, a single, clear, determinate meaning should be given to each term from which conclusions can be drawn. In its scientific use, then, a "spirit" is a body that cannot be sensed, because it is too fine to stimulate a sense organ. (*See* BODIES AND ACCIDENTS.) Since every body is material and occupies space, spirits are material and occupy space even though they are imperceptible (*L* 34.2). (It follows from Hobbes's principles that God is a spirit and material.) Spirits are part of the universe. In a lost letter to Descartes, Hobbes equates his own understanding of spirit with Descartes's notion of "subtle matter" (To Mersenne for Descartes, 21 January, 1641), in *The Philosophical Writings of Descartes*, p. 170). But Descartes rejected the equation.

In the ordinary, vulgar understanding of the term, spirits are not thought of as bodies. "Common people" do not think of the universe as consisting only of bodies; for them, only the parts of it that they can perceive are bodies. They mistakenly think of bodies as only those things that can be felt to resist their force or be seen to hinder their clear sight of a "farther prospect," so that the wind, for example, has been taken to be a spirit, not the movement of a body, air. People also use the word "spirit" to refer to causes of phenomena that mystify them, such as the images produced in dreams and hallucinations which, as with the images in a mirror, "represent bodies to us where they are not." Hobbes's own view about such phenomena is that they are "nothing but tumult" in the brain (*L* 34.3). Hobbes summarizes the proper meaning of "spirit" in the ordinary sense in this way: "a subtle, fluid, and invisible body, or a ghost, or other idol or phantasm of the imagination" (*L* 34.3). He then adds as an afterthought that people also use the word "spirit" to mean a disposition of the mind, as in the phrase "unclean spirit," which means being disposed to be unclean.

In the Bible, "spirit" is used in many different ways. In Genesis 1:2, the spirit of God is said to have moved upon the face of the waters. Hobbes might have taken this opportunity to argue that the Bible must mean that God is a body since only bodies move, but instead he takes the sensible position that the passage only means that God caused the waters to move (*L* 34.5). The "spirit of God" sometimes means an extraordinary wisdom or zeal, the power of predicting by dreams or visions, life, a submission to authority, or "an aerial body" (*L* 34.5–15). The last meaning is assigned on the basis of certain stories told about Jesus. Since several of his disciples

289

saw him walking on water, the vision could not have been an hallucination, which affects only one person at a time (*L* 34.15). All of these interpretations are plausible and well supported by the texts Hobbes chooses; all or most of them would be accepted by biblical scholars today.

(2) Angels. Etymologically, an angel is a messenger. The term is usually restricted however to messengers of God. Although they are usually thought of as persons, angelic messengers should be construed as anything that indicates that God is present or revealing Himself to human beings. Thus, an angel may be an image in a dream or a vision (*L* 34.16–17).

When angels are substances, they have to be bodies, since all substances are bodies. They are called spirits, but then "spirits" in the proper sense of the term, as explained above, are imperceptible bodies.

The Bible does not describe the creation of the angels, and the origin of the belief in angels was the same among the Jews as it was among non-Jews. Not having any scientific explanation for the striking figures in dreams and other apparitions, the Jews jumped to the conclusion that they must be some sort of substance, and since they seemed to be very different from ordinary substances, they often called them "incorporeal substances" even though that term is self-contradictory (*L* 34.18, 34.23). Since some dreams and visions are good and some bad, the Jews distinguished between good angels and bad angels, as non-Jews distinguished between good demons and bad demons.

There is little or no scientific evidence for the existence of angels; so Hobbes tries to explain them away as much as possible. He thinks that all of the texts in the Old Testament can plausibly be explained without positing the existence of a special angelic creature. In some biblical passages, "angel" signifies the presence of God, sometimes the voice of God or whatever caused someone to believe that she heard the voice of God; sometimes they are supernaturally caused images or apparitions in dreams. In every Old Testament passage and in some New Testament passages, some such explanation is plausible (*L* 34.19–23). There are some New Testament passages however that resist all such de-mythologizing tactics. Certain passages can be sensibly interpreted only as asserting or presupposing the existence of angels as substances. Hobbes says,

> I was inclined to this opinion, that angels were nothing but supernatural apparitions of the fancy, raised by the special and extraordinary operation of God, thereby to make his presence and commandments known to mankind, and chiefly to his own people. But the many places of the New Testament and our saviour's own words and in such texts wherein is no suspicion of corruption of the Scripture have extorted from my feeble reason an acknowledgment and belief that there be also angels substantial and permanent. (*L* 34.24)

Further, in these cases, angels must be understood to be material substances. For example, the second epistle of Peter says, "God spared not the angels that sinned but cast them down into hell." It would be pointless to put an incorporeal substance, if there were such a thing, into a fire for punishment, since only bodies burn.

(3) Demons. Demons are the heathen analogs to the angels of the Jews and Christians. Demonology is the study of demons. It is not a science, because the demons themselves do not exist; they are mythological creatures imported into Christian doctrine from pagan myths. What Hobbes offers is a critique of demonology. He discusses demons in part four of *Leviathan*. Demonology is the second of the four main categories of deceptions purveyed by the KINGDOM OF DARKNESS. Hobbes begins the chapter on demonology with a paragraph that summarizes his theory of sensation: "Lucid bodies," either in a direct line or reflected from opaque objects or refracted through "diaphanous bodies," strike the eye and cause motions that cause "an imagination of the object" from which the lucid bodies proceeded (*L* 45.1). Internal motions continuing from this initial sensation are called memory, imagination, and dreams.

The purpose of this brief mechanistic account of sensation is to prepare the way for a dismissive account of demons. Belief in demons is the result of ignorance of the true causes of sensation as discovered by modern science. Ancient thinkers could not think of any better explanation for certain odd images that people experience than that they were objectively existing but immaterial beings. So they thought that what are in fact certain internal motions of the brain were extraordinary external beings (*L* 45.2). But modern people do not have that excuse.

According to Hobbes, the mythology of demons begins with the ancient Greeks, who spread their stories to the surrounding areas, including Judaea and Alexandria where it corrupted post-exilic Judaism (*L* 44.4). The Greek priests and poets thought of some demons as good and some as bad, but the Jews called only the bad ones "demons" or "devils." The good ones were called the spirit of God (*L* 45.2, 45.4). People with various disabilities ranging from insanity to deafness were diagnosed as demoniacs, that is, people possessed by a demon (*L* 45.4).

One might object that demons cannot be mythic beings, because Jesus believed that they existed. Hobbes denies the claim. Jesus did not believe in them. His apparent addresses to them, such as "Go out, evil one," are uses of figurative language, analogous to the language he used when he addressed the wind and the sea when he calmed them (*L* 45.5). This is not to say that Jesus did not believe that spirits exist. Hobbes seems to think that, while Jesus did believe in spirits, he knew that they were material. Recall, for example, that the devil, who is a spirit, led him into

291

the wilderness, presumably by walking with him; and only material objects can walk. However, there is also evidence that the spirit referred to was only a vision (*L* 45.5–6). Jesus had been abstaining from food and drink for forty days. Hobbes goes through several other texts with the purpose of showing that talk about spirits and the devil can be interpreted figuratively (*L* 45.7). Nonetheless, he concludes the discussion by affirming the existence of corporeal spirits and angels (*L* 45.8).

To the question why Jesus did not straightforwardly tell people that he did not believe that spirits were immaterial, Hobbes says that analogous questions could be raised about all sorts of things that are left out of the Bible: "Why didn't Moses report the creation of spirits in Genesis?" and "Why didn't Jesus give faith and the other virtues to all people?" Hobbes calls such questions "more curious than necessary for a Christian man's salvation." Although human beings cannot know the answers, "probable and pious reasons" can be suggested. Hobbes says that the reason that God did not supply people with the answers to questions about the nature of the physical world was that He wanted them to exercise their "industry and reason." The mission of Jesus himself was only "to show us this plain and direct way to SALVATION" and beliefs about spirits are irrelevant to this (*L* 45.8). Hobbes's view is consonant with the spirit of Galileo's remark that the Bible shows not how the heavens go but how to go to heaven.

state of nature (*status naturae*)   The state of nature is the condition that human beings are in when there is no civil state ("the time men live without a common power to keep them all in awe" (*L* 13.8)). The thought of this condition inspired Hobbes to write some of his most memorable prose: It is the condition of war "where every man is enemy to every man . . . and the life of man [is] solitary, poor, nasty, brutish, and short" (*L* 13.9). The concept of the state of nature is largely a heuristic device that Hobbes uses to explain the need for government and to justify its existence. But there are circumstances in which the state of nature is actually realized, even though he does not think that there was ever a time when everyone in the whole world was in the state of nature (*L* 13.11; *QLNC,* pp. 214–15).

One might first approach the idea of the state of nature through a thought-experiment. Think about what human beings are like in society; then conceptually remove all laws and consider what human behavior would be like if completely unconstrained by any law whatsoever. That is the state of nature arrived at by analytic or resolutive thinking. One might also begin by thinking about what human beings are like in themselves, that is, by considering only their physical nature. This is what they are like in the state of nature. One might then add a certain kind of law, say the law of nature, in order to determine how that addition would change the

292

behavior of the people and what new kind of behavior might then be possible. This way of thinking about the state of nature uses the synthetic or compositive method.

There are three situations in which people are actually in the state of nature: (1) the kind of primitive conditions in which there is no government at all, such as America before the arrival of Europeans, as Hobbes conceived it; (2) civil war, when a government has collapsed and no other has replaced it; (3) the condition of each government with respect to every other government (*L* 13.11–12).

About eighty percent of all occurrences of the phrase "the state of nature" appear in *De Cive*; about fifteen percent are in *The Elements of Law*. The phrase does not occur in *Leviathan* at all, where Hobbes speaks instead of the "natural condition of mankind." It makes sense then to begin with the concept as it occurs in the first two works. In both *De Cive* and *The Elements of Law*, Hobbes begins by mentioning four natural powers of human beings: bodily strength, experience, reason, and passion (*DC* 1.1; *EL* 1.14.1). Although people differ with regard to the degree to which they have each of these four powers, the sum total of these powers that virtually every person possesses is sufficient to make any person able to kill any other. The power to kill would not be a problem for everyone if people did not have motives to kill others. But they do. In the state of nature, everyone may need to kill someone in order to survive or at least to enhance the chances of her own survival. In other words, scarcity of resources causes people to become a threat to each other (*DC* 1.6; *EL* 1.14.5). To make matters worse, some people have a natural desire to dominate others even though their own survival does not require it. Since no one knows who may need or want to kill her, everyone must fear everyone else: "For though the wicked were fewer than the righteous, yet because we cannot distinguish them, there is a necessity of suspecting, heeding, anticipating, subjugating, self-defending, ever incident to the most honest and fairest conditioned" (*DC* "Preface" 3). Finally, since everyone knows that everyone should fear everyone else, one has a still further reason to fear everyone else (*DC* 1.4; *EL* 1.14.3–6).

Although the phrase "the state of nature" does not appear in *Leviathan*, the concept is there in a more sophisticated form than in the two works just discussed. It occurs in chapter 13 as a preliminary to the discussion of the laws of nature in the following chapter. Hobbes begins chapter 13 by asserting the (virtual) equality of all human beings "in the faculties of body and mind." He thinks that the differences between people that appear if only intelligence or physical strength is considered tend to disappear if both are taken together (*L* 13.1). The presupposition is that intelligent people tend to be physically weak, and that physically weak people tend

293

to be stupid. Hobbes need not depend upon that presupposition, and he immediately goes on to argue in a different way. It does not take much strength and intelligence to kill another person in the state of nature. The job can be done by simply waiting until the prospective victim goes to sleep; one then sneaks up on her and bashes her brains out with a rock, or, if necessary, one may conspire with others long enough to kill a stronger or cleverer person (*L* 13.1). These temporary alliances are possible in the state of nature.

The equality of all people, combined with scarcity, is sufficient to make them enemies, according to Hobbes. Scarcity can be defined in two ways. Something is scarce either when two or more people need the same thing that cannot be shared, or when two or more people want the same thing that cannot be shared. It is not necessary for Hobbes to argue that there is in fact scarcity in the sense of insufficient goods to go around. Given the acquisitive nature of some human beings, there would be scarcity (in the second sense) even in a land flowing with milk and honey.

There is another reason why equality, together with scarcity, guarantees enmity. Hobbes thinks that the equality of all human beings gives rise in each person to an "equality of hope" that she will achieve her aims (*L* 13.3). Hobbes's reasoning however seems dubious and ultimately irrelevant. It seems dubious because it is perhaps not actual equality that would give rise to equal hope but rather everyone's belief that she is equal to all others, whether or not that is so. Two people of equal ability may have unequal estimates of their own abilities, and vice versa. Further, a person's general attitude of mind affects that estimate. *Ceteris paribus* pessimists are less hopeful of attaining their goals than optimists, and Hobbes does not consider that fact.

In any case, hope seems largely irrelevant to the issue of the inherent conflict between people. If a person wants something badly enough, then she is going to try as hard as possible to get it, no matter what she thinks the chances of success are. The same point holds if scarcity is understood in terms of need. If the only way to escape starvation is to fight an expert in the martial arts, then one will fight even though one has little hope of winning. In short, scarcity alone is enough to make people enemies.

At some level, Hobbes may have realized this, because he lists "competition" as the first of three causes of war found in the nature of human beings. The other two are distrust of other people ("diffidence") and the desire for glory. Distrust follows from competition. Since a person can never know who will need or want what she has, she must not only distrust everyone, but also pre-emptively strike at anyone who could possibly become a competitor. This distrust is intensified by the fact that some people get pleasure from conquering others even when it is not necessary or even

294

desirable for their own survival. Thus, the desire for glory is a third cause of war (*L* 13.6–7).

Hobbes often gives the impression that he holds that in the state of nature every person thinks that every other person is an actual threat, as when he says that, even in a civil state, to lock one's doors for protection is to "accuse mankind" (*L* 13.10). But that is not correct. People lock their doors not because they think that everyone is dangerous, but because they think that some people are dangerous and they do not know who they are or when they may threaten. This was in effect the point, noted above, that he made in the "Preface" of *De Cive*. It is the combination of some dangerous people and ignorance that makes it necessary to take precautions and perhaps to fear everyone. But to fear everyone because some people are dangerous does not entail that one believes that everyone is dangerous.

The state of nature is a dangerous place, but it is not a place of injustice or wickedness; justice and injustice depend upon the existence of law, and law depends upon the existence of a common power, and there is no common power in the state of nature (*L* 13.13). This position is slightly problematic because in other places Hobbes says that the laws of nature exist before the civil state and can be broken at that time. He also says that covenants can be made and broken in the state of nature, and that to break a COVENANT is unjust.

Any solution proposed to this difficulty is interpretive and conjectural. It is worth suggesting one here merely for clarificatory purposes. A distinction is drawn by some scholars between a primary and a secondary state of nature. In the primary state of nature, human beings are considered in abstraction from law of any sort, including the laws of nature. In this primary state of nature, it is impossible for there to be any injustice. In the secondary state of nature, human beings are considered outside of the laws of any civil state, but not in abstraction from the laws of nature, which in fact always hold at least in the minimal sense of binding in the court of conscience. In the secondary state of nature, a person can be unjust by taking more than she believes is needed for her survival or by breaking some other law of nature.

Since there is no common power in the primary state of nature, there is no way to protect things from other people. There is thus no such thing as private property in this state. PROPERTY only begins with and is guaranteed by the sovereign of a civil state (*L* 13.13). Hobbes said this consideration was crucial in his thinking about justice: "my first enquiry was to be, from when it proceeded that any man should call anything rather his *own*, than *another man's*. And . . . I found that this proceeded not from nature, but consent" (*DC* "Dedication"). Hobbes was strongly attacked for holding this position. The standard seventeenth-century view was that property rights

295

were natural and not dependent upon the sovereign. The issue was not academic but timely and political. Both James I and Charles I had difficulties raising sufficient taxes to conduct their policies. Absolutists like Roger Manwaring in 1626 argued that the king had the right to everyone's property. Hobbes told his biographer John Aubrey that his own view was the same as Manwaring's. The doctrine of *De Cive* and *Leviathan* bears out Hobbes's words.

(*See also* LAW OF NATURE; RIGHT OF NATURE.)

substance   *See* BODIES AND ACCIDENTS

superstition   Superstition is defined in *De Cive* as "fear of invisible things when it is severed from right reason" (*DC* 16.1). It is associated with atheism, which arises from "an opinion of right reason without fear." Notice that atheism is the belief that one has right reason, not the possession of it. These are definitions or descriptions that, far from offending clerics, might inspire them to praise their author. Not so for the definition of "superstition" in *Leviathan*. After having said that religion is fear of power invisible, which is a fair definition, Hobbes says that superstition is religion that is not allowed. Earlier, he had indicated that religion and superstition signify the same thing, fear of power invisible, and differ only in regards to the attitude one takes to that fear. Religion is approved of; superstition is not approved of.

In order to understand, partially, why Hobbes gives such an odd explanation of superstition in *Leviathan*, it is necessary to distinguish between the (cognitive) meaning of a word and the criterion by which the word is applied. For example, thinking is a mental activity but the criterion by which "thinking" is applied to a person has to be some observable bodily activity. Again, measles is a disease caused by a certain virus but the criterion by which "measles" is applied is the presence of characteristic red blisters, a fever, and so on. The definitions and the criteria just articulated are correct and sensible. It is possible however to confuse the criterion for the definition. Naive behaviorists confuse the criterion for thinking with thinking itself. And if someone confused the red blisters, fever, and so on with measles itself, the same kind of mistake would be made.

Also, it often happens, when people have some emotional stake in a topic, that not only does the criterion for applying a word get confused for the thing itself, but the criterion that is applied is nonsensical. For many people in the late nineteenth century, belonging to a labor union was confused with being a communist, even though union membership is not even a reliable criterion for being a communist. For many people in the seventeenth century, belonging to a religion that was not permitted was confused with being superstitious. Thus, after the Reformation, Protestants in England often called Roman Catholics superstitious; and puritans during the 1640s called the members of the establishment Church of England superstitious. My suggestion is that Hobbes is sarcastically playing with this confusion of criterion and meaning. Under the rubric of defining "superstition" in *Leviathan*, Hobbes is actually explaining how most people use the term, because they confuse their mistaken criterion for superstition with superstition itself. This interpretation is buttressed by Hobbes's remark that "this fear of things invisible . . . every one in himself calls religion, and in them that worship or fear that power otherwise than they do, superstition" (*L* 11.26).

Given his correct definition of "superstition" in *De Cive*, written in 1642 with warnings about the impending civil war, it is plausible that Hobbes had a correct understanding of it. Further, given that his warnings were not heeded during the religious turmoil of the 1640s, immediately preceding his writing of *Leviathan*, it is understandable that frustration would have led someone like Hobbes to write sardonically about the matter.

Bramhall in particular was unhappy with Hobbes's treatment of superstition. After quoting Hobbes's remark that superstition proceeds from fear without right reason and that atheism proceeds from an opinion of right reason without fear, Bramhall wrote that Hobbes makes "atheism more reasonable than superstition" (*BCL*, p. 289). Hobbes's reply is persuasive. He says in part:

> I said superstition was fear without reason. Is not the fear of a false God or fancied demon contrary to right reason? And is not atheism boldness grounded on false reasoning, such as this, *the wicked prosper, therefore there is no God*? He [Bramhall] offers no proof against any of this; but says only I make atheism to be more reasonable than superstition; which is not true: for I deny that there is any reason either in the atheist or the superstitious. And because the atheist thinks he has reason, where he has none, I think him the more irrational of the two. (*BCL*, p. 291)

Idolatry is related to superstition. In *De Cive*, Hobbes says that idolatry cannot be the worship of false gods, because these gods do not exist; rather, it is must be a defective worship of the one God that exists. Idolatry is "a worship of one God, yet under other *titles, attributes,* and *rites* than what were established by Abraham and Moses; for this was to deny the God of Abraham . . ." (*DC* 16.18). Hobbes must subsequently have thought that this treatment of idolatry was either imprecise or unnecessarily inflammatory, because in *Leviathan* he holds that nonexistent objects, and not the one true God, are indeed the targets of idolatry. Idolatry is the worship of a nonexistent object that is represented by some physical object such as a statue or a painting (*L* 45.10, 45.20). Connected with idolatry is typically an image that is believed to resemble the object that is believed to be divine (*L* 45.14; cf. 45.16). In an extended sense, idolatry is the worship of any creature such as the sun or a star as divine (*L* 45.18). Idolatry is forbidden by the second commandment (*L* 45.10, 45.19). (*See also* WORSHIP.)

T

Ten Commandments The Ten Commandments were the first written laws that God gave to human beings; they were delivered directly to Moses (*L* 42.37). Hobbes discusses the meaning of the commandments several times in different contexts. In *Leviathan*, chapter 42, it occurs as part of his discussion of the teaching function of the church. God gave the Ten Commandments to the Jews when He became their civil sovereign. (Before that time God's only law was the law of nature "written in every man's own heart" (*L* 42.37).) Hobbes casts his discussion of the Ten Commandments in such a way that it becomes part of his general design to secularize certain religious concepts. For example, he transfers various divine attributes to the sovereign. Just as God is omnipotent and the judge of all, the sovereign has overwhelming power and is the judge of all facts and events. Also, just as eternal salvation from the ravages of sin comes from God, worldly salvation from the wretchedness of the state of nature comes from the sovereign. Similarly, the Ten Commandments are reinterpreted within a secular, political framework. Hobbes interprets the first four commandments, which are usually thought of as applying distinctively to God, as analogous to what is required of any civil sovereign: "the first [table of stone] contains the law of sovereignty." The commandment not to have foreign gods, for example, is in fact an assertion of the unity of the sovereign. The commandment not to take the name of God in vain is in fact the law that the people "should not speak rashly of their king nor dispute his right" (*L* 42.37).

Scholars often do not sufficiently emphasize that Hobbes thought that the selfish behavior of human beings can and should be curbed by education, and that it was the sovereign's job to do so. In answer to the objection that ordinary people are incapable of understanding their political obligations, Hobbes illustrates how easy it is by expressing those obligations in terms of the Ten Commandments. The decalogue is usually divided into two groups: those commandments that dictate one's relations to God and those that dictate one's relations to other human beings. In

Hobbes's political rendering of them, the first group of commandments are secularized analogs of the biblical ones.

Concerning the first commandment, Hobbes says that subjects should not try to change their form of government, and in particular they should not try to model their form of government on that of a neighboring nation; to do so is analogous to breaking this commandment, which forbids a person to worship alien gods (L 30.7).

The political analog of the second commandment, which condemns idolatry, is that the sovereign should not allow his subjects to admire or honor any other subject in such a way that it may lead them to compromise the obedience that is owed to the sovereign himself. This attitude of the sovereign is the political analog of the biblical description of God as jealous (L 30.8).

The political analog of the third commandment, Thou shalt not take the name of the Lord thy God in vain, is that the sovereign should not allow any subject to criticize his policies or challenge his authority (L 30.9).

The political analog of the fourth commandment, Remember to keep holy the Lord's Day, is that time should be set aside to instruct the subjects of their duties (L 30.10). One cannot expect the people to be obedient unless they have been taught what they are supposed to do and why. Hobbes illustrates this commandment by describing the practice of the ancient Jews. He could have used a more recent example. He was in effect endorsing the standard Elizabethan practice of having government-approved sermons read to congregations. The practice continued during the reigns of the early Stuarts, though less extensively.

The political analog of the fifth commandment, Honor thy father and mother, is that children should be taught that they ought to respect the sovereign because originally the father and the sovereign of the child were identical, "with power over him of life and death" (L 30.11). However, when the father transferred his sovereignty to someone else, he did not also give up his claim to be honored by his children. Hobbes's talk here about the "father" is refined when he discusses PATERNAL GOVERNMENT explicitly; there he is more sensitive to the fact that in the state of nature the mother has a better claim to sovereignty over the children than does the father. When fathers have sovereignty over a family, it is usually due to some covenant by which the mother has transferred her right to the father.

The sixth, seventh, eighth, and ninth commandments do not need to be adapted to the political sphere since they already directly relate to it. Justice requires that people not be deprived of what is dearest to them: their life, their spouse, their property. Similarly, the things that lead to the loss of these things, such as fraud and corrupt judicial proceedings, are outlawed (L 30.12).

The tenth commandment is that one should not covet one's neighbor's wife and property (*L* 30.13). Hobbes has elsewhere pointed out that laws cannot regulate a person's beliefs or other mental states, because only behavior can be controlled. In this context, the tenth commandment, like the others, is part of what the sovereign is teaching the people, not what he is commanding them to do.

In *De Cive* there is a brief derivation of the last six commandments that occurs as part of the discussion of the ways that laws can be divided (*DC* 14.9). (*See* LAWS, DIVISION OF.)

In *De Cive* 16.10, Hobbes's treatment of the division of the commandments into those that belong to the laws of nature and those that do not is novel. Eight commandments are said to belong to the former and only two to the latter. The first commandment, Thou shalt not have any other gods before me, and the fourth, Remember to keep holy the Lord's Day, are not laws of nature but unique to Judaism. (Hobbes came to this view after reading Peter Heylyn's book *The History of the Sabbath* in 1636.) The second, not to have false gods, and the third, not to take God's name in vain, are part of the law of nature because they are part of "natural worship" and "natural religion" (*DC* 16.10).

Later in the same work, when he is explaining the KINGDOM OF GOD by the new covenant, Hobbes indicates that the Ten Commandments are not detailed enough to serve as a complete system of morality. Take the sixth commandment, Thou shalt not kill. This does not exclude all killing. The question arises then how can one figure out who may kill whom and in what circumstances. If each person could decide such issues for herself, then one would be in the state of nature. Only the sovereign can make the practical decisions necessary to make that commandment fully useful. Similarly, the seventh commandment, Thou shalt not commit adultery, does not prohibit all sexual intercourse. It prohibits, says Hobbes, only sexual intercourse with "another man's wife"; but the laws of the state have to determine when a women is a wife and when not; whether monogamy is lawful or not, and so on (*DC* 17.10).

time　*See* SPACE AND TIME

transubstantiation　Transubstantiation is the Roman Catholic theory of the eucharist, according to which the bread and wine that are consecrated at Mass are changed into the physical body and blood of Jesus. Hobbes considers this theory to be one of the deceptions of the KINGDOM OF DARKNESS. The motive behind the doctrine, according to Hobbes, is to gain control of people. If a priest can turn bread into Jesus, then it is plausible that the priest has control over a person's eternal destiny and consequently ought to be obeyed (*L* 46.18). Also, if a person can be persuaded that a priest has turned bread into Jesus, then she can be persuaded to believe anything.

One of Hobbes's philosophical objections to the doctrine is that a substance cannot be in more than one place at one time. But, if transubstantiation were true, Jesus could be in many places at many times (*L* 46.23). One clue to the absurdity of the doctrine is the absurdity of the explanation of it:

> And particularly in the question of transubstantiation; where after certain words spoken, they that say, the white*ness*, round*ness*, magni*tude*, quali*ty*, corruptibili*ty*, all which are incorporeal, &c. go out of the wafer, into the body of our blessed Saviour, do they not make those *nesses, tudes, and ties*, to be so many spirits possessing his body? For by spirits, they mean always things, that being incorporeal, are nevertheless moveable from one place to another. So that this kind of absurdity may rightly be numbered among the many sorts of madness . . . (*L* 8.27, 44.11, 45.24)

One of Hobbes's complaints against Descartes was that he accepted the doctrine of transubstantiation even though it was not only absurd in itself but obviously inconsistent with his own theory, as Antoine Arnauld and others showed. In one of his several defenses of his view, Descartes wrote, "Mindful of my own weakness, I make no firm pronouncements, but submit all these opinions to the authority of the Catholic Church, and the judgment of those wiser than myself. And I would not wish anyone to believe anything except what he is convinced of by evident and irrefutable reasoning" (*Principles of Philosophy*, part 4, sect. 207). Hobbes should have been sympathetic to this response since he himself made several statements to similar effect (*L* 32.2–4).

Hobbes's philosophical attack on the doctrine of transubstantiation is in tension with his political theory that the sovereign can dictate doctrine. Whatever the sovereign commands in religion must be professed. It is possible that this realization is behind Hobbes's conditional claim that, if Christ's words, "This is my body," mean that he himself is what appears to be bread, then it is not idolatry to worship it. However, it may be that this claim is in fact part of an implication that the worship of the eucharist is a form of idolatry and SUPERSTITION (*L* 45.24).

Transubstantiation is also treated as the second general abuse of the Bible; it is an example of transmuting "consecration into conjuration" (*L* 44.11). To consecrate something is to change its use from something secular to something religious, while to conjure something is to pretend an alteration of nature by the words spoken.

treason   Treason is any word or deed by which a subject signifies that she will no longer obey the sovereign. It is a renunciation of the covenant that established the civil state, and because the covenant "contains in itself all the laws at once," treason is the disobedience of all laws, which is much worse than disobeying any single law (*DC* 14.20). Hobbes's discussion of treason occurs as part of his explanation of SIN (*peccatum*); so treason is said to be a sin.

One way to signify that one will no longer obey the sovereign is "to do violence to the sovereign's person, or to them who execute his commands" (*DC* 14.20). Since this was written in 1642 just before the time that the Civil War officially began and after Lord Strafford had been executed and Archbishop Laud imprisoned, Hobbes is in effect calling the parliamentary opposition traitors. His words are somewhat prophetic in mentioning "regicides" as traitors. That Hobbes is talking about parliament is confirmed by his catalog of the kinds of persons who are treasonous. In general, it is "he who should say that he [the sovereign] had no right to wage war at his own will, to make peace, list soldiers, levy monies, electing magistrates and public ministers, enacting laws, deciding controversies, setting penalties, or doing aught else without which the state cannot stand" (*DC* 14.20). This is a fairly good catalog of the issues dividing Charles and parliament in the late 1630s and early 1640s; it is also a list of the sorts of things that Hobbes says are the rights of a SOVEREIGN.

Treason, properly speaking, is a sin against the natural law that obliges people to keep their covenants; the sovereign-making covenant implicitly or explicitly includes one's alienating the right to govern oneself. A sovereign may however enact a law that makes specific actions, such as coining money or copying the privy seal, treason. But to commit such statutory treason is to break only one law, not, like natural treason, to break every law. If a sovereign were to try to enact a law that duplicated the treason that is a sin against the natural law, he would fail for logical reasons: for the subjects were already obliged not to act treasonously by the sovereign-making covenant; a specific law forbidding rebellion adds nothing to the obligation; it is, in a word, "superfluous" (*DC* 14.21).

In *De Cive*, Hobbes thinks that the basis for punishing traitors must be different from the basis for punishing (ordinary) criminals since traitors break the law of nature while criminals break civil law (*DC* 14.22). Traitors are punished by "natural right" as enemies, while criminals are punished by "civil right." This view does not accord with the way that Hobbes explicitly defends the institution of PUNISHMENT. According to that doctrine, the sovereign punishes in virtue of the right of nature, according to which he has the right to all things. The reason Hobbes makes this his ground for justifying punishment is that giving up one's right to self-defense cannot be one of the rights alienated when one covenants to become a subject of a sovereign, since self-defense is the purpose of the covenant (*L* 28.2). The sovereign remains in the state of nature and thus he punishes criminals and traitors by the same right.

Trinity *See* PERSON

truth Truth is in propositions only and not in things (*DCo* 3.7–8). For this reason, a "man that seeks precise truth" needs to remember what the words he uses stand for "or else he will find himself entangled in words, as a bird in lime-twigs; the more he struggles, the more belimed" (*L* 4.12). Geometry was the first science because it begins with definitions that specify the meanings of words.

Sometimes "truth" is used in contexts that might suggest that it is facts or events that are true; but in such cases, there is a straightforward paraphrase of the expression that makes it clear what proposition is being said to be true. For example, the phrase "truth of the resurrection of Christ" should be understood to mean "the truth of this fundamental article of Christian religion, that Jesus was the Christ" (*L* 42.12). (*See also* LANGUAGE AND SPEECH; PROPOSITIONS.)

Notwithstanding this explicit treatment of "truth," there are places in which truth is explicated differently. When the book of Exodus says that the high priest was given "evidence and truth," truth is tantamount to infallibility (*L* 42.93).

U

***

understanding (*intellectus*)   There is a broad and a narrow sense of "understanding." In the broad sense, understanding is the "imagination that is raised . . . by words or other voluntary signs . . . and is common to man and beast" (*L* 2.10). We know that beasts respond to voluntary signs, because they respond to the call of their master. (Of course, in recent years anthropologists and linguists have shown that some beasts respond to rather sophisticated symbol systems. But Hobbes does not pursue this issue.)

For the most part, Hobbes uses "understanding" in the narrow sense, in which human beings have their thoughts caused by "the sequel and contexture of the names of things into affirmations, negations, and other forms of speech" (*L* 2.10). In short, human beings have language and no other animal does. While LANGUAGE AND SPEECH have their advantages, there is a drawback. They make ABSURDITY possible (*L* 4.22, 11.18). (*See also* REASON.)

In scholastic philosophy, there are two main faculties of the mind: understanding and WILL. Hobbes does not think that either of these things is a faculty. Neither will nor understanding is a compartment or power of the mind. Will is the last desire before an action is performed. Understanding is an extension of IMAGINATION. Hobbes rejects the view that an idea of something can be in the imagination in one way (say, as a "phantasm") and in the understanding in different way (say, as an "intelligible species"). ("Phantasm" and "intelligible species" are part of the scholastic philosophy that Hobbes rejects as nonsensical.)

Bishop Bramhall expounded at length about the relationship between will and understanding, and asserted that the will commands the understanding. Hobbes gives Bramhall's position short shrift (*QLNC*, pp. 73–6). Hobbes does not accept much of the traditional doctrine about will and understanding. In particular, he does not accept that what people understand is under their control. This has an implication for religious faith. Christians, Hobbes says, are commanded to captivate their understanding to the words of Scripture; but "by the captivity of our understanding is not meant a submission of the intellectual faculty . . . but of the will to obedience . . ." (*L* 32.4). In order to preserve his view that people do not have a choice about what they understand, Hobbes radically reinterprets the idea of a religious admonition.

In *De Corpore*, Hobbes says that the understanding of propositions is the cause of the understanding of the propositions that are logically inferred from them (*DCo* 3.20), because he wants some kind of MOTION to explain everything.

universals (*universales*)   Hobbes is a nominalist. He holds that universals are names, "there being nothing in the world universal but names; for the things named are every one of them individual and singular" (*L* 4.6; *AW*, p. 35). The words that are universals are common nouns, because they are used as the names for many things (*L* 4.7). Thus "human being" is a name for Socrates, Xanthippe, and many other things. Nominalism of course is inconsistent with realism construed as the view that, in addition to particular objects, there exist things that are not individual and singular but are common to many things. Hobbes also wants his nominalism to exclude conceptualism, the view that universals are individual ideas in a person's mind.

Since Hobbes holds that universals are names, it is not surprising that some of what he says about them in *De Corpore* in the chapter "Of Method" seems to apply to words. Most universals can be analyzed into simpler universals, just as most words can be analyzed into simpler ones, according to the standard view of analytic philosophy. Thus he says that a square can be resolved into a plane, bounded by a certain number of straight lines equal to one another, and right angles. But some of what he says about them there does not seem to apply to linguistic entities. He says that universals are contained in the nature of individual objects (*DCo* 6.4). He also calls universals "components of every material thing." How could a name be contained in a body, be a component of a material thing? Some of what he says about universals seems to apply to ideas, and some seems to apply to accidents. Universals seem to be ideas when he says, "let any conception or idea of a singular thing be proposed," in order to present an example of a universal to be analyzed. It makes sense for an idea to be analyzed. But ideas cannot be causes, and he implies that universals are. What seem to be causes are accidents, and he does call universals accidents: "those accidents that are common to all bodies" (*DCo* 6.4). Later in the chapter, he says that a cause is "the sum or aggregate of all accidents," and there are other passages to the same effect (*DCo* 6.10, 9.3).

V

vacuum   There is no vacuum (*DCo* 26.2). Hobbes was adamant about this point in the 1650s and the 1660s, especially after Robert Boyle published his results about the airpump in 1660, even though he had accepted the idea of a vacuum in 1643 (*AW*, pp. 47–9). In *De Corpore*, his discussion of it occurs as part of his discussion of the nature of the universe and stars, towards the end of the book. Hobbes describes a common watering-bucket used by gardeners. At the top it has one small hole, which serves as a mouth into which the water is poured. At the bottom, there are numerous tiny holes out of which the water flows. If, however, the mouth is securely stopped up, then water does not run out of the tiny holes in the bottom. The standard explanation today, as it was for Torricelli and Boyle in the seventeenth century, is that the water does not flow out because of air pressure. Hobbes did not accept this explanation. He claims that the water does not flow out because, the world being completely filled, there is no place for it to flow to. If the mouth of the bucket were open, then air could fill the top of the open bucket and allow the water to flow out of the bottom by leaving its place on the outside and filling the place left by the water on the inside (*DCo* 26.2).

Hobbes then refutes the arguments presented by Epicurus and Lucretius for the existence of a vacuum. For Hobbes, there is no need to conceive of fluids as being in their smallest bits "small grains of hard matter" which would prevent each other from moving unless there were a vacuum. Rather, a fluid is fluid all the way down: "its own nature [is] . . . homogeneous as either an atom or as vacuum itself" (*DCo* 26.3; *OL* 4:244).

Hobbes also reinterprets Torricelli's experiments concerning air pressure with the same sort of argumentation. According to Hobbes, the reason that a cylinder filled with mercury does not completely drain out when quickly overturned into a dish of mercury is that it has no place to go. The reason that the mercury flows out until it reaches a height of about twenty-six inches is that the mercury has only that amount of force and no more to push the air it displaces around the dish into the space at the top of the cylinder (*DCo* 26.4; *OL* 4:255).

More important than these arguments are the ones Hobbes developed to refute Boyle. Many of Boyle's experiments involved a large glass sphere. At the bottom of the sphere was a device consisting of a cylinder and piston ("sucker"), and a cock which controlled the opening between the sphere and cylinder. Pulling the piston back when the cock was opened caused air to be drawn out of the sphere, according to Boyle. Since the cock was closed when the piston was pushed forward again, no other air could get into the sphere. Thus, Boyle maintained, the sphere contained less and less air as the cylinder/piston pump was worked. A large part of Hobbes's attack was directed at the integrity of the machinery. Hobbes suspected that the sphere leaked at the point where the cock joined the sphere and cylinder. Since particles of air are very small, much smaller than droplets of water, they could get into the sphere undetected. Hobbes conjectured that there was "pure air," which consisted of much smaller particles than those of gross air. Also, retracting the piston would cause the cylinder to expand ever so slightly, again compromising the supposed tightness of the seal. Finally, since nothing is perfectly or infinitely smooth, there would always be some space between piston and the cylinder by which air could get into the sphere (*Dialogus Physicus*, pp. 354–5; *OL* 4:244–6).

victory Victory is power gained over another person as the result of a war. Victory is not the same as conquest. Conquest is victory plus consent (*L* 20.11, "Review and Conclusion" 7). A vanquished person has the liberty to choose to die or to make the victor her sovereign (*L* 20.11). Hobbes thought that any behavior, even constrained behavior, is free so long as it is caused by a desire.

virtue A virtue is a habit or disposition that tends to human preservation. Vice is the opposite; it is a habit or disposition that tends to human destruction (*EL* 1.17.14). The essence of virtue is "to be sociable with them that will be sociable, and formidable to them that will not. And the same is the sum of the law of nature . . ." (*EL* 1.17.15; cf. *EW* 6:436). Justice is the virtue which helps people to keep their covenants; injustice is the vice that causes people to break them. Equity is the virtue that causes people to treat others equally; arrogance is the corresponding vice. Gratitude is the virtue that causes people to repay benefits given to them; ingratitude is the corresponding vice (*EL* 1.17.14; *L* 15.10; *EW* 6:436–8). Glory is the reputation of virtue (*EW* 6:429). In *Behemoth*, Hobbes mentions several specifically "royal" virtues, such as fortitude, frugality, and liberality (*B*, p. 45).

Moral philosophy is "the science of virtue and vice" (*L* 15.40).

Hobbes does not see any foundation for Aristotle's doctrine that virtue is "mediocrity," that is, a mean between two extremes. Courage is a virtue even when it involves an extremely daring action, so long as the cause is worthwhile; and extreme fear is not a vice when the threat is extreme (*EL* 1.17.14). Virtue always requires a disproportionate amount of some characteristic that is "valued for eminence" (*L* 8.1).

In *Decameron Physiologicum* (see Bibliography [36]), magnetism, following Kepler's terminology, is said to be a virtue (*EW* 7:102, 151, 157).

W

war (*bellum*)   "War" and "peace" are correlative terms. One must be taken as basic and defined; the other may then be defined as the negation of the other. Most people would take "peace" as basic because they think of peace as the standard condition. However "peace" would be defined, "war" would be defined as "not peace." Hobbes is different from most people. For him, war is the natural condition of human beings, and "war" is the basic term. War is the condition of people in the STATE OF NATURE. It does not necessarily consist of actual fighting; it resides essentially in the disposition or inclination to fight (*L* 13.8; *DC* 1.12).

will   Will is the last desire an animal has before it acts; it often follows deliberation, which is simply a succession of alternating appetites and aversions (*L* 6.53; *DCo* 25.13; *DH* 11.2). (*See* DESIRE.) Hobbes is quite aware of the fact that, by his definition, beasts will actions as much as human beings do, because they have desires every bit as much as human beings do.

Hobbes gives the impression that his definition of "will" is descriptive of how people use the term. It is certainly not how most people think of their will; so his definition is better construed as theoretical. That is, it fits the phenomena it is designed for and is explanatorily superior to the ordinary way of thinking of them. Considered as a theoretical term, Hobbes's definition of "will" has merit. It is metaphysically economical in that it does not commit him to any entity, such as a mind or soul, other than bodies and it coheres with his definitions of other cognitive and affective terms.

Hobbes's analysis of will is part of his attempt to give a thoroughly naturalistic and mechanistic account of human psychology. Wills are desires, and desires are immeasurably small motions of bodies. As a motion, instances of will are caused by other motions over which the agent has no control. An agent does what it wills but does not will what it wills. Agents are free to act but not free to will, and hence there is no such thing as free will (*DH* 11.2). The scholastic definition of will as a rational appetite cannot be correct, because it entails, according to Hobbes, that no act of will is contrary to reason, and that is obviously false (*L* 6.53). (*See* LIBERTY

AND NECESSITY.) The scholastic theory of will is an example of the kind of false metaphysics that is taught by the KINGDOM OF DARKNESS for its own purposes. According to that theory, will, under such names as "volitio" and "voluntas," is said to be a power or faculty that causes actions. But it is absurd to hold that a power or faculty causes anything. It is not the ability to do evil that causes evil, but some motion (*L* 46.28).

wisdom A wise person is one who "knows how to bring his business to pass (without the assistance of knavery and ignoble shifts) by the sole strength of his good contrivance. A fool may win from a better gamester, by the advantage of false dice, and packing of cards" (*B*, p. 38).

women Hobbes is relatively enlightened about women. In the state of nature, they are equal to men: "some have attributed the dominion to the man only as being of the more excellent sex; they misreckon in it. For there is not always that difference of strength or prudence between the man and the woman, as that the right can be determined without war" (*L* 20.4). Inequality arises in the civil state. Nonetheless, women are less fit for labor and danger than men (*L* 19.22); they are more timorous than men (*L* 21.16).

Hobbes has no problem with women being sovereigns (*L* 20.6). Theoretical considerations, plus the memory of Elizabeth's glorious reign, make this quite understandable.

world The world or universe is the aggregate of all bodies, which are either visible, like the earth and stars, or invisible, like the smallest atoms (*DCo* 26.5; *AW*, pp. 32, 318, 491). Every part of the world is "body, and that which is not body, is no part of the universe." It seems to follow that God, who is a body, is part of the universe; otherwise He does not exist: "And because the universe is all, that which is no part of it is nothing and consequently nowhere. Nor does it follow from hence, that spirits are nothing: for they have dimensions and are therefore really bodies" (*L* 46.15). Some scholars have used Hobbes's definition of the world to argue that he was either an atheist or a pantheist. It's at least equally possible that he was not aware of the consequences of his definition, since he did not even see that the consequences of some of his geometrical proofs led to absurdity.

Sometimes Hobbes says there are three worlds. The first, called "the Old World," goes from the creation to the flood; the second, "the Present World," goes from the flood until the return of Jesus ("the day of judgement"); the third, "the World to Come," also referred to as the KINGDOM OF GOD, goes from the day of judgement to eternity (*L* 38.24, 44.32). All three of these worlds belong to the earth: the first was on earth, the second is, and the third will be. (*See also* KINGDOM OF GOD, PROPHETIC.)

worship (*cultus*)   Worship is an outward act that is a sign of the inward attitude of HONOR, where honor is the opinion that someone is both good and powerful (*DC* 15.9; *L* 45.12). As a sign of honor, genuine worship can be feigned; that is, one may go through the motions that conform to the worship that may be commanded without genuinely believing that the object of worship is either good or powerful. This is important since subjects owe to their sovereigns obedience as to how to worship even when the object or method of worship conflicts with their own beliefs (*DC* 15.12). For Hobbes, such a conflict does not compromise one's conscience; on the contrary, he thinks that his view explains how people can preserve their religious beliefs without violating their civic duties.

Hobbes gives two related reasons why people want to be worshipped. The first is that people enjoy glory, that is, the belief that they are powerful. Second, people enjoy increasing their power; and being worshipped actually adds to one's power because people tend to think that a person who is worshipped actually is powerful, and when they believe this, they treat her as if she were powerful: thus "honour is increased by worship" (*DC* 15.13). In *Leviathan*, Hobbes contrasts the human desire for worship with God's indifference towards it. Because God has no "ends," He does not desire to be worshipped. Nonetheless, human beings owe Him worship from the "duty" that the weak owe the strong "in hope of benefit, for fear of damage, or in thankfulness for good already received" (*L* 31.13). Hobbes's explanation of why human beings ought to worship God is similar to that of Aquinas, who said that people ought to worship God because they owe it to Him and because it is good for them: it reminds them of their dependence on Him.

Some things intrinsically signify honor; some signify it only by convention (*arbitrarius*) (*DC* 15.11). For example, calling someone virtuous or good is intrinsically worshipful, as are obeying, thanking, and praying to her. In contrast, the honor signified by words such as "communist," "entrepreneur," and "philosopher," like that signified by deeds such as bending at the waist, kneeling, and gesturing in a certain way with one's hand, depends upon the customs and attitudes of the community. Because of this variability, what is conventionally worshipful is not a philosophical topic. Consequently, Hobbes restricts his discussion to what is intrinsically worshipful.

Hobbes says that worship can be divided into that which is done by words and that which is done by deeds. Hobbes's distinction can be criticized by considering each of its terms. Since talking is a kind of action, the categories words and deeds are not mutually exclusive. Also, many of the things that Hobbes would consider deeds involve some prayers, which consist of words. These theoretical objections notwithstanding, we shall

312

keep the terms (1) worship by words and (2) worship by deeds, as an organizational device.

(1) Hobbes explains what it is appropriate to say about God and what is not appropriate. He begins with the attributes that are to be said of God. Existence is to be attributed to God since no one can honor what she thinks does not exist (*L* 31.14). Will, knowledge, understanding, sight and other senses may be attributed to God but not in any anthropomorphic sense. In human beings, will is a desire, and God has no desires. Applied to God, will means the power to cause everything. "Understanding" should not be literally applied to God, because understanding is nothing but a "tumult of the mind, raised by external things that press the organical parts of man's body" and nothing like this goes on in God (*L* 31.27; *DC* 15.14). Hobbes does not explicate what the other terms mean, but the thrust of his remarks is clear. Like Anselm of Canterbury, Hobbes realizes that human beings are accustomed to say things about God that are acceptable but not literally true (*Proslogion*, cc. 6–9).

Given the limitations of human knowledge, people need to apply to God "negative attributes, as *infinite, eternal,* [and] *incomprehensible* . . . or superlatives, as *Most High, Most Great,* and the like, or indefinite, as *good, just, holy, creator*" (*L* 31.28; *DC* 15.14). (Hobbes uses the term "indefinite" in two ways. It can refer either to a categorematic term prefixed with an existential quantifier, for example, "some dog," or to one with no quantifier at all, for example, "dog" (*DCo* 2.11, 3.5; *EL* 1.5.6; cf. *DCo* 3.5).)

There are many things that should not be said about God. He should not be said to be the Soul of the World, because that is tantamount to denying His existence. Since a cause must precede its effect and God is the cause of the world, He cannot be identical with it or any part of it, (*L* 31.15). Similarly, to say that the world is eternal is to say that there is no God; for then the world would have no creator. And to say that God does not care for or govern the world is also tantamount to atheism. Hobbes also explains why other epithets should not be applied to God (*L* 31.16–25). (*See also* GOD.)

Hobbes insists that the purposes of speaking of God should be worship, not description. God is not an object of natural science; it is presumptuous to think that human beings can understand the nature of God when they cannot understand the nature of even "the smallest creature living" (*L* 31.33). Having disputations about the nature of God is "contrary to his honour." When selecting attributes to assign to God,

> we are not to consider the signification of philosophical truth, but the signification of pious intention, to do him the greatest honour we are able. From the want of which consideration, have proceeded the volumes of disputation

about the nature of God that tend not to his honour, but to the honour of our own wits and learning; and are nothing else but inconsiderate and vain abuses of his sacred name. (*L* 31.33)

Hobbes has a very moving passage in which he identifies those terms that best express the human conception of God: "For there is but one name to signify our conception of his nature, and that is I AM: and but one name of his relation to us, and that is *God*; in which is contained Father, King, and Lord" (*L* 31.28). The phrase "I am" is the English version of the Hebrew "Yahweh"; it is the name that God revealed to Moses on Mount Sinai and that the Jews thought was too sacred to be spoken by anyone except the high priest on certain select occasions. Hobbes's treatment of what words people should use when they talk about God and why they should is Protestant and biblical.

(2) Let's now consider worship by deed. Prayers, thanksgiving, gifts, and swearing only by God when swearing is required are inherently worshipful. Hobbes says that thanksgivings are actions performed after a benefit is received and that prayers are actions performed before benefits are received from God. He should have said that prayers are actions that are performed in hope of obtaining a benefit. Gifts, that is, sacrifices and oblations, are a kind of thanksgiving. All of these actions should involve "words and phrases, not sudden nor light nor plebeian; but beautiful and well composed" (*L* 31.34, 31.29–32, 44.21; *DC* 15.15).

Hobbes is not coming down strongly on either the puritan or non-puritan side although his words are skewed towards the Laudian liturgy of the Church of England. During the Interregnum, there was much greater variety of worship officially tolerated than before. There was in fact no state church. Hobbes comments on this lack of uniformity: "where many sorts of worship be allowed, proceeding from the different religions of private men, it cannot be said there is any public worship, nor that the commonwealth is of any religion at all" (*L* 31.37). Hobbes did not like such a situation: "But seeing a commonwealth is but one person, it ought also to exhibit to God but one worship" (*L* 31.37). Of course, the sovereign ought to be the one to specify the liturgy, just as Charles I through Laud and the other bishops had tried to do in Scotland and England. Without referring explicitly to Charles, Hobbes makes this point unequivocally (*DC* 15.16).

Hobbes's last serious discussion of worship is in *De Homine* (1658). There he says that worship is half of religion, the other half being faith in God, which is tantamount to what Hobbes calls "honour." Worship is divided into two kinds, public and private (*DH* 14.9). Public worship is worship commanded by the sovereign. It need not be voluntary, in the sense that a subject may go through the motions of the ritual without doing it as the expression of her own belief that the object of worship is either powerful or good (*DC* 15.12). Private worship is any other worship, and may be performed by one or more people (*DH* 14.8; *L* 31.9–12).

Worship can also be divided into the rational and the superstitious. Rational worship consists of prayers, thanksgiving, public fasting, and offerings; it involves most of the things that belong to ritual (*DH* 14.10). Concerning superstitious worship, Hobbes says that it has a "greater variety than can be told." Specific instances of it are polytheism, astrology, and Roman Catholic doctrines such as transubstantiation and free will (*DH* 14.11–13). The discussion of superstitious worship in part four of *Leviathan* is more subtle. Superstitious or false worship is part of demonology, which is one of four general categories of deceptions propagated by the KINGDOM OF DARKNESS.

For much of the first half of the seventeenth century, the proper mode of worship was a hotly debated topic in England. The puritans wanted a simplified liturgy that emphasized biblical readings and preaching. The non-puritans wanted a richer liturgy that emphasized various sacramental elements. In the eucharistic celebration, the consecration of the bread and wine was the central event. Hobbes preferred the richer liturgical practice of the Laudians. When he was near death, he asked to have the sacrament administered to him according to the rite of the Church of England, and late in life he said that he liked the rites of that church above all others. Puritans thought that the rich liturgy of the Church of England was inseparable from certain Roman Catholic doctrines such as transubstantiation and sacramental grace. But Hobbes, like other Anglicans, disagreed (*DH* 14.13), and he thought that the disputes between the puritans and the non-puritans was a dispute over inessentials.

Bibliography

The most complete source for information about first and other early editions of Hobbes's works is Hugh Macdonald and Mary Hargreaves's *Thomas Hobbes: A Bibliography* (London: The Bibliographical Society, 1952). The most complete bibliography of works about Hobbes before 1980 is William Sacksteder's *Hobbes Studies: A Bibliography* (Bowling Green, Ohio: Philosophy Documentation Center, 1982). There is also a bibliographical survey of important research done between approximately 1970 and 1986 in Europe, North America, and South America in *Bulletin Hobbes I* in *Archives de Philosophie* 51 (1988).

Works by Hobbes

Collected works: *The English Works of Thomas Hobbes of Malmesbury*, edited by Sir William Molesworth (London: John Bohn, 1839–45, 11 vols.; reprinted by Scientia Aalen, 1962) [*EW*]

Thomae Hobbes Malmsburiensis Opera Philosophica Quae Latine Scripsit Omnia in Unum Corpus, Guilielmi Molesworth (Londini: Apud Joannem Bohn, 1839–45, 5 vols.; reprinted by Scientia Aalen, 1962) [*OL*]

Molesworth's edition contains most of Hobbes's major and minor works; but it is not a critical edition. Oxford University Press is in the process of putting out a critical edition of all of Hobbes's works. Four volumes have appeared: the Latin and English versions of *De Cive*, edited by Howard Warrender; and Hobbes's complete correspondence in two volumes, edited by Noel Malcolm.

1 *Eight Books of the Peloponnesian Warre Written by Thvcydides the sonne of Olorvs. Interpreted with Faith and Diligence Immediately out of the Greek By Thomas Hobbes Secretary to ye Late Earle of Deuonshire* (London: Imprinted for Hen: Seile, 1629); *EW* 8 and 9

Reprinted during Hobbes's lifetime in 1634, 1648, 1676 by various printers. A recent edition is *The Peloponnesian War: Thucydides*, The Complete Hobbes Translation, with notes and a new introduction by David Grene (Ann Arbor: University of Michigan Press, 1959; reprinted Chicago: University of Chicago Press, 1989).

2   *Ad Nobilissmvm Dominvm Gvilielmvm Comitem Devoniae, &c. De Mirabilibus Pecci, Carmen* (n.p.: n.pub., n.d.); *OL* 5:319–40

A poem about a trip Hobbes took with the second earl of Devonshire between 1626 and 1628 up 'the Devil's Arse of the Peak'. It was published in London in about 1636 and reprinted in 1666 and 1675; a translation done without Hobbes's permission was published in 1678.

3   *A Briefe of the Art of Rhetorique. Containing in substance all that Aristotle hath written in his Three Bookes of that subject, Except onely what is not applicable to the English Tongue* (London: Printed by Tho. Cotes, for Andrew Crook, and are to be sold at the black Bare in Pauls Church-yard, 1637); *EW* 6:419–510

This is Hobbes's translation of his own Latin summary of Aristotle's *Rhetoric*. It is the first translation of Aristotle's book into English. The Latin was prepared as an exercise for his tutee, the young third earl of Devonshire. Hobbes was not involved in the publication of two other editions, each of which had slightly different titles, that appeared in his lifetime. In Molesworth's edition, the work has the title *The Whole Art of Rhetoric*. Hobbes is not the author of *The Art of Rhetoric, plainly set forth with pertinent examples for the more easy understanding of the same*, which also appears in Molesworth's edition. A recent edition of Hobbes's translation is in *The Rhetorics of Thomas Hobbes and Bernard Lamy*, ed. John T. Harwood (Carbondale: Southern Illinois University Press, 1986).

4   *Elements of Law Natural and Politic. By Thomas Hobbes* edited with a preface and critical notes by Ferdinand Tönnies, Ph. D. To which are subjoined selected extracts from unprinted mss of Thomas Hobbes (London: Simpkin, Marshall, and Co., 1889)

Circulated in handwritten copies in 1640 shortly after the Short Parliament was dissolved in May; Hobbes's original manuscript is at Chatsworth, as are a manuscript copy dedicated to the earl of Newcastle and a third manuscript copy. The British Library has five manuscript copies. Harley MSS. 4235 is signed by Hobbes himself and contains some corrections by him. The other four manuscripts are Harley MSS. 1325, 4236, 6858 1325, and Egerton 2005. *The Elements of Law* was published in two parts in 1650 without Hobbes's permission, under the titles *Humane Nature* and *De Corpore Politico*. The work was not published as a whole until 1889, as the result of Ferdinand Tönnies's work on the manuscripts in the British Museum. References by part, chapter, and section number follow Tönnies's edition.

5   *Renati Des-Cartes, Meditationes De Prima Philosophia, in Qva Dei Existentia, & animae immortalitas demonstratur* (Parisiis: Apud Michaelem Soli, via Iacobaea sub signo Phoenicis. M. DC. XLI); *OL* 5:249–74

Hobbes is the author of the third set of objections. He was invited to contribute them by Marin Mersenne, who had been impressed by Hobbes's comments on Descartes's *Discourse on the Methods of Rightly Conducting the Mind* a few years earlier.

6   *Elementorvm Philosophiae Sectio Tertia De Cive* (Parisiis: n.p., 1642)

Usually known as *De Cive*. It was written in Latin in 1641 in Paris; and published in a limited edition in 1642; a second, expanded edition, with a "Preface to the

Reader" and explanatory footnotes, was published by Elzevir in Amsterdam in 1647. Many other editions were published during Hobbes's lifetime, especially on the Continent. Samuel Sorbière, a friend of Hobbes, translated it into French and published it in 1649. A manuscript copy, presented to the third earl of Devonshire, is at Chatsworth. *De Cive* was supposed to be the third section of a trilogy, containing a complete philosophy, but it was the first to appear. The first English translation was published in 1651 under the title *Philosophical Rudiments Concerning Government and Society*; it is disputed whether Hobbes translated this work himself.

7   *Thomas Hobbes: Critique du De Mundo de Thomas White*, ed. Jean Jacquot and Harold Whitmore Jones (Paris: Vrin, et Centre national de la recherche scientifique, 1973)
  This manuscript was probably written in 1642–43 and contains some material that is tantamount to a first draft of *De Corpore*. The manuscript, untitled, is listed as *fonds latin 6566A* in the Bibliothèque Nationale in Paris. It is a critique of Thomas White's book *De Mundo* and was first published in 1973. It is now usually referred to as *Anti-White*. A translation of it is *Thomas White's De Mundo Examined*, tr. Harold Whitmore Jones (London: Bedford University Press, 1976).

8   *Tractatus Opticus* in *F. Marini Mersenni Minimi Cogitata Physico Mathematica* (Parisiis: Sumptibus Antonii Bertier, via Iacobea, M. DC. XLIV); *OL* 5:215–48
  There is a recent edition of this work, edited by Franco Alessio, in *Rivista Critica Di Storia Della Filosofia* 18 (1963), pp. 147–228.

9   *A Discourse Upon Gondibert. An Heroick Poem Written by Sr. William D'Avenant. With an Answer to it by Mr. Hobbs* (A Paris, Chez Matthiev Gvillemot, ruë Sainct Jaques au coin de la ruë de al Parcheminerie, à l'Enseigne de la Bibliotheque, M.DC.L); *EW* 4:441–58

10   *Humane Nature: or, The fundamental Elements Of Policie. Being a Discoverie Of the Faculties, Acts, and Passions of the Soul of Man, from their original causes; According to such Philosophical Principles as are not commonly known or asserted* (London: Printed by T. Newcomb for Fra: Bowman of Oxon., 1650)
  Published without Hobbes's permission, it consists of the first thirteen chapters of Part One of *The Elements of Law, Natural and Politic*. (See [4] above.)

11   *De Corpore Politico, Or The Elements of Lavv, Moral & Politick, With Discourses upon Several Heads; as Of The Law of Nature, Oathes and Covenants, Severall kind of Government. With the Changes and Revolutions of them* (London: Printed for J. Martin, and J. Ridley, 1650)
  Published without Hobbes's permission, it consists of chapters 14–19 of Part One and all of Part Two of *The Elements of Law, Natural and Politic*. (See [4] above.)

12   *Philosophical Rudiments Concerning Government and Society. Or, A Dissertation Concerning Man in his severall habitudes and respects, as the Member of a Society, first Secular, and then Sacred. Containing the Elements of Civill Politie in the Agreement*

which it hath both with Naturall and Divine Lawes. In which is demonstrated, Both what the Origine of Justice is, and wherein the Essence of Christian Religion doth consist. Together with The Nature, Limits, and Qualification both of Regiment and Subjection (London: Printed by J.G. for R. Royston, at the Angel in Ivie-lane, 1651)

This is a translation of *De Cive*; it is disputed whether it was done by Hobbes. There is evidence on each side. This is the only book of Hobbes published by Richard Royston, a royalist, and *Philosophical Rudiments* was generally accepted as a defense of the royalist position. This translation is available in *Man and Citizen*, edited with an introduction by Bernard Gert (Garden City, NY: Anchor Books, 1972; reprinted Indianapolis: Hackett Publishing Company, 1991).

13 *Leviathan, or The Matter, Forme, & Power of a Common-wealth, Ecclesiasticall and Civill* (London: Andrew Crooke, 1651); *EW* 3

Written in Paris in late 1650 and early 1651. There are three editions dated 1651 and supposedly printed for Andrew Crooke. They are known respectively as the Head, Bear, and 25-Ornaments editions. The Head is the authentic first edition. The actual dates and publishers of the other two editions cannot be firmly established. (For details see Macpherson's Introduction to his edition of *Leviathan.*) A copy of *Leviathan*, handwritten on vellum, which is believed to have been presented to Charles II ("a presentation copy"), is in the British Library. A Latin translation was published in 1668. (See [27] below.) Part of it appears to be earlier than the English version and part appears to be later.

There are several good, recent editions: *Leviathan*, edited with an introduction by C. B. Macpherson (Harmondsworth: Penguin Books, 1968). Based upon the Head edition, this is a popular, reliable, and inexpensive edition. It also contains the original pagination inserted into the text.

Leviathan, edited with an introduction by Michael Oakeshott (Oxford: Basil Blackwell, 1957) The introduction presents a unique interpretation of Hobbes and is well respected.

Leviathan, edited with an introduction by Richard Tuck (Cambridge: Cambridge University Press, 1991). Based upon the Head edition, it also was compared against the presentation copy in the British Library. It also contains the original pagination inserted into the text.

Leviathan, with selected variants from the Latin edition of 1668, ed. Edwin Curley (Indianapolis: Hackett Publishing Company, Inc, 1994). Currently the best edition available. Among its many valuable features, it contains notes about variations in the Latin version and translations of chapters 9, 46, 47, and the three chapters of the Appendix.

14 *Of Libertie and Necessitie, a Treatise, Wherein all controversie Concerning Predestination, Election, Freewill, Grace, Merits, Reprobation, &c. is fully decided and cleared, in answer to a Treatise written by the Bishop of London-derry, on the same subject* (London: Printed by W.B. for F. Eaglesfield, 1654); *EW* 4:229–78

Written in 1645 at the request of the marquis of Newcastle after Hobbes's debate with John Bramhall; published without Hobbes's knowledge in 1654.

15 *The Questions Concerning Liberty, Necessity, and Chance. Clearly Stated and Debated Between Dr. Bramhall Bishop of Derry, And Thomas Hobbes of Malmesbury* (London: Printed for Andrew Crook, 1656); *EW* 5

This contains the complete text of item [14], Bramhall's reply, and Hobbes's reply to the reply.

16 *Elementorum Philosophiae Sectio Prima De Corpore* (Londini: Excusum sumptibus Andreae Crook sub signo Draconis viridis in Coemeterio B. Pauli, 1655); *OL* 1

Usually known as *De Corpore*. For a complete translation see [17]. Part one of *De Corpore* is available in a new translation: *Thomas Hobbes: Computatio sive Logica*, tr. Aloysius Martinich (New York: Abaris Books, 1981). It contains a detailed introduction and commentary on Hobbes's philosophy of language by Isabel Hungerland and George Vick.

17 *Elements of Philosophy, The First Section, Concerning Body. Written in Latine by Thomas Hobbes of Malmesbury. And now translated into English. To Which are Added Six Lessons to the Professors of Mathematicks of the Institution of Sr. Henry Savile, in the University of Oxford* (London: Printed by R. & W. Leybourn, for Andrew Crooke, at the Green Dragon in Pauls Church-yard, 1656); *EW* 1

This is a translation of [16]. The extent of Hobbes's involvement in the translation is disputed. Chapters 18 and 20 were rewritten in reaction to criticisms leveled by John Wallis about Hobbes's attempts to square the circle.

18 *ΣΤΙΓΜΑΙ Αγεωμετριας, Αγροικιας, Αντιπολιτειας, Αμαθειας, Or Markes Of the Absurd Geometry, Rural Language, Scottish Church-Politicks and Barbarismes of John Wallis Professor of Geometry and Doctor of Divinity* (London: Printed for Andrew Crooke, at the Green Dragon in Pauls Churchyard, 1657); *EW* 7:357–400

19 *Elementorum Philosophiae Sectio Secunda De Homine* (Londoni: Typis T.C. sumptibus Andr. Crooke, & vaeneunt sub insigni viridis Draconis in Caemetirio Paulino, 1658); *OL* 2:1–132

Usually known as *De Homine*; written in Latin. None of it was translated into English until the Dedication and chapters 10–15 were published in the following: Thomas Hobbes, *Man and Citizen*, ed. Bernard Gert (Garden City, NY: Anchor Books, 1972; reprinted Indianapolis, Hackett Publishing Company, 1991).

20 *Examinatio & Emendatio Mathematicae Hodiernae. Qualis explicatur in libris Johannis Wallisii Geometriae Professoris Saviliani in Academia Oxoniensi. Distributa in sex Dialogos* (Londini: Excusum sumptibus Andreae Crooke, sub signo Draconis viridis in Coemeterio B. Pauli, 1660); *OL* 4:1–237

21 *Dialogus Physicus, Sive De Natura Aeris Conjectura sumpta ab Experimentis nuper Londini habitis in Collegio Greshamensi. Item De Duplicatione Cubi* (Londini: Typis J.B. & prostant Venales apud A. Crook sub insigne Draconis in Caemeterio Paulino, 1661); *OL* 4:238–96

A translation of this work is "Hobbes's Physical Dialogue (1661)," tr. Simon Schaffer, in Steven Shapin and Simon Schaffer, *Leviathan and the Air-Pump* (Princeton: Princeton University Press, 1985). Both Wallis and Robert Boyle wrote replies to this work. Boyle's is *An Examen of Mr. T. Hobbes his Dialogus Physicus De Natura Aëris.* (1662).

22 *Problemata Physica. De Gravitate. Cap. I. De Aestibus Marinis. Cap. II. De Vacuo. Cap. III. De Calore & Luce. Cap. IV. De Duro & Molli. Cap V. De Pluvia, Vento, aliisq; Coeli varietatibus. Cap. VI. De Motuum Speciebus. Cap. VII. Adjuncatae sunt etiam Propositiones duae de Duplicatione Cubi, & Dimensione Circuli* (Londini: Apud Andream Crooke in Coemiterio D. Pauli sub signo Draconis viridis, 1662); *OL* 4:297–359

23 *Seven Philosophical Problems, and Two Propositions of Geometry. By Thomas Hobbes of Malmesbury. With an Apology for Himself, and his Writings. Dedicated to the King, in the year 1662* (London: Printed for William Crook at the Green-Dragon without Temple-Bar, 1682); *EW* 7:1–68
Written in 1662, this was published only posthumously.

24 *Mr. Hobbes Considered in his Loyalty, Religion, Reputation, and Manners. By way of Letter to Dr. Wallis* (London: Printed for Andrew Crooke, and are to be sold at his Shop, at the Sign of the Green-Dragon in St Paul's Church-yard, 1662); *EW* 4:409–40
Usually known as *Considerations upon the Reputation, Loyalty, Manners, and Religion of Thomas Hobbes of Malmesbury*, the title of the edition published in 1680. It is a largely plausible defense of Hobbes's behavior and beliefs.

25 *De Principiis & Ratiocinatione Geometrarum. Ubi ostenditur incertitudinem falsitatemque; non minorem inesse scriptis eorum, quam scriptis Physicorum & Ethicorum. Contra falsum Professorum Geometriae* (Londini: Apud Andream Crooke in Coemiterio D. Pauli sub signo Draconis viridis, 1666); *OL* 4:385–484

26 *A Dialogue between a Philosopher and a Student of the Common Laws of England,* ed. Joseph Cropsey (Chicago: University of Chicago Press, 1971)
Written in about 1666, at the suggestion of John Aubrey, this book was first published in a 1681 edition of [3] with the title *The Art of Rhetoric, With a Discourse of the Laws of England* by Hobbes's publisher, William Crook.

27 *Thomae Hobbes Malmesburiensis Opera Philosophica, Quae Latinè scripsit, Omnia. Antè quidem per partes, nunc autem, post cognitas omnium Objectiones, conjunctim & accuratiùs Edita* (Amstelodami: Ioannem Blaeu, 1668)
This contains the first publication of the Latin version of *Leviathan.*

28 *An Answer to a Book Published by Dr. Bramhall, late Bishop of Derry; Called The Catching of the Leviathan. Together With an Historical Narration Concerning Heresie,*

And the Punishment Thereof (London: Printed for W. Crooke at the Green Dragon without Temple-Barr, 1682); *EW* 4:279–384
This work was written in about 1668 but published posthumously.

29 *Quadratvra Circuli, Cubatio Sphaerae, Duplicatio Cubi, Breviter demonstrata* (Londoni: Excludebat J.C. Sumptibus Andraeae Crooke, 1669); *OL* 4:485–522

30 *Three Papers Presented to the Royal Society Against Dr. Wallis. Together with Considerations on Dr. Wallis his Answer to them* (London: Printed for the Author; and are to be had at the Green Dragon without Temple-bar, 1671); *EW* 7:429–48

31 *Rosetum Geometricum. Sive Propositiones Aliquot Frustra antehac tentatae. Cum Censura brevi Doctrinae Wallisianae de Motu* (Londini: Excudebat J.C. pro Guilielmo Crook, ad Signum Draconis viridis in vico vulgo vocata Without Temple-bar, 1671); *OL* 5:1–88

32 *Lux Mathematica. Excussa Collisionibus Johannis Wallisii Theol. Doctoris, Geometriae in celeberrima Academia Oxoniensi Professoris Publici, et Thomae Hobbesii Malmsburiensis. Multis & fulgentissimis aucta radiis Authore R.R. Adjuncta est Censura Doctrinae Wallisianae de Libra, Una Cum Roseto Hobbesii* (Londini: Excudebat J.C. pro Guilielmo Crook, ad Signum Draconis viridis in vico vulgo vocata Without Temple-bar, 1672); *OL* 5:89–150

33 *The Travels of Vlysses; As they were Related by Himself in Homer's Ninth, Tenth, Eleventh & Twelfth Books of the Odysses, to Alcinous King of Phaecia* (London: Printed by J.C. for William Crook, 1673); *EW* 10:382–427
Written when Hobbes was eighty-five because, he said, "I had nothing else to do. Why publish it? Because I thought it might take off my adversaries from showing their folly upon my more serious writings, and set them upon my verses to show their wisdom." A second edition appeared in 1674 and another the next year.

34 *Homer's Iliads in English. Translated by Tho. Hobbes of Malmsbury. With a Large Preface Concerning the Vertues Of An Heroique Poem. Written by the Translator* (London: Printed by J.C. for William Crook, 1676); *EW* 10:1–301
A second edition of this work appeared in 1677 and included the translation of the *Odyssey* and "With a large Preface concerning the Vertues of an Heroick Poem."

35 *Principia et Problemata Aliquot Geometrica Antè Desperata, Nunc breviter Explicata & Demonstrata* (Londini: Excudebat J.C. pro Gulielmo Crook, ad signum Draconis Viridis in Vico Vulgo Vocato Without Temple=bar, M. DC. LXXIV); *OL* 5:151–214

36 *Decameron Physiologicum: Or, Ten Dialogues of Natural Philosophy. By Thomas Hobbes of Malmsbury. To which is added The Proportion of a straight Line to half the Arc of*

a *Quadrant. By the same Author* (London: Printed by J.C. for W. Crook, 1678); *EW* 7:69–180

37   *The History of the Civil Wars of England. From the Year 1640, to 1660* (Printed in the Year 1679); *EW* 6:161–418

The earliest editions of this book were not authorized by Hobbes and did not have "*Behemoth*" in their title. No place, publisher or date is given on the title page. The book was written in the middle to late 1660s, but Charles refused to give Hobbes permission to publish it. Several other unauthorized editions appeared in 1679 shortly after Hobbes died. Some of these have the title *Behemoth, The History of the Civil Wars of England from the Year 1640, to 1660.* Other early editions had the title *Behemoth; Or an Epitome of the Civil Wars of England, From 1640, to 1660.* The first edition that can be considered authorized is that of William Crook, who in 1682 published *Tracts of Mr. Th. H. of Malmsbury*, which included a version of *Behemoth* that Hobbes had given to Crook in about 1670. A manuscript copy, neatly written, probably by Hobbes's amanuensis James Wheldon, who was also the executor of Hobbes's estate, is held in the library of St John's College, Oxford. This copy contains a dedication to "Sr Henry Bennet, Baron of Arlington," one of Charles II's closest advisers. A critical edition based upon it was edited by Ferdinand Tönnies in 1889 under the title, *Behemoth or The Long Parliament* (London: Simpkin, Marshall, and Co., 1889). A reprint of this edition is published by University of Chicago Press, 1990, with an introduction by Stephen Holmes.

38   *Thomae Hobbessii Malmesburiensis Vita. Authore Seipso* (Londoni: Typis, Anno Dom. CIↃ IↃC LXXIX); *OL* 1:lxxxi–xcix

A translation of this autobiographical poem was published in 1680. A recent translation is "The Life of Thomas Hobbes of Malmesbury," tr. J. E. Parsons, jr. and Whitney Blair, *Interpretation* 10 (1982), 1–7.

39   *Thomae Hobbes Angli Malmesburiensis Philosophi Vita* (Londoni: Apud Guil. Crooke, ad Insigne Viridis Draconis juxta Portam vulgo dictam Temple=Bar); *OL* 1:xiii–xxi

This prose autobiography was published in November 1680.

40   *The Last Sayings, or Dying Legacy of Mr. Thomas Hobbs of Malmesbury, Who Departed this Life on Thursday, Decemb. 4. 1679* (London: Printed for the Author's Executors, 1680)

This broadsheet consists for the most part of quotations from *Leviathan.* The quotations, taken out of context, give the distinct appearance that Hobbes was anti-religious.

41   *An Historical Narration Concerning Heresie, And the Punishment thereof* (London: Printed in the Year 1680); *EW* 4:385–408

The content of this work is similar to chapter 2 of the Appendix to the Latin edition of *Leviathan*, published in 1668.

42   *Historia Ecclesiastica Carmine Elegiaco Concinnata* (Augustae Trinobantum: Anno
      Salutis, MDCLXXXVIII); *OL* 5:341–408
This was published in London. A translation appeared in 1722 with the title
A True Ecclesiastical History, From Moses, To the Time of Martin Luther, In Verse.

Select Seventeenth-Century Works Relevant to Hobbes

Ascham, Anthony, *Of the Confusions and Revolutions of Goverment* [*sic*] (London,
      1649)
Aubrey, John, *Brief Lives,* 2 vols., ed. Andrew Clark (Oxford: Clarendon Press,
      1898)
Bramhall, John, The *Catching of Leviathan or the Great Whale* (London, 1658)
——, *Works,* 4 vols. (Oxford, 1842–4)
Chillingworth, William, *The Religion of Protestants* (Oxford, 1638)
Clarendon, Edward Hyde, Earl of, *A Brief View and Survey of the Dangerous and
      Pernicious Errors to Church and State in Mr. Hobbes's Book, Entitled Leviathan* (Lon-
      don, 1676)
Coke, Roger, *Justice Vindicated From the False Focus Put Upon It – By Mr. T. White
      Gent, Mr. T. Hobbes, and Hugo Grotius* (London, 1660)
Cotton, John, *Gods Mercie Mixed with His Justice* (London, 1641)
Cudworth, Ralph, *The True Intellectual System of the Universe . . . Wherein All the Reason
      and Philosophy of Atheism is Confuted and its Impossibility Demonstrated* (London,
      1678)
Descartes, René, *The Philosophical Writings of Descartes,* 3 vols., tr. John Cottingham
      et al. (Cambridge: Cambridge University Press, 1984–91)
Dowel, J., *The Leviathan Heretical* (London, 1683)
Eachard, John, *Mr. Hobbes's State of Nature, in a Dialogue Between Philautus and
      Timothy* (1672)
——, *Some Opinions of Mr. Hobbs Considered in A Second Dialogue Between Philautus
      and Timothy* (1673)
Filmer, Robert, *Observations Concerning the Originall of Government of Mr. Hobbs Le-
      viathan; Mr. Milton Against Salmasius; H. Grotius De Juri Belli, Mr. Hunton's Treatise
      of Monarchy* (London: Printed for R. Royston at the Angel in Ivie-Lane, 1652)
Hunton, Philip, *A Treatise of Monarchy* (London: Printed for John Bellamy and
      Ralph Smith, and are to be found at the three Golden-Lyons in Corn-hill, 1643)
——, *A Vindication of the Treatise of Monarchy* (London: Printed for John Bellamy, at
      the sign of the three Golden Lyons in Cornehill neare the Royal-Exchange, 1644)
Lawson, George, *An Examination of the Political Part of Mr. Hobbs His Leviathan*
      (London: Printed by R. White for Francis Tyton at the three daggers in Fleet
      Street, near the Inner Temple Gate, 1657)
——, George, *Politica Sacra et Civilis* (London, 1660)
Locke, John, *An Essay Concerning Human Understanding* (1st edn 1690), ed. Peter
      H. Nidditch (Oxford: Clarendon Press, 1975)
——, *Two Treatises of Government* (1st edn 1690); Student Edition, ed. Peter Laslett
      (Cambridge, Cambridge University Press, 1988)

Lucy, William, *Observations, Censures, and Confutations of Notorius Errors in Mr. Hobbes his Leviathan and other of his books* (London, 1663)

Preston, John, *The Cuppe of Blessing* (London, 1633)

Pufendorf, Samuel, *De Jure Naturae et Gentium Libri Octo* (1688); English trans., *The Law of Nature and Nations,* tr. C. H. and W. A. Oldfather (Oxford: Clarendon Press, 1934)

Tenison, Thomas, *The Creed of Mr. Hobbes examined; in a feigned Conference between him and a Student of Divinity* (London, 1670)

Tyrrell, James, *A Brief Disquisition of the Law of Nature* (London: Printed and are to be sold by Richard Baldwin, near the Oxford Arms in Warwick Lane, 1692)

Wallis, John, *Due Correction for Mr. Hobbes: Or school Discipline, for not saying his lessons right. In answer to his Six Lessons directed to the professors of mathematics* (Oxford: Printed by L. Lichfield, printer to the university for T. Robinson, 1656)

Ward, Seth, *Vindiciae Academiarum containing some brief animadversions upon Mr. Websters book stiled, The examination of academies: together with an appendix concerning what M. Hobbs and M. Dell have published on this argument* (Oxford: Printed by Leonard Lichfield, printer to the university for Thomas Robinson, 1654)

Twentieth-Century Works

Ashcraft, Richard, "Hobbes's Natural Man: A Study in Ideology Formation," *Journal of Politics* 33 (1971), pp. 1076–171

Barry, Brian, "Warrender and His Critics," in *Hobbes and Rousseau,* ed. Maurice Cranston and Richard Peters (Garden City, NY: Anchor Books, 1972), pp. 37–65

Bowle, John, *Hobbes and His Critics: A Study in Seventeenth-Century Constitutionalism* (London: Jonathan Cape, 1951)

Brandt, Frithiof, *Thomas Hobbes' Mechanical Conception of Nature* (Copenhagen: Levin & Munksgaard, 1928)

Brown, Keith (ed.), *Hobbes Studies* (Oxford: Blackwell, 1965)

Burns, Norman T., *Christian Mortalism from Tyndale to Milton* (Cambridge, Mass.: Harvard University Press, 1972)

Cranston, Maurice, and Richard Peters (eds), *Hobbes and Rousseau: A Collection of Critical Essays* (Garden City, NY: Anchor Books, 1972)

Curley, Edwin, "'I Durst Not Write So Boldly'," *Hobbes e Spinoza* (Naples: Bibliopolis, 1992), pp. 497–593

Damrosch, Leopold, jr., "Hobbes as Reformation Theologian: Implications of the Free-Will Controversy," *Journal of the History of Ideas* 40 (1979), pp. 339–52

De Beer, G. R., "Some Letters of Hobbes," *Notes and Records of the Royal Society* 7 (1968), pp. 5–42

Debus, Allen, *Science and Education in the Seventeenth Century* (New York: American Elsevier, 1970)

Dietz, Mary (ed.), *Thomas Hobbes and Political Theory* (Lawrence, Kansas: University of Kansas Press, 1990)

Drummond, H. J. H., "Hobbes's *Philosophical Rudiments,*" *The Library,* 5th series, 28 (1973), 54–6

Eisenach, Eldon J., "Hobbes on Church, State and Religion," *History of Political Thought* 3 (1982), pp. 215–43

Gauthier, David. *The Logic of Leviathan: The Moral and Political Theory of Thomas Hobbes* (Oxford: Oxford University Press, 1969)

——, "Why Ought One Obey God? Reflections on Hobbes and Locke," *Canadian Journal of Philosophy* 7 (1977), pp. 425–46

Gert, Bernard, "Hobbes and Psychological Egoism," *Journal of the History of Ideas* 28 (1967), pp. 503–20

Glover, Willis, "God and Thomas Hobbes," in *Hobbes Studies,* ed. Keith Brown (Oxford: Blackwell, 1965), pp. 141–68

Goldsmith, M. M., *Hobbes's Science of Politics* (New York: Columbia University Press, 1966)

——, "Hobbes's 'Mortal God': Is there a Fallacy in Hobbes's Theory of Sovereignty?" *History of Political Thought* 1 (1980), pp. 33–50

——, "The Hobbes Industry," *Political Studies* 39 (1991), pp. 135–47

Halliday, R. J., Timothy Kenyon, and Andrew Reeve, "Hobbes's Belief in God" *Political Studies* 31 (1983), pp. 418–33

Hamilton, J. J., "Hobbes's Study and the Hardwick Library," *Journal of the History of Philosophy* 16 (1978), pp. 445–53

Hampton, Jean, *Hobbes and the Social Contract Tradition* (Cambridge: Cambridge University Press, 1986)

Hood, F. C., *The Divine Politics of Thomas Hobbes: An Interpretation of "Leviathan"* (Oxford: Clarendon Press, 1964)

Jacoby, E. G., "*Thomas Hobbes* in Europe," *Journal of European Studies* 4 (1974), 57–65

Johnson, Paul J., "Hobbes's Anglican Doctrine of Salvation," in *Thomas Hobbes in His Time,* ed. Ralph Ross, Herbert W. Schneider, and Theodore Waldman (Minneapolis: University of Minnesota Press, 1974), pp. 102–28

Johnston, David, *The Rhetoric of Leviathan: Thomas Hobbes and the Politics of Cultural Transformation* (Princeton: Princeton University Press, 1986)

——, "Hobbes's Mortalism," *History of Political Thought* 10 (1989), pp. 647–63

Kargon, Robert Hugh, *Atomism in England from Hariot to Newton* (Oxford: Clarendon Press, 1966)

Kavka, Gregory, *Hobbesian Moral and Political Philosophy* (Princeton: Princeton University Press, 1986)

Kraynak, Robert P., *History and Modernity in the Thought of Thomas Hobbes* (Ithaca: Cornell University Press, 1990)

Kroll, Richard, Richard Ashcraft, and Perez Zagorin (eds), *Philosophy, Science, and Religion in England, 1640–1700* (Cambridge: Cambridge University Press, 1992)

Lloyd, S. A., *Ideals as Interests in Hobbes's Leviathan: The Power of Mind over Matter* (Cambridge: Cambridge University Press, 1992)

Macdonald, Hugh, and Mary Hargreaves, *Thomas Hobbes: A Bibliography* (London: The Bibliographical Society, 1952)

Macgillivray, Royce, *Restoration Historians and the English Civil War* (The Hague: Martinus Nijhoff, 1974)

McGrath, Alister, *Iustitia Dei: A History of the Christian Doctrine of Justification, volume II: From 1500 to the Present Day* (Cambridge: Cambridge University Press, 1986)

McNeilly, F., *The Anatomy of Leviathan* (New York: St Martin's Press, 1969)

Macpherson, C. B., *The Political Philosophy of Possessive Individualism: Hobbes to Locke* (London: Oxford University Press, 1962)

Malcolm, Noel, "Hobbes, Sandys, and the Virginia Company," *Historical Journal* 24 (1981), pp. 297–321

Marshall, John, "John Locke and Latitudinarianism," in *Philosophy, Science, and Religion in England, 1640–1700,* ed. Richard Kroll, Richard Ashcraft, and Perez Zagorin (Cambridge: Cambridge University Press, 1992), pp. 253–82

Martinich, A. P., *The Two Gods of Leviathan: Thomas Hobbes on Religion and Politics* (Cambridge: Cambridge University Press, 1992)

Mintz, Samuel, *The Hunting of Leviathan* (Cambridge: Cambridge University Press, 1962)

——, "Hobbes on the Law of Heresy: A New Manuscript," *Journal of the History of Ideas* 29 (1968), pp. 409–14

Moore, Stanley, "Hobbes on Obligation: Moral and Political," *Journal of the History of Philosophy* 9 (1971), pp. 43–62

Nagel, Thomas, "Hobbes's Concept of Obligation," *Philosophical Review* 68 (1959), 68–83

Peters, Richard, *Hobbes* (Harmondsworth: Penguin Books, 1956; 2nd edn, 1967)

Reik, Miriam M., *The Golden Lands of Thomas Hobbes* (Detroit: Wayne State University Press, 1977)

Robertson, George Croom, *Hobbes* (Edinburgh and London: William Blackwood and Sons, 1886; repr. Bristol: Thoemmes, 1993)

Rogers, G. A. J., and Alan Ryan (eds), *Perspectives on Thomas Hobbes* (Oxford: Clarendon Press, 1988)

Ross, Ralph, Herbert W. Schneider, and Theodore Waldman (eds), *Thomas Hobbes in His Time* (Minneapolis: University of Minnesota Press, 1974)

Schoneveld, Cornelis W., *Intertraffic of the Mind: Studies in Seventeenth-Century Anglo-Dutch Translation with a Checklist of Books Translated from English into Dutch, 1600–1700* (Leiden: E. J. Brill, 1983)

Shapin, Steven, and Simon Schaffer, *Leviathan and the Air-Pump: Hobbes, Boyle and the Experimental Life* (Princeton: Princeton University Press, 1985)

Sherlock, Richard, "The Theology of *Leviathan*: Hobbes on Religion," *Interpretation* 10 (1982), pp. 43–60

Skinner, Quentin, "Hobbes's *Leviathan*," *Historical Journal* 7 (1964), pp. 321–33

——, "History and Ideology in the English Revolution," *Historical Journal* 8 (1965), pp. 151–78

——, "Thomas Hobbes and His Disciples in France and England," *Comparative Studies in Society and History* 8 (1965–6), pp. 153–67

——, "The Context of Hobbes's Theory of Political Obligation," in *Hobbes and Rousseau,* ed. M. Granston and Richard Peters (Garden City, NY: Anchor Books, 1972), pp. 109–42

——, "The Conquest and Consent: Thomas Hobbes and the Engagement Controversy," in *The Interregnum,* ed. G. E. Aylmer (London: Macmillan, 1972), pp. 79–98

——, "Thomas Hobbes on the Proper Signification of Liberty," *Transactions of the Royal Historical Society,* 5th series, 40 (1990), pp. 121–51

——, "Thomas Hobbes: Rhetoric and the Construction of Morality," *Proceedings of the British Academy* 76 (1991), pp. 1–61

Sommerville, Johann P., *Thomas Hobbes: Political Ideas in Historical Context* (New York: St Martin's Press, 1992)

Sorell, Tom, *Hobbes*, The Arguments of the Philosophers (London: Routledge, 1986)

Spragens, Thomas A., *The Politics of Motion: The World of Thomas Hobbes* (Lexington, KY: University of Kentucky Press, 1973)

State, Stephen A., "Text and context: Skinner, Hobbes, and Theistic Natural Law," *Historical Journal* 28 (1985), pp. 27–50

——, "The Religious and the Secular in the Work of Thomas Hobbes," in *Religion, Secularization and Political Thought: Thomas Hobbes to J. S. Mill,* ed. James E. Crimmins (London: Routledge, 1989), pp. 17–38

Stephen, Leslie, *Hobbes* (London: Macmillan, 1904; repr. Ann Arbor: University of Michigan Press, 1961)

Strauss, Leo, *The Political Philosophy of Thomas Hobbes* (Chicago: University of Chicago Press, 1952)

Strong, Tracy, "How to Write Scripture: Words, Authority, and Politics in Thomas Hobbes," *Critical Inquiry* 20 (1993), pp. 128–59

Taylor, A. E., "The Ethical Doctrine of Hobbes," *Philosophy* 13 (1938), 406–24; reprinted in *Hobbes Studies*, ed. Keith Brown (Oxford: Blackwell, 1965), pp. 35–55

Tuck, Richard, *Natural Rights Theories* (Cambridge: Cambridge University Press, 1979)

——, "Warrender's *De Cive,*" *Political Studies* 33 (1985), pp. 308–15

——, "Hobbes and Descartes," in *Thomas Hobbes,* ed. G. A. J. Rogers and Alan Ryan (Oxford: Clarendon Press, 1988), pp. 11–41

——, "Optics and Sceptics: The Philosophical Foundations of Hobbes's Thought," in *Conscience and Casuistry,* ed. Edmund Leites (Cambridge: Cambridge University Press, 1988), pp. 235–63

——, "Hobbes and Locke on Toleration," in *Thomas Hobbes and Political Theory,* ed. Mary Dietz (Lawrence, Kansas: The University of Kansas Press, 1990), pp. 153–71

——, "The 'Christian Atheism' of Thomas Hobbes," in *Atheism from the Reformation to the Enlightenment,* ed. Michael Hunter and David Wootton (Oxford: Clarendon Press, 1991), pp. 111–30

——, *Hobbes* (Oxford: Oxford University Press, 1991)

——, *Philosophy and Government 1572–1651* (Cambridge: Cambridge University Press, 1993)

Walton, C., and P. J. Johnson (eds), *Hobbes's "Science of Natural Justice"* (Dordrecht: Martinus Nijhoff Publishers, 1987)

Warner, D. H. J., "Hobbes's Interpretation of the Doctrine of the Trinity," *Journal of Religious History* 5 (1968–9), pp. 299–313

Warrender, Howard, *The Political Philosophy of Hobbes: His Theory of Obligation* (Oxford: Clarendon Press, 1957)

——, "The Place of God in Hobbes's Philosophy," *Political Studies* 8 (1960), pp. 48–57

Warrender, Howard, "Hobbes and Macroethics: The Theory of Peace and Natural Justice," in *Hobbes's "Science of Natural Justice,"* ed. C. Walton and P. J. Johnson (Dordrecht: Martinus Nijhoff, 1987), pp. 297–308

Watkins, J. W. N., *Hobbes System of Ideas: A Study in the Political Significance of Philosophical Theories* (London: Hutchinson, 1965)

Wolin, Sheldon, *Hobbes' and the Epic Tradition of Political Theory* (Los Angeles: Clark Memorial Library, 1970)

Wootton, David (ed.), *Divine Right and Democracy: An Anthology of Political Writing in Stuart England* (Harmondsworth: Penguin Books, 1986)

Yolton, John W., *A Locke Dictionary*, The Blackwell Philosopher Dictionaries (Oxford: Blackwell Publishers, 1993)

Zagorin, Perez, "Hobbes on Our Minds," *Journal of the History of Ideas* 51 (1990), pp. 317–35

Index

Note to reader

Page numbers in **bold** refer to the main entries or to especially significant discussions of given terms.